MARIANNE
As Years Go By
Faithfull

Mark Hodkinson

OMNIBUS PRESS

London / New York / Paris / Sydney / Copenhagen / Berlin / Madrid / Tokyo

DEDICATION:

For my best friend Peter Read (1962–1988)

By the same author (selected titles)
Thank Yer, Very Glad (Omnibus Press, 1990)
Life Sentence (Parrs Wood, 2001)
Believe In The Sign (Pomona, 2007)
The Last Mad Surge Of Youth (Pomona, 2009)

www.markhodkinson.com

Copyright © 2013 Omnibus Press
(A Division of Music Sales Limited)

Cover designed by Fresh Lemon
Picture research by Jacqui Black

ISBN: 978.1.78038.837.3
Order No: OP55044

Exclusive Distributors
Music Sales Limited,
14/15 Berners Street,
London, W1T 3LJ.

Music Sales Corporation
180 Madison Avenue, 24th Floor,
New York,
NY 10016,
USA.

Macmillan Distribution Services,
56 Parkwest Drive
Derrimut, Vic 3030,
Australia.

Every effort has been made to trace the copyright holders of the photographs in this book but one or two were unreachable. We would be grateful if the photographers concerned would contact us.

Typeset by Phoenix Photosetting, Chatham, Kent

A catalogue record for this book is available from the British Library.

Visit Omnibus Press on the web at www.omnibuspress.com

Preface

*A*s *Years Go By* (this book) was originally titled *As Tears Go By* (that book). It's only a single letter changed but a world of difference. I was in my early twenties when I was first commissioned to write the life story of Marianne Faithfull, back in 1990. I was overwhelmed, both by the gravitas of the subject matter and its actual framing – tasteful typesetting, hardback, top-whack price. I responded by adopting an outlandish authorial voice, one that belonged to a haughty faux-posh older gentleman. He might well have worn a cloak. And, unlike the rest of us, he didn't, for example, 'go upstairs', but 'defected to the uppermost portion of the residence'.

Within a few months of publication I grew to dislike *As Tears Go By* and its tortuous tautology. Marianne Faithfull didn't like it either. She called it 'scaly'. She uses this word frequently. People are scaly; ideas or plans are scaly. It's an adjective that is clearly meant to suggest unpleasantness but to meet it straight-on you have to look it up. I have. It's a slang term denoting shabby and despicable. I think we disliked the book for different reasons.

I was asked several times whether I wanted to update *As Tears Go By* but it didn't feel right to revisit the past. I'd moved on. I was proud of the solid journalistic research I had done but embarrassed by the earnest tone and the malapropisms. In truth, I wanted the book to disappear, fade away. But nothing disappears or fades away any more, not in the age of the Internet. So, one day, it suddenly became an easy decision. I would revise and update a piece of work that had caused me so much unease over the years, and make good a bad job. Very seldom in life are we offered such an opportunity.

The commission was to undertake a six-week revision. It became six months. In that time I could not fundamentally alter the 'shape' of the book or overlay a different narrative but it allowed me to tighten the grammar, excise the fanciful and, most importantly, chase away the condescending fool who had possessed my insecure twenty-something self. Although at first glance it may seem to follow the same outline, I doubt there are more than a handful of sentences that remain unchanged and, of course, there is a heavy poundage of new material. I was delighted when the publisher decided to change the title, for this is a richer, better book and deserves to stand alone.

I remember, back in 1990, being a little bit hurt when Marianne's long-standing friend, Christopher Gibbs, referred to me as 'an earnest young chap'. Now, I'm glad I was earnest and diligent and enthusiastic. I walked down the street where Marianne grew up. I spoke to her former neighbours. I sat on the grass in the grounds of her school, St Joseph's. I stood on the car park at the Progress Theatre in Reading and imagined it was 1960 and 13-year-old Marianne might appear from among the maze of privet hedges and houses, on her way to rehearsal with the youth group. I did all this without the aid of the Internet. I had to write letters and make phone calls, knock on doors and meet people in cafes and pubs. It meant the research was pure, first-hand.

Sadly, in some cases it will no longer be possible to retrace my trail of research. A number of the people I interviewed have died. I was probably the only writer to spend time talking about Marianne with her father, Glynn Faithfull. We spent a pleasant few hours walking the grounds of Braziers College. I was pleased he had agreed to speak to me, especially when others within her circle had refused. I think he did so because he wanted to register formally his part in Marianne's life. I did not realise then the complexity of their relationship. Through the book

I have tried to avoid second-rate psychoanalysis but I think it is fair to say that the father-daughter dynamic is the most important of her life. To understand this is to properly understand her story.

Another advantage of beginning the research more than two decades ago was that I got there first. Many were speaking of Marianne and the times she lived through for the first time. They were fresh and candid. The 'Swinging Sixties' and Marianne's part in it was already a media fascination but it was nothing like today where it is raked over again and again across hundreds of television channels, radio stations and magazine articles. Barely a few months pass without another book or revelation forming an excuse to bathe deep in nostalgia.

I find it heartening when asked if Marianne co-operated with this book. It shows that even in a supposedly cynical world where we are each arch and savvy, some still believe that a well-known figure such as Marianne would give up time to support a project over which she will not have ultimate control or stand to make financial gain. These days artists offer themselves for interview only when they have a product to promote. The media understands and accepts implicitly that no one is available 'out of season' any more. So, no, she didn't co-operate.

She was asked, of course, back in 1990 and again for this book; not to do so would have been discourteous on my part. I exchanged e-mails with her manager. At first he said he would have a 'chat' with her but pointed out that she was 'really busy'. He later asked to see the manuscript; clearly this was the required brokerage for her possibly agreeing to an interview. My editor, a man with great experience in such matters, envisaged a fraught exchange developing. There would be discussions, requests, compromises, complaints, tantrums and, inevitably, deadlines flouted.

His standpoint may have been coloured by how Marianne reacted to the original book. She wrote in her autobiography that I was 'counting on her keeling over at any moment'. She also reported that I had told the 'British press' I expected to hear that 'any day now' she had 'overdosed in some street corner lavatory'. Her next attack (contained in two tart paragraphs) was on the publisher. She claimed it had delayed publication in the hope of coinciding with her death. None of these statements was true and, I have to admit, it made me distrustful of an otherwise well-written and entertaining book.

To Marianne's credit she did not put an embargo on the co-operation of others. Several who had been extremely close to her – her ex-husband, Ben Brierley; former fiancée, Oliver Musker; best friend, Henrietta Moraes; 'stepbrother', Chris O'Dell; and, of course, her father, among them – all put time aside for an interview and none requested payment. I'm sure they contacted Marianne first and she left the decision to them. I had much less success with the revision. Scores of my e-mails were ignored or I would make partial headway but after presenting my written questions or trying to arrange a meeting, subsequent e-mails remained unanswered.

When I undertook the first book I did not properly grasp the magnitude of the life Marianne had lived. I was born after she released her first record and my main cultural frame of reference was punk and new wave. I was a little dismissive of her generation. Much of the music was blues-based, which I saw as derivative and formulaic. I failed to recognise that, regardless of where the music originated, the concept of young people and pop music was so new – the recording process, the marketing, the idolatry, the travelling, the media enthrallment, and then the speedy acceptance of the format as a true and valid art form. Marianne was a pioneer, especially as a girl in a male-dominated world, and she was denied the shelter of falling within a group format. Was anyone at such a young age truly prepared for that kind of attention, that kind of test? If she, and many more, went a bit dotty or suffered various degrees of damage, who would be surprised?

A quick perusal of the book's index will reveal the sheer breadth of her life. At times it can feel as if there is no cultural or historical figure of the last century, possibly longer, who is not ultimately interwoven with her story: Leopold von Sacher-Masoch to Jimmy Savile; William Burroughs to Will Self; Jim Morrison to Heinrich Himmler; Kate Moss to Francis Bacon; Christopher Walken to Cecil Beaton; Nick Cave to Robert Mitchum; Bob Dylan to Sid Vicious. That these disparate figures should be linked through merely one person seems absurd but it is an absurd story, an absurd life.

The person with whom Marianne is most associated is Mick Jagger. If theirs was the first generation to coalesce both the pop and the media age, they were its royalty. I have tried to relate the energy and excitement of those years while placing them in the context of the whole of Marianne's life. Even today, more than 40 years since they parted, almost every article about Marianne mentions Jagger. No wonder she sighs when asked about him on the television or radio. And that bloody Mars bar story! As Marianne's biographer I am teased constantly, asked to confirm or deny its veracity. I have endured this episode only by proxy but it has worn me down. The world should let it be.

Unlike most life stories, Marianne's is interesting from the outset. As a reader, I am prone to skip the early chapters of biographies. One childhood is pretty much the same as another. Marianne's isn't, and neither are the families from which she emerged. Many of her ancestors are also worthy of greater study, for they are each similarly beguiling.

I have tried my best to avoid producing another book that could be considered 'scaly', though not at the cost of circumventing the truth, at least as I see it. The story is told straight and journalistically. It is remarkable enough without my driving through an attitude or adopting any literary chicanery. I have covered Marianne's drugs and down-at-heel years but I have also focused on the more recent period where she has accomplished a sturdy creative output. The pace dips a little towards the end, commensurate with the relatively humdrum nature of Marianne's current career: record, tour, film, play, record, tour, film, play. She has said many times, as people often do, that she has no regrets but, equally, a bit of the routine so late in life must bring good cheer.

Reading it back once more, I can plot the chain of charismatic and connected people who have propelled Marianne into such a fantastic life – John Dunbar to Andrew Oldham to Mick Jagger to Ben Brierley to Mark Miller Mundy to Chris Blackwell to Hal Willner to François Ravard. Most of us would consider ourselves lucky to have met one of these influential figures. But Marianne made her own luck by running hard and fast at life while others shilly-shallied.

Mark Hodkinson
May, 2013.

1

The 1960s has become the most written about and eulogised decade of modern history. The claim, no less, was that a 'new kind of people' were said to walk among us. They weren't strictly 'new' of course – history is replete with similar dandies and hedonists – but the difference was their time coincided with the media age. This meant that unlike previous generations they did not exist in isolation and remain of limited influence. Everyone got to know of these young, savvy, sharp-dressed free spirits. In their bangles and bright colours, they were easy to spot. If they looked different, they also acted and thought different. They made it cool to be cultured and independent, creative and reactionary. Though many at its epicentre were educated, privileged and wealthy, the attitude and mind-set was accessible to all.

Distilled to a single scene the decade is a golden sun blazing down upon a skinny girl as she sashays through London. Long hair frames her face and sways rhythmically with her miniskirt. The passing cars are white, long and sleek. Their owners, street-smart young men, pop their haircuts out of the side window and ask if the skinny girl is all right, darling. Meanwhile, across the Atlantic, a flower-powered dream stems from California in glorious Technicolor. 'It's not the hair on top but the mind underneath' and 'Beethoven in a crew cut?' are among slogans daubed on placards carried by students in Connecticut where 53 of their contemporaries are suspended for wearing their hair long. The youth of the world were liberating their hair before moving on to their minds and bodies.

Time magazine, with a worldwide readership of 25 million, devoted much of its issue of Friday April 15, 1966, to celebrating 'Swinging London'. The phrase 'swinging' had been coined earlier by the socialite and former Tiller girl Diana Vreeland, editor-in-chief of *Vogue* who noted: 'London is the most swinging city in the world at the moment.' This astute commentator had previously conjured a similarly apposite term when she wrote of a 'youthquake' hitting the world. The media appropriated the epithet 'Swinging Sixties' to summarise the period. Only one other decade, the 'Roaring Twenties', had been defined so concisely.

Obviously the 1960s did not swing in the sense that people succumbed en masse to hedonism. Otherwise, trains and buses would not have run on time (did they ever?); dustmen would not have emptied bins; shops would have run out of stock and no one would have voted at elections. The vast majority lived a life largely unchanged from previous decades. They travelled to work on public transport. Young married couples ate ham sandwiches at their in-laws' on Sunday evenings. Football fans were soaked watching drab matches in the teeming rain on open terraces. On television Sergeant George Dixon (played by Jack Warner) proffered a stolid and paternal version of police work in *Dixon Of Dock Green,* closing each episode with a homely, philosophical direct-to-camera speech. If the decade was swinging it was on the periphery of most lives – the music coming out of radios, films shown at the local cinema, programmes broadcast on television, clothes featured in magazines, advertisements on billboards.

The 'Swinging Sixties' is not, however, a falsehood A tiny percentage really did live life to the brim, overflowing. By chance or design they found themselves at the core of a seismic cultural and social shift. Youth was celebrated and valued as never before. They formed bands, opened art galleries and shops, wrote novels and plays, directed films. Everything they achieved or attempted was considered inherently hip, vital. The intelligent and shrewd walked with the beautiful and the handsome, everyone a star in their own film. They

2

The surnames of Faith, Faithful and Faithfull were used originally to mark out a person considered to uphold this very quality. The first Faithfull on record was William Faythful (as the name was then spelt), a burgess [municipal official] in the town of Chichester in 1492. Fifty years later, a will was issued in Hampshire by a married couple called Hugo and Margaret Faythfull. Marianne's authentic patriarchal surname is Davies. The last member of the paternal line to have Davies as part of his name was Marianne's great-grandfather, the Rev Richard Mervyn Faithfull-Davies, who had been a vicar in Australia and Melanesia (a group of islands off the north-east coast of Australia) before returning to London in the 1900s. Interestingly, church records reveal that at a farewell party held when he left All Saint's Church in South Wimbledon in April 1914, 'Musical entertainments, some including the illustrious clergyman himself, took up much of the evening.' The Davies section of the family name was jettisoned by the Rev Faithfull-Davies' son, Theodore James. Theodore, Marianne's paternal grandfather, began his working life as a veterinary surgeon tending mainly farm animals in East Anglia. He was restless and radical and in a bid to distance himself from his family's ecclesiastical background he abridged the surname to Faithfull. He served in the Veterinary Corps during the First World War and afterwards became founding principal and self-styled 'resident psychologist' of Priory Gate School in Sudbury, Suffolk. A colleague of his at this time, the respected psychologist John Bowlby, described him as 'a rather mercurial character, very intelligent, very unstable really, but with an analytic orientation'. The private school catered for up to 30 children and was based on Boy Scout woodcraft principles, combining love of the outdoors with the involvement of pupils in running the school. Swearing was permitted and Faithfull encouraged nudity, which he termed 'sun battling'. Between 1921 and 1934 Priory Gate moved to five different locations in East Anglia but ultimately proved unsustainable and closed.

During the 1920s and 1930s and now referring to himself as a 'sexologist', Theodore published several books on the psychology of sex and gender, each with a compulsive title: *Bisexuality: An Essay On Extraversion And Introversion* (1927); *Plato And The New Psychology* (1928);

The Re-Education Of The Invert (1932); *Psychological Foundations, A Contribution To Everyman's Knowledge Of Himself* (1933); and *The Mystery Of The Androgyne* (1938). The preface of *Bisexuality* contains the passage: 'Sunlight, both real and artificial, will be used to bathe our bodies, and the light of understanding will profoundly alter our attitude towards sex and the reproduction of the species and of Love.' He invented a device he called the 'Frigidity Machine' to unlock primal libidinal energy and had a policy of not taking baths. Theodore was considered a pioneering influence on an ideology known as 'New Psychology', a term used to embrace theories popularised by Sigmund Freud and Wilhelm Reich. He collaborated with the famous educationalist A. S. Neill, the principal at the similarly progressive school, Summerhill, based in nearby Leiston.

In 1910 Theodore married a woman whose father had also been a parson. Frances Newman Channer was born in Shepherd's Bush, London, in 1885 and worked variously as an artist, calligrapher and embroiderer. In 1912, the year of the Stockholm Olympics and the sinking of the SS Titanic, Frances gave birth to Marianne's father, Robert Glynn Faithfull. There was a surfeit of Roberts, Bobs and Bobbys in the family so he became known as Glynn. His parents had four more children: Alfred Bernard (1913), Margaret Elaine (1914), Vera (1919) and Stephen (1921). Theodore Faithfull died in 1973. His passion for controversy barely waned. He left his wife, Frances, and, according to family legend, took up with a circus dancer. In later life he submitted florid articles to underground magazines such as *International Times*.

Glynn Faithfull, together with his brothers and sisters, was educated under his father's freestyle methods. "I do not think he did anything courageous or striking in his life but he was certainly a rebel against his strait-laced family. I think he has left us with a nice, unique name and I believe it is unusual that we followed the family's female line," said Glynn Faithfull. This 'line' boasted another notable personality in the publisher and women's rights activist Emily Faithfull, born in 1835. She too was from a church background, the daughter of the Reverend Ferdinand Faithfull of Headley, Surrey. She set up the printing company the Victoria Press and published a monthly magazine for 18 years, *The Victoria*. She also lectured on women's rights across the United States and published a novel in 1869. Among Emily's nephews were the successful music hall comedian Rutland Barrington and John Faithfull Fleet, an expert in epigraphy (the study of inscriptions), especially in India where he lived for many years.

The education proffered at Priory Gate gave Glynn Faithfull a thirst and an impressive ability to absorb knowledge. After finishing his formal schooling at Beckenham Grammar School in Kent he entered London University to study modern languages, specialising in Italian. He attained an honours degree in 1934 and for the next three years taught Italian on a part-time basis at the university where he had himself studied. He completed a PhD in the same subject and when he left London in 1937, he was also fluent in French and German and spoke Russian to a good standard. Although his family had moved from East Anglia to Bristol to Essex, and back to East Anglia, his first move north was to take up a full-time lecturing post at Liverpool University, which he held until the outbreak of World War Two in September 1939. Glynn Faithfull joined the intelligence unit of the British Army where his main duty was to interrogate prisoners of war. "It seemed to me we had no choice. We were going to either help or hinder Hitler," he said. "When one got to know what was happening in Nazi Germany, and his plans to attack England, there was only one option and that was to defend one's country." He spent the first year of the war in the Middle East but was later transferred to Europe. The army reflected the class structure of civilian Britain and he enjoyed privileges generally afforded to a member of the educated middle-class. He rose quickly to the rank of Major and there was consternation at the War Office when, at the end of the war, he left the Army.

In the autumn of 1945 Faithfull found himself on the outskirts of Vienna, which had been liberated by the Russian army and was to be occupied briefly by the British. In the back pocket of his trousers he carried a letter written several months earlier by an Austrian refugee and Count's son, Alexander Sacher-Masoch. Originally a chemist, Alexander was a left-wing activist who later worked for the Communist Party. When the war ended he became a writer and his books, *The Parade* and *The Oil Burning Gardens*, were popular in Austria. He had been interned on the island of Korcula in the Adriatic Sea, which was occupied by the German army until 1944. The two men had met earlier at Bari in the heel of Italy. Alexander had spent most of the war hiding in Yugoslavia, passing on information to the Allies about the movements of enemy forces. At their meeting they reminisced about their families and home countries and Alexander wrote a letter of introduction for Faithfull. He told him to produce it if he should ever pass through Vienna and wish to visit the other aristocratic Sacher-Masochs, whom he assured were excellent company. In some versions of this story it has been said Faithfull saved Alexander's life and in return was advised to head to Vienna forthwith and claim his prize, Alexander's beautiful sister, Eva. "It's a good story but I'm afraid it's not true," said Faithfull. "I certainly didn't save his life and, to be frank, I was not particularly close to Alexander. I thought he was a friendly chap and it was jolly decent of him to write a letter introducing me to his family."

The address on the letter led Faithfull to an institute in Vienna put aside for displaced Hungarians. Graf Artur Ritter Wolfgang von Sacher-Masoch, an Austrian Count, had been allowed to take refuge in a self-contained flat within the institute because his wife, Elisabeth Flora Ziprisz (known as Flora), who he had married when she was 18, was of Hungarian-Jewish parents. She had converted to Christianity when she married the Count, 14 years her senior. They lived among the remnants of the Count's salvaged riches with their only daughter, Eva, who was granted the title of Baroness because of her father's status. His full title was Count von Sacher-Masoch of Apollonia and Erisso. "To some extent they had a kind of diplomatic privilege. It must have been a frightening war for the family because Eva's mother was 100 per cent Jewish. When Hitler invaded Austria, life would have been terribly dangerous. I'm sure if they had been anywhere else they would have been taken to Auschwitz. It was a convenient hide-out in a threatening world," said Faithfull.

Glynn Faithfull recognised many similarities between the cordial Austro-Hungarian family and his own, whom he had seen for just a two-week period in the five years up until 1945. "Their flat was a very pleasant set-up. It had three rooms and seemed to take up the whole of

to America." Marianne's first school was Ormskirk Church of England Infant School, a few hundred yards from their home. She was one of the first pupils to enter the single-storey building, which had been built to meet the demands of the postwar baby boom. The Faithfulls were eager to expand their family and Eva became pregnant three times but miscarried on each occasion. Although she remained at the school for less than a year, Marianne developed a peculiar accent, a mixture of patrician English picked up from her father, a Teutonic edge from her mother and a Lancashire burr from her classmates. The Faithfulls were obviously vastly different from other families in the neighbourhood and it was inevitable they would soon move on.

2

The Faithfulls duly returned to the south of England in 1952 although Glynn remained in Liverpool, working at the university. Eva, Marianne and Eva's mother, known as 'Nona', moved into Milman Road, Reading. The road is about a mile from the centre of Reading in a traditional working-class area. A cul-de-sac, it has several large detached houses at its entrance and then two rows of parallel Victorian terraces. A line of elegantly curved lamp posts stops at a high wooden fence across the bottom where there is a patch of grassy wasteland. The Faithfulls lived approximately halfway along the row of terraces, opposite Christ Church School where Marianne became a pupil.

Locals were intrigued by the new arrivals. "They just didn't belong there and a lot of people thought that. Marianne's mum wore sheepskin coats and high heels. I remember she used to walk along with two pedigree dogs. They were quite big and used to pull her along. It was quite comical really," says Paul Privitera, a resident of one of the larger houses at the top of the street. As an adult Marianne told writers she used to long for the prosperity to complement her family's noble past. She dreamed of leaving the house, which she referred to as 'Reading Gaol' after the prison made famous by Oscar Wilde. Other times, when distance lent enchantment, she recalled Milman Road as the 'most perfect, most beautiful place in the world to grow up'.

Glynn Faithfull joined the family on occasional weekends and at the end of university terms. The marriage was beginning to fail and they separated a year or so after the move to Reading. "There was a certain amount of excitement, I suppose, about marrying foreign girls," said Glynn Faithfull. "It was only after a few years that we found we were not getting on very well. I think it was a hell of a lot of upheaval when Eva left her home country. It might have worked if we had stayed in Vienna. The break-up was an unhappy event and one on which I do not wish to dwell." Marianne, in her book *Memories, Dreams And Reflections*, recalled their differing personalities: 'Eva was much warmer than my father and I'm more like her in that respect. But of course the emotional side of her had a downside. She could erupt in irrational fury. My father's detachment was oddly soothing compared to my mother's rages. He didn't get so emotionally involved, and his remoteness, which I often lamented, was reassuring amidst the family turmoil,' she wrote.

Soon after they parted Glynn asked Eva to grant him a divorce so he could marry his new partner, Margaret Elizabeth Kipps. Eva held out but finally agreed to an uncontested divorce in the early 1960s, seven years after they had separated. "I think to Eva marriage was sacred and she didn't think it should end," said a close friend. "For her it was a life-long pact. I think that is why she never married anyone else." Glynn married Margaret in 1963 and they had twin sons, Simon and Timothy, and a daughter, Hazel. Glynn died in March 1998 and on Margaret's death her ashes were scattered on his coffin when he was buried in Ipsden, Oxfordshire.

Despite straitened circumstances Eva Faithfull did not compromise her lifestyle. She rearranged the terraced house to create an illusion of the splendour of her earlier gentrified life. The stairway was pulled out and relocated to make more space. Ornate furnishings salvaged from Vienna gave the home an idiosyncratic touch. The family's history was recorded on pewter plates scattered throughout the house. Marianne would find coats-of-arms obliterated by tobacco ash flicked into the dishes by her mother. "The children from our terrace wouldn't come into our house because they were frightened of the tapestries in the hall, while the girls from school would come for the weekend, then go back and say I lived

talk to my mother for ages. They cooked together. She was a perfectly normal little girl. She always seemed happy and I remember her singing all the time. She seemed to wear funny clothes quite a lot. They would be weird colours, like she had a dress that was half red and half blue."

Marianne's grandmother, Nona, died two years after they moved to Reading, aged 65. She had rarely been seen out of doors. "She was a really typical grandma figure. She had rosy cheeks and was a lovely old lady," said Maryan Robson. She remembers the two girls would ask her for a 'Valentine'. "She used to give us a gift of a piece of chocolate or a bar of soap. It must have been an Austrian tradition," she said.

Eva remained on speaking terms with Glynn Faithfull and tried to shield Marianne from the distress of their failed marriage. Neighbours say Marianne seldom saw her father and the infrequency of his letters meant Eva often had to write hasty notes reminding him to drop a line to his daughter. He would then call to collect Marianne and take her out for the day. Glynn sometimes required a partner to accompany him to official engagements at the university. Eva's former next-door neighbours, Cyril and Ida Rapley, recall an occasion when he turned up unannounced. "He called round to see Eva one afternoon and said he wanted her to go with him to a ball. She didn't have a dress to wear so she took down the curtains and made one by the time he arrived in the evening. She was incredibly resourceful," said Ida Rapley. Glynn Faithful said he could not recall the episode and thought it unlikely because he did not involve himself with the university's social scene.

Acquaintances sometimes set up home with the Faithfulls. They were often teachers or artists, whimsical friends of Eva who was prepared to open up her miniature palace and accommodate poor souls finding themselves temporarily homeless. Chris O'Dell, then 17, moved in with them in 1960 when his parents fell gravely ill. His father had become paraplegic after a viral infection and was attended for many years by his mother. Chris left the family home when his mother became afflicted with motor neurone disease. Both his parents died soon afterwards. Eva, a friend of his family, invited O'Dell to share their home. "I was absolutely delighted. I was very fond of them. I went through a difficult period of my personal life, losing my family and everything that went with it. I was in a terrible state. The family home and the furniture was sold. Every last thing went and I didn't even salvage a book. It was a fantastic act of generosity by Eva, as they never really had any money. They saved my life actually."

Marianne referred to O'Dell as her older brother and they developed a strong platonic friendship. He was often mistaken for a brother and became a surrogate son to Eva. He redecorated the house and put up shelves. "She became just like my mother and she did extremely well because she was quite a wise person," he said. "She took me in because of a combination of being sorry for what had happened to my parents and because there might have been a tiny element that a male figure added something to the home." During most of his stay O'Dell was at college and could only contribute to the stretched household finances when he took on temporary jobs outside term times. "Eva never asked for a penny. I became part of the family, like a son. I worked at a brewery in Reading delivering beer at Christmas but otherwise I wasn't really working." Apart from her mother, O'Dell was the closest person to Marianne during her early teenage years. "She had a terrific personality – very bright and clever, which you would expect coming from a family like that. There was a long ancestry of intellectuals on both sides, academics on the side of her father and intellectual aristocrats on the side of her mother. There were hundreds of years of writers and artists on her mother's side. Marianne was very happy and extremely well balanced. She had taken the divorce of her parents well and always seemed motivated. This is really why it got so tragic later on when we all watched this remarkable child turn into a vegetable, as the drugs thing took over. She became in a terrible state. We had a terrible, dreadful time with her."

Chris O'Dell saw at close quarters how Eva was schooling Marianne. There was little infringement on her freedom and in later years Marianne remarked that she lived as if in a Renoir painting. "I think it was a sort of bohemian household in a way. It was quite artistic," said Chris O'Dell. "There were paintings all over the place. People listened to music and there were frequent gatherings of Eva's friends who were mostly in arts or teaching. It was a very pleasant, slightly bohemian atmosphere: nothing crazy. It was a lively place, everything was discussed: political issues of the day, population, religion. It was very stimulating to be there."

While Marianne was encouraged to seek out literature and art, other matters such as etiquette or housework were considered banal. "Eva was a real aristocrat but she had no time or inclination to do basic jobs around the house," said Ida Rapley. "I don't think she had any experience of things like that. Eva would host parties in her back garden and ask to borrow butter or sugar. That was really typical. She'd have bottles of wine but forget to get the butter for the bread. She was always on the tap but she was a good sort and I liked her very much." Ida was known to Marianne as 'Aunty Ida'. "Marianne was a very, very naughty child. I remember one time she had magazines all over the floor and her father had arrived to take her out. I told her to tidy up before she saw him. She hated being told what to do and kept saying, '... but Daddy's here'. I told her I didn't care if the Queen of England was here: she had to tidy up the magazines. She got very angry and said: 'I hate you Aunty Ida'."

As a teenager Marianne developed a high-minded manner that was an almost inevitable outcome of her upbringing. "To be so insecure and at the same time so sort of grand and arrogant is an odd mixture. I was trying to hide my fear. When I was 17 and really snotty it drove people wild with fury," she told *The Guardian* in 1990. Ida Rapley remembered Marianne's precociousness. One afternoon, Marianne, aged nine, was playing in the garden with Ida Rapley's daughter, Linda, three years her junior. Ida was shocked to hear Marianne informing her daughter of the facts of life. "She was a little madam. She would not take anything seriously. Everything seemed to be boring to her. I know a lot of the neighbours used to think: 'Who does she think she is?'"

Glynn Faithfull left Liverpool University to join a group of progressive thinkers who had settled into communal living among the cornfields and solitude of Ipsden, near Wallingford in Oxfordshire. The group had bought the handsome country residence of Braziers Park in 1950 for £8,000 as a base to study 'ideological theory and live out an integrated life'. Glynn was the creative force behind the 'school of integrative social research' but did not devote himself to it on a full-time basis until he left Liverpool. Braziers Park was built in 1688 and remodelled 100 years later in Strawberry Hill Gothic, complete with a turret and castellated roofline. Although it is situated only half a mile from the busy A4074 Oxford to Reading road, it forms a peaceful hush among swathes of mature beech trees and has been designated an 'area of outstanding natural beauty', one of only 33 in England. The commune was inspired by the ex-cancer surgeon-turned-sociologist, Wilfred Trotter, known for identifying two distinct types of people in an article published in the *Sociological Review* – the 'resistive' who formed the conservative majority and maintained the status quo and the 'sensitive', a radical minority willing to embrace change. He predicted that unless mankind reconciled these two sectors, disaster would result. A resolution was needed for people to reach their full potential and he called this state 'multimentality'. The psychiatrist John Norman Glaister further developed Trotter's theories. Glaister had worked previously with Theodore Faithfull at Priory Gate and was a committed member of the Order of Woodcraft Chivalry, a pacifist, camping movement that encouraged children and adults to work together learning woodcraft skills and the study of evolution and psychology. Glaister was also an advocate of 'New Commerce', a system of barter for goods and work.

These days Braziers Park refers to itself as a 'community and residential college' and claims to be a 'continuing experiment in the advantages and problems of living in a group. As one of the oldest secular communities in the UK, we endeavour to create a space which enables people to integrate both learning and teaching, and to find and develop their full potential in all aspects – intellectual, physical, emotional and spiritual. We strive to understand more fully our relationships with each other and with nature and society so we can co-operate in taking constructive action in the world today.' A dozen or so permanent members run the mansion house (a Grade II listed building) and oversee 55 acres of land, an organic kitchen, garden and tend livestock. They also organise courses and events assisted by volunteers from around the world. The college's tag line is: 'Making conscious the process of which we are part, so we may facilitate its development more efficiently.' Braziers receives finance from hiring out its rooms and grounds, and its courses on herbal medicine, yoga, singing, peace studies and sound healing. These are much broader themes than those offered when Glynn Faithfull was convenor of studies and his wife, Margaret, secretary – positions they held from the early 1960s. Typical courses in their time were 'transpersonal psychology', 'the poetry of Rainer Maria Rilke' and 'Hegel and collective consciousness'. One visitor said of Brazier's back then: "It was a peculiar place if ever there was one. It was one of those places run by a certain type of academic coterie who know lonely, elderly ladies who want to do strange things. It was very much of the 1950s. There were these very odd, Bloomsbury-type characters wandering around, surrounded by these strange ladies and all kinds of slightly batty looking people."

Considering the liberal outlook fostered by Eva Faithfull it seemed peculiar that she should switch Marianne from Christ Church School to the relative austerity of a nearby Catholic convent school, St Joseph's, especially as her old school was literally yards from their home and she had settled well after the move from Ormskirk. Eva met opposition from Glynn Faithfull who was uneasy about the overt religious element of St Joseph's. "I was not terribly religious but it was very important to Eva that Marianne was educated in a convent school, like she had been. There was not a lot of friction. I think when you have a child it makes you more conventional and one is anxious to do the proper thing for one's child," he said. Typically, Glynn viewed the issue with a pseudo-sexual slant. "This will give her a problem with sex for the rest of her life," he told Eva. Many years later Marianne recalled that her parents had a 'blazing row' over the issue and said her father considered the Catholic Church 'an abomination'. Marianne was not surprised at Eva's resolve. They had often gone to church together when Marianne was a child and she witnessed her mother becoming incredibly emotional, praying loudly with tears streaming down her face. She saw that the church provided peace, an escape from the issues that tormented her – the failed marriage, an ambition thwarted by war and a longing for her homeland. On a more phlegmatic level, Eva had befriended a local priest, Canon

Murphy, and they had become good drinking pals. Chris O'Dell, whose parents were also Roman Catholic, barely noticed the religious artifacts at the Faithfull home and was largely oblivious of Eva's religion. "The difference is basically if you are from a non-denominational Protestant background, the things missing from people's homes are the icons of religion – the sacred heart, crosses and stuff like that, lying about all over the place. They were familiar to me anyway, so I didn't notice it, but I suppose there were probably small things around which had religious connections. They went to Mass and we had a wonderful priest who came to see us but religion didn't impose itself too much on my consciousness."

Marianne began at St Joseph's in September 1953, first in the day-school and soon afterwards as a weekly boarder. She was made a charitable boarder at reduced fees because she was of a one-parent family. She stayed at the school through the week (although it was just over a mile from her home) and returned to Milman Road at weekends. As an adult, Marianne pondered whether her being away facilitated Eva's sexual liaisons. 'She still had the odd girlfriend – and certainly boyfriends. I can see that one of the reasons I was sent to the convent was so my mother could have a sex life,' she wrote.

St Joseph's Convent School, known as St Joseph's College since September 2010, is still standing and thriving in Upper Redlands Road, Reading. It was established by the sisters of Saint Marie Madeleine Pastel and housed in a tall, magnificent sandy-brick building. Marble carved images of the Virgin Mary cradling baby Jesus stand high over immaculate grounds where every car park space is marked in brilliant white. The school describes itself as a 'vibrant, independent Catholic day school for boys and girls aged three to 18. It was founded over 100 years ago, retaining an important sense of tradition whilst embracing new thinking in teaching and learning.' The annual cost of sending a child to the school is equivalent to the purchase price of a new small family car. The school appointed its first secular head teacher in the early 1980s. It was, for many years, a girls' school but is now co-educational and accepts pupils of all denominations. Marianne has been critical of the school's starchy values while at other times praising its nurturing qualities. She was taught that nakedness was shameful and self-denial was the route to godliness. At bath times girls were made to wear shifts to conceal themselves. "I didn't fit in," she told the writer Nik Cohn in 1970. "I didn't want to play hockey or any of that. Everyone thought I was stuck up and I had no friends until I was 13. I was very precocious and very sort of, you know, a misfit, and I used to spend all my time alone, reading. I read all the time, Milton and Shakespeare. I was a proud little soul, terribly proud. I was happier as a teenager. I wasn't so much alone. I had a friend and, when everyone else was playing hockey, we used to walk round and round together, discussing existence."

Marianne missed a couple of terms at St Joseph's when she suffered tuberculosis. The illness was advanced when properly diagnosed and she was sick and pale for many weeks as she lay on the settee at Milman Road. Eva accompanied Marianne to school when she volunteered to hold dance classes for the pupils. At the age of 14 Marianne played the lead in *The Snow Queen*. She had her first period during a performance and the white costume became dabbed in blood. She could hear her mother's stage whisper: "Just ignore it."

At school Marianne's aim was to finish third in all subjects. She avoided the top two positions because she considered those in them to be sycophants, but if she slipped to fourth or fifth she put in extra work because it dented her pride. At home she could read books and view paintings that were banned from school and she was allowed to explore all types of literature. Marianne later talked of the confusion caused by this meeting of bohemianism and Catholicism, and the convent school was a convenient scapegoat. "I was taught I had to marry the first man I made love to," she said. Within a few years of leaving St Joseph's she was satirising its primness. At a launch party for the underground magazine *International Times* held at The Roundhouse, London, in October 1966 she wore a nun's habit with most of the back cut away, winning first prize for the 'barest fancy dress costume'. The habit was back on again seven years later when she sang a duet with David Bowie, *I Got You Babe*, at his *1980 Floor Show*, a revue filmed by NBC at The Marquee Club, London, for broadcast in the United States. After many years of lamenting her school days, she told Eamon Carr of the *Dublin*

Evening Herald in February, 1990: "I didn't really have such a bad time. I have rather fond memories of it. I sort of think it was good for me in a way." She recalled passing time in lessons scribbling down potential stage names and pseudonyms for her debut novel. She also praised the school's music teacher who recognised her fine singing voice and spent many hours teaching how best to blend it with piano. Glynn Faithfull also came to view the school in a more positive light. "I can see the training and poise it gave her. When I saw her speaking on television I could see she had that polish about her," he said. Nik Cohn, in his book *A Wop Bopa Loo Bop A Lop Bam Boom*, explored the same theme: 'She might be shocking, but she did it in a nice accent. She wasn't vulgar with it. She could be coped with. Even in disgrace, she was a lady.'

3

Progress Theatre was established in 1946 by a team of young actors wishing to bring challenging and thoughtful drama to Reading. In their youth the BBC newsreader John Edmunds and the radio actress Rosalind Shanks were members but most famous among its alumni is the actor and film director Sir Kenneth Branagh. He made his theatrical debut as a teenager in the mid-1970s at the company's 96-seat venue housed in a former Co-op building in The Mount. He is now patron of the company. Another former member is Marianne Faithfull. In 1960, Marianne, aged 13, spent most Wednesday evenings with other teenagers in the youth section.

"She was a young girl when she was with us," said Freda Keep, a stalwart of the theatre. "She did various little things. She was quite a good singer and a very attractive girl who knew how to use her looks and voice. I remember she took part in a revue and sang the old music hall song 'The Boy I Love Is Up In The Gallery' accompanied by a piano. I didn't know her very well, but I remember her being confident." Betty Bishop, one of the theatre's founders, said, "She was keen and mucked in with everyone else. She was lively and bright and obviously an intelligent girl." Marianne appeared in Thornton Wilder's challenging play *Our Town*, staged by the senior players. "I don't know why she didn't play the main role of Emily. I think at the time we thought it would be better for her if she did a character part. Marianne had a great deal more potential than some of the others. She was one of the better ones," said Betty Bishop.

On one occasion Vanessa Redgrave, then aged 23, was invited to address the youth section. Marianne was among the audience as she recounted tales of playing opposite Charles Laughton in *A Midsummer Night's Dream* and Laurence Olivier and Albert Finney in *Coriolanus*. Eva Faithfull attended shows and afterwards discussed Marianne's performances with her, suggesting how she could improve. Marianne listened intently, recognising that the theatre was one of her mother's foremost passions. She sensed too that Eva wanted for her a career she had been denied.

As Marianne entered her mid-teens she grew ever more pretty. She learned quickly how to draw attention, a skill passed on by her mother. "She taught me that to be beautiful – as I knew I was – shouldn't be a passive thing. It was something to be put to use, the way that, in the past, she'd put her own beauty to use. I was taught by a highly trained professional," she told Philip Norman, The Rolling Stones' biographer. She had several dates with local youths including a few with the son of the headmaster of a local Quaker school, Leighton Park. Marianne attended a Valentine's Ball at Churchill College, Cambridge, in February, 1964. A party was being held on a staircase at the college and on the way up Marianne passed a student's room with the Da Vinci drawing on it, *The Vitruvian Man*. She was pondering who lived there when John Dunbar opened the door and the pair immediately began an animated conversation. She decided to ditch the boy with whom she had gone to the party. "It was one of those things where everything pales around you, except that one person," she said. Dunbar was studying at Churchill for a degree in Natural Sciences (he switched to History of Art in his final year). He had unkempt hair and horn rimmed glasses and seemed, to Marianne, exceptionally worldly and rebellious. "I met my catalyst, my Virgil. A world opened up when I met John," she said.

Dunbar was of an extremely prominent family. His grandfather, also called John, had been managing editor of the publishing firm Odhams Press, which owned *Woman* and *Ideal Home* magazines and, in 1930, had taken over the *Daily Herald*, the best-selling daily newspaper at the time with sales of two million copies per day. Dunbar's father, Robert – known as Bob – had graduated from and later taught at the Royal College of Arts and founded the London School of Film Technique [now the London Film School], run from a warehouse in Covent Garden. Bob Dunbar had left England for Hollywood in 1937 after struggling to find work with the near-collapse of British film production. On an extended stay in Mexico he met his future wife, Tatiana (known as Tania) Blagovieschensky, the daughter of wealthy Russian émigrés. John was born in Mexico in 1943 but moved in November 1944 to Moscow when his father was put in charge of press, public and cultural relations at the British Embassy. He also edited the newspaper, the *British Ally*. On returning to England in 1947, Bob Dunbar began a long career in the film industry working mainly as a producer with stellar actors, among them Orson Welles and Richard Attenborough.

John Dunbar had attended the same school as his father, Bryanston School in Dorset, set in 400 acres and designed in a neo-Georgian style by the architect Richard Norman Short, complete with its own outdoor Greek Theatre and 50 tennis courts. "At 17 I was chucked out for getting pissed. I did my entrance exams for Cambridge from Harrow Tech, started going to Hampstead parties and met lots of cool people," said Dunbar. While Marianne was schooled mainly in drama and singing by her mother, Dunbar had been encouraged by his liberal parents to love pictures, both still and moving. "He was fine – very cocky; a cocky graduate. He moved in a completely different world than me," said Chris O'Dell, who had studied under Robert Dunbar at the film school.

Marianne soon began visiting Dunbar regularly at Cambridge. She introduced him to her parents and although her mother was unsure about her first proper boyfriend, Glynn Faithfull thought him a 'nice chap'. Marianne continued to perform with the Progress Theatre and also appeared at coffee bars in Reading such as Shades and Café au Lait. She sang mainly a capella – 'House Of The Rising Sun', 'Blowin' In The Wind' (Bob Dylan had just made his first appearances in the UK, playing at a couple of London folk clubs in December 1962 and January 1963) and 'Babe I'm Gonna Leave You', the Anne Bredon song covered by Joan Baez. Chris O'Dell had a small car and during his holidays from Brighton Art College he ferried Marianne and her friends to venues. One of Marianne's closest friends was Sally Oldfield, sister of the musicians Mike and Terry Oldfield, and a fellow pupil at St Joseph's. Sally sometimes backed Marianne on guitar and Mike, although only 10 years old, tagged along too. Sally was from a similarly eccentric family as the Faithfulls and the pair often walked the school grounds discussing death, their favourite subject.

One of the first records Marianne owned was *Sketches Of Spain* by Miles Davis. She also bought singles by Buddy Holly, the Everly Brothers and Chuck Berry. The main influence on her was the darling of the bohemian set, the French singer Juliette Greco. Marianne imitated her look, wearing white lipstick, smoking Galoises and drinking strong black coffee. She hunted out books by Jean-Paul Sartre, Simone de Beauvoir, Albert Camus, Franz Kafka and Céline Arnauld. Dunbar took it upon himself to further shape her taste in music, playing her jazz records by the likes of John Coltrane.

While at Cambridge, Dunbar had met the folk singer and botanical artist, Rory McEwen. The son of a knighted MP, Eton-educated McEwen was typical of the associations made by Dunbar. "He introduced me to his family and all their cousins and Lord Thingummybob... oh, you know, that whole posh crowd," said Dunbar. At a party held in Chelsea, Dunbar met Princess Margaret who informed him that he had a hole in his jeans, putting her finger through it as she did so. Dunbar told Marianne of a scene developing in London among young people embracing drugs, music, photography and film. He was able to sample the high end of this nascent movement through his friendship with Peter Asher (the brother of actress Jane Asher) whom he had known since a child. Peter Asher, then 19, was a singer and guitarist and had formed a duo, Peter and Gordon, with a fellow former pupil of Westminster School, 18-year-old Gordon Waller. At the time, Waller was dating Dunbar's sister, Jenny [a future wife of the American 'Black Mountain' poet, Ed Dorn], an identical twin to Margaret. Dunbar, whose parents lived in a palatial house in Bentinck Street, Marylebone, regularly visited the Asher family home at nearby 57 Wimpole Street, where

Peter Asher shared the top floor with The Beatles' Paul McCartney, while Jane (McCartney's girlfriend) and her younger sister, Clare, had another floor.

On Friday 27 March, 1964 Marianne travelled from Reading to spend the weekend with Dunbar in London, staying at his parents' house. Dunbar told her Peter Asher had invited them to a party that evening at a flat in Seymour Place, Bayswater. Asher and Gordon Waller were in a celebratory mood because 'World Without Love', written for them by Asher's prospective brother-in-law, Paul McCartney, and his fellow Beatle, John Lennon, had reached the charts. Within a month it would displace The Beatles' 'Can't Buy Me Love' at number one. The party was to launch the singing career of former Italia Conti Stage School graduate Adrienne Poster (later known as Posta). Her father, Sid, had made a fortune in the furniture business and the party was held at his flat. As an eight-year-old Posta had appeared in the film *No Time For Tears*, a hospital drama starring Anna Neagle, Anthony Quayle and Sylvia Sims. Decca had released her debut single, 'Only Fifteen', in 1963 when she was actually 14. She was a protégé of Andrew Loog Oldham, manager of The Rolling Stones, who had asked Mick Jagger and Keith Richards to write a suitably cheery ditty for Posta. Oldham was set on creating a songwriting team to rival Lennon and McCartney. The pair proffered 'Shang A Doo Lang' as a follow-up to 'Only Fifteen' and Oldham, taking a cue from his hero Phil Spector, had produced. The record, much the same as the other seven singles subsequently released by Posta, failed to chart. Still, at the very party where she was being fêted, Oldham found someone with whom he would have far greater success.

Marianne and Dunbar had caused a stir as they arrived. "When we went in with Peter and Gordon there was a whole group of girls there," said Marianne. "They thought John was John Lennon and I was Cynthia. And I went 'Wow!' Very pleased about this!'" Members of The Rolling Stones turned up after their performance at the Windsor Ex-Servicemen's Club, a sell-out with more than 200 fans turned away. A few weeks earlier the band had finished recording their debut album and the single 'Not Fade Away', a cover of a Buddy Holly song, had entered the Top 10. The Stones and their entourage filtered through the large house but made only fleeting contact with Dunbar and Marianne. When he finally spoke to them, Jagger put on a slovenly voice to counter Marianne's refined tones. In his book, *Stone Alone*, former Stones' bass-player Bill Wyman wrote that Jagger deliberately spilled his drink onto Marianne's dress. 'The eyes of Mick and Andrew fell upon her immediately, for different reasons,' he wrote. 'Andrew saw her charismatic potential as a pop star, without ever hearing a note, and told her so during the opening conversation. Mick vied for her attention for a more obvious reason, but she was clearly attached to Dunbar. So Mick 'accidentally' spilled champagne down her dress to make an impression: she would not forget that. At this stage, Mick was still attached to Chrissie Shrimpton [sister of the famous model Jean Shrimpton and, at that point, Jagger's girlfriend of one year]; his obvious enthusiasm for Marianne had to be put on ice'. Others at the party did not recall the incident with the champagne and reported that the initial contact between two people later to become celebrated lovers was curt and largely unmemorable. A similar episode did occur, however, at another party a year or so later. Marianne claimed later to be initially unimpressed with The Rolling Stones, considering them coarse and vulgar.

The one associate of the band to focus on Marianne was the man at its epicentre, Andrew Oldham. As he came into view she recalled that he looked like 'a strange creature, all beaky and angular like some bird of prey'. He had known Dunbar from when they were both involved briefly in Labour Party politics in Hampstead. Marianne viewed Oldham, 20, and resplendent in mascara, eyeshadow and pancake make-up, with the same initial disdain as The Rolling Stones. He was brash but, as she listened to him speak, she realised he was personable and urbane [he had been public school-educated and expelled from the prestigious Wellingborough School, one of the oldest schools in England with historical links to the armed forces]. When Marianne told him her full name, Oldham remarked that it was the perfect name for a pop star. "He had spent most of the evening talking to John and then, at the end, he said he wanted to record me," said Marianne. "He didn't want to know if I could sing; he said it didn't matter. Why me? I don't know. I was very poor and very bohemian, I suppose, and I must have been very pretty and very unconscious of it. I think he thought I had star quality. I thought he was a spotty youth." Oldham was not too concerned about Marianne's singing ability because he was aware multi-tracking and echo chambers could bolster the weakest of voices.

At the same party Keith Richards met the 17-year-old model, Linda Keith. She became his girlfriend for several years before taking up with Jimi Hendrix. "The big excitement of the evening was Marianne sitting at a piano very coyly," said Linda Keith. "That was her thing, to be this coy, sweet child." The weekend was made even more memorable for Marianne because she later met Paul McCartney. He said: "I knew Marianne directly she came out of the convent. I'd met her at the Ashers' house so I'd see her there socially. She was such a pretty, virginal little thing. Then I remember reading an interview with her and she said, 'I want to experience anything and everything,' and I remember thinking, 'Ooh, hold on now, Marianne. Come on, girl – straight out of the convent to anything and everything?" Marianne later told friends she and Dunbar had made love for the first time that weekend.

Two days after the party Marianne was summoned to Andrew Oldham's office. She took with her an acoustic guitar and sang a couple of 'Joan Baez-style' songs. 'Technically, Faithfull couldn't sing – still can't – but she reminded me of Grace Kelly,' wrote Andrew Oldham in his book, *Stoned*. 'Or rather Kelly's voice in the duet she sang with Bing Crosby, 'True Love', in the 1956 film, *High Society*. Kelly was almost speaking her part in a captivating and sensual monotone.' Oldham was fixated by this Grace Kelly association and mentioned it often to friends when 'talking up' Marianne. He had, in his words, 'fallen' for Kelly several years earlier, claiming he admired 'tramps that passed for pure'. In hindsight it seems a peculiar link because in the film Kelly sings only a few lines of the Cole Porter song and then as an accompaniment to Crosby. Her voice is barely discernible. Oldham had probably made the connection because of the atmosphere evoked by the song – the two lovers are alone in a small boat on the sea – and a similar impression he had of Marianne.

Back in Reading, Marianne was planning to do A-Levels in English, Divinity and History at St Joseph's before, if accepted, starting a degree course at Cambridge University. She was enthralled by Dunbar and already imagining marriage and a life together. She saw him as a tormented youth, a hero of a Fyodor Dostoyevsky novel, talking endlessly of his angst and plans to kill himself. She would be his muse and her love would save him from himself. Meanwhile, Andrew Oldham was also lost to reverie. "The minute I saw Marianne, I knew she was something special," he said. "She had this fantastic virginal look. I mean, at a time when most chicks were shaking ass and coming on strong, here was this pale, blonde, retiring, chaste teenager looking like the Mona Lisa, except with a great body. I didn't care whether she could sing or not, I could sell that look, and I'd learned what miracles could be achieved by clever engineers in a recording studio."

Although Jagger later referred to him as a 'dilettante', Oldham had, in fact, served a thorough apprenticeship, albeit at breakneck speed. In the three years since leaving college with three O-Levels, he had done promotional work for the fashion guru Mary Quant and the 'King of Carnaby Street', John Stephens – one of the first to identify a market for fashionable clothes for young men; booked bands for the well-regarded Manchester music agency, Kennedy Street Enterprises; plugged records by Gerry & The Pacemakers and Billy J. Kramer & The Dakotas for The Beatles' manager, Brian Epstein (on a weekly retainer of £6); and been tour manager of Mark Wynter who had scored two hits, 'Venus In Blue Jeans' and 'Go Away Little Girl', in the winter of 1962. Oldham was proud of his hustler status and talked his way into acting as publicist for the producer Joe Meek, and Bob Dylan when he made his first visit to Britain. Between music business jobs he worked as a waiter at the Flamingo Club and doorman at Ronnie Scott's Jazz Club, both in Soho.

Rumours circulated that before embarking on impresario roles Oldham had tried to establish himself as a performer. He dismissed the notion many years later. "I got rid of any desire to be a performer when I sung in a school concert at the age of 12 and the sound that was louder and more in tune than my voice was the sound of my knees knocking," he said. "Bios [biographies] on me always state that I was a performer called Sandy Beach and had a group called The Chancery Lane Trio. Here I'm rewarded with my own PR. I used to tell Peter Jones of the *Record Mirror*, incidentally the journalist who first sent me to see The Rolling Stones in April of 1963, that I had been a compère called Sandy Beach and had played piano in a jazz group called The Chancery Lane Trio. Nonsense. Anyone familiar with London will know that Chancery Lane is a Tube station and a famous street in the City. As for Sandy Beach, I don't think there are any of those in England. Well, not without pebbles."

Throughout the spring of 1964 Oldham presented The Rolling Stones as the antithesis of the presumed soft-edged cuteness of The Beatles. He was originally against the Stones' renegade stance but had seen its potential mass appeal. In a famous stroke of PR genius he asked the question 'Would you let your daughter marry a Rolling Stone?' Meanwhile, he had seen Brian Epstein assemble a roster of young protégés with The Beatles at the vanguard but with others such as Cilla Black and Gerry & The Pacemakers, and speculative signings, The Rustiks, The Cyrkle and The Remo Four, part of the portfolio. Oldham was keen to do the same, realising a combination of acts would complement each other in artistic and financial terms and provide an effective insurance policy against fluctuating trends. Marianne Faithfull was an ideal act for Oldham for three distinct reasons: Jagger and Richards could write for her and establish themselves as a bona fide songwriting 'team'; her virginal look and convent school background was a counterpoint to the Stones' bad-boy persona and, thirdly, he had noted the chart success of a string of girl singers, among them Dionne Warwick, Dusty Springfield, Millie, Julie Rogers, Cilla Black and Mary Wells. On a personal level he wanted to emulate Phil Spector who had largely made his name working with female performers.

Without Marianne being aware, Oldham began looking for a song to mark the debut of his new discovery. "From the moment I had caught sight of her I'd recognised my next adventure. In another century you would have set sail for her – in 1964 you recorded her," he said. He was already mentally writing the press release: 'Marianne Faithfull is 16, beautiful, unblemished, and straight out of convent school...' Oldham had struck up a friendship with Lionel Bart, 14 years his senior, a prolific writer of chart hits, winner of nine Ivor Novello awards and most famous for creating the successful stage musical *Oliver!* The pair had nebulous plans for a joint project called 'Forward Sound' where they would present new talent to the British public. Marianne was considered the perfect opening act and Bart was on standby to write a song should Jagger and Richards fail to deliver. Oldham was apprehensive because as well as the Adrienne Posta flop, two Jagger/Richards songs written for the Decca-signed artist George Bean had also failed to chart in January 1964 – the rocky 'It Should Have Been You' (on which Richards also played guitar) and the anaemic 'Will You Be My Lover Tonight?'

Six weeks after the party Marianne passed the voice test held at Decca's studios in Broadhurst Gardens, West Hampstead, but had difficulty singing the number supplied by Bart, 'I Don't Know How (To Tell You)'. She made several attempts but, according to Oldham, sounded like an 'inbred hyena'. Tony Calder, Oldham's business partner, later referred to the song as 'the biggest pile of dog shit you've ever heard in your life'. Oldham had no option but to draw on Jagger and Richards for Marianne's debut single. He ordered them to compose a ballad he felt appropriate to Marianne's convent girl background. "I want a song with brick walls all around it, and high windows and no sex," he told them. Keith Richards recalled later: "So what Andrew Oldham did was lock us up in the kitchen for a night and say, 'Don't come out without a song.' We sat around and came up with 'As Tears Go By'. It was unlike most Rolling Stones material, but that's what happens when you write songs, you immediately fly to some other realm. The weird thing is that Andrew found Marianne Faithfull at that time, bunged it to her and it was a fuckin' hit for her – we were songwriters already! But it took the rest of that year to dare to write anything for the Stones."

Mick Jagger recalled it differently: "Keith likes to tell the story about the kitchen, God bless him. I think Andrew may have said something at some point along the lines of 'I should lock you in a room until you've written a song' and in that way he did mentally lock us in a room, but he didn't literally lock us in." Despite Oldham's claim that it was written specifically for Marianne, she said the song, originally titled 'As Time Goes By' but later changed to 'As Tears Go By' (to avoid confusion with the Herman Hupfeld song featured in the film *Casablanca* and sung by Sam [Dooley Wilson]), already pre-existed and was an out-take from the Stones' early repertoire. "All that stuff about how Mick wrote it for me was awfully nice but untrue," she told *Penthouse* magazine in 1980. Ten years later, on the sleeve notes for the *Blazing Away* album, Marianne contradicted herself by referring to it as, 'the song Mick Jagger and Keith Richards wrote for me'. Whatever the true circumstances surrounding the genealogy of 'As Tears Go By', Oldham was delighted because, unlike previous compositions by the pair, it was neither derivative nor anaemic. In his own snappy terminology he described it as 'absolute knockout'. With its sad, nostalgic refrain, it was a peculiar song to be sung by someone so young. "I thought at the time it was a very odd song for a girl to sing with those lyrics about watching people 'Doing things I used to do/They think are new,' Marianne told Kris Kirk of *Melody Maker* in August 1987. Most of the emerging group of girl singers generally went in for boisterous ditties such as 'Shout' by Lulu and '(There's) Always Something There To Remind Me' by Sandie Shaw, two songs released at a similar time.

Marianne recorded the single in May 1964 at Olympic Studios in London's Baker Street. The session followed a series of missed appointments. Oldham had difficulty making contact with Marianne because there was no telephone at Milman Road. Telegrams were sent backwards and forwards: 'Can't do three o'clock, Wednesday. Have to come after finishing school'. The musical director working with Oldham on the record was Mike Leander. Although only 23, Leander had studied orchestration and conducting at Trinity College of Music in London and partly completed a law course before joining the Decca empire in 1963. Within the company he was seen as a straight man with an ability to create songs to a deadline from scraps of musical ideas. Sometimes he supervised the recording and mixing of three singles in a day on primitive four-track equipment, with concrete echo chambers positioned on the studio roof. "I was happily married and settled down," he said. "My hair wasn't very long and I *was* quite straight really. I took

35

it all very seriously and wanted to have a serious career. I did not do drugs and I think I was viewed as reliable, dependable and respected for whatever musical skills I had."

Leander had worked on numerous projects with Oldham, most recently in January 1964 when they recorded, as The Andrew Oldham Orchestra, the track '365 Rolling Stones (One For Every Day Of The Year)', which was released as a single and became the theme tune to *Ready Steady Go!* for two years. "As far as Andrew was concerned Marianne was the Virgin Mary. She not only had that fresh innocence but she looked like the Virgin Mary," said Leander. He shared many hours in close quarters with Oldham, usually trying to interpret his unorthodox production ideas. "Everything about Andrew was commercial. He had great vision and it would be unfair to call him a dilettante. He probably didn't grow up and that is the nicest way of putting it. He wasn't a great businessman but he had tremendous flair and was a great entrepreneur." Leander was keen to blend orchestral music with pop and used harps, oboes and harpsichords at sessions. Marianne was perfect for his indulgence because she had no real views of her own about how she wanted her record to sound. "She was terrified and very slow to make her presence felt," said Leander. "She was nervous. Andrew could be very intimidating when he fired on all cylinders but I have always been good with girl singers. She had no experience at all. It was not as if she had even been in a band for a couple of years. She was the last person who knew what we were trying to do. With Marianne, I soon learned to take what I could get. She was never a brilliant singer but a wonderful creator of musical moods. If Andrew and I ever got a sound for Marianne, I suppose it was a plinky-plunky orchestral one."

On the day of the session they tried again to record the song written by Lionel Bart. Once more, they failed. "I remember the musicians' sigh of relief at not having to play Lionel's fart-stopper," said Oldham. "That feeling of release can be heard in the very playing of 'As Tears Go By', making it so magical." It took Marianne 30 minutes to place a vocal on the track and only the slight rasping of her over-stressed 'S's' and 'T's' might have suggested it was done by a novice. On the B-side of Decca F11923, Marianne, at Oldham's request, laid down an impressive version of the traditional folk song 'Greensleeves', recorded with the help of Decca's in-house sound engineer, Harry Robinson. Oldham's name appeared on both sides of the record. He was listed as arranger of 'Greensleeves' and, cryptically, co-writer of the A-side. Theoretically this meant he was due a share of publishing royalties but he later claimed David Platz of Essex Music, with whom he had a business arrangement, directed the income elsewhere.

In interviews Marianne has given differing accounts of her first recording session. In one she claimed to have travelled to and from the studio alone while in the other she said Sally Oldfield was with her, and Jagger and Richards had been present during a small part of the recording. Afterwards they offered the girls a lift to the railway station in their car where Jagger suggested Marianne should sit on his knee because it was a tight fit. She refused politely and Sally had to position herself awkwardly on his leg while Jagger grinned and gave a wink to Marianne. It is likely that the incident occurred at a later session because the Stones spent most of May 1964 on a British tour.

Andrew Oldham held a party at a London club to launch Marianne's career and turned up in a pristine white suit. He was said to be going through his 'Tom Wolfe period'. Oldham's publicist and fellow carouser, Andy Wickham, formerly a press officer at EMI, had brought along the charismatic American impresario Kim Fowley. Oldham revered Fowley because he had worked with Phil Spector and Berry Gordy, the founder of Motown Records. Fowley had relocated to England temporarily to oversee the career of PJ Proby and undertake various side-projects. "And there was Marianne Faithfull," said Fowley. "The whole big-titted Aryan Goddess, the peak of wet-pussy goddess. I came on hard and hit on her immediately. Andrew controlled the room with her. We were both there with our pieces of meat. Mine was Proby, his was Faithfull. Andrew was a great hustler. He was old-school Broadway-Beverly Hills. He had his 'I'll kill you, I'll charm you, I'll leave you for dead' act."

'As Tears Go By' first appeared in the charts on Thursday August 13 and Saturday August 15, 1964, reflecting the different days *Record Mirror* and *Record Retailer/Music Week* were published. Oldham had negotiated with Decca to make the record a priority and in the weeks preceding its release, the marketing and press departments worked assiduously to acquaint the public with Marianne Faithfull. "She was a superstar at Decca. She took a bit of stick because there was a degree of hype about her, as there usually was when Andrew Oldham was involved. She did one TV appearance and blew everyone away. The kids loved her. She suffered at first for being a figment of Andrew's imagination but she soon threw it off and got a strong following," said Leander.

Marianne had joined Decca during its most prolific period since it had begun releasing records in June 1929. In the year she signed to Sir Edward Lewis' company it had scored 39 Top 30 hits from 247 releases, a remarkable ratio of almost one hit per six records. The label had been prominent in the 1950s with established artists Vera Lynn, Winifred Atwell, Jimmy Young, The Stargazers, Mantovani, Ted Heath and Dickie Valentine. These were superseded by the next wave – Anthony Newley, Tommy Steele, Billy Fury, Tom Jones and, of course, The Rolling Stones. By the time Marianne joined Decca it was a showbiz institution, a who's who of British pop.

If the record label was right, so was the timing. Britain had six million teenagers in 1964 with previously unrivalled spending power. Government figures showed teenagers were spending £1,500 million per year, of which a large proportion was devoured by the record industry. In 1964 alone more than 100 million records were bought and Marianne's chances of survival in such a bracing market place were strong, especially with her link to one of the market leaders, The Rolling Stones. Their fourth single, 'It's All Over Now', had become the first of five consecutive number ones just weeks before the release of 'As Tears Go By'. Across Britain the summer of 1964 was particularly turbulent. Mods and rockers clashed in May, assaulting each other with broken deck chairs at several South Coast resorts. Police made 76 arrests at Brighton, while in Margate two youths were stabbed and 51 arrested. The youth of the country was restless and for possibly the first time identified itself as a distinct group, caught between childhood and adulthood. Henry Brooke, the Home Secretary, promised 'firm action'.

One of Marianne's first promotional trips was to Tyne Tees Television in Newcastle. She travelled there with Andrew Oldham in Lionel Bart's two-seater Lamborghini, squeezed uncomfortably into a 'ledge seat' at the back. She returned to London by train and met Jeremy Clyde of the pop duo Chad and Jeremy, in the first-class compartment. On arriving in London they went to Clyde's flat and had what Marianne later referred to as 'great sex'. Over breakfast the next day, Clyde counselled Marianne on the difference between sex and love, warning her to be careful with her emotions. Around this time Marianne had her first lesbian relationship, with an Indian girl called Saida. After taking Tuinal [a sedative], Marianne said she was seduced by 16-year-old Saida who was 'absolutely gorgeous'. They remained occasional lovers for several years.

Oldham had drawn up a contract that needed the signature of Eva Faithfull because Marianne was not old enough to sign a legal document. The only clause Eva requested was that Marianne should have a chaperone while on tour. Marianne, encouraged by Eva, was determined to complete her studies, convinced the record was a one-off, a pleasant but short diversion. She viewed the pop world as trivial and transient and believed she was destined for a more significant life as an actress or possibly a journalist. Eva was interviewed about her daughter's fledgling pop career by a local paper and provided fantastic copy: "I feel I may have to put a cannon outside the front door and train our Dalmatian to be fierce. Shall we have fans around the door writing 'I love Marianne' over our dustbin?" Oldham chose Peter Jones as the journalist to introduce Marianne in print. Jones, the first writer to interview The Beatles in the national music press, was known for his ability to unearth new talent. On Saturday July 11, 1964, Marianne was featured in Jones' weekly column, 'New Faces' in *Record Mirror*. Under the headline 'Marianne is a "real" nice person' Jones assembled cheery prose to appease Oldham and set the tone for a succession of similarly flimsy articles. The piece opened with: 'She's a seventeen-year-old blonde who causes male heads to swivel approvingly (especially mine) even when she does something simple like walk across a room. She's so shy, rather wistful, with unspoiled charm.' He informed readers that 'the long-haired lovely' was the daughter of a Baroness, attended a convent school and 'digged' folk stars. He closed the feature: 'Marianne is a sweetie, a doll, a dish. Is everybody getting the message?'

Another writer, Keith Altham, had recently joined the staff of *New Musical Express* after a stint with *Fabulous* magazine, and was assigned to interview Marianne. "We had a policy of interviewing people when they got into the charts. Interviews were unmemorable in those days. They weren't particularly substantial or intrusive. It was more like finding out their favourite colour and things like that." He too was taken by Marianne's good looks and grandeur. "She was incredibly beautiful. She had very pale skin and took your breath away. She was one of the most beautiful women I have ever seen. It was difficult to concentrate during the interview. Even in the early days, when people tried to present her as a bimbo, although that word wasn't around then, she was bright. She was never pretentious, just slightly upper class and slightly snobby, but it made her more lady-like if anything."

In an interview with *Record Mirror*, Marianne revealed an unusually candid side when asked about her single: "Well, I don't honestly like it all that much. Some critics have said it's folksy. Well, I'm a folk fanatic. People like Joan Baez impress me – and I know I could never sing in the same class as her. So for me there's something phoney about my disc."

'As Tears Go By' debuted at number 27 in the *Record Mirror* chart. Decca moved swiftly and its marketing department created an advert to help keep the record on an upward course. Filling nearly half a page across the music press, it contained 10 small photographs of Marianne, all hair and hazy sultriness. The caption read: 'Any way you look at it... Marianne Faithfull's "As Tears Go By" is No. 27'. The other chart entries that week were The Kinks' first hit and an eventual number one, 'You Really Got Me', which came in seven places below Marianne and The Bachelors' 'I Wouldn't Trade You For The World', which was also on Decca, as were a quarter of all the acts in that week's Top 20. 'As Tears Go By' made a steady weekly climb of the charts, to numbers 19, 16, and 15.

On Wednesday September 2 1964 Marianne made her first appearance on *Top Of The Pops*, appearing live at the former church where it was recorded in Rusholme, Manchester. The DJ David Jacobs introduced her and the other live guests, The Kinks, Herman's Hermits, Manfred Mann, Dave Berry and The Honeycombs. Her appearance helped the record move up a place. The following week it slipped back to number 10 but then made a slight reverse and returned to number nine on September 25. The first time Marianne spoke on television was on *Juke Box Jury* on October 31, 1964. She was the 'mystery guest' and had to wait off-screen while a panel including Gene Pitney and Petula Clark made remarks about her record. After they had finished she was introduced to the viewers. She said later that she looked like 'an angel with really big tits'. 'As Tears Go By' enjoyed a chart life of more than three months and finally slipped out in November, 1964. As it left the British chart, it was released in the United States and reached a creditable number 22 by Christmas 1964, which was to be her highest ever placing in America's *Billboard* singles chart. *Billboard* magazine, incidentally, deemed Marianne 'the greatest discovery of the year'.

Eva Faithfull was nonplussed by the record's success. "I will be glad when she goes back to school. This is getting serious and Marianne looked upon it from the start as a bit of fun," she told reporters. Eva found herself discussing Marianne's pop career with a good number of people in 1964 because it was often the main topic of conversation at a coffee bar where she worked, The Carillion in Harris Arcade close to Reading railway station. "It was very much a place for ladies going shopping. It was in a respectable area. We all took turns at working there," said Chris O'Dell. Eva had undertaken several other low-paid jobs including spells in a shoe shop and as a bus conductor. John Dunbar, meanwhile, had missed the commotion. He spent most of the summer of 1964 hitch-hiking around Greece. Earlier in the year he had done the same in the United States.

'As Tears Go By' would later be seen as an abridged narrative of Marianne's life. The song title or a modified version – As Years Go By or As Time Goes By – provided apposite headlines, year on year, for

Marianne's story. "I once said that, if it hadn't been for that song, I'd be happily married with six kids now, but I've never wanted that. In fact it's one of the most absurd things I've ever said, but I do sometimes make those kind of remarks for the hell of it. I always have and I hope I always will," she said.

4

The success of *As Tears Go By* left Marianne bemused. At first she planned a return to studies ("If I get good marks I'll stay on at school" – August, 1964); then she wanted to act ("I think this record will help me in my ambition to become an actress" – August, 1964, again); but sometimes she would commit herself to singing, though she was unsure of the genre, whether to revert to her first love of folk or continue with pop. She recognised the flimsy nature of the music business but was captivated by it. "You see, I've lived a sheltered life, what with the convent schooling and so on. Now I'm getting a chance to meet 'real' people outside, if you see what I mean," she told *Record Mirror*. At other times she told friends she wanted to be back home with Eva and their Dalmatian, Sarah. "When I was about 15, before it all happened, I was happy, with my mum, with my school friends, really innocent," she told the *Jewish Chronicle* in 2008. "I mean, the naughtiest thing I was doing was reading Oscar Wilde and Baudelaire."

Soon after *As Tears Go By* became a hit Andrew Oldham put Marianne on a weekly 'wage' of £80. At the time the average weekly wage for women in manufacturing was £9 and men working in white collar jobs were earning £24 per week. Marianne was fond of shopping and began commissioning clothes from feted fashion designers such as Caroline Charles, an ex-protégé of Mary Quant famous for eccentric creations which included dresses made from bedspreads. Marianne's first taste of life on the road came on a tour supporting Freddie & The Dreamers and The Hollies, two bands who between them had scored more than 10 hits by September 1964. These package tours were popular in the mid-1960s and up to 10 different acts often comprised a bill. The young artistes clambered on board a coach outside Andrew Oldham's office and set off for scores of unlikely destinations throughout Britain. Marianne later referred to these tours as 'brutal'. She had told Oldham about Chris O'Dell's love of photography and secured him a job taking pictures on the tour for possible use on record sleeves.

"They were very early days in the pop business," said O'Dell. "It was run very badly by a lot of really terribly dishonest people. Everything was done on the cheap. We'd bundle on to the bus and trundle on this bloody thing to the most appalling, clapped out, smelly, old rotten places in towns like Skegness and Redcar – awful places. The accommodation was fairly squalid. There weren't any roadies or tons of back-up gear. It was terribly primitive and as a way of life it was foreign to everyone." The first show of the 22-date tour – effectively Marianne's first bona fide concert performance – was at the Adelphi in Slough on Saturday 19 September, 1964. She was fifth on the bill behind the two main headliners, plus The Four Pennies and Tony Jackson & The Vibrations. In the official programme it stated that she was the daughter of 'Diana Erisso' and her 'likes' were: folk music, Marlon Brando, long evening dresses and the skin off custard. The notice closed: 'She is all set for a promising future.'

During the tour Marianne had a fling with Allan Clarke, the singer with The Hollies, who was married at the time. 'The awkward bit came with the arrival of his wife, as he then pretended not to know me,' she wrote in her autobiography, *Faithfull*. 'I don't know what I thought he should have done, maybe introduce me enthusiastically: "Darling, I want you to meet this lovely girl I've been fucking on the road. She's been a super stand-in for you."' That night, Marianne got drunk for the first time and had to be helped on to the stage to perform. Graham Nash, The Hollies' guitarist, revealed that the song 'Carrie Anne', a number three hit for the band in May 1967, was about Marianne. "The story with 'Carrie Anne' is that we wrote it – started it – as a song for

Marianne Faithfull. We'd all seen her and we all wanted her. She was a deliciously sexy young Catholic schoolgirl with all of the baggage that comes along with that. We loved Marianne, so we started it out to be a song about her, then chickened out. We tried to find a name that was kind of similar and one that would not give the game away, shall we say. We came up with Carrie Anne. Me and Tony [Hicks, the band's other guitarist] started writing it mainly and then Allan came and joined in."

The tour closed on 18 October, 1964 at the Rank Ballroom, Hanley, Staffordshire. Marianne had quickly developed her own idiosyncratic way of performing. She approached the microphone nervously and with her hands dangling loosely at her sides, sang primly and clearly very close to the microphone, backed usually by a lone guitarist. "I'm not aloof. I'm terribly shy and fantastically introvert. I don't see myself as anything. I stand still and just sing when I'm on stage because I'm too terrified to move," she told *New Musical Express*. She said her innate sense of stillness was appropriated from the nuns at St Joseph's. At a concert held at an RAF camp in Scotland, Marianne appeared on the same bill as Alma Cogan and the contrast in performances was marked. Cogan, then in her early thirties, had emerged a decade or so before with similarly mainstream female singers such as Rosemary Clooney, Ruby Murray and Anne Shelton. In their extravagant dresses and with ready smiles, they were about to be superseded by a generation of girls epitomised by Marianne who were perceived as more street level and cute-sexy. After the upbeat projection of Cogan, the airmen in the crowd were met by matchstick Marianne shuffling fearfully towards the microphone stand, her dress buttoned to the top. "I'm going to sing my next record," were the only spoken words in her performance.

By 1964 the four major record companies each had successful British girl singers. EMI had Cilla Black; Pye, Petula Clark and Sandie Shaw; Philips, Dusty Springfield; and Decca, Kathy Kirby and Lulu. The exuberance of this new girl talent distinguished them from their more established peers but they were still marketed largely as 'girls next door' with little suggestion of sex or real artistic worth. Outside these flagship acts, girls in pop were often little more than novelty turns. Some dressed in tartan, others wore horn-rimmed glasses or had silly names such as

Polly Perkins and recorded songs with witless titles like *Oo-Chang-a-Lang* (The Orchids) and *Ya Ya Twist* (Petula Clark). Their management teams were habitually male and the few women in the industry were secretaries or personal assistants. Male domination was reflected in the end-of-year sales figures for 1964. Only three girls appeared in the list of 20 best-selling artists and even Cilla Black with two number ones – 'Anyone Who Had A Heart' and 'You're My World' – could not find a place within a Top 10 dominated by solo male performers and all-male groups, among them The Bachelors, The Searchers and, of course, The Beatles and The Rolling Stones.

Only days into her first tour, newspapers were tracking down Marianne and expressing surprise, and joy, to find her quotable and photogenic. Under headlines such as 'Talent Doesn't Count' Marianne was remarkably frank. "I don't know whether I'm a success as a singer," she said. "I don't really care because success in the pop world can't be had by wanting it. The only things I want to succeed in are marriage and acting. You can make yourself a good actress. But you can't make yourself a good singer because in the pop business talent doesn't count." She was already able to deconstruct a business in which she was a novice. "What makes me furious is that everybody forgets they are only there by courtesy of a few thousand kids. They think they are talented – but they are not. They listen to the people that tell them they are wonderful and they lap it all up. If only they would have the humility to appreciate the kids who buy their records and put them where they are. It's all the fault of the managers and the hangers-on." She then showed playfulness towards Andrew Oldham. "Andrew's different. He's sincere. Well, he says so, anyway, so let's pretend he is."

In September 1964 she told Cordell Marks of *New Musical Express*: "Most people are in music just for the money but they don't admit it." A few weeks later she told the same paper: "What I dislike about the pop business, from what I've seen so far, is quite basic. I hate being told to be sociable to people whom I couldn't really give a damn about." No other artist, male or female, solo or group member, had spoken before in such direct and truthful terms about the business of pop, and rarely have they done so since.

Oldham quickly began to find his hold over Marianne slipping. "When a human being is controlled it's always a two-way street," she told *Melody Maker* in 1987. "Little Marianne had as much power in her own way as Andrew did. Dependency always cut both ways and you never really know who's depending on whom, who really has the power, in a situation like that. And naturally, the tendency is for any human being to abuse that power." Although she often spoke of leaving the business in the early days, Chris O'Dell understood why she didn't. "I think she enjoyed it. Looking back, it is hard to see why she stuck it out but like a lot of people she is quite egocentric and I think she loved the attention. She had a lot of attention as a child from her mother and from me and everyone else around her because she was an attractive child with a nice personality. I think she instinctively knew how to make people like her and I think she managed quite well in the business as far as getting on with everybody," he said.

At the end of September 1964 Marianne returned to the Decca studios to record a follow-up to 'As Tears Go By'. Mike Leander was working in the United States so the sessions were supervised by an acquaintance of Oldham's, David Whitaker, who had previously worked as a songwriter for the producer Bunny Lewis and the Denmark Street publisher Freddie Poser. Marianne was anxious to show off her folk slant and chose Bob Dylan's 'Blowin' In The Wind'. Dylan had established himself as the leader of America's wave of folk/protest with his second album, *The Freewheelin' Bob Dylan*. His visit to Britain in 1963 had been noted by the hip cognoscenti but since then the chief players in Greenwich Village and beyond had adopted Dylan as their leader and this led to an intense scramble to record his material. Unfortunately, Marianne missed out to a trio that attended the same clubs and socialised with Dylan. Peter Yarrow, Paul Stookey and Mary Travers, collectively known as Peter, Paul & Mary, released a version of 'Blowin' In The Wind' a few weeks before Marianne's. While theirs reached number two in the United States and 13 in Britain, Marianne's mannered rendition did not chart. On the B-side she covered 'House Of The Rising Sun' which had been a number one for The Animals three months earlier. Marianne's version, heavily orchestrated by Whitaker (under Oldham's supervision) and featuring backing vocals by The Ivy League, was a peculiar hybrid of classical and folk with more than a passing nod to Ennio Morricone whose soundtracks to spaghetti westerns were proving popular across Europe in the mid-1960s.

The commercial failure of 'Blowin' In The Wind' was the catalyst to Marianne parting company with Andrew Oldham. She blamed Decca and Oldham for choosing the wrong song, saying she wanted to release a track she had recorded called 'Strange World'. She referred to the single as a 'total disaster' and complained she had been hurried into the studio straight from a tour and this made her sound 'dreary'. 'I did my best to blame Andrew and Decca at the time but it was my own doing entirely,' she wrote in her autobiography, *Faithfull*. 'I was having problems with Sir Andrew. It was the fog-and-amphetamine factor that bothered me. He was really out there at that time. I was intimidated by the cool, mystifying jive speak that passed for chat. I had no idea what he was talking about. He was too hip for me.'

Marianne turned to Oldham's business partner, Tony Calder, and asked him to become her manager. "Decca was crying out for more Marianne," said Calder. "It had all got a bit big and Andrew decided he was the star. He said, 'I'm not going to record her any more,' like it was the end of the world as we'd known it. I said, 'Don't be a cunt.' He was going off on drugs, pills, liquid speed. He didn't want to know about Marianne; he'd had it with her. Things might have been different if he'd wanted to fuck her like the rest of the world. She bored him. He said, 'She's not cred; I can't work with her any more.'"

Calder and Oldham had formed Image – widely thought to be the first PR company to specialise in pop – in 1963 when they were 20 and 19 respectively. They had declared war on the existing orthodoxy. "Our attitude to the business in the UK was fuck them all, they were old men," said Calder. He had moved to London from his home town of Southampton to work in the sales and marketing department at Decca where he quickly built up a reputation for antagonism. "I remember Calder rubbing his hands together and saying, 'Who can we screw up now, who can we cut up?'," said Tony Hall, the head of promotions. Calder left Decca after he became frustrated with colleagues who did not share his obsession with the Del Shannon song 'Runaway'. He felt they were slow to promote it, though, in March 1961, it reached number one in the British charts. He spent evenings working with the DJ Jimmy Savile, who was having success with his 'Off The Record' nights where he toured venues playing records, effectively heralding the birth of the discothèque.

After leaving Decca, Calder was able to spend more time promoting Savile's ventures and learned a great deal about the industry from a man almost 20 years his senior. Calder was hustling on behalf of Steve Marriott (later of The Small Faces) when he met Andrew Oldham early in 1963. They agreed to pool contacts and clients and set up office as Image in July 1964 at Ivor Court, a few streets from Regent's Park in Marylebone, London. They handled the PR for all the acts signed to the two northern management heavyweights, Brian Epstein's NEMS Enterprises in Liverpool and Kennedy Street Enterprises in Manchester, as well as Oldham's established clients The Rolling Stones, Gene Pitney, Georgie Fame, Phil Spector, The Beach Boys and Marianne Faithfull. They had formed by far the most powerful independent company in the music business and revelled in their status as a formidable double-act. They formed a pincer movement on their quarry, talking fast and finishing one another's sentences. They were aware that they complemented each other physically – Oldham was extremely tall, fair and slim while Calder, usually in a suit, was dark, stocky and wore thick-rimmed glasses.

"Tony was not a bad guy," said Marianne, "but a bit sleazy in the nicest possible way." Andy Wickham, who left EMI to work at Image, agreed: "Tony was a dog-track bookie who seemed to only think in terms of deals and reeked of danger." Indeed, there was a coalescence of charm and menace about both men. Oldham, usually with his chauffeur in tow, Reg 'The Butcher' King – a name given to him by Keith Richards – was well known for occasional strong-arm tactics and violence-tinged escapades. He had slammed down sash windows on journalists' fingertips, roughed up promoters and cruised across London in his powder blue Chevrolet, smashing car windows and punching pedestrians. In a two-page article in the *Daily Mirror* in September 1964 headlined 'The Strange man who set the Stones Rolling: NUT OR GENIUS?' Oldham revealed: "I don't dig that 'hello' bit. The record companies are only interested in money. The artists only love you so long as you're making money for them." In the same piece he admitted he had visited a psychiatrist and undergone group therapy. "It was all very funny," he said.

While Oldham was on business in the United States, Marianne confided to Calder that she wanted him to be her manager. Although he knew it would affect his relationship with Oldham, at least on a temporary basis, he agreed. "Marianne had caused a real sensation, just the pictures alone," he said. "David Bailey fell in love with her and did those famous pictures with the ankle socks on and everybody wanted to fuck her." Oldham feigned indifference but in his book *2Stoned* written many years later, he claimed *he* had left Marianne and smarted: 'She embarrassed me and for that I left her. On vinyl she was my audiophile Grace Kelly, a siren slut from the top drawer to undermine a nation's hard-on. But away from my vinyl screen, on stage and alone, Marianne was not very good. She was no longer true-hearted Kelly and I was no longer Bing. I found it too painful to contemplate Marianne alone on the stage with an acoustic Jimmy Page in some pop fodder treadmill. And so the eggshell broke, and I abandoned her.'

In terms of record sales Marianne had made only a small impact in her debut year. She trailed the three top-selling girl performers of 1964 – Cilla Black, Brenda Lee and Dusty Springfield – by a considerable distance. She had also sold fewer records than Kathy Kirby, Doris Day and Millie whose *My Boy Lollipop* was to remain her solitary hit. Marianne, however, had established her individuality in a few short months. She was in a field of one in Britain as a girl singer who spoke in refined tones, giggled a great deal and personified a bohemian, free-spirited outlook and dress sense that was about to be replicated by literally millions of girls. By chance she found herself the most famous epitome of a newly formed teenage girl, one who was collegiate, bookish, dreamy, independent, politically aware (defiantly pro-CND), folk and jazz influenced and, in appearance, simultaneously unkempt and glamorous. Marianne, without really trying, had got there first. The sound of her records was also original, the blend of baroque, folk, pop and the close-to-the-microphone near whisper of the vocals. There was felt to be a pureness in her music too, a fragile honesty suiting a time when 'keeping it real' was suddenly crucial.

Her next major package tour, of 26 dates, was promoted by Brian Epstein and began at the Granada, Walthamstow, on Saturday 7 November, 1964. She was fourth on the bill behind Gerry & The Pacemakers, Gene Pitney and The Kinks. Joining the line-up on the northern leg on December 1 were The Manish Boys, the band fronted by Davie Jones, later to become David Bowie. They were promoting their one and only single, 'I Pity The Fool'. The novelty of life on the road was already fading for Marianne. "I was told at the start of my very first tour – you will either love touring or hate it. I hate it. I hate leaving home, I hate the travelling, I hate the packing, I hate it!" she told the *New Musical Express* in May 1965.

During the tour she befriended Barry Fantoni, a friend of The Kinks' Ray Davies and later a regular contributor to *Private Eye* magazine as writer and cartoonist. "On camera, she never looked like she did in real life," he said. "She is blessed, like so many blondes, with those kind of features that actually improve when they are being photographed. It was always incredible to watch her walk from the dressing room, looking rather ordinary, and watch the transformation take place on screen. There was something about the cheekbones and mouth in particular, and her big eyes. She was blessed with an appearance that responded to being under lens scrutiny."

On his return from Greece, John Dunbar arranged to meet Marianne in a coffee bar in South Kensington. She imagined he would be condescending about her pop career. While she was thinking how to broach the subject 'As Tears Go By' came on the radio in the café. They were both speechless. Dunbar was not as dismissive as expected and they resumed their relationship although they squabbled before Marianne's next package tour. She was downcast and Gene Pitney became a keen suitor. He was six years older than Marianne and, at 25, already had a wealth of experience in the music business. As a songwriter he had provided hits for Bobby Vee ('Rubber Ball'), Ricky Nelson (the million-selling 'Hello Mary Lou') and The Crystals' classic 'He's A Rebel'. Pitney and Marianne had an affair while on tour but she was later excoriating about him, writing that he was a 'complete arsehole', 'nitwit', 'pompous' and 'fake'. In her book *Memories, Dreams And Reflections* she paid him one small compliment, conceding that he was 'a great shag'. As a consequence of their relationship she fell pregnant and had an abortion – an experience she has not spoken about in interviews and mentioned only in passing across two autobiographies.

Dunbar, perhaps stirred by rumours, intercepted the tour party before a show at the ABC in Wigan on December 1, 1964. He proposed marriage. 'I saw myself as a good girl and suddenly I was being very promiscuous,' wrote Marianne. 'The convent girl reappeared. I started to think I was a bad woman, a whore and a slut. I'd better get married and then I'd be good again.' Hours after the announcement of her engagement Marianne was besieged by reporters. "Can he sing?", "Does he buy your records?", "Is he a good investment?" She answered: "All I am saying is that John studies psychology at university and we're very happy together. Long before I ever met Gene Pitney, I was going out with John. Sorry to spoil all those alley cats!" Many of Marianne's music business friends had not met Dunbar but after the engagement he was around more often. "I found it hard to like Dunbar," said Barry Fantoni. "I didn't dislike him but he was part of a smart university set and I was working with a very smart university set at *Private Eye,* but they had a kind of self-effacement and an eccentricity and anarchy that was so wonderful. The second generation did not have that. They had seriousness and a protective self-seriousness and it was interesting to see Marianne sucked into it."

Marianne continued to confound the press with eccentric ideas and opinions. Keith Altham found that while he could discuss trifling matters with Sandie Shaw such as a shared love of fish and chips or her possible affair with Adam Faith ('They are constant companions'), it was not so elementary with Marianne. "I believe in living on several different planes at once. It's terribly important," she told him. In their next interview, which ran in *New Musical Express*, Altham forged Marianne's maverick image in an article headlined, 'Marianne never does what a pop star should.' After the interview, Marianne donned her sunglasses and dashed off into the street. Altham was astounded when she returned with a small gift, a volume of the light opera, *Big Ben* by A. P. Herbert, bought from a nearby second-hand book shop. He simply had to have it, she said.

Richard Green of *Record Mirror* caught Marianne in a reflective mood in a Kensington park. She was wearing a large pair of horn-rimmed glasses and clutching a copy of Lawrence Durrell's *Bitter Lemons.* "When I'm so rich I don't have to make more than one good record a year, I'll have a house in Venice and a place in the Greek Islands. I'll be a female Beatle and only come over to England to do TV and concerts," she said. "We'd have Radio Marijuana near the coast of Mousehole. We'd bring brandy, wine and fine cigarettes into the country. We'd land at the dead of night, rowing into little coves." Marianne was voted seventh best 'British Female Singer' in the end-of-year readers' poll in *New Musical Express* with 1,512 votes. Dusty Springfield was top with 7,771.

Mike Leander returned from the United States at the end of 1964 and began working with Marianne on tracks for her debut albums – for there would be two, not the conventional one. He was astonished by the progress she had made. "She really seemed to know what she wanted. It was hard to believe the difference just a year later. She was a pleasure to work with. There were no artistic tantrums or anything," he said. "She did not suffer fools gladly and if she did not respect someone musically she would tell them. I personally think she had great taste. She became a perfectionist and gained my respect, I did not regard that as a problem." Jon Mark, an accomplished guitarist, had been drafted in to back Marianne in the studio and at shows. He was another member of the Decca family, having recorded a folk album for the label in 1963 under his real name, Jon Michael Burchell, with a former school friend, Alun Davies (later to work extensively with Cat Stevens). They had recorded under the name Jon and Alun.

Marianne continued her hectic live schedule, teaming up for a series of dates in February 1965 on a package tour headlined by Roy Orbison on his second visit to Britain. The tour, this time comprising 29 shows, again started in Slough and followed a route familiar to Marianne. At one hotel Orbison appeared at her door in his usual regalia – shades, cowboy boots and black leather waistcoat – and told her his room number. The intimation was obvious but Marianne did not take up the offer because she found him 'large, strange and mournful-looking, like a prodigal mole'. After the tour she was invited to take part in a BBC 2 programme combining folk, pop and comedy called *Gadzooks! It's All Happening*. She was keen to broaden her career options and agreed to become guest host but had to drop out after falling ill with nervous exhaustion. Another teenage singer, Jan Panter, took her place.

The third single of Marianne's career was perhaps the most important. Oldham and then Calder, with their gifted team of movers and shakers, had ensured her profile was high but they needed hit records to maintain the position. If her next single were to fail in the manner of 'Blowin' In The Wind', the momentum would be lost and her future as a recording artist possibly under threat. Tony Calder claimed to have played a decisive role in finding Marianne a suitable song. He was with her in a hotel room during the tour in support of Roy Orbison. In the next room were Jimmy Page, who had been taken on as an arranger by Andrew Oldham, and Jackie DeShannon; they had recently become a couple. DeShannon, then only 20, was already established as one of the first and most talented female singer/ songwriters of the post-rock'n'roll era. Calder is reported to have shouted through: "As soon as you two are finished in that room fucking each other's brains out, why don't you write Marianne a song?" Within an hour, said Calder, they had delivered 'Come And Stay With Me'. The story is probably apocryphal because the single was released on Tuesday 5 January, 1965, a month before the tour began, unless the episode occurred during Marianne's first or second package tour, earlier in 1964. Nevertheless, DeShannon delivered a demo version to Marianne who, while fond of the song, said she wanted to make it more understated. Leander was unsure but was eventually persuaded by Marianne. "It's a far better record than 'As Tears Go By' and has much more guts," she told *New Musical Express*. The B-side was 'What Have I Done Wrong' written by Gary Farr of the Sussex-based rhythm and blues band Gary Farr & The T-Bones.

Marianne's instinct was vindicated when the song charted in February, 1965. It entered the *Record Mirror* chart at number 26 and climbed to number four by the end of March. Marianne, at 18 years old, had already reached the apex of her career in terms of singles chart success; she would never chart so highly again. In the United States 'Come And Stay With Me' peaked at number 26. Almost 45 years later the song was chosen by Morrissey when he appeared on BBC Radio 4's *Desert Island Discs* in November, 2009.

5

The move to London was almost mandatory in the mid–1960s for the young newly rich with artistic leanings. Chelsea, especially, was the vogue place of residence with its mews, dashes of parkland, its exclusivity and affluence. The pop nouveaux set up home in lordly flats with tiled vestibules, fronted by tall marble colonnades. The beat scene that began with a handful of people listening to be-bop records, reading American poets and discussing abstract surrealism, had caught on, caught fire. They painted Pop Art on the walls. They burnt joss sticks and smoked hashish. London was about to swing, with the rest of England and the world soon to follow.

Marianne was keen to embrace this burgeoning scene and escape small-town Reading. In the Mini car bought by grateful bosses at Decca, she shifted her belongings from Milman Road and Dunbar's flat in Cambridge to her new address at 29 Lennox Gardens, Belgravia, in the heart of the Royal Borough of Kensington & Chelsea. Shopping missions were undertaken to tasteful emporiums in the King's Road a few hundred yards away and the even closer Harrods where most purchases came with a designer label. Her nesting instincts were honed because, in April 1965, she discovered she was pregnant. Almost immediately Dunbar and Marianne decided to marry, as quickly as possible. Their relationship had been punctuated with sporadic disagreements and several of their friends were apprehensive about the forthcoming union.

"She was one of the first on the scene to get married," said Barry Fantoni. "John offered strong and stabilising links with the intellectual world and one of the things unfortunately true of popular music is that the people who are capable of offering a great deal intellectually are few and far between."

On Tuesday May 4, 1965 Marianne found herself, via the help of various intermediaries, at the Savoy Hotel on The Strand with Bob Dylan. She, like most of Britain's literate youth, was in thrall to Dylan who had acquired almost messianic status. 'He was nothing less than the hippest person on earth. The zeitgeist streamed through him like electricity,' she wrote in her autobiography, *Faithfull*. Dylan's seven British concerts had sold out within an hour. His English tour manager, Fred Perry, had noted the reverence shown by fans. "I had never seen anything like it," he said. "The audience acted as if they were going into a church. You could see the awe on their faces." *The Guardian's* reviewer concurred: 'The audience radiated a religious fervour. It was the second coming of Bob Dylan, their singing messiah.'

Dylan was enjoying a rest day before appearing at Birmingham Town Hall when Marianne dropped by. A few minutes of their get-together were featured in the documentary film *Don't Look Back*, shot by D.A Pennebaker. Dylan jabs away at a typewriter while Marianne (trying, she said later, to 'look beautiful') is curled up on a settee a few feet away. Also in the room is Albert Grossman, Dylan's manager, and Joan Baez, Dylan's former girlfriend, who accompanied him on the tour but did not perform at his concerts. In the footage Baez picks up an acoustic guitar and sings 'Percy's Song'. At various times the room was full of hipsters, either chatting away pretentiously or drifting off to the bathroom to take drugs. Dylan rarely engaged with them but on the few occasions he drawled a cryptic pronouncement, everyone fell hushed and his words were received as if nuggets of gold. Marianne was almost catatonic in such company and the only person she felt comfortable speaking to was the American poet Allen Ginsberg.

Marianne returned to Dylan's suite several times while he was staying at the hotel and soon found herself what she called 'Chief Prospective Consort'. Dylan's girlfriend (and later wife of 12 years), Sara Lownds, was absent and, anyway, Dylan had dismissed her as 'some girl I know from somewhere'. In the early hours of one morning everyone had moved on, leaving Marianne and Dylan together in the room. He sat across from her and stared 'so long I thought I was going to dissolve and evaporate into the smoky air of the room', she wrote. He put his new album, *Bringing It All Back Home*, on the record player. After almost every song he asked whether she 'got it' and told her they were 'snapshots of the inside of my brain'.

She revealed later: "Apparently Bob spent days and days writing a poem for me and I think it was understood in his circle that I would go to bed with him. I mean, I presume that's the intention when you're a very pretty girl and you go to a big star's bedroom, isn't it? But I didn't realise this at the time because I was a silly teenager and it was all a bit much." He asked her to make love but she refused. "I very much wanted to go to bed with him," she said. "But I was pregnant and about to get married at the time. I told him all this and he was furious and ripped the poem up in front of me." She said he turned into Rumpelstiltskin and ordered her out of the room, eventually throwing her out. Undeterred she returned to his suite the next day and he began quizzing her about Dunbar. She told him a little about John, how he had been at Cambridge and was a poet who wrote in the style of Ted Hughes [Dylan had not heard of Hughes]. "He's just a goddam student, what d'ya want to marry a damn student for?" he asked. He told her she couldn't marry someone who wore glasses [Dylan is himself short-sighted]. He continued his rant and Marianne told him he could meet Dunbar if he wished because he was outside the Savoy at that very minute, walking the pavement in the rain waiting for her; she had long missed their rendezvous time. Most of the people in the room went to the window and stared down at Dunbar, making sarcastic comments. One suggested dropping a bottle on his head. Dylan eventually met Dunbar at a party held a few days later by Rory McEwen. He was even less sympathetic, telling Marianne she was about to marry an 'intellectual jerk, the worst kind of jerk there is'. "Bob's not terribly witty and takes himself very seriously. Really, he's a poet," she told Q magazine in 1990.

Marianne and Dylan remained in contact afterwards. "We are still very fond of each other and still talk about that night," said Marianne. "I'll say to him, 'But Bob, I was only 17' [she was actually 18] and he always says, 'Yeah, but I was only 22 [he was 23, almost 24] myself!'" Incidentally, another rising folk singer, Dana Gillespie, accompanied Dylan during his stay in England. Just 16, she too was of Austrian descent – the daughter of Baron De Winterstein Gillespie.

A few days after her summit with Bob Dylan, Marianne married John Dunbar at Cambridge Register Office. The excitable party travelled around Cambridge picking wild flowers before the ceremony. It had been the traditional 'well kept secret' and even the *Cambridge Evening News* did not learn about it until three weeks later. Dunbar told reporters his wife would not be singing for a while but had no plans to retire. Marianne fibbed that they would have six children and live in Cornwall. Eva was upset the marriage had taken place outside the auspices of the Catholic Church so, six weeks later, a second ceremony took place at St Mary's RC Church, Knightsbridge. The best man was Peter Asher, Dunbar's friend who had taken them to the party that had changed their lives a year earlier. After the formalities, the group moved on to Lennox Gardens. Peter Asher's singing partner, Gordon Waller, attended, as did the Jamaican singer Millie, but otherwise the reception consisted of Dunbar's student friends and the usual mixture of family, friends and neighbours.

Barry Fantoni looked on ruefully. "I was torn apart, not from any personal involvement but because I felt that for her it was a step in the wrong direction," he said. "I thought if she should marry at all, it should be someone with slightly more charm and slightly less self-satisfaction. She was very accessible; hugely warm and uncontaminated. There was a lineal fragrance to her that everybody immediately became seduced by because it was genuine. There was that quality of taking an orchid out of the right environment. It is there for a while but it looks unusual in its new environment and you know something terrible is going to happen unless it goes back, but human beings cannot go back. You've simply got to go on. I can hear her laughter being very spontaneous. When she laughed, her face was very different. Suddenly, this perfect blonde country maid face would burst into a clown's face of genuine laughter and enthusiasm. It was terrifically infectious and very unguarded. I thought she was incredibly gracious with everybody."

After the excitement of meeting Dylan and the wedding, Marianne had to fulfil a much more downbeat arrangement. Two days after the wedding she was booked to appear at the Imperial Ballroom in Nelson, Lancashire, one of many typical provincial venues on the circuit. The former roller-skating rink held 2,000 people. Steve Chapples, author of *Goin' Down Th' Imp* [a biography of the venue], attended, paying the equivalent of 35p for a ticket. "Once inside, I noticed the place was full to capacity," he said. "The place was crawling with lads, with barely a girl in sight. Marianne was wearing a long dress and as she began singing we all lurched to the front. Lads were sitting on other lads' shoulders and drooling. I heard one say to his mate: 'It's no good, I can't stand it. I'm off to the bogs for a wank.' We were spellbound."

The next day, Sunday May 9, Marianne completed a momentous week by attending Bob Dylan's concert at the Royal Albert Hall. Allen Ginsberg accompanied her and the crowds parted as they entered, almost as if they were royalty. Inside the venue she saw Brian Jones of The Rolling Stones with his new girlfriend, Anita Pallenberg. They were dressed outlandishly in silks and feathers and meandered through the hall clearly on LSD. After the concert Marianne was among a party invited back to the Savoy and witnessed members of both The Beatles and The Rolling Stones in self-conscious deference to Dylan. She commented later that Dylan 'adored' John Lennon, was 'very cool' to Paul McCartney and barely looked at The Rolling Stones who sat there 'like little teddy bears'.

Marianne and Dunbar had an unconventional honeymoon, sharing it with a group of Beat poets in Paris. Allen Ginsberg travelled with them along with fellow American Lawrence Ferlinghetti, the poet and activist. Several nights were spent in the company of Gregory Corso, another Beat poet and great friend of Ginsberg's, at the Hotel La Louisiane which had long been a hangout for jazz musicians and freethinkers. Corso would take a breakfast cocktail of morphine and cocaine.

The flat at Lennox Gardens became a popular meeting place, the equivalent of a Paris salon but in more salubrious surroundings. Friends and acquaintances dropped by keen to discuss art with Dunbar and smoke his Moroccan dope or take stronger drugs. Dunbar usually began the day by adding Methedrine [a stimulant] to his morning coffee. Paul McCartney was a regular visitor with his fiancée, Jane Asher. 'There used to be certain places where you could light up a joint and not be frowned on,' wrote McCartney in his authorised biography, *Many Years From Now*. 'This meant you could go there for the evening and generally hang there, and 29 Lennox Gardens was one of those early formative little pads.' Dunbar had collar-length black hair and in his blue pinstripe suits with waistcoats he was considered hip, speaking the lingo of 'cool', 'man' and 'far out'. He enthused about his favourite artists and sculptors, the likes of Marcel Duchamp, Jean Dubuffet, Yves Klein, Arman, César Baldaccini and Christo. He played his favourite music: Beethoven's late quartets, Chicago blues and the jazz improvisation of Thelonius Monk, John Coltrane and Ornette Coleman. "We talked a lot about the music, all of the time," said Dunbar. "We used to play stuff and record stuff. Old blues, Jimmy Reed, Muddy Waters, all the old blues blokes. Mason [Hoffenberg, the American writer] lived with us, six months, maybe it only seemed like that but he lived there for a while. Shawn Phillips [American folk/rock musician], Donovan, Marc Bolan, he was called Mark Feld then. Everybody who was around came around."

When the talking stopped, ethnic instruments were pulled from wardrobes and the twanging reverberated through open windows and across London's skyline. Marianne's copper-bottomed pots were dragged from the kitchen and used as bongos. Another occasional pastime was playing wine glasses, wetting their rims and rubbing gently to produce a clear ringing note. Paul McCartney experimented at the flat and used the technique on the tail-out of the instrumental 'Hot As Sun/Glasses' on his first solo album, released in April 1970. "It was a very comfortable flat with a well-furnished front room. It did seem to be a place of meeting," said Fantoni. "Marianne enjoyed people calling round. It is hard to remember how vulnerable she must have been, given she was so incredibly beautiful, being in a world of slightly scurrilous people, not to mention lots and lots of people getting quite horny about her. She was a sex symbol in a sophisticated way, where I don't think anyone really fancied Sandie Shaw or Cilla Black. Marianne cried out to be mothered, to be loved."

Dunbar did not want a conventional job or lifestyle. He began writing a fortnightly arts column for the national Scottish newspaper, *The Scotsman*. He was keen to open an art gallery and early in 1965 an American poet, Paolo Leone, introduced him to Barry Miles who quickly became a friend and then, business partner. Miles had completed a four-year course in design and was working at Better Bookshop in Charing Cross Road. He developed the shop around his own interests, inviting modern poets to give readings and stocking the shelves with work by Jack Kerouac and Allen Ginsberg. Miles had embraced the counterculture since the beginning of the decade and by 1965 had seen it grow from a few hundred like-minded activists on CND marches to a street level movement offering countless opportunities. As Leone imagined, Dunbar and Miles were soon discussing a wide range of interests and ideas, from existentialism to expressionism.

"I thought John was very self-confident and very self-consciously hip in a swinging London way, even though he had only just moved down from Cambridge," said Miles. They agreed to work towards a joint venture of an art gallery embracing a bookshop. Dunbar told Miles he would be able to secure the cash from his wife, the famous Marianne Faithfull. "We decided to set up together almost immediately. We went about it in a naïve 60s way. It all seemed a lot of fun," said Miles. Marianne was unable to secure enough cash in time to finance her husband's plans and was reticent about doing so, anyway. Dunbar and Miles approached Peter Asher, a better choice because he had a strong interest in the project. He agreed to put a portion of the profits from hits such as 'A World Without Love', 'Nobody I Know' and 'True Love Ways' into the scheme – £700 as his own share and a loan of £700 each to Dunbar and Miles, which they agreed to pay back later. The trio formed a company called 'MAD', an acronym of the first letters of their surnames.

During 1965 Miles spent a great deal of time in the company of Marianne and Dunbar, usually at their flat. "It was obviously a strange period for Marianne. She was very young and very much like a teenager in her attitude. It was very obvious John cared for her enormously and was very protective towards her. He knew the rock'n'roll world was totally corrupt and did not know how to deal with it." Dunbar took his first acid trip at the flat, the drops absorbed in sugar cubes. "I was resting in the bed," said Marianne. "And suddenly there's John, gleaming-eyed, and he wants the pillows." She gave him the bedding and then the mattress. When Eva found her lying on the bed-springs she explained that Dunbar was doing an 'experiment' in the other room.

Eva Faithfull called regularly and would usher Marianne into the kitchen to have long conversations, out of view of the others. "She seemed to be around all the time. She behaved like a diva, like an opera singer. She had very great pretensions. She would ask for a cigarette and then take the whole packet," said Miles. Marianne smoked marijuana but resisted heavier drugs because, unlike most of their visitors or house guests, she usually had to be up the next morning to take a taxi to a television studio or label meeting. She decorated the flat to very fine detail, with a taste owing more to middle age than a teenager. Napkins were placed on tables and ornate chandeliers hung down from the ceiling. She continued to patronise feted clothes designers and invited upmarket interior designers to make recommendations. Dunbar was often at her shoulder, reminding her that the money would eventually run out.

The darker side of life at the flat was that some of Dunbar's friends were addicts. At the time pharmaceutical heroin was legal in Britain, which is why many drug-dependent Americans had converged on London. 'My main recollection of Lennox Gardens is a rather chilling thing,' wrote Paul McCartney. 'Being at John Dunbar and Marianne's house when one of their friends came around who was a heroin addict. And we are in the corner smoking a little bit of pot here. And he is over there, and suddenly he pulls out a big red rubber tube thing and he tightened his arm up, putting a tourniquet on. And he's tapping, and he's got needles and he's got spoons and he's got a little light. And I'm going, 'Uhhhhhh!' You get the kind of shock of horror through you. I thought, 'My God, fucking hell! How did I get here? I'm in a room with a guy who's shooting up!' He had a big rubber tourniquet, which smacked to me of operations. I'd always been fearful of red rubber as a kid. And me mum was a nurse, so enemas and things, it was all red rubber. Very frightening sort of thing to me, not pleasant at all, that shit.'

Several visitors stayed for weeks or months in the case of Mason Hoffenberg. A long-term junkie, he co-wrote *Candy* with Terry Southern and later published his own novels, *Until She Screams* (1968) and *Sin For Breakfast* (1971). At 43, he was older than most of the regulars at the flat and had moved to London from Paris after the breakdown of his marriage. His long stay was tolerated because of his outlandish humour and a raconteur style many felt was similar to Lenny Bruce. Marianne was less enamoured by the American folk singer Sandy Bull. The son of a high-ranking New York family, Bull was plagued with drug problems and, according to Marianne, was a 'dreadful' person. Another long-term house guest was drummer Charlie Moffett, who had played with a host of leading jazz figures such as Sonny Rollins, Archie Shepp and Ornette Coleman.

On Thursday April 15, 1965 Marianne released *two* debut albums – the 'folk' record *Come My Way* and *Marianne Faithfull*, which was predominantly 'pop' (apart from 'What Have They Done To The Rain' written by the American folk/blues songwriter and political activist Malvina Reynolds). It was a curious move for Decca to sanction because it divided sales of each and ran the risk of confusing the public. The albums were recorded over a three-month period at Lansdowne Studio in Holland Park and Decca Number Two Studio. As her time was filled by promotional activities and concerts, recording sessions often began at midnight and finished at about 3am. This was routine at the time and revealed the industry's prevailing attitude towards the recording process, which often appeared an afterthought.

The cover shot for *Come My Way* was taken by Gered Mankowitz and became an iconic image of the decade. Marianne, wearing a knee-length dress and white socks pulled up almost to her knees, was pictured reclining beneath a tall window with her legs resting on a cushioned bench. Shot in monochrome, the setting and mood was everything. Marianne's apparent indifference to the camera played defiantly against type for the period when artists, especially girls, routinely jumped, danced, frowned or clown-smiled into the lens. Chris O'Dell complemented the picture with a subtle and tasteful cover design. Another of Andrew Oldham's contacts, Mankowitz used the session to announce his arrival, though he was only 18 at the time. His studio, which he opened in 1963, was in Mason's Yard in the heart of London's West End, close to the Scotch of St James, one of the scene's foremost clubs. He later photographed scores of leading pop acts, among them The Rolling Stones, Jimi Hendrix and Traffic. He befriended Marianne during the shoot. They had much in common. The son of Wolf Mankowitz, the author, playwright and film writer, and Ann Mankowitz, the Jungian psychotherapist, he had attended various progressive public schools.

In the album's sleeve notes, Andy Wickham, Oldham's trusted wordsmith, summarised the record as: 'Most of all it signifies the extent of what Marianne Faithfull has done for the advancement of folk music in this country.' The claim was typically grand but not without substance. As a debut record it was full of confidence and there had been few, if any, similarly assured arrivals on the English folk scene and certainly not from an artist so young. Marianne's sweet, controlled voice held firm against Jon Mark's sturdy acoustic twang. All but two of the songs were traditional standards arranged by Mark, including 'Portland Town', 'Fare Thee Well' and 'Once I Had A Sweetheart'. "Beware the jab jab bird" warned Marianne on 'Jaberwock', a spirited run-through [though spelt differently] of the Lewis Carroll nonsense verse from his novel *Through The Looking-Glass And What Alice Found There*. The title track 'Come My Way' was written by Mark while 'Lonesome Traveller' was composed by the renowned American folk singer Lee Hays and had already been a minor hit for Lonnie Donegan in 1958.

The 'pop' album, *Marianne Faithfull*, called on more than 20 established songwriters from Britain and the United States, with material ranging from Lennon and McCartney's 'I'm A Loser' and Bacharach/David's 'If

I Never Get To Love You' to compositions by Mike Leander with his Decca colleagues. Marianne's first attempt at lyric writing was 'Time Takes Time', set to music composed by Barry Fantoni: 'Today will end when the sun will rise/ When I shall laugh to your blind eyes/ The world can break/ And time takes time to realise.' "It ended up being a very different song than I envisaged," said Fantoni. "I wanted it to be a gentle cello and harpsichord piece but the album didn't have any fast numbers on it and it ended up like a *Rawhide* number." Marianne told *Fabulous* magazine that the lyrics were nonsensical. "Most of the words I write are what I call 'frumious'. You know: intense rubbish. 'Life is like a currant bun' and all that. It's awful but it makes the money."

Fantoni suspected the words were not solely Marianne's. "I think she got them from somewhere. I think they are from someone's poem – heavily edited. It didn't rhyme particularly well." The album was an eclectic mixture of styles. The brash pop numbers such as 'Down Town' and 'Can't You Hear My Heartbeat' did not best suit Marianne's voice while on others, most notably 'If I Never Get To Love You', the combination of classical, folk and pop was well accomplished. "In the early years, she was projected, invested in, given a role to play and she played it," said Fantoni. "She wasn't great at putting a song over but she was great at letting a song happen to her and I think that is where she's good. She is one of those people whose journey of self-discovery gave her a real presence. It gave her something she could perform and work with. It is an awful truth that she had to go through all that. In the beginning her talent was very fragile."

Record Mirror awarded both debut albums four stars out of a possible five. Its reviewer said of *Come My Way*: 'Graciousness seems the keynote, a sort of royal approach,' and of *Marianne Faithfull*: 'Nice and clean-cut arrangements from a variety of sizes and shapes. Sometimes she seems to lack a little confidence, but it really all adds to her charm. Not everybody's cuppa, but we liked it. Quaintly effective.' Sales of both albums were strong and they entered the Top 30 on June 5, 1965. *Marianne Faithfull* stayed a fortnight and reached number 15 while its sister record peaked at number 12, spending seven weeks on the charts and possibly indicating a slight public preference of a folksy Marianne.

In the United States *Marianne Faithfull* contained extra tracks and first showed in the *Billboard* chart on July 14, 1965. It stayed in the charts for more than three months and its highest position was number 12. The album, released on London Records, was the first and last by Marianne to enter the *Billboard* Top 40.

Marianne's next single was 'This Little Bird', a song written by John D Loudermilk, the American songwriter who had supplied 'Sittin' In The Balcony' for Eddie Cochran and 'Waterloo' for Stonewall Jackson, a number one in the United States. Unknown to Marianne, Andrew Oldham was recording the same song with The Nashville Teens elsewhere in the Decca studios. It was fairly common for records of the same song to be released simultaneously in the 1960s but unusual for both versions to be on the same label. Marianne kept a noble silence (in public, at least) but Oldham spoke out in *Record Mirror*. "There have been arguments about my advertising campaign on the Teens' behalf. Some negative people say I have malicious intent. This upsets me. This song does have a special meaning. All I say is that EVIL, as well as beauty, is obviously in the eye of the beholder. As a producer, I believe today's sound – a sphere I'm proud to belong to – has as much to say as the music of Chopin or Mozart, or the wonderful sets of Sean Kenny. We in the industry belong to an art form which can hold its head as high as any other art forms. And that when we create, we say something worthwhile, as does my 'Little Bird'." The Nashville Teens had a greater call than Marianne on 'This Little Bird'. They had covered another Loudermilk song, 'Tobacco Road', and taken it to number six in Britain the year before.

The music press heralded both versions with typical anodyne approval. Marianne's was predicted by *Disc* to do 'very well indeed' while the Teens' 'might well be a gigantic hit'. Marianne's delivery was mannered, bordering on deadpan and, at just over two minutes, the song was very short. The Teens' had a warmer, richer arrangement and the vocal harmonies better disguised the slow pacing. Marianne performed the song on *Gadzooks, It's The In Crowd* in June, 1965 on which her Decca contemporary, Lulu, also appeared, singing her Top 10 hit, 'Leave A Little Love'. They posed together for a BBC photographer:

Lulu smiling pleasantly, Marianne staring through the lens, her mind seemingly elsewhere. Marianne's 'This Little Bird' considerably outsold the Teens' and reached number six, compared to their placing of 38. Marianne's fared better in every territory except Japan and Australia. In the United States, hers reached number 32 and the Teens' did not chart. She had won the sales battle but Oldham had registered his injured pride at being jettisoned by one of his discoveries.

Marianne had accrued 26 weeks on America's *Billboard* singles chart, just four singles and a little over a year into her career – an impressive achievement for a newcomer and vital groundwork. The two debut albums had marked an unconventional start but soon afterwards Marianne threw in another rogue element; she wanted to go jazz. "I've changed. The more I hear of modern jazz records, and I've only recently bought a gramophone, the more I become involved in the possibility of creating that sort of atmosphere on my records. It's not the technical aspect that appeals to me, it's the atmosphere the sounds create," she told David Griffiths of *Record Mirror*.

During the summer of 1965 the press had a new line on which to quiz Marianne. Babies made an agreeable change to either her good looks or eccentric views across all manner of subjects. "You've no idea how difficult nannies are to find. I've got the choice of one of those Yorkshire varieties with a stiff white cap and starched collar or some gorgeous blonde from a French college. Well, I'm not having the first, and John's not getting the second," she told the *New Musical Express*. The couple announced the baby was to be called Lisa if a girl and Nicholas, a boy. Marianne was adamant she would be a dependable wife, mother and pop star. "I'll just keep making records and having babies," she said. She ruled out one-night stands in clubs and ballrooms though because she was 'through with dirty dressing rooms and draughty stages'. Relations between Marianne and Dunbar were generally fine but a recurring issue was their differing attitude towards money. "Before she got into smack and all the other drugs, her big kind of 'out' was to spend money," Dunbar told the writer A.E. Hotchner, the author of *The Rolling Stones And The Death Of The Sixties*. "She'd go into clothes shops and buy mountains of stuff she'd never wear, thousands of pounds. She was making loads of loot but was in debt, so unnecessarily. It was just clothes, clothes, clothes, which I think she even started hiding somewhere outside the house."

Marianne appeared at the Uxbridge Blues and Folk Festival on Saturday, June 19, 1965 held at Hillingdon Borough Showground. She was part of a bill that included The Who, The Spencer Davis Group and John Mayall's Bluesbreakers, with whom Eric Clapton also performed. During the summer package tours were suspended and artists appeared instead at seaside towns on revue bills. On Sunday, August 1, 1965, Marianne, now almost six months pregnant, collapsed on stage in Morecambe, Lancashire. Concerts and television appearances and a short tour of the United States, where she was due to appear at state fairs in Michigan and Ohio, were cancelled.

The union between Marianne and Tony Calder became strained when he objected to her pursuing a parallel acting career. She was also dissatisfied with how income appeared to be divided between them. At the end of 1964 he had advised her not to audition for a role in the John Osborne play *Inadmissible Evidence*, which was due to open at the Royal Court Theatre – one of the capital's most progressive theatres at the time. She would have been paid £18 per week, a considerably smaller sum than she could earn touring Britain. Marianne regretted her acceptance of Calder's counsel because she was desperate to escape her 'pop nightmare'. Her disgruntlement increased as she tramped around Britain's backwaters and seaside resorts as part of the latest package tour. She longed to be back in London playing alongside Nicol Williamson in a role for which he became famous, playing the embittered solicitor, William Maitland. On the night Marianne informed the Royal Court she would not be joining them, she attended a party hosted by the production team behind *Ready Steady Go!*. Mick Jagger was there and had been drinking. He tried to attract Marianne's attention, smiling and winking at her. She failed to respond and so, pretending to raise his glass in a formal toast, he tipped the drink down Marianne who was wearing a low-cut top. She drifted off to another room in the studios. It was barely lit but she could make out Keith Richards sitting at a piano playing quietly. She stayed there for some time but they did not speak.

"My mother taught me that to be beautiful—as I knew I was—shouldn't be a passive thing. It should be something to be put to use..." *(Philip Glassborow Collection)*

Left: Glynn Faithfull with his baby daughter in the garden of their first family home in Hampstead, North London. *(Glynn Faithfull Collection)*

Below: Marianne's mother, the former Eva Von Sacher-Masoch, with her daughter in the grounds of Braziers College. *(Glynn Faithfull Collection)*

Left: Braziers College, near Wallingford, the home of Glynn Faithfull since the early fifties, where Marianne spent part of her childhood. *(Glynn Faithfull Collection)*

Above: Marianne, aged three, at her parents' second home in Ormskirk, Lancashire. *(Glynn Faithfull Collection)*

Right: The matrilineal Faithfull family home at 41 Millman Road, Reading. *(Paul Privetera)*

Above: Marianne, aged 10, at Braziers. *(Glynn Faithfull Collection)*

Above: St Joseph's Convent School, Reading, where Marianne was educated from 1953 to 1962. *(Paul Privetera)*

Above: Marianne, aged 15. *(Rex Features)*

Above and below left: Marianne's first publicity shots for Decca Records: "... 16, beautiful, unblemished and straight out of convent school..." *(Terry Rawlings Collection/Showbiz Photo Collection)*

Right:
John Dunbar.
(Graham Keen)

Above and below: Marianne with her son Nicolas at Lennox
Gardens, 1965. *(Gered Mankowitz/Rex Features)*

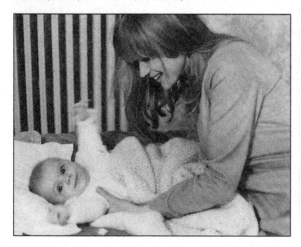

Above: Producer Mike Leander working
with Marianne in Decca's Hampstead
Studios in 1965. *(Gered Mankowitz)*

Above: The opening of the Indica
Gallery, January 28, 1965. Left to
right: Barry Miles, John Dunbar,
Marianne, Peter Asher, Paul
McCartney. *(Graham Keen)*

Right: "I didn't care whether she
could sing or not—I could sell that
look"–Andrew Oldham.

(Gered Mankowtiz)

Above: Marianne with Mick Jagger, in Italy for the San Remo Song Festival, during the first weeks of their relationship in 1966. *(Rex Features)*

The contract Marianne had signed with Calder gave him an unusually high commission. On certain earnings it was thought to be more than 30 per cent. She considered a high rate was perhaps fair had he launched her career (which required excessive man hours and heavy expenses) but that had been undertaken by Andrew Oldham. Calder chiefly took on an executive role since a team had formed around Marianne including a publicist, lawyer, accountant and chaperone. Barry Fantoni met many of the impresarios on the scene and was aware of Calder's racy reputation. "People said a lot of things about him, but he sent me one of the biggest royalty cheques I have ever received, for the track 'Time Takes Time'. He was all right to me." Fantoni, however, held a contemptuous view of most of the background players of the 1960s. "These guys were people suddenly with huge amounts of money and power and they didn't really know how to handle it. The fact that Andrew Oldham had funny glasses and long hair did not make any difference at all. They were basically upper-class people who thought everybody else were twits and could be exploited in some way."

In an interview in *Fabulous* magazine Marianne again provided a seldom revealed insight into the music business and her own character, oblivious as to how she might be perceived. "I'm quite a patient person and I don't often get angry," she said. "I'm more likely to get nasty in a quiet way – but really nasty. It makes me angry when I've been on the go, on and on and on, travelling, playing, travelling, until I can't do any more. I hate things going wrong, things that should be organised properly. I get cross when people don't do their jobs properly and, I suppose it's beastly, but if I don't want anyone working for me any more I write them a short polite note saying 'that's that'." Tony Calder no doubt received such a note because in the summer of 1965 he was relieved of his duties. Marianne decided to continue without a manager but recognised the need for a music industry professional to handle the paperwork. She took on Gerry Bron at a flat rate of 10 per cent. He was referred to as her 'agent' but became her manager in all but title. The brother of actress Eleanor Bron, he ran a small and homely management company called Bron Artists with his wife, Lilian. Gene Pitney and Manfred Mann were its two main acts. "I remember Marianne ringing my wife and she was in tears about something," said Bron. "I don't know exactly why she came to us but she was complaining about the Terrible Twosome of Oldham and Calder. I think she felt they owed her money. I remember her being very confused."

Bron was 32 years old and this relative maturity appealed to Marianne. "I think I was a bit of an uncle figure to her. She used to sometimes actually call me Uncle Gerry," he said. Bron organised a series of dates in the United States for Marianne at $1,000 per show. He was surprised when the promoters increased their offer to $1,500 without prompting. "I rang Marianne to tell her we'd had an offer of fifteen hundred dollars rather than a thousand. I was surprised when she asked me if it were a greater sum than a thousand. I don't think she'd heard of 'fifteen hundred'. She obviously expected me to phrase it as 'one thousand, five hundred'," he said. In the event the tour was cancelled because of Marianne's pregnancy. Marianne told Bron she wanted to leave Decca because she was suspicious of the company's accounting. He asked his friend, the American Ken Glancy, who had taken over as managing director at CBS Records, to examine her royalties. He found no grounds for concern and reported that there was little chance of Marianne being freed from her contract.

As Marianne was playing significantly fewer concerts, the income tailed off and Bron's return from Marianne was negligible. Nevertheless, he became fond of her and saw she was struggling with the pressure of pop stardom. "She was very naive and probably still is. I felt she missed some help in her domestic background. Dunbar was inexperienced. He tried to help but he was not able to and he got in the way more than anything. I know my wife jollied her along and she seemed to get on easily with her. I think she thought our set-up was more natural than what she had been used to."

The few times Eva Faithfull contacted Bron were invariably peculiar encounters. He was awoken once at 4 a.m. by Eva who told him her daughter would not be able to attend filming for a television programme later that day because she had walked into a pane of glass. "I asked her what she expected me to do about it at that time of the night. I don't know why she just didn't wait a few hours," he said. Bron was impressed by Marianne's professionalism, especially in television studios where she was often invited back. "I felt she was a very, very talented artist and had a unique talent. I hoped we could be a stabilising influence on her career because she had had a bad time of it. I think she has more talent than she has ever been given credit for."

Marianne was less complimentary about Bron. In her autobiography she said he was 'a straight, boring, Jewish showbiz agent'. She had hoped he would be wiser than both Oldham and Calder. 'I thought if you were older it meant you had more sense. Was I wrong on that one! Gerry Bron was a fool and I ended up playing the lowest dives and the stupidest places imaginable,' she wrote.

In the mid-1960s the mainland European market was opening up to British artists and unlike today when English (or more accurately, American-English) is established as an international musical language, performers sang their songs in different languages to generate additional foreign sales. It was a comparatively inexpensive operation because the same backing track and sleeve artwork (with the obvious change of title) was used and the only extra expense was the remastering and pressing costs. Marianne's first song specifically for Europe was 'Summer Nights' or, as it appeared in France, 'Nuit D'éte', released in July, 1965. The song, lasting one minute and 47 seconds, was written by Lesley Pauline Strike and Brian Thomas Henderson. Strike, better known as Liza Strike, was the singer with The Jet Set who were signed to Parlophone and Henderson, another band member, was the group's chief songwriter. Strike later became a session singer working with Pink Floyd, The Who and many others. On the single, Marianne sang blithely of her happiness that winter had passed and she was now able to enjoy summer nights with her intended, either at the beach, the bay or staring at the moon. She rhymed café with play ('There's a little ca-fay, where we can hear music play'). The single reached number 10 in the British charts and number 24 in the United States. It was to be her last ever hit single.

6

Paul McCartney called regularly at Lennox Gardens during 1965 and it was almost inevitable he should offer a song to Marianne. "I did write a song but it was not a very good one," he said. "It was called 'Etcetera' and it's a bad song. I think it's a good job it's died a death in some tape bin. Even then, I seem to remember thinking it wasn't very good. There was always the temptation to keep your better songs for yourself and then give your next-best songs to other established people, so when it was someone like Marianne, who at that time was a newcomer, those people tended to end up with fairly dreadful offerings of mine."

Others within The Beatles' circle took a more positive view. "It was a very beautiful song," said their engineer, Alan Brown. "I recall it was a ballad and had the word 'etcetera' several times in the lyric. I only heard it twice: when he recorded it and when we played it back to him. The tape was taken away and I've never heard of it since." In June 1965 McCartney had put down a song called 'Yesterday' at Abbey Road Studios. The melody had come to him in a dream while sleeping at the Ashers' house in Wimpole Street. On waking, he played it repeatedly on the piano for fear of forgetting it. He told Marianne The Beatles had decided not to release it as a single because it sounded more like a solo effort than a group. They also felt it didn't 'fit with the band's image'. He suggested, however, that it would be perfect for Marianne. "I suppose, thinking back on it, after 'As Tears Go By' maybe they were looking for more sort of a 'Yesterday', something more poignant, more baroque," said McCartney. "I probably thought, well, this is really all I've got at the moment. I'll send it round and maybe they'll put a baroque thing on it and that'll make it OK. She probably did 'Yesterday' because they figured it was better than 'Etcetera'."

Mike Leander gave the song elaborate orchestration, drafting in 300 backing singers from the Royal College of Music. McCartney pointed out that since The Beatles' *Help!* album, which was to feature the track, was released on August 6, other artists would also be recording versions of 'Yesterday'. He attended Marianne's sessions at the Decca studios. "Those kind of sessions tended to be off duty for me. So I might be in a little bit of a party mode and sort of swinging by. Marianne certainly wouldn't have welcomed outside suggestions, even from a Beatle," he said.

Her version of 'Yesterday' was released on October 22 1965 and McCartney helped with its promotion. On November 1 and 2, Granada Television filmed a 50-minute special, *The Music Of Lennon And McCartney*, featuring Peter and Gordon, Billy J. Kramer & The Dakotas, Lulu, Cilla Black and other artists famous for singing their songs, with The Beatles themselves introducing acts and miming to 'Day Tripper' and 'We Can Work It Out'. Marianne was invited to perform 'Yesterday' with McCartney. "Paul really helped me by putting me on the thing The Beatles did with Granada. It was really great, because he started it off," she said. McCartney began the song alone, strumming his guitar and singing while sitting on a stool. After 30 seconds it faded to Marianne's version, complete with choir and orchestra. She was eight months pregnant. In an era when few pregnant women appeared on television, especially entertainers, McCartney insisted she took part, though only her head and shoulders were filmed and angled shots from above.

Paul McCartney was correct when he predicted a race to make 'Yesterday' a hit. Matt Monro, another singer with a strong Beatles affiliation, released the song at the same time. His version was arranged and produced by The Beatles' producer, George Martin, and released by

Parlophone. Unlike Marianne's orchestrated rendition, it relied chiefly on Monro's strong voice and he handled it with poise. Effectively ensnaring two generations of record buyers (fans of The Beatles and his own older, more traditional fan base), Monro outsold Marianne considerably and made number eight in the charts while hers reached 36. Neither was aware, of course, how popular the track would later become – covered by 2,200 different artists and voted the best song of the 20th century in a BBC poll.

Throughout the summer of 1965 Marianne had continued to work but in the early autumn she retreated, heavily pregnant, to Lennox Gardens. Plans to extend the summer by visiting Mexico and the United States were abandoned when her doctor warned that the sun and stress of travelling might affect her health. Dunbar was teaching at the capital's Central School of Arts and spending his spare time with Barry Miles working towards the opening of their art gallery and bookshop. The baby was due at the end of November but after a slight accident at their flat when Marianne stumbled down a few stairs, she was taken to a Harley Street clinic and the baby arrived prematurely, weighing less than six pounds. They had told friends they were hopeful of having a boy and, on November 10, their hopes were realised. The baby was given the full name of Robert Nicholas Dunbar, but would be known as Nicholas. Barry Miles visited Marianne clutching a bouquet of flowers. While he was at the clinic a nurse approached the bed and told Marianne a man calling himself Loog Oldham had telephoned from New York and wanted her to look out of the window, where she would find a present. Marianne saw a new Mini parked in the clinic's car park. "She was absolutely knocked out by it," said Miles. "In those days a phone call from America was a big deal. It was the kind of thing that was going on at the time. Andrew was making a lot of money out of The Rolling Stones and I am sure he made a lot out of her."

The plan to return to work hastily was scotched after the birth. Marianne wanted to rest and spend time with Nicholas. She announced that she would take a six-month break from the pop business and on her return shun package tours and play sporadic concerts instead. Eva Faithfull, realising the baby had been born earlier than expected, thought she had discovered a way of concealing the fact that her daughter had conceived outside wedlock. She was hoping to convince everyone Nicholas had arrived two or three months early. "She was silly trying that one," said a former neighbour. "When she told me he was conceived just after they were married, I said to her: 'Eva, who are you trying to kid?' I felt sorry for her having to lie like that. I think the whole thing really upset her." A nanny was hired, a model called Maggie McGivern, but her presence in the flat soon began to cause tension. "John and Marianne were friendly, liberal people who naturally treated Maggie as an equal," said Barry Miles. "They were also very young to be hiring staff of any kind, so in the evening there would be an embarrassing situation when they never knew how to tell her they were entertaining and that she should leave the living room." Maggie befriended Paul McCartney and sometimes attended art gallery openings with him. In 1997 she revealed that this led to a three-year clandestine relationship with McCartney. She also had an affair with Dunbar while at Lennox Gardens. "The household turned into a three-act farce," said Miles.

Despite the managerial changes and her ambivalent attitude to the industry, 1965 was a magnificent year for Marianne. In terms of record sales, the only solo female performer to sell more was Sandie Shaw and although Marianne trailed the likes of The Seekers, Cliff Richard, The Rolling Stones and The Beatles, she outsold other established artists such as Tom Jones, P. J. Proby and Jim Reeves.

Books and paintings were stored at the Ashers' home in Wimpole Street during the winter of 1965 and spring of 1966, ready to be moved into premises Dunbar and Miles had secured on rent of £19 per week at Mason's Yard, off Duke Street, London. Dunbar had noticed the building was empty one evening while on his way with Marianne to the Scotch of St James Club. Miles bought stock for the bookshop, concentrating on American small-press imports and avant-garde literature. Paul McCartney, on his way downstairs from the attic flat he shared with Peter Asher, often unloaded books from the back of a Bedford van and helped paint the gallery walls. He also lent his Aston Martin to Miles and Dunbar to collect wood for shelving. They called their enterprise the Indica Gallery, named after cannabis indica, a plant cultivated in the production of hashish. McCartney was the bookshop's first customer and sometimes visited at night to browse, leaving a note for books to be put on his account.

The opening night was famously chaotic. "Everyone was trying to get the place ready – John, Barry Miles, Paul McCartney, Jane Asher, our friend David Courts, so many people," said Marianne. "But nobody had thought to clean the lavatory, which was, of course, filthy. I remember I was wearing a beautiful dress and very pale tights, and there I was, on my hands and knees, scrubbing the loo. Because of John, I was very much a part of it all, and I'm so proud I was."

The first exhibition, *Indications And 2*, opened on Saturday, June 4, 1966 and was by the collective the Groupe de Recherche d'Art Visuel de Paris (G.R.A.V), featuring neon sculpture, light boxes and Op Art constructions by Julio Le Parc, François Morellet and others. Le Parc's work was influenced by fairgrounds and circuses – he made distorting spectacles and hand-held mirrors that warped the reflection in the manner of a funfair hall of mirrors. One of his pieces, *Passage Accidente*, was displayed outside in Mason's Yard – a set of eight unstable black wooden boxes. When visitors stood on them they wobbled like loose stepping stones across a stream. One lunch time, dustmen mistook them for rubbish and loaded them on to a cart, never to be seen again.

A stream of visitors from pop's elite visited Indica to view the outlandish exhibitions and buy books recommended by Miles. Various members of The Moody Blues dropped by and John Lennon met his future bride, Yoko Ono, there when he attended her exhibition, *Unfinished Paintings And Objects By Yoko Ono* in November 1966. Ono's exhibits included an apple on a pedestal with a price tag of £200 pinned next to it; a stepladder with a spyglass attached to the top step by chain; and a board covered in nails bearing the petition: 'Hammer A Nail In'. At another time the gallery was filled with handbags, lumps of cement and pieces of machinery. Upstairs, Miles was selling Ono's book, *Grapefruit*, containing a flippant suggestion on each page: 'Draw a map to get lost' or 'Stir inside your brains with a penis until things are mixed well. Take a walk.' When Dunbar introduced Lennon to Yoko, she handed him a card which read: 'Breathe'. He panted like a dog. "Indica gave me a space where I could be free and express my ideas," said Yoko. "It was a comfort zone in an otherwise cold and snobby art world that didn't get me yet." The gallery was patronised by others from the burgeoning Underground. Film director Roman Polanski sometimes called in the early hours to peruse the latest objects d'art and Allen Ginsberg was so taken by the atmosphere that he moved for a short period into a flat next to the gallery.

Throughout early 1966 there were two distinct levels of 'alternativism' existing in parallel, one rooted in elitist intellectualism, politics and art, propelled by drugs (mainly LSD and hashish) such as the activities at the Indica Gallery, and the other, a populist lightsome version of boutiques, short dresses, bright colours and the so-called 'swinging' set. They soon converged but were initially unconnected, apart from their focus on youth. Before then, children appeared to become adults, both in dress and attitude, almost as soon as they left school. The 1960s highlighted what became known as the generation gap and children no longer wished to immediately embrace adulthood. In a noteworthy piece by columnist Arthur Helliwell in the *Sunday People* he looked out from beneath his trilby hat and wrote: 'The swinging, switched-on, with-it world of young people in the UK... a world as remote and unpredictable as Mars. A world beyond our ken. It's slick and glossy. Bold and brash. Defiant and vital.' Helliwell told the paper's readers [its circulation in 1966 was 5.5 million] that the kids were 'living tremendously exciting lives at a breathless, breakneck pace that completely baffles their perplexed and confused mothers and fathers'.

The American magazine *Time* played a pivotal role in heralding London as the core of this swinging scene. Its correspondents ambled down Carnaby Street and saw sharp-dressed youths wearing clothes bought from Biba in Kensington High Street where designer Barbara Hulanicki offered a 'total look', and haircuts from Vidal Sassoon's in Bond Street. In an editorial in its issue of April 15, 1966, *Time* gave a breathtaking account of the scene which quickly permeated through to tourist brochures and Sunday supplements. Readers were informed:

'In a decade dominated by youth, London has burst into bloom. It swings; it is the scene. This spring, as never before in modern times, London is switched on. The city is alive with birds (girls) and Beatles, buzzing with Mini cars and telly stars. In a once sedate world of faded splendour, everything new, uninhibited and kinky is blooming at the top of London life'. The secret was no more and film crews rushed to the city to make movies that would appear 18 months after the event.

Meanwhile, London's counter-scene was flourishing and about to reach street level. Its first promulgation had been at the International Poetry Incarnation held at the Royal Albert Hall on Friday 11 June, 1965. Radical poets and writers such as William Burroughs, Alexander Trocchi – who compèred the event – and Michael Horowitz recited their works to 7,000 people, many holding aloft joss sticks and flowers. The anti-psychiatrist, R.D. Laing, author of *The Divided Self* and *Knots*, had brought along some of his patients who became lost to reverie, 'dancing' to the poets' readings. Lawrence Ferlinghetti performed *To Fuck Is To Love Again*. John Latham, the conceptual artist, painted his body and stuck torn paper to himself but passed out before reaching the stage. Simon Vinkenoog, a Dutch poet, attempted to perform while high on mescaline. The audience became unsettled so he began shouting 'Love' repeatedly until the crowd fell quiet again. "The underground was suddenly there on the surface," said Jeff Nuttall, author of *Bomb Culture*.

Barry Miles also felt it was a key gathering. "There was a sense of constituency that was never there before. All these people recognised each other and they all realised they were part of the same scene," he said. One of the organisers, Steve Stollman, who had left his home city of New York specifically to immerse himself in the London scene [and to seek out venues where bands signed to his brother's record label, ESP-Disk, could perform] was inspired by its success and began hosting a series of events known as 'Spontaneous Underground' at the Marquee Club in Wardour Street every Sunday afternoon. It was invite-only and alcohol-free. Jugglers and magicians performed and avant-garde musicians 'played' everything from transistor radios to African drums. Word spread across London about the Marquee shows and a committee was formed comprising the Underground's prime movers. John 'Hoppy' Hopkins, later the founder of *International Times* and the UFO Club, shared drugs and ideas with the likes of Miles and an assembly that had formed around Pink Floyd – the band's co-managers Andrew King and Peter Jenner and their producer Joe Boyd, who had overseen the set-up of Elektra's British office.

The Marquee was superseded by All Saints Hall in Powis Square, Notting Hill, where Hopkins ran a community self-help organisation. Elsewhere, radicalism thrived among other art forms. Ralph Ortiz, the American artist, organised the first Destruction in Art Symposium (DIAS) to 'focus attention on the element of destruction in Happenings and other art forms, and to relate this destruction in society'. Ortiz performed a series of seven public events, including piano destruction concerts filmed by the BBC. On a similar theme, Gustav Metzger established Auto-Destructive Art and the Art Strike movement. In 1964 art students interrupted a lecture taking place at the Architectural Association School of Architecture in Bedford Square, London, and declared it a 'happening'. The Who, heavily influenced by the Auto-Destructive Art movement, trashed their equipment on stage and Jeff Beck did the same before film cameras in Michelangelo Antonioni's *Blow-up,* the film which best distilled the ambience of the times with its focus on youth, fashion, art and music.

Marianne was one of a handful privy to the many tributaries of London life. To the media she epitomised the swinging scene of Twiggy, Sandie Shaw and the Mini car but through her husband and her own wide eye on the world she was heavily connected to the Underground. She was also part of a group of pseudo-aristocrats, a stately set from high families who had largely eschewed their ancestral piles (temporarily at least) to submerge themselves in the cultural revolt. These had appended themselves chiefly to The Rolling Stones and to a lesser degree The Beatles, and included, among many others, the fashion designer Michael Fish; antique dealer Christopher Gibbs; art gallery owner Robert Fraser; photographer Michael Cooper; model agency owner Mark Palmer; illustrator Michael English; socialite Tara Browne; men's fashion store owner Michael Rainey; film director Donald Cammell; experimental film maker Kenneth Anger; and fashion designers Ossie Clark and Celia Birtwell, the subjects of David Hockney's famous painting of 1970, *Mr And Mrs Clark And Percy.*

Christopher Gibbs was a former Etonian and had studied at the Sorbonne. The nephew of Sir Humphrey Vicary Gibbs, the former Governor of Southern Rhodesia, he was almost 10 years older than Marianne. They had first met at an exhibition by a group of South American kinetic sculptors. "There was this pale, ethereal, slightly tipsy charmer and before very long we got talking. From then onwards I saw her quite a lot over a period of about five years," he said. "We talked about the sculptures. They were lovely trembling things with wavy bits of steel and lights. Although she was already a mother, she was dazzlingly beautiful. I was bewitched by her mix of innocence and knowingness and also by the fact she knew about and was interested in a lot of things I was – literature, art and architecture; manifestations of ancient decadence. She had a very good nose for a freak and appreciation for it."

The dedicated wife-and-mother phase was all but over for Marianne by the early months of 1966. "I was bored, I felt trapped and I was exhausted," she said. "I developed an irrepressible need to get out of the flat. I would get up in the morning; there'd be no heat. I'd have to step over several people crashed in the living room. I'd go into the kitchen to warm up a bottle for Nicholas and find the draining board strewn with bloody needles." One morning she toured the flat and collected up hundreds of pills and flushed them down the toilet. 'I had begun to find John and his cerebral junkies tiresome, and all around me was the centrifugal whirls of the Sixties. I wanted to see what all the fuss was about," she wrote in *Faithfull.* "She was always being torn in these directions. There was a definite pull to earthing herself in the things womankind are taught – motherhood, household chores, bringing up the children, attending her man – but there were much stronger pulls, exerting much more potent influences on her," said Gibbs.

Marianne had been switched on to marijuana and dabbled in various colourful tablets. Another former Etonian and school friend of Gibbs, Robert Fraser, known as 'Groovy Bob', introduced her to cocaine. Marianne, like many in the 1960s, entered the world of drugs with an impression coloured by the wondrous and romantic visions fashioned by literary and artistic figures. William Blake had written: 'Prudence is a rich, ugly old maid courted by Incapacity' and 'The road to excess leads to the palace of wisdom'. The main players of the counterculture scene held particular books as tablets of absolute truth, especially Hermann Hesse's *Journey To The East* and *Steppenwolf,* and Aldous Huxley's *The Doors Of Perception.* They quoted key sentences: "Christianity and mescaline seem to be much more compatible" *(The Doors Of Perception).* They believed drugs were tools to free themselves from conventionalism into unbridled creativity and had historical evidence to prove it. Robert Louis Stephenson had written 60,000 words of *The Strange Case Of Doctor Jekyll And Mister Hyde* in just six days while supposedly on a binge of cocaine or the hallucinogenic fungus, ergot. Lewis Carroll's *Alice's Adventures In Wonderland* contained fantastical imagery that many speculated was inspired by drugs. Carroll (the pen-name of Charles Lutwidge Dodgson) suffered from migraines and epilepsy and may have taken opium, which was then a legal drug, to alleviate the symptoms. Jean Cocteau, the French polymath, endorsed opium and wrote of its fetishist appeal: 'It is reassuring. It reassures by its luxury, by its rites, by the anti-medical elegance of the lamps, stoves, pipes, by the secular setting of this exquisite elegance.'

This was Marianne's dream world. Since school days she had read the works of Oscar Wilde, De Qunicey and Algernon Swinburne. Her heroes had been decadents, aesthetes, doomed Romantics, mad bohemians and opium-eaters. Christopher Gibbs viewed the explosion of drugs use among the youth with the clarity provided by relative maturity. He took LSD 'now and then' and evolved from a strand of social class that had been indulging in raffish behaviour for many years. "I should think a lot of the swinging was to do with the chemical flowering that was happening at the same time," he said. "The frontiers of the imagination were being pushed forward by people dropping acid. You could definitely say there was a feeling of spiritual renaissance, stepping out of some tired old cocoon into a fresh, rather frightening, beautiful world. Everyone was throwing away their dreary old clothes and peacocking around."

Marianne frequently visited the flat shared by Brian Jones and Anita Pallenberg in Courtfield Road, off Gloucester Road. It contained a hotchpotch of artefacts – a stuffed goat mounted on an amplifier, silk sunflowers, a huge painting of demons, Moroccan rugs – and was seldom cleaned or renovated so magazines and newspapers were scattered everywhere and paint peeled from the walls. Jones had met Pallenberg a year before, backstage after a Rolling Stones concert in Munich. She was the daughter of an Italian artist, Arnaldo Pallenberg, and Paula Wiederhold, a secretary to the German Embassy in Rome. At an early age Anita could speak four languages and before turning 20 had lived in Rome, Germany and New York where she had associations with Andy Warhol. Marianne said she was the most incredible woman she had ever met: 'dazzling, beautiful, hypnotic and unsettling'. Pallenberg and Jones would dress up in furs, satins and velvets and either parade around the flat or sit on rugs and talk through their kaleidoscopic ideas. Joints were handed around and Marianne joined in enthusiastically. Dunbar had objected to her smoking hash at their flat, which she considered chauvinistic. Another regular visitor to Courtfield Road was Keith Richards who had broken up with Linda Keith and, according to Marianne, 'exuded lonely bachelordom'.

Sexual liberation was a crucial element of the times. The youth imagined they had discarded the politics of sex and used it as a greeting card, a statement to express participation in the rebellion. "It was a way to show you were part of the club, a member of the swinging generation," said Barry Fantoni. "Almost everyone on the scene was making love to each other, even those that were really deeply unhappy and would have preferred to settle down with one partner. As in the use of drugs and the appreciation of polemic music, there was plenty of charlatanism at play."

Marianne had become intrigued by The Rolling Stones. She was initially attracted to Keith Richards whom she considered the most handsome. She liked his reserved manner, that he did not assert himself on situations, or women. She imagined it concealed a charm and strength of character – in her words, 'a tortured Byronic soul'. She had grown fond of Brian Jones who she considered the most cultured. She soon saw his vulnerability and the psychosis that eventually led him to lose much of his power in the band. "Brian was more like the sort of young men I knew," she said. "He had more education than the others; more culture, a little more sophistication. He could talk about almost anything. I got less interested in the superficial snobs and pseudo-intellectuals I had known – John Dunbar's friends – and I was also losing interest in the life I was leading," she said in an interview in 1985. Mick Jagger had made several clumsy plays for Marianne and been rebuffed. Within the early Stones set-up he was viewed as the straight man, outside the inner controlling core of Richards and Jones, who were more earnest about sampling the scene to its fullest. In comparison Jagger seemed reticent of letting slip his veneer of self-assurance.

On one occasion, in September 1966, Marianne called at Courtfield Road and Jones was there by himself. They talked for a while on his favourite subjects: trains (he collected train and bus magazines), Ingmar Bergman films and mystical links between druidic movements and UFOs, a topic greatly discussed at the time. They smoked a great deal of dope and Jones, who had also taken Mandrax, led Marianne to the attic, which they reached by pulling down a metal ladder. They lay on a mattress and Jones unbuttoned her blouse. They groped one another but did not have sex. 'He was a wonderfully feeble guy, quite incapable of real sex,' wrote Marianne.

Marianne quickly became aware of the volatile nature of Jones and Pallenberg's relationship. They were deeply in love but prone to mood-swings exacerbated by the large amounts of hashish and LSD they took. Anita often had bruises on her arms and although nothing was said, everyone was aware Jones had inflicted them. Many of Jones' drugs trips were fraught with frightening hallucinations that set off his paranoid tendencies. He became fidgety, scribbling in notebooks, hurling reels of tape across the room. People were talking about him, plotting. He needed constant reassurance. One day he started work on a huge mural of a graveyard on the wall above their bed, with a large headstone positioned above the pillows. "Poor Brian was somewhat uncool. He could summon coolness up, but fundamentally he wasn't cool at all," said Marianne. "His was a false cool. Keith [Richards], on the other hand, really was cool, ice cool, always."

The route that led to Marianne and Jagger becoming lovers had similarities for them both. Their previous partners, Dunbar and Chrissie Shrimpton, had helped take them from suburban life, in Reading and Dartford respectively, and mix in more refined circles. Chrissie was occasionally mentioned in articles about her sister, the model Jean Shrimpton, with whom she shared the same dark attractive looks. Jagger revelled in the loose association with the fashion world, its David Baileys and Mary Quants. They had first met at Windsor's Ricky-Tick blues club early in 1963. Chrissie, then 17, was a secretary working in Covent Garden and 19-year-old Jagger was a student at the London School of Economics. The Rolling Stones were hardly known at the time and, of the pair, friends considered Shrimpton the better catch. "Mick would come and meet me for lunch," she said. "One day, as we walked through the fruit and veg market in Covent Garden, a stall-holder threw a cabbage at Mick's head and shouted 'You ugly fucker'."

They had made vague plans to marry soon after meeting. As the Stones' adulation grew with every record and tour, the relationship became strained and by late 1965 they rowed often, sometimes in public. Chrissie told Jagger's biographer, Philip Norman, in 2012, that he was possessive and controlling. "When I was with Mick, I wasn't allowed to look at anyone else or even be friends with girls he considered tarts," she said. Mick Jagger had seen Brian Jones with the vibrant Anita Pallenberg, a girl oozing self-confidence and dark exoticism, and Chrissie, a builder's daughter with a famous sister who craved marriage, children and a stable home, quickly lost her lustre.

Jagger was linked in 1965 with the French singer Françoise Hardy. "I have a very strong memory of London in the 60s," she said in an interview in 2006. "I was walking down one of those small streets where you could find shops selling boots. And suddenly, there stood Mick Jagger right in front of me. I was totally flabbergasted. I have rarely met anyone with such charisma, such beauty. He gave me an enchanting smile, which left me petrified, speechless." Later, the photographer

Jean-Marie Perier brought the pair together for a shoot. They were photographed against a white-painted brick wall, Jagger wearing a rugby shirt and Hardy in a two-piece pinstriped suit. Jagger told friends and the press she was his 'ideal woman' but Hardy said she felt 'too clean' to fit comfortably into his lifestyle. Friends thought Jagger had earmarked the actress Julie Christie – another who had been educated at a convent school, the same as Marianne and Chrissie Shrimpton – as his next girlfriend but she was engaged to the lithographer Don Bessant, whom she had met two years earlier when he was working as a part-time postman. Jagger realised his chances of being with her were slim when, through 1965, pictures of Christie and Bessant ran in the press as they stepped out at the official openings of acclaimed films *Darling* and *Doctor Zhivago*.

Increasingly Jagger found himself meeting Marianne at parties and after concerts. At first he held out little hope of a relationship because he knew of her marriage and child and, indeed, admired Dunbar, whom he considered personable and intelligent. Barry Miles had noticed Marianne's drift away from Dunbar and her growing friendships with those in and around The Rolling Stones. "I wouldn't say she flirted but she was clearly attracted to people that were strong and overpowering," he said. Brian Jones and Keith Richards invited Marianne to a concert the band were playing at the Colston Hall, Bristol, where Ike and Tina Turner were the support act. Marianne was driven to the venue on Friday, October 7, 1966 by a chauffeur in a Ford Mustang she had bought. As the evening developed she was to see several contrasting sides of Jagger. Soon after arriving she spotted him with Tina Turner in the corridor outside the Stones' dressing room. Turner was teaching him to dance the 'Sideways Pony'. While Jones and Richards looked on giggling, he tried earnestly to copy the movements and Marianne enjoyed his playfulness. Afterwards, during the concert, she was bewitched by the primal energy of Jagger's performance. She wrote later that he was 'Dionysus, the dancing God'. In that weekend's edition of the *Sunday People*, Jagger explained his approach to performing: "I entice the audience. What I'm doing is a sexual thing. I dance and all dancing is a replacement for sex. My dancing is pretty basic sexuality."

Marianne went back to Jagger's hotel room after the show for an impromptu showing of Roman Polanski's new film *Repulsion*, screened by Michael Cooper who was working with the Polish director. Reefers were passed around and Marianne had more than ever before. She was unable to speak for a while and in her vacant state all she could grasp was that people were leaving the room on a sporadic basis. As the night passed she regained composure and began to wonder with whom she would be left, hoping it would be Keith Richards. Eventually only two others remained, Mick Jagger and a member of Ike and Tina Turner's backing group of singers, the Ikettes. Although never revealed, this was probably P. P. Arnold with whom Jagger had begun a loose association a few weeks earlier, at the start of the tour. "Mick was dating Marianne and me at the same time," she said in an interview in 2010. "We were quite friendly about it and I wasn't expecting Mick Jagger to marry me or anything like that. And Marianne was aware of me and I was aware of her."

After a long period of near-silence the other girl departed, leaving Marianne alone with Jagger for the first time. The room was clogged with smoke and Marianne suggested they go for a walk in the hotel grounds. The grass was sodden with dew and, in their dreamy, doped state, the talk was fantastic. They spoke of King Arthur, Stonehenge, Merlin, the Holy Grail and Joseph of Arimathea. Jagger joked that it was as if Marianne was setting him a test. She was: "You would ask your date, 'Do you know Genet? Have you read *A Rebours*?' and if he said yes, you'd fuck." Back at the hotel Jagger noticed Marianne's boots had become wet in the grass. He untied them and put them on a radiator to dry. She was impressed by his kindness and thoughtfulness. They climbed into bed and as the couple made love the sun rose to perfectly conclude their encounter.

One of the first times Jagger and Marianne were seen together publicly was at the all-night rave held on October 15, 1966 to mark the launch of the seminal underground newspaper *International Times*. They had gone with other friends so did not appear necessarily to be a couple. Arrivals were welcomed with a free sugar cube, which many wrongly believed to be coated with LSD. Pink Floyd topped the bill and Soft Machine also appeared at the event organised by Miles and John Hopkins at The Roundhouse, Camden Town. More than 2,000 packed into the former engine shed. Many had taken LSD beforehand and wandered aimlessly through the cold, cavernous building, facing queues of more than an hour to use one of only two toilets. Jagger did not enjoy the party and said afterwards: "I thought everyone would be freaking out and wearing weird clothes but they were all wandering around in dirty macs. It was the most boring thing I've ever seen." Paul McCartney attended dressed as an Arab but it was Marianne's adapted nun's habit that drew most attention.

A few days later Marianne took off with Nicholas for a holiday in Positano, a picturesque village on Italy's Amalfi coast. A nanny, Diana, Marianne's roadie, Pat and a model called Kelly who Marianne had met a few days earlier in a boutique in Oxford Circus, accompanied them. They stopped off in Paris en route where hotel staff handed Marianne a letter from Dunbar pledging his love and seeking reconciliation. "Wonderful letter. I threw it out of the window," she said. While in Positano, Kelly was visited by her boyfriend, a handsome American model. He and Marianne had an instant attraction and made love under a full moon on the terrace of the villa where they were all staying. Marianne received three letters from Jagger and he phoned her regularly at the villa. She had taken with her The Rolling Stones compilation album *Big Hits (High Tide And Green Grass)* and played the 14 tracks continually as if trying to understand and draw closer to Jagger. She pondered later whether she had willed herself to fall in love with him to move on from Dunbar who 'never made a penny' and was 'incredibly selfish' and to also leave behind a pop career that had quickly become a 'horrible millstone'. She still maintained strong feelings for Keith Richards and telephoned the Stones' new business manager, Allen Klein, from Positano and told him of her dilemma. Klein was a curious choice of confidante but she had warmed to him on the few occasions they had met, and considered him clear-minded. He warned her Jagger would be devastated to hear this and perhaps she should wait until her thoughts were more definite.

Marianne flew back from Italy but the rest of the party, including Nicholas, endured a fraught journey back in the Mustang, which broke down and had to be repaired. She booked herself into the Mayfair Hotel and phoned Brian Jones. He said he was at his flat with Richards and Tara Browne, who had just separated from his wife, Nikki. They picked up Marianne and went back to Jones' to take acid. While they were tripping Jones asked Marianne to accompany him again to the attic. He fondled her but it did not go further because Marianne wanted to maintain the intensity of the trip. She decided this would be best achieved alone and returned to Lennox Gardens. She had not been there long before Keith Richards phoned and told her it was important for their psychic well-being that they 're-connected'. Richards met her cab and told Marianne that Brian had passed out and Browne had left. He climbed into the taxi and they returned to the hotel. They slept together and Marianne had what she described in her autobiography as 'the best night I've ever had in my life'. The next morning, as The Four Seasons played on the record player, Marianne was in a state of exhilaration. Richards, though, was in a much more phlegmatic mood. "You know who really has it bad for you, don't you?" he asked. When he told her it was Jagger, he added: "He's not that bad when you get to know him, you know."

In his book, *Life*, Richards wrote that soon after making love in the morning they realised Jagger had arrived at the hotel. 'My head was nestled between those two beautiful jugs and we heard his car drive up. I did one out of the window, got my shoes, through the garden, and I realised I'd left my socks. Well, Mick's not the type of guy to look for socks,' he wrote. The episode became an in-joke between Richards and Marianne for many years when he would ask if she had found his socks yet. Marianne said later that she was 'too English' and conventional for Richards who preferred his women more glamorous and 'exceptional'. Marianne also sensed he was deeply in love with Anita Pallenberg at the time.

Once Jagger learned of Marianne's return from Italy he began to phone her regularly. They went on shopping trips together in Bond Street. Their meetings were clandestine because Jagger had not ended his relationship with Chrissie Shrimpton (on her part, Marianne was now largely estranged from Dunbar). She saw quickly that Jagger disliked confrontation and was slow to take decisive action, especially in his emotional life. Chrissie knew of Jagger's promiscuity but believed it was restricted to inconsequential one-night stands while touring. Theirs had been a volatile relationship with rows and brief separations but she became aware of a material change in November 1966 when she learned bills could no longer be charged to his bank account. They had planned to spend a holiday together in Jamaica over the Christmas period, flying out from Heathrow on Thursday December 15, 1966. She claimed that she only found out the tickets had been cancelled by ringing the Rolling Stones' office.

On that day, Jagger was Christmas shopping with Marianne. They bought a tricycle for Nicholas at Harrods and lunched together at Lorenzo's, the Italian restaurant in Beauchamp Place frequented by stars from the pop and film world. Three days later Jagger finally told Chrissie he wanted to end their three-year affair, though he did not tell her about Marianne. Chrissie returned to their flat at Harley House, Marylebone Road, close to Regent's Park, which they shared with a dog, six cats and three birds. She overdosed on sleeping pills. "It wasn't just attention-seeking or a cry for help," she said. "I really wanted to die. I thought my life was over." Chrissie regained consciousness at St George's Hospital at Hyde Park Corner and discovered she had been admitted under a false name, presumably to keep the episode out of the press, a ruse which was successful. After a few days she was taken in a wheelchair to Greenways Nursing Home, Hampstead, and kept under heavy sedation until well enough to recuperate further at her parents' in Buckinghamshire. While there she learned for the first time about Jagger's affair with Marianne through newspaper articles. When she eventually returned to Harley House to collect her belongings the locks were changed. She had to ring the Stones' office and book an appointment to gain admittance. She later claimed she did not feel animosity to Jagger. "You can't help going off people, and we were both very, very young," she said in 2012.

Many of Jagger's feelings about Chrissie Shrimpton had been channelled into The Rolling Stones' songs. The shifting change in the balance of power was famously summarised in 'Under My Thumb' ('The squirming dog who's just had her day') and her mental state exposed in '19th Nervous Breakdown' ('Oh, who's to blame, that girl's just insane'). Jagger, though, claimed neither song was autobiographical. Marianne was convinced she would not be portrayed so negatively in future songs Jagger might write. 'Unlike Chrissie, I would have no trouble at all handling whatever came along,' she wrote. 'Here was a nice man whom I loved and who loved me. He would take care of me and we'd live happily ever after.' On the subject of Chrissie's suicide attempt, Marianne wrote: 'I can't pretend that I was sympathetic with her plight. On the contrary, I was feeling pleased with myself and I was quite secure.' The first song thought to be about Marianne was 'Let's Spend The Night Together', recorded by The Rolling Stones at Olympic Sound Studios weeks after Marianne and Jagger had first made love at the hotel. In the lyric Jagger appears to be describing that very night: 'I'm off my head and my mouth's getting dry. I'm high, but I try, try, try, oh my'.

On a whim, Marianne invited Jagger to join her in Italy where she was due to appear at the ill-fated San Remo Music Festival held over three days on January 26, 27 and 28, 1967. The televised event featured visiting singers from around the world and indigenous Italian talent. Marianne met Jagger at Cannes airport and they hired a boat to sail on the Mediterranean, docking overnight in Nice and Villefranche-sur-Mer. The boat was shared with a crew of two and a nanny to take care of Nicholas. During a storm, Marianne, Jagger and Nicholas climbed into a bunk and held one another, waiting for it to pass. Marianne stated later that this was the precise moment she fell in love with Jagger.

Back at San Remo they did a short interview with the tenacious and influential journalist Don Short of the *Daily Mirror*, who was renowned for scoops, mainly about The Beatles. They posed for a series of photographs for Dezo Hoffman, the Slovakian émigré with similar Beatles connections. They were pictured eating at a restaurant, Jagger in a collarless white shirt, Marianne in a floppy wide-brimmed hat. In another shot they walked arm-in-arm along the seafront, Marianne in voluminous flared trousers and wearing small heart-shaped glasses. The pictures became famous throughout the world and announced that Mick Jagger and Marianne Faithfull were now together and in love, a couple.

With her mind clearly on other matters, Marianne did not excel at the festival, which also featured two singers with whom she'd had flings,

Gene Pitney and Allan Clarke of The Hollies. She lost out in her first round 'sing-off' to Milan's Riki Maiocchi whose version of 'There Are Those Who Hope' ('C'è Chi Spera' – Marianne sang in Italian) was considered the better. The festival, however, was overshadowed by the suicide of one of the participants, 28-year-old Luigi Tenco. He shot himself through the head after learning his duet with his fiancée, Dalida, of 'Bye Love, Bye', had been eliminated. A note found near his body said he had killed himself as a protest to 'the jury and public's choices' during the competition.

On returning to England, Marianne moved into Harley House with Jagger, leaving Nicholas in the care of his nanny, Diana, at the flat in Lennox Gardens, which Marianne had decided to keep on. Marianne redecorated the flat at Harley House in opulent style, spending hours in Chelsea's foremost shops. The most expensive purchase was a chandelier costing £6,000 – more than five times the annual wage of a manual worker in 1967. John Dunbar told friends he had not given up hope of getting back with Marianne. He confronted Jagger on one occasion and they had a row which closed with Dunbar telling him he was 'nothing but a cheap Beatle imitation'.

"John adored Marianne but he could not hold her," said Christopher Gibbs. "He had great joy out of his brief time with her. I don't think there was joy without the other side. There was a bit of agony along the way. I love John Dunbar. He is a very gentle person and has worn very well. I wasn't looking for signs that their marriage was breaking up but I was aware life was changing for all concerned. If you are a friend of both it is very dangerous to take a view that one person is in the right or whatever. Who are we to comment on these kinds of divine arrangements that shake everything up all the time?" Barry Miles saw Dunbar often during this period. "I didn't really get to know his emotional state when Marianne left him. John was a smart guy and he was always switching people on to new ideas, new drugs and new artists. He did not have any shortage of girlfriends afterwards," he said.

Dunbar used his friendship with an artist who had exhibited at the Indica Gallery as a possible route to being reunited with Marianne. John Alexis Mardas (born, Yanni Alexis Mardas) had arrived in England from

Athens in 1965 with his one-man show, *Kinetic Light Sculptures*. He built up a friendship with many on the scene including John Lennon who was fascinated by his 'Nothing Box', a small plastic box with randomly blinking lights. Lennon gave him the nickname 'Magic Alex' and elevated him to 'guru' status, announcing him as such to friends. Dunbar had first met the charismatic Mardas when he was fixing television sets at a London shop. They shared a flat for a while, making vague plans to go into business together. Dunbar introduced him to The Rolling Stones and Mardas was soon installed as the band's quasi-lighting engineer. One of his inventions was a light that changed colour in time to music. Dunbar travelled with him to several of the Stones dates on their three-week European tour beginning in Malmo, Sweden in March 1967. "Dunbar and Mardas managed to get various sums of money for these projects, but there always seemed to be a problem when we asked to see examples of their work," said Bill Wyman. "As far as I could see, the only magic Mardas performed was making our money disappear. Maybe John Dunbar was getting his own back."

On learning of her union with Jagger some of Marianne's friends were concerned. "The Rolling Stones were all middle-class yobs, except for Charlie and Bill, who were just yobs," said Barry Fantoni. "Brian was brighter, but he suffered. He was much too sensitive. I think Mick is a deeply unpleasant person and I feel there is something quite repellent about his personality. He is a posturer, a man who postures. He is absolutely obsessed by wealth but he had great power and I think Marianne was seduced by that. I think that kind of rootless, wealthy power is incredibly seductive."

Before giving birth to Nicholas, Marianne had made a series of recordings during September and October 1965 and these sustained her career throughout 1966 when she was otherwise preoccupied. 'Tomorrow's Calling', written by Eric Woolfson, later to found The Alan Parsons Project, was a spirited follow-up to 'Yesterday' but failed to chart in any of the countries where it was released, including France, a market for which she sang the version 'Si Demain'. The same fate befell her other single released in 1966, 'Counting'. A wordy song performed in a high register, it was written by Bob Lind, the American folk singer/ songwriter who had scored a hit in both Britain and the United States with 'Elusive Butterfly'. The hierarchy at Decca was not particularly perturbed by the poor sales of both singles because there was a strong feeling that Marianne's folksy introspection was better suited to the ever-growing albums market.

Unfortunately the album *North Country Maid*, released in April 1966, did not support the perception. Despite containing several of Marianne's most accomplished vocal performances, it did not chart. Standards such as 'Scarborough Fair' were merged with newer folk songs – Bert Jansch's 'Green Are Your Eyes'; Tom Paxton's 'The Last Thing On My Mind' and Ewan MacColl's 'The First Time Ever I Saw Your Face'. Her voice, sometimes brittle, at other times rich, proved conclusively that she could sing – a criticism made often during her early recording career. The album was largely stripped down to voice and guitar with occasional percussion but did not become repetitive. On numbers such as 'Cockleshells' (written by Mick Taylor, later of The Rolling Stones) where her range was fully tested, she accommodated the key shifts and also supplied heart to the excellent 'Sally Free And Easy' and Donovan's 'Sunny Goodge Street', written especially for her. *North Country Maid* was a brave statement, digging deep into the British and Irish songbook. Working again with Mike Leander, she was proving a fine interpreter of songs and revealed an authentic desire to explore the genre, which effectively made her Britain's premier female folk singer.

The Rolling Stones, meanwhile, were selling millions of records throughout the world. Their album *Aftermath*, released in the spring of 1966, the first composed entirely of Jagger/Richards songs, had reached number one in the UK and number two in the United States. The single '19th Nervous Breakdown' had reached number two on both sides of the Atlantic and its follow-up, 'Paint It, Black', went to number one in both countries. They were a global phenomenon and fascination, and so was anyone associated with them.

7

Marianne and Jagger's first outing as a couple back in England came early in 1967 when they attended the 20th birthday celebrations of Decca's American sister label, London Records. In his best velvet jacket Jagger sat down for dinner at the Savoy Hotel with fellow London and Decca recording artists such as Tom Jones and Cat Stevens. Squeezed between Jagger and Marianne for part of the evening was the hyperactive and now disgraced disc jockey Jimmy Savile. He tugged at Marianne's hair, pulled funny faces and generally larked around, especially when a photographer was in their vicinity. Andrew Oldham arrived in shades with an empty milk bottle, which he placed tenderly on the banquet table hoping to antagonise more than a few guests.

A media tumult began when The Rolling Stones released their twelfth single, 'Let's Spend The Night Together', on, aptly enough, Friday, January 13, 1967. The suggestive title led many radio stations to either ban the song or bleep out the word 'night'. Jagger teased *Melody Maker*: "If people have warped, twisted, dirty minds, I suppose it could have sexual overtones. The song isn't really very rude." The Stones were due to appear on the *Eamonn Andrews Show* where they expected to conform to the usual protocol and mime. The Musicians' Union insisted they played live, a move the band felt was designed to make an example of them [in the event they performed 'She Smiled Sweetly' because they had not fully rehearsed 'Let's Spend The Night

Together']. The show ended with a panel discussion section where Jagger was joined by fellow guests, the sitcom actor Hugh Lloyd and the singer Susan Maughan, famous for her version of 'Bobby's Girl'. Andrews asked Jagger if he felt any responsibility to his fans – a typical examination of the band's values and lifestyle. "Everyone is fallible, but the teenager of 16 to 18 knows their own mind," replied Jagger. "I don't have any real moral responsibility to them. They'll work out their own moral values for themselves."

In the United States the song became 'Let's Spend Some Time Together' when they appeared on the *Ed Sullivan Show*. Sullivan was resolute about the change of title and lyric. "I've hundreds of thousands of kids watching my show. I won't stand for anything like that with a double meaning. Either the song goes or the Stones go," he said. Stanley Dorfman, producer of *Top Of The Pops*, took a more sanguine view. "I don't disapprove at all. I don't think it's corrupting – it might be a very innocent night!" he said.

Another row broke out when the Stones refused to take to a revolving stage on *Sunday Night At The London Palladium*, a television variety staple of 12 years' standing, presented that week by Irish comedian Dave Allen [guesting for Jimmy Tarbuck] and watched by up to 10 million viewers every Sunday. The show routinely ended with the show's host and guests smiling and waving to the theatre audience and viewers as they stood on a revolving stage, a convention in which the Stones were unwilling to participate. The whole day had been fraught. Featured acts were asked to be at the theatre for 4pm to rehearse the show, which was broadcast live four hours later. When the Stones, and Jagger in particular, refused to 'revolve' because it made them 'part of a circus' it understandably caused anxiety with show time looming. Andrew Oldham was called for and, perhaps surprisingly, said the band should do as they were asked. "I was so disappointed in my dealings with them," said Albert Locke, the show's producer. "Not only were they late for rehearsal but I was confronted with ill-mannered, studied rudeness." The reaction across the media bordered on hysterical. Letters were sent to the press and leader writers attacked the band's 'arrogance'. Miss Joan H Gadd's letter to the *Daily Mirror* was typical: 'They should take a lesson from the real stars like Gracie Fields, Margot Fonteyn and Frankie Vaughan. None of them would dream of being so rude to either their fellow artists or the public.' Bill Wyman, the Stones' bass player, commented: "It was as if we'd committed a major crime."

The news stories about The Rolling Stones that appeared in January 1967 were little more than hors d'oeuvres before a feast. In a series of articles, the *News Of The World* published a five-part exposé under the heading: 'Pop Stars and Drugs – Facts That Will Shock You'. The instalment implicating the Stones was based on an interview that had supposedly taken place with Jagger at Blaises, a night club in Kensington. It was reported that as he spoke with the journalists 'Jagger' took Benzedrine tablets and offered hashish to a couple of girls. It was actually Brian Jones they were writing about – he habitually claimed to be the 'leader' of The Rolling Stones and this probably led to the misidentification. Known for his lack of discretion and flattered by almost any kind of attention, Jones would talk freely and fantastically on a range of subjects, oblivious to the impact it might have on the band. He would also agree to bizarre stunts such as the photo session he did with Anita Pallenberg for the left-leaning German weekly news magazine, *Stern*. Anita had starred in the film *A Degree Of Murder* to which Jones contributed the soundtrack. They thought it would help promote the film if Jones was pictured in a Nazi SS uniform while Anita crouched at his feet cradling a doll and an ornamental swastika. "These are realistic pictures," explained Jones. "The meaning of it all is there is no sense in it."

In the issue dated February 5, 1967, Mick Jagger was wrongly exposed in the six million-selling *News Of The World* as a user of LSD (the paper's staff assumed hashish and LSD were different names for the same drug). Jagger was understandably piqued and issued a writ for libel against the paper. The battle lines were drawn but Jagger was mistaken if he thought it was going to be a hasty, bloodless skirmish. He did not receive an immediate letter of apology and the paper continued on the offensive. It had to substantiate that Jagger indeed took drugs and, therefore, the article was truthful, an absolute defence of libel. Just a week later, Jagger provided the substantiation the paper required when he attended the most celebrated house party of modern times.

The host was Keith Richards, the guests a close circle of friends including Marianne and Jagger, who descended on Richards' Redlands home in West Wittering, Sussex, with the intention of a weekend's revelry beginning on the Saturday night of February 11. Also present were the art dealer Robert Fraser with his personal assistant, the Moroccan Ali Mohammed; Christopher Gibbs; Michael Cooper; George and Pattie Harrison; David Schneiderman [in several books it has appeared as Schneidermann] a.k.a David Britton or David Henry but better known as 'Acid King David', a 24-year-old (or 27) Californian (or Canadian, no one was quite sure – Robert Fraser had only met him a few days earlier) with an attaché case packed with an LSD-type drug called variously 'White Lightning' and 'Sunshine'; and Nicky Cramer, a 'Kings Road loon', one of many flamboyant characters who attached themselves to the Stones' party on an intermittent basis. On the Friday before travelling to Redlands, Jagger, Richards and Marianne had attended a Beatles recording session that turned into a grand party. Mike Nesmith of The Monkees and Donovan had also dropped by at the chaotic session that lasted until 1am. The Beatles had hired a 40-piece orchestra comprising members of the Royal Philharmonic and the London Symphony to play in the 24-bar gap in 'A Day In The Life'. Novelty hats, red noses and masks were donned and snippets were filmed, possibly to include in a proposed television special to tie in with the forthcoming *Sgt. Pepper's Lonely Hearts Club Band* album.

On the Saturday night Jagger drove Marianne in his new Mini Cooper through the snaking lanes to Redlands where dinner was prepared by Ali Mohammed. The next day they all drove around in a van, stopping off at West Dean House, set in 8,000 acres, the former home of the poet and patron of the surrealist movement Edward James. They skipped around the grounds but could not gain entry to the grand house, which James had given over to a charitable trust three years earlier. Afterwards they walked in the woods that fringed Richards' estate and had a short outing to a nearby shingle beach. They had each taken acid provided by Schneiderman. As he had passed over the tablet with their morning cup of tea he told them it was 'the Tao of lysergic diethylamide, man' and promised it would help them 'navigate the cosmos'. During the weekend they found him pompous and opinionated but were in forgiving mood because his drugs were incredibly strong. George and Pattie Harrison did not arrive until late on Sunday afternoon and left in the early evening, heading back home to Esher, Surrey. The rest sat around talking while Mohammed cooked dinner. Marianne, whose clothes were covered in sand and dirt, went upstairs for a bath and when she left the lounge the men were listening to a Bob Dylan record. She did not have a change of clothing so, after leaving to dry the ones she had been wearing, she bathed and wrapped herself in a large, thin rug, returning to the living room where ethnic instruments were leaning against the walls. "I remember her demurely wrapped in fur lying on the sofa," said Christopher Gibbs. "It was an elegant and appropriate garment to wear among old friends after a bath. She was a charming, modest girl on occasions, and she was on this evening. She was not flaunting herself, certainly not. She was among close friends relaxing." They chatted amiably, smoking joints and sipping wine, the effects of the LSD gradually diminishing. "We were sitting down quietly, nothing at all untoward; a nice, quiet evening in the 60s," said Gibbs.

The group's tranquil, spaced-out reverie was disturbed in formidable fashion. Eighteen police officers trampled into the house. Chief Inspector Gordon Dineley stood among the startled guests, empty wine bottles, overflowing ashtrays, decorated cushions and discarded musical instruments and announced that he possessed a warrant under the Dangerous Drugs Act (1964) that entitled him to search the premises. Unknown to the group, someone had phoned the West Sussex Regional Police Headquarters in Chichester at 5pm and told the officer answering the phone, DC John Challen, that a 'riotous party' was being held at Redlands involving drug-taking. In little over an hour the police had organised the first ever drugs bust to take place in the division. Initially Marianne thought the scene was part of a bad LSD trip. Detective Constable Rosemary Slade, one of three police women who had travelled with other officers to Redands in seven vehicles, said she wanted to search Marianne who immediately let slip the rug. "It wasn't one bit lascivious, a quick flounce done very gracefully, almost like a curtsey," Marianne said. Detective Sergeant Stanley Cudmore would say later that Marianne let the rug slip several times 'showing portions of her nude body'. At the time Marianne thought it all 'hysterically funny' but conceded later that she had misjudged the gravity of the situation. "It didn't seem quite so funny later. I certainly got paid back in spades," she said. Keith Richards was also unable to take it seriously. He began rolling on the carpet laughing and then, much the same as the others, answering the officers' questions with – according to Marianne – 'grandeur and disdain'. Despite Richards' attitude, the police were surprised at his articulacy and Jagger's, too. "They weren't morons like we expected them to be," said DC Challen. "They were both intelligent and pleasant."

Marianne was naked beneath the rug so was clearly not in possession of any drugs. The other guests were more fretful. Robert Fraser had 24 heroin 'jacks' in his pocket; Schneiderman had an envelope packed with cannabis and a case full of LSD; and Jagger had four capsules of amphetamine in a pocket of his green velvet jacket. The tablets were the remainder of a quantity given to Marianne by a disc jockey to help her stay awake after she had smoked too much hashish in San Remo. They were inside a plastic phial with the word 'Stenamina' stamped on it. They were legal in Italy and most other European countries but not in Britain. All three men made valiant attempts to delude Dineley and his team. Schneiderman handed over the cannabis but implored officers not to touch the briefcase because it was full of exposed film. They left it unopened. Fraser almost had a similar reprieve when an officer appeared to believe that the white capsules were insulin for his diabetes. After returning them to Fraser the officer took one back 'just for analysis'. Fraser knew immediately his chicanery had failed. Jagger told officers: "The tablets were prescribed for me by my doctor, Dr Dixon Firth of Wilton Crescent, Knightsbridge. They help me to stay awake and work." Dr Firth later corroborated this, telling police they had been prescribed because his patient had suffered 'a period of intense personal strain'. While the raid was taking place Keith Richards had put on to the record player 'Rainy Day Women # 12 & 35', the Bob Dylan track with the refrain 'Everybody must get stoned'. When the police left, Fraser, Mohammed and Schneiderman returned immediately to

London. Marianne, Jagger and Richards stayed behind to discuss how they should respond.

The next day, Richards' solicitor, Timothy Hardacre, and the Stones' publicist, Les Perrin, joined them at Redlands. Another meeting was held a few days later at the Hilton Hotel in London attended by Jagger; Richards; Hardacre; the high-ranking QC, Victor Durand; and Allen Klein who had flown in especially from the United States. The Stones' coterie, with its expansive connections, was suspicious as to why the police had swooped at such an opportune time. It might have been a remarkable coincidence but there was a growing hunch that Richards' phone had been tapped. The more probable explanation was a tip-off and it was generally agreed the bust had been instigated by an act of treachery. As most were long-standing and trusted friends, there were only two real suspects. Nicky Cramer was 'visited' by David Litvinoff, a heavy who sometimes 'helped out' the Stones. He had connections to London's gangland and was an associate of the Krays. He systematically beat Cramer until he was convinced he had nothing to do with the raid. Schneiderman, therefore, was the prime suspect.

"He was a Pied Piperish character," said Gibbs. "Who the hell he was and where he came from, nobody knew. He had just popped up. He was able to tune into everybody's wavelength and was seductive, satanic, the devil in his most beguiling of disguises. After the bust he vanished as devils do, in a puff of smoke, and was never seen again." Michael Cooper told Tony Sanchez, author of *Up And Down With The Rolling Stones*: "The guy was much more than an ordinary pusher. He had a whole collection of different passports in different names and with different nationalities on them. I saw them when I was looking through his bag for some dope at Redlands. And he talked to me about guns and weapons in the same sort of way most guys talk about chicks. I know it sounds fantastic but I reckon he was something much more than a creep hired by the *News Of The World*. He was like some kind of James Bond character and someone right at the top put him in because the Stones were becoming too powerful. They really were worried that they could spark off fighting in the streets if they tried. I'm sure the newspaper was in on it somewhere, but it was this guy using them – not the other way around."

David Schneiderman fled the country unimpeded. It was thought he had telephoned the news desk of the *News Of The World* where a dutiful news editor had informed the West Sussex Constabulary, therefore assuring the paper police co-operation when the story broke. "I think it was likely it was a set-up," said Gibbs. "Schneiderman was a charming, personable hipster. I suppose he knew all the passwords, and anyway, people then were more open to new people and experiences. They were more innocent. He had a little suitcase with drugs in it and I suppose he was a kind of Candy Man figure." Marianne shared the same view. "In retrospect, it was obvious to all of us that somebody had set us up. At the time this conspiracy theory business sounded like your typical, drugged-out paranoid hippy ravings, but if you read the recent revelations of what MI5 was up to around this time, it doesn't seem quite so far-fetched," she said.

The following Sunday, the *News Of The World*, which had much to gain from an explicit link between Jagger and drugs, ran an exclusive front page story headlined: 'Drugs Squad Raids Pop Stars Party'. The article, written in the first person, was purposely ambiguous as court proceedings against Jagger, Richards and Fraser were about to become 'active' and to name them might have prejudiced a fair trial. The piece began: 'Charges alleging illegal possession or use of drugs may be made as a result of a police raid on a pop stars' [sic] house-party last week. Several stars, at least three of them nationally known names were present at the party. It was held at a secluded country house near the South Coast'. Few people were left in any doubt it was referring to members of The Rolling Stones because the story appeared so soon after the earlier allegations about Jagger. After it broke in the *News Of The World*, Fleet Street decided en bloc to breach the Contempt of Court Act and reveal details of the raid, although there was an absence of hard facts. The article in the *Daily Express* was typical: 'A village was talking yesterday about the night a drugs squad raided Rolling Stone Keith Richards' country hideaway.' It continued, quoting Richards' cleaner, Mrs Dyer of Malthouse Cottages, West Wittering. "I saw nothing unusual when I went to clean," she said.

During the meeting at the Hilton, Klein said it was vital the band and its entourage escaped the media clamour. Morocco was chosen as the place of refuge. They travelled to North Africa separately on Monday February 27, 1967, to reduce the risk of detection by the press. Jagger and Marianne flew from Paris while Richards, Anita Pallenberg, Deborah Dixon (the American girlfriend of their film director friend, Donald Cammell) and Jones were driven in Richards' Bentley Continental through France and Spain by Tom Keylock, the Stones' chauffeur and 'fixer'. The plan was for everyone to meet up at the lavish El Minzah Hotel, a favourite haunt of film stars such as Rita Hayworth and Rock Hudson, overlooking the Bay of Tangier.

Brian Jones took ill en route with pneumonia and as he recovered in the Centre Hospitalier d'Albi, near Toulouse – where he spent his 25th birthday alone – the rest continued the journey. The flirting between Richards and Anita that had begun several months earlier developed into a full-blown affair when they stopped off for three days at Marbella. Jones joined the party in Morocco several days later and harboured a suspicion that remained unspoken until Anita refused to participate in a sex session with two local prostitutes. Drunk and drugged, in a jealous rage he punched Anita. Her face became swollen and her eyes were blackened. "He whacked Anita," said Keylock. "I said, 'If you ever do that again, I'll punch your lights out. You don't go round hitting women. It ain't on.' 'I'm sorry,' he said. 'I don't know what came over me.' It was no use putting it down to pills this time. He knew what he was doing."

Richards met Anita by the hotel's pool the next day and his feelings of guilt dissipated when he saw her injuries. Although Keylock was Jones' designated driver, he took Richards and Anita to the ferry terminal so they could travel to Malaga. From there they headed to Madrid and then home to London. Jones, meanwhile, distraught with grief, guilt, loss and self-pity, visited Donald Cammell in Paris. He was still unsure whether Richards and Anita were lovers and hoped any affection from Richards to her was paternal rather than passionate. Jones eventually called at Richards' flat and the two men were left confounded when Anita left the country to begin filming in Spain where she had a part in the space fantasy *Barbarella*. She told Richards she was not ready to live with him, and Jones that she no longer wished to be considered his girlfriend.

While in Morocco, Jagger took part in a photo session around the hotel swimming pool with royal photographer Cecil Beaton, whom Marianne found to be 'bitchy and insufferable'. Beaton later said of Jagger: "He is sexy, yet completely sexless. He could nearly be a eunuch. As a model he is a natural." On a walk into the Atlas Mountains with Jagger and Gibbs, Marianne broke down crying. She told them it was merely 'existential anguish' but she was really pining to be alone with Jagger and away from their omnipresent circle of friends and associates. She also sensed for the first time that Jagger was 'bringing out all my feelings of worthlessness'. One evening Marianne paid a local prostitute called Yasmin to come back to the hotel with them. The three of them had sex, which finished with Jagger rolling a joint while watching the two girls continue. "It was part of an intensely sexual period of my life," said Marianne.

Marianne had taken Jagger to visit her father in Ipsden and he approved of her new partner. "He was a very pleasant chap. He was quite charming," said Glynn Faithfull. "He told me he had attended the London School of Economics but didn't finish his course. I was glad he was taking her under his wing because he seemed such a level-headed, cool thinking chap." Jagger's primal on-stage persona had initially made Marianne apprehensive of her new lover but she was heartened that he was 'nice and cuddly', as she told friends. Jagger's circle noted that he suddenly appeared more learned and interested in culture. Marianne took him to the theatre, opera and ballet. Her bedtime reading included Eliphas Levi, the French occult author and ceremonial magician, and Aleister Crowley, the famous English occultist. Jagger was keen to know more of these eccentric figures and, in response, played his favourite records to her – Motown's The Miracles; the master of the blues harmonica, Slim Harpo; and Robert Johnson, whose Mississippi Delta blues records, originally recorded in the 1930s, had been recently reissued. Friends noticed Jagger was speaking in measured tones and his clothes were better cut and more expensive. Many noted the couple's child-like manner, especially when they were together at Harley House. Gina Richardson of the *Sunday Telegraph* wrote that they were like two children left in charge of the house while the grown-ups were out.

In the early spring of 1967 Marianne and Jagger moved from Harley House to 48 Cheyne Walk by the banks of the River Thames, positioning themselves in the middle of London's élite Chelsea set. Marianne had custody of 18-month-old Nicholas and Jagger accepted him wholeheartedly. John Dunbar was understandably upset at being estranged from his son and Marianne admitted he 'hardly saw him for years'. One time Nicholas left the house in his slippers and dressing gown, presumably on his way to see his father. He was found later at a local police station. Marianne and Jagger tried to retreat into domesticity but it was almost impossible. At the time, and unlike today, there were no other trans-global rock groups. The rest were largely also-rans, which meant the focus on The Beatles and The Rolling Stones was fierce and unremitting. The notion of acts seeking sporadic and bespoke attention to tie in with an album and tour did not exist: The Beatles and The Rolling Stones were pursued continually.

"There was a grotesque circus around the Stones when they arrived in town," said Keith Altham. "It was like a gravy train. It left a lot of people in its wake. I think Mick was constitutionally stronger than Marianne. Keith [Richards] is a strong person, mentally and physically; you have to be to ride such a crazed horse. I don't think the scene around them has been exaggerated. It has been underestimated. The intensity was sensational. The attention on Mick Jagger especially was colossal and anyone who attached themselves to him was obviously going to be under a great deal of stress. Certain things frightened me, like the drugs. The whole LSD bit was scary. It was mistakenly thought to provide a creative insight. Marianne and Mick had their faces on lots of magazine covers. They were treading new areas. They were only in their mid-twenties [Marianne was actually 19 when she became involved romantically with Jagger] and it was heaped upon them. To get through, people had to create a second person, but you have to make sure the real person is not taken over."

Jagger revealed chauvinistic traits that irritated Marianne and led to petty rows. She noted too that he was occasionally 'tight with money' though after she had convinced him it was his duty to complement status with good taste, he began to spend 'a small fortune', especially on items for their flat. Sometimes she felt she was merely a trophy, a beautiful, intelligent doll to parade. When they rowed she would grab a £5 note and a lump of dope and race from the flat. It was her way of asserting her independence, showing him this was all she needed to survive. She soon became aware of the gulf between their standing in the media. She was granted plenty of space and precedence in newspaper articles about Jagger but securing column inches in her own right for her musical output was difficult to acquire.

Marianne's fourth album, *Love In A Mist*, with Mike Leander again producing, moved away from the delicate backing of *North Country Maid* and featured heavy orchestration to varying success. Decca advertised the LP as: 'A beautiful singer sings 14 beautiful romantic songs in wistful mood.' It opened with her downbeat rendition of 'Yesterday' and was followed by a passable version of Jackie DeShannon's 'You Can't Go Where The Roses Go'. Chris Andrews, who had previously supplied hits for Sandie Shaw and Adam Faith, wrote the lukewarm and shrilly sung 'Our Love Has Gone'. Other songs that caught Marianne sounding lacklustre were Bob Lind's 'Counting' and 'I Have A Love', lifted from Leonard Bernstein and Stephen Sondheim's *West Side Story* and sounding particularly incongruous among Marianne's canon. The songs supplied by Donovan and Tim Hardin were far more successful. Most of the yearning was taken from Hardin's 'Don't Make Promises' and replaced with a typical 1960s swing-beat shuffle, replete with brass punches and deranged lead guitar. 'Reason To Believe', also by Hardin, which later became a folk standard, was more subdued and better fitted the mood created by such forlorn lyrics – 'You lied straight-faced, while I cried'. Donovan's contributions, 'In The Night Time' and 'Good Guy', were excellent, smattered in harpsichord, harmonica, plinky guitar riffs, unlikely backing vocals and pumping organ. Several astute reviewers observed that *Love In A Mist* sounded as if it had been made by someone with their mind on other matters. It was to be Marianne's last studio album for a decade.

At Andrew Oldham's insistence – he was back on the scene – Marianne recorded a version of 'Is This What I Get for Loving You?' The track was written originally for The Ronettes by Gerry Goffin and Carole King, with help from producer Phil Spector. Decca released Marianne's version as a single, although it was not included on the album. She sang it in her perfectly pronounced English, over-emphasising every last letter of words ending in 'T' (Don't tell me that you don't want my love') with a trumpet solo included apparently at random. It reached number 43 in the UK charts and a derisory 125 in the United States.

Marianne had spoken often of her desire to act. She felt she merely had to look pretty and sing sweetly in the pop world and had not made best use of the training from her mother and Progress Theatre. "I thought that nothing I did was important," she said in a magazine interview in April, 1977. "I felt the music the Stones were making was relevant, whereas mine was not. Secretly I liked my little songs but in the end I affected not to." The agent, Robin Fox, the father of actors James and Edward Fox and film producer, Robert Fox, took on Marianne as a client. He represented the top tier of young British acting talent. Dirk Bogarde, Maggie Smith, Paul Scofield and Julie Christie were on his roster. Marianne began her acting career with a particularly challenging role, securing the part of Irina Sergeyevna Prozorova, the youngest, at 20, of the siblings in Anton Chekhov's play *Three Sisters*. She was to appear at the Royal Court in Sloane Square, London, alongside established actors such as Glenda Jackson and George Cole. A rumour circulated that auditions had been rigged and Marianne offered the part merely as a publicity stunt. It emerged later that she had been second choice but the other actress had pulled out before production began. Marianne accepted a weekly wage of £30 from the theatre, which contrasted sharply with the £250 she earned per pop concert at that time.

At first Equity was reluctant to grant her membership, which added to the pressure on her and fuelled the media's cynicism. The busy rehearsal schedule meant there was little time to promote *Love In A Mist* and the few interviews she did focused mainly on the play. *Three Sisters* opened at the end of April and Jagger sent a small orange tree to the dressing room on the first night. He had earlier helped with her lines, reading aloud the parts of the other sisters played by Glenda Jackson (Masha) and Avril Elgar (Olga). Marianne was by far the most inexperienced of the three 'sisters'. Avril Elgar was 14 years her senior and had been trained at the Old Vic Theatre School while Glenda Jackson, 10 years older, was a protégé of the Royal Academy of Dramatic Art and already had an established film and theatre career. Marianne's performance was greeted as solid if a shade too ardent. David Benedictus, the well-known reviewer, wrote a piece in the trade magazine *Plays And Players* that typified the general response: 'Whatever you think of her union membership, she remains the best we can do for a symbol of radiance and innocence, a rubbing post for our itchy souls... Marianne is unable to conserve her emotions, must offer them up (but with a charming awareness of the audience and anxiety to please) wholesale, at once.'

During the run of *Three Sisters* Marianne had heroin for the first time. She was travelling back to London after a jaunt with Jagger, Gibbs and Mason Hoffenberg. They had to stop several times because Hoffenberg was unwell. Marianne was worried they would not make it to the theatre in time so, to calm herself, took some of Hoffenberg's heroin when they called at a pub in Newbury. She arrived before the curtain call but was ill during the performance, vomiting into a bucket every time she came off stage. 'All the other drugs I had taken in a quest for sensation, this was the cessation of all sensation. The thing that's so seductive about heroin is that there is an absolute absence of any kind of pain – physical or otherwise,' she wrote.

On March 18, 1967 the *Daily Mirror* confirmed what most had long suspected, when it revealed that Jagger and Richards, and two of their 'friends', Robert Fraser and David Schneiderman, were due to appear before Chichester magistrates on May 10 facing drugs charges. Richards was charged with knowingly permitting his house to be used for drugs consumption and the others for possessing substances unlawful under the Dangerous Drugs Act of 1964. During the weeks leading to the court case, Marianne pleaded with Jagger to disclose that the tablets found in his pocket belonged to her, but he refused. Jagger and Richards expected a mild rebuke in the form of a token sentence and had no inkling it was their lifestyle and what they represented that was about to go on trial.

The trio (Schneiderman was suspiciously absent, thought to be back in the United States) elected trial by jury at the West Sussex Quarter Session and their cases were adjourned until June 27. They were granted bail at the sum of £250 each. Hours after their brief court appearance, officers from the Scotland Yard Drug Squad called at Brian Jones' flat and seized 11 items for chemical analysis. He appeared before a stipendiary magistrate at Great Marlborough Street Court the following morning and elected trial by jury on charges of possessing cocaine, cannabis resin and Methedrine.

On a night out to take their minds off the impending court case, Marianne and Jagger visited the Speakeasy Club in Oxford Circus to see a performance by Jimi Hendrix. Marianne had seen him in January 1967 at the Seven and a Half Club in Mayfair when she was among a crowd of about 20 people. Since then he had scored hits with 'Hey Joe' and 'Purple Haze' and his new single, 'The Wind Cries Mary', had entered the charts. They sat at a table in front of the stage and were extremely close to his sexually charged antics. After the performance Hendrix threw down his guitar and, ignoring the cheers of approval from all around, immediately sat at their table. He squeezed between them and positioned his chair so his back was towards Jagger, and stared hard at Marianne. The sound system had already kicked back into life and he had to shout into her ear. He was a friend of Brian Jones whom he felt was being ostracised from the Stones by Jagger. Hendrix reportedly told Marianne her boyfriend was a 'cunt' and she should leave him and be his girlfriend instead. The Who's Pete Townshend witnessed the episode and said afterwards that for a minute or two it looked as if Marianne was considering Hendrix's proposition. She admitted to friends afterwards that she had wanted to go with him 'more than anything' but did not think Jagger would have forgiven her. She maintained a lifelong love of Hendrix's music. She chose 'Hey Joe' as one of her Desert Island Discs when she appeared on the BBC Radio 4 programme with Sue Lawley in May, 1995.

The Rolling Stones toured Europe through the spring of 1967. On April 9 Marianne flew out to join Jagger in Genoa, where the band was playing at the Palazzo Dello Sport. The tour had been marked by crowd mania: 154 fans were detained after a riot in Vienna; 200 tried to storm the band's dressing room in Rome; and police had to disperse a crowd of 2,000 in Paris. Marianne was waiting for Jagger back at the hotel after the group had finished the second of two performances at the venue. She said he was 'possessed' and began slapping her across the face. He followed her around the room and, according to her autobiography, 'beat me quite badly'. She said he was never again violent during their time together and it was as if he had been taken over by a 'demonic force' brought on by the various hostilities while on tour.

On the first day of the trial, Tuesday 27 June, 1967, Marianne remained in London. She visited the Richmond home of Steve Marriott of The Small Faces with her 'girlfriend', Saida. They took acid with Marriott and his fellow band members, one of whom claimed to have turned into a frog during the trip. Jagger was concerned about her whereabouts and sent Tom Keylock to take her to Redlands where she had more acid and slept with Michael Cooper, out of 'loneliness and lostness'.

The next day, as she pushed through the television crews, fans and T-shirt sellers on her way to the court in Chichester, Marianne had no idea her reputation was about to be shredded. In an open court, Jagger, Richards and Robert Fraser could speak for themselves and also had highly paid counsel to do their bidding. Marianne, who unexpectedly became a central figure in it all, had to remain silent and look on as her character was besmirched.

If it really was the Establishment v The Rolling Stones, the Establishment could not have chosen a more formidable ambassador to preside over the case. Judge Leslie Kenneth Allen Block's distinguished legal career had been interrupted by an equally distinguished wartime naval service. On retirement he had settled down to run a Sussex dairy farm and accepted a part-time role as Chairman at Chichester Quarter Sessions, which required a few days each year of his time. As the trial progressed, Michael Havers, a future Attorney General, issued a strong defence for Jagger. The drugs had been prescribed by a doctor and in Europe, where Jagger often performed, they were sold openly for mild ailments such as fatigue. He told the jury they were also widely available on prescription in Britain and 150 million similar drugs had been supplied in the previous year. The sole defence witness, Dr Raymond Dixon Firth, said Jagger had phoned him to ask about some tablets he had bought on the way back from the San Remo Pop Festival and when he realised they were amphetamines, the doctor gave Jagger permission to use them in emergencies. Before the jury retired, Judge Block effectively tried the case on its behalf by announcing that Dr Firth's verbal approval to take the tablets did not constitute a prescription and was therefore no defence to the charge. After six minutes the jury returned and its foreman pronounced Jagger 'Guilty'. He was remanded in custody until after Richards' trial the next day, when he would be sentenced. Fraser, on the advice of his counsel, had earlier pleaded guilty to possessing heroin. They were each handcuffed to a police officer and led into a van with four other Chichester felons to be driven the 40 miles to the Victorian prison at Lewes, East Sussex.

Marianne arrived in Chichester early the next day in a jacket, open-necked shirt, trousers and sandals. A hot day was expected. She was allowed to enter the court building by a rear entrance because a crowd of more than 100 fans had gathered at the front. Vans had parked up selling ice creams and hot dogs. She was anxious to see Jagger as she had heard he had broken down the previous evening. She too was in a fragile state. She had collapsed during the third act of *Three Sisters* and her place was taken for the final few shows by her understudy, Janette Legge. Marianne was told she would have some time with Jagger after Richards' trial. She made her way to the public gallery where she sat between Les Perrin and Allen Klein.

The prosecuting counsel, Michael Morris QC, needed to heighten the air of dissolution at Redlands on the night of the raid to influence the jury into believing Richards had allowed cannabis to be smoked at the premises. A naked girl wrapped only in a rug more than sufficed. The women police officers were called to give evidence and Havers quickly detected the prosecution's tactic. Detective Constable Rosemary Slade said the young lady had let the rug slip from time to time, exposing her body. "The woman was in a merry mood and one of vague unconcern," confirmed Detective Constable Evelyn Fuller.

Havers looked across at Marianne and realised he stood between her and public ridicule. "She is well known to many. Her name is bandied around Fleet Street. Her name has been blackened in a way that could affect her career," he said. The court had referred to Marianne under the transparent alias of 'Miss X'. Rather than offer anonymity, it served to increase the mood of impiety. Havers' entreaty on Marianne's behalf went unheeded and the slander continued. "She was taken upstairs and when she got to the bedroom door, she allowed the rug to fall to the ground. She had nothing on. I heard a laugh from the man in the bedroom who was using the phone. I saw her naked back," said Sergeant John Challon. Malcolm Morris introduced a new, blatantly sexual inference when he suggested Marianne was finding the experience pleasurable. "She was unperturbed and apparently enjoying the situation," he told the jury.

The press corps scribbled enthusiastically and reporters were soon scampering to nearby phones. The story had everything – pop stars, drugs, an enigmatic 'Miss X' and sex. The attention placed on the rug caused Havers to have it sent for so he could prove it more than adequately covered a woman of Marianne's stature (five feet, four inches tall). The brown and white rug with orange lining was unfurled across desks in the court room and Havers said: "It's enormous. You can see – it's about eight-and-a-half feet by five." Keith Richards later told the court it was 'large enough to cover three women'. Havers again defended Marianne from the prosecution's dirtying tactics. "She's not on trial. She is a girl who remains technically anonymous and I hope she will remain anonymous. She is described as a drug-taking nymphomaniac with no chance of saying anything in her defence. Do you expect me to force that girl to go into the witness box with no chance to refute the allegations? I am not going to tear the blanket aside and subject her to laughter and scorn." His speech did little to save Marianne's honour and, in fact, aggravated the situation. He had unwittingly crystallised the prosecution's innuendos by referring to her as a 'drug-taking nymphomaniac'. The press now had a juicy, succinct phrase to use in headlines. Havers' claim that Marianne was nothing of the sort had no effect; the association had been made. In the minds of the British public she was soon to become the 'drug-taking nymphomaniac' and the more Havers refuted it, the more he inadvertently damned her by repetition.

The court adjourned for the day and Marianne was led down a flight of stairs to be with Jagger. She was allowed 12 minutes, in which time she gave him, as the newspapers anxious for trivia revealed: a draughts set, a science fiction novel, newspapers, 60 tipped cigarettes and fresh fruit. Michael Cooper was also granted a few minutes with Jagger and took a quick shot of him behind bars. The Stones' publicity machine was still in motion despite the temporary impediment and Cooper had been advised that a suitably forlorn Mick staring sad-eyed through bars could make the band's next album cover. An attentive police officer saw Cooper surreptitiously place the camera into his pocket and as he was about to re-enter the courtroom, the film was confiscated.

On the journey to Redlands, where Marianne was staying with others during the three-day trial, she stopped off at a newsagent's shop to buy an evening paper. The front-page headline read 'Naked Girl At Stones' Party'. As she walked through the garden towards the house afterwards, she was unaware that a photographer had a lens trained on her. He was positioned at waist level, above the foliage, and his shot caught her head bowed. She carried the newspaper in her left hand with its sonorous front page on show. The tableau was the final indictment of pop's maverick and elite class. Marianne Faithfull had, until very recently, been a beautiful, free, young woman surrounded by intelligent, handsome, wealthy men, but in that famous second in the garden, she was alone, afraid and ordinary.

Within hours of the revelation about Marianne and the rug, an outlandish story began to spread. It was said that at the time of the raid Jagger was performing cunnilingus on Marianne who had a Mars bar inserted in her vagina. The rumour was believed to have originated either from one of the police officers involved in the raid, a reporter in the courtroom or a fellow prisoner at Lewes eager to embroider the tale of his meeting with Jagger. *Private Eye* magazine printed on the cover of its next issue: 'A Mars bar fills that gap'. Sniggering adolescents began asking shopkeepers for a 'Marianne Faithfull' instead of a Mars bar. The story took on a life of its own and grew increasingly fantastic. Some versions had all the members of The Rolling Stones taking part (even though three of them were patently not at Redlands on the night) and in the United States the very same incident was supposed to have taken place at Woodstock.

After the trial Christopher Gibbs consented to several newspaper interviews in which he rebutted the smutty claims. "I thought it was all a lot of nonsense, all the stupid Mars bar jokes. It was rather childish and ungallant," he said. "It was all down to the glamour of the participants and the nature of vulgar journalists. The way everyone was painted by the press was ridiculous. I found it hard to understand at the time, but now, of course, I realise people *are* always looking for victims to get their teeth into, and victims offer themselves up unknowingly all the time. I don't think Marianne and Mick comprehended it all. I don't suppose you do until you've had the full glare of the searchlight on you. I did what I could to protect them. I protested, but one is made to feel useless. Their lives and destinies were being interfered with by forces outside anybody's control and there was nothing anyone could do about it."

Unfortunately for Marianne, the smear became part of her biographical fabric and was to surface ad nauseam throughout her life. She has refuted the legend every time: "I sat there in my fur rug, with no Mars bar. It's a folk legend, and if people want to believe that when the cops walked in there was this incredible orgy going on, they will, but get it straight," she said. "It's a dirty old man's fantasy, some old fart who goes to a dominatrix every Thursday afternoon to lick her boots and get spanked."

On the last day of Richards' trial a final mention was made of Marianne's alleged immorality. Morris asked Richards whether he expected a young girl to be embarrassed if she had nothing on but a fur rug in the presence of eight men. "We are not old men. We're not worried about petty morals," was his famous response. Judge Block closed proceedings by asking the jury to ignore the evidence it had heard about Marianne – Miss X – and said the revelations should not cause any prejudice. His comments rang hollow after he had previously allowed Morris to expostulate the debauched details for hours, without a hint of censure.

The jury found Richards guilty. He was sentenced to a year's imprisonment with £500 costs. Robert Fraser was told he must spend six months in prison and pay £200 costs. Michael Philip Jagger put his head in his hands when Judge Block told him he must spend three months in prison and pay £200 costs. A girl fled from the court and shouted to the crowd outside: "Mick's been sent to prison". Jagger later told the *Daily Mail* afterwards: "I just went dead when I was sentenced. I could think of nothing." He was driven to Brixton Prison, and Richards and Fraser were taken to Wormwood Scrubs. Marianne visited Jagger and found him crying uncontrollably in his cell. She admonished him, which she later regretted, telling him he was acting like a 'spineless, pampered pop star'. It was the only time during their relationship that he would reveal such raw emotion and she had not appreciated his candidness or responded to his need. Havers made an application for bail the next day. Jagger and Richards were granted bail of £5,000 with further sureties totalling £2,000 each. They were told their appeal would be heard when the new law term opened in September.

Fellow musicians and fans were outraged at the severity of the sentences and support was quickly mobilised. A gang of about 200 teenagers gathered in Fleet Street with placards reading 'Free the Stones' and 'We Want Love'. They were dispersed by police officers using dogs. Keith Moon of The Who was among the protestors and had taken along a home-made banner on which he had roughly daubed: 'Stop! Pop Persecution'. The Who were steadfast allies and took out an advert in the music press asserting: 'Mick Jagger and Keith Richards have been treated as scapegoats for the drug problem'. They called for action against 'the savage sentences imposed on them'. In a further show of solidarity they recorded two Stones tracks, 'The Last Time' and 'Under My Thumb', and released them as a single. A grand but unfeasible plan surfaced to hold a concert for up to 100,000 people with all proceeds used to buy flowers for Judge Block; any left over would be distributed to hospitals throughout the country. Allen Ginsberg wrote a letter to *The Times* saying: 'The Rolling Stones are one of Britain's major cultural assets who should be honoured by the Kingdom instead of jailed.' The New York-born cartoonist Bud Handelsman supplied the most caustic response in the London *Evening Standard*. He drew a stereotypical courtroom scene with the judge announcing: 'Let us weigh without prejudice the defendants' insolence, flamboyance, wealth, youth and the fact we would love to put them behind bars'.

During the trial there had been a noticeable reduction in the amount of opprobrium directed at the Stones and even some expressions of sympathy. Several newsmen, habitually the scourge of Jagger's life, had protested on his behalf to police when they saw him handcuffed as he came to and from court. In print the London *Evening Standard* had questioned the need for such excessive measures. The rumblings swelled in the space of a few days until the Establishment did a glorious about turn and The Rolling Stones metamorphosed into ill-treated underdogs. Fittingly, Jagger and Richards' staunchest ally was the newspaper long considered the Establishment's most loyal advocate, *The Times*.

Jagger was awoken on Saturday July 1 by Marianne hurling a mound of newspapers on to their bed. He detected the forgiving air blowing through the pages but its acme lay within three columns of editorial in *The Times* beneath a quotation borrowed from the satirical English poet Alexander Pope. 'Who Breaks A Butterfly On A Wheel?' was the question posed by the paper's editor, William Rees-Mogg. 'If after his visit to the Pope, the Archbishop of Canterbury had bought proprietary airsickness pills at Rome airport, and imported the unused tablets into Britain on his return, he risked committing precisely the same offence,' he wrote. He criticised Judge Block's harsh penalty for 'about as mild a drug case as can ever have been brought before the courts' and closed by suggesting Jagger would not have been sentenced so if he were 'a purely anonymous young man'. The rest of the media followed *The Times*' lead and the new-found compassion for Jagger and Richards was such that the Lord Chief Justice, Lord Parker, moved forward their appeal to July 31, the final day of the law term.

By appearing on drugs charges The Rolling Stones had accidentally became freedom fighters for the hippy generation (as it was now often termed) and their outlaw image enhanced. Convictions for marijuana possession doubled between 1966 and 1967 to 2,238 in Britain and two-thirds of offenders were under 25. Artists who had broken through amid the suits and forced smiles of performers launched in the 1950s and before became figureheads of a new generation. The Beatles and The Rolling Stones were at the forefront but, behind them, were others from all strands of music, spanning the new soul of Smokey Robinson & The Miracles to the hyperactive rock of The Who and psychedelic blues of The Yardbirds. The Vietnam War, aired on British television mainly in the form of fractured, forlorn monochrome images, fostered a tremendous feeling of solidarity among the youth and melded a collective anti-war stance. The civil rights movement and the riots in the United States' black ghettoes heightened political consciousness in Britain. Increasing numbers studied at universities, which became a breeding ground of polemic thought. The economy was relatively buoyant so the enlightened youth had jobs and money to pursue greater individualism.

The components for cultural detonation were nurtured through the earlier underground and swinging scene and its apogee came in the summer of 1967. The record that was said to best distil the ambience of those preciously short months was released on June 1 and stayed at the top of the albums chart for the rest of the year. The Beatles' *Sgt. Pepper's Lonely Hearts Club Band* took 700 hours to record at a cost of more than £25,000. Beneath its irresistible melodies was a sturdy intellectualism that elevated pop music to a new, considered and credible artistic level. Traditional acts were not washed away though. Engelbert Humperdinck had the three best-selling singles of the year and other places in the year's Top 20 were taken by fellow mainstays of light entertainment – Anita Harris, Frankie Vaughan, Topol and Vince Hill. The year's top-selling album was *The Sound Of Music* soundtrack.

The court case meant that the Stones took a secondary role in Jagger's life during most of 1967. He had more time to commit to his relationship with Marianne and participate in the social scene. Friends noted that he appeared at ease as he visited exhibition openings, theatrical performances, rock concerts and parties. He was already established in his own right but Marianne provided additional glamour and elegance. When she began speaking in her splendid posh voice and discussed literature or art with acquaintances, Jagger sensed an inferred gentlemanly status. She took him to the ballet and afterwards he said he admired Rudolf Nureyev. There were frequent trips to the Indica bookshop. Marianne would leave with armfuls of trippy underground literature such as *The Secret Of The Golden Bough* or *The Book Of The Damned*. She soon began to secretly rue introducing Jagger into theatrical circles. He watched numerous performances of *Three Sisters* and became transfixed by the theatre. He was enticed by its bourgeois import. Marianne, who was far more insecure and hesitant than she appeared, secretly took exception to his acting ambitions. She saw it as an attempt to compete with her and inflict further defeat.

The Redlands bust had its finale on July 31 at the High Court in Fleet Street. Jagger and Richards were taken from a black Austin Princess, through the crowd and the court precinct, to the Lord Chief Justice's Court. Richards' conviction and sentence was dropped completely and Jagger's sentence reduced to a one-year's conditional discharge. In total Jagger had spent three nights in jail and Richards less than 12 hours. Fraser's sentence remained and his time in prison affected him deeply. He lost his art gallery and his sunny outlook on life. He died in 1986 from AIDs after many years as an alcoholic and heroin addict.

Another casualty of Redlands unnoticed by the public was Eva Faithfull. She suffered snide remarks about Marianne's supposed promiscuity and constant jibes about Mars bars. She had begun a teachers' training course and was set to embrace a new career but her plans were abandoned after Redlands. She began drinking heavily and seldom left the house. After she died in 1991, Marianne found letters among her belongings from the college, concerned as to why she was no longer attending lectures.

Les Perrin had organised a press conference directly afterwards and Jagger, sedated by Valium, was in a vague, bewildered state. Marianne was at his side wearing a mini skirt that held the pressmen's attention when Jagger's words almost dried up. Marianne told reporters she was 'really happy now everything had turned out all right'. Afterwards they were picked up in a Jaguar and driven at speed to a helicopter pad in Battersea. Jagger had agreed to take part in a television debate billed as 'a dialogue between generations' for Granada's *World In Action* programme. He would face several members of the Establishment, namely the editor of *The Times,* William Rees-Mogg, who was to act as chairman since he was of the Establishment [educated at Charterhouse School, former president of the Oxford Union, owner of the palatial country estate Ston Easton Park] but also a defender of Jagger; the former Home Secretary, Baron Stow Hill (or as he was known while incumbent, Sir Frank Soskice); the Anglican Bishop of Southwark, Dr Mervyn Stockwood; and Father Thomas Corbishley, a Jesuit.

The showdown took place at Spains Hall near Finchingfield, Essex, an Elizabethan country house then owned by the Lord Lieutenant of Essex (but now primarily a venue for weddings). The programme's producer, John Birt, a future director-general of the BBC, accompanied Marianne and Jagger in the helicopter and was abashed as they touched one other fondly. On arrival they were asked to wait in a bedroom until filming began. Birt called on them unexpectedly early and as he knocked on the door he suspected they had been overtaken by ardour. Jagger, in an embroidered open-neck smock, finally appeared to joust verbally with the soberly dressed and earnest pillars of society, sitting on chairs in the landscaped garden. Almost as soon as the debate began he abdicated any actual or assumed position as 'leader of youth'. He spoke of himself in the patrician first-person 'one' rather than 'I' and confounded his adversaries with his wide vocabulary – using the words 'fallacious' and 'curtailed' at various points. His smile and smirk and quick brain crushed easily their pomposity, and obtuse questions – 'Is it freedom or intensity of living that you are seeking?' – were swatted with ease.

A disillusionment with Western materialism led many to look East during the mid-1960s. They saw a more basic, uncontaminated life in India where the colourful clothes matched their own, the music was organic and an endless supply of inexpensive but potent hashish was available. Vans painted with gigantic sunflowers and large multi-coloured eyes set off from towns and cities across Britain heading to the Indian sub-continent. Some became ill en route, others were robbed or ran out of money. Few stayed very long in India but this hardly mattered because they believed the answers to life's questions lay in the journey itself. Many Hindus made the reverse journey, dancing on Britain's streets in saffron robes, seeking converts. The most illustrious visitor was the Maharishi Mahesh Yogi, boasting an unprecedented ability to enthrall pop's elite, from The Beach Boys to The Beatles. The heavily bearded guru with a wide smile and infectious giggle was the founder of Transcendental Meditation, a process whereby devotees repeat a mantra for up to 20 minutes twice daily to invoke feelings of peace and restfulness. He invited The Beatles to undergo a tutorial at a teacher training college in Bangor, North Wales, on the August Bank Holiday weekend of 1967.

The Beatles and The Rolling Stones had been drawing ever closer through the summer of 1967. Jagger and Marianne, with Brian Jones and Keith Richards, had sat in during the television transmission of The Beatles' *All You Need Is Love* on July 6, when assorted friends joined in the final chorus. McCartney and Lennon had sung backing vocals on the Stones' single 'We Love You'. Marianne and Jagger often visited McCartney at his Regency house in Cavendish Avenue, close to Lord's Cricket Ground in St John's Wood. "I believe I turned Mick on to pot in my little music room at Cavendish Avenue," said McCartney. "Which is funny because everyone would have thought it would have been the other way round." McCartney and Jagger regularly checked with one another to make sure their groups did not release a new single within the same few weeks, which would have split sales. "We would go and see Paul a lot but I don't remember him coming to us," said Marianne. "Mick always had to come to his house, because he was Paul McCartney and you went to him. I was very curious about how Mick saw him, how Mick felt about him. It was fun to watch. There was always rivalry there. Not from Paul, none at all. Paul was oblivious, but there was something from Mick. It was good fun. It was like watching a game on the television." The Beatles imagined the Stones would enjoy a weekend away in the company of the giggling guru, so invited them along.

Marianne and Jagger shared a deep interest in astrological data and, as many others did at the time, they often consulted the Chinese predictive text, *I Ching*, before making decisions. Their natural enthusiasm for a weekend in the company of a mystical Eastern guru was tempered when they were alerted by Barry Miles that the word from the Underground, especially in India, was that the Maharishi was suspected of financial impropriety [on his death in 2008 he was said to have personal holdings exceeding $1 billion] and the odd sexual transgression. As the two groups and their entourages boarded the specially chartered train at Paddington Station to take them to Bangor, they were besieged by reporters. They shouted out their questions: "What's he like?" "Do you think you will all be changed by next Tuesday?" Jagger, his scepticism honed by Miles' counsel, spent the few days with the man *Private Eye* later dubbed the 'Veririchi Lotsamoney Yogi Bear', smirking at what he considered a suspect and hollow manifesto. "It was more like a circus than the beginning of an original event," he said. The party, especially the Beatles' faction, *was* changed by Tuesday, however, when news reached them that their manager, Brian Epstein, had died. The 32-year-old 'Beatle-Making King of Pop', as the *Daily Mirror* dubbed him, was found dead in London after an overdose of barbiturates.

Andrew Oldham, keen to maximise publicity from the Redlands trial, asked counterculture film-maker Peter Lorrimer Whitehead to make a promotional film to accompany the single 'We Love You'. Based on the trial of Oscar Wilde, it was shot in a church hall in Essex. Jagger was Wilde in a frilly shirt and tails; Marianne was Lord Alfred Bruce Douglas (Bosie) in a wig and Richards was the Marquis of Queensberry. The infamous rug played a starring role and the final shot was of a naked Jagger casting it aside with a sardonic grin. The other Stones were seen playing their instruments in the studio. Marianne's elevated role caused friction. Bill Wyman pointed out that it had long been understood that girlfriends were to remain outside band projects.

The class of young, wealthy and famous were susceptible to the lure of all elements new and exciting. Diabolism and occultism were widely embraced and The Rolling Stones were at the forefront. The American magus Kenneth Anger infiltrated the band's network via the Indica Gallery. He claimed to be a disciple of Aleister Crowley and his tall stories enraptured Jagger in particular. Anger was infamously mischievous. He sent a razor blade to Robert Fraser as a 'cure' for his stuttering. Another time he threw a William Blake book tied to a brick through a window of Jagger and Marianne's flat in Cheyne Walk. Jagger was invited to appear in Anger's film *Lucifer Rising* after the first choice for the role of Lucifer was imprisoned for murder in California. Jagger declined but agreed to compose a musical score in which his brother, Chris Jagger, and Marianne were to have parts.

Marianne bought Jagger *The Master And Margarita* by Mikhail Bulgakov and saw many of its ideas and imagery channelled into the Stones' track 'Sympathy For The Devil' [though Anger claimed later he was the primary influence on the song], which was featured on the album *Beggars Banquet*, released in 1968. She routinely felt her ideas were being appropriated and her talent subsumed, as she serviced her boyfriend's career and artistic development.

8

Acting was still foremost in Marianne's mind through 1967 and after several failed auditions she landed her first major film role, opposite French idol Alain Delon, in *Girl On A Motorcycle*. A year earlier, the Roger Corman film *The Wild Angels*, starring Peter Fonda and Nancy Sinatra, had been a cult hit with its tag-line: 'Their credo is violence... their God is hate... and they call themselves the Wild Angels'. The film had established the motorcycle, the Harley-Davidson especially, as a symbol of the counterculture, representing independence, power and reckless energy. *Girl On A Motorcycle* was an Anglo-French production due to be filmed in France, Germany and Switzerland. Marianne imagined it would mark a low-key but credible, potentially art-house start to her film career.

Days after confirmation of the role, Marianne, Jagger and Christopher Gibbs accepted an invitation from the brewery heir and former Etonian Desmond Guinness to take a holiday with him in Ireland. Soon after arriving they took LSD and spent the morning snapping branches from trees and arranging them in huge vases in the empty rooms of Castletown House in County Kildare, the vast Palladian country house which Guinness had recently bought. They returned to Guinness' main place of residence, Leixlip Castle, where he asked them to accompany him to a prestigious civic function. Lord Ormonde was about to hand over Kilkenny Castle to the state and had invited different generations of the Butler family, who had owned the castle since 1391, to the ceremony. As the guests politely inquired as to which strand of the Butler family they were connected, Marianne and Jagger were having difficulty standing because of the LSD and dope they had taken. "It was like people from Mars landing among them on this great day," said Gibbs. "This very old lady latched on to us, Lady Freda Valentine. She had rotten teeth and one of those hats which has pheasant feathers sticking off it in every direction, getting in people's eyes. We were tripping strongly. The effects had reached their full throttle. Desmond was, of course, in great disgrace for having brought all these raffish disreputables who had nothing to do with the event. We had a lot more Irish jaunts, driving about Ireland, staying in fishing hotels on the west coast. It is a quiet, never-never land. In the remote parts of Ireland they did not know who Marianne was." Guinness later took them to meet the Smithwicks, a wealthy family who owned Ireland's oldest operating brewery. "The family were very kind of Irish and Catholic and uptightish," said Gibbs. "And I have this vivid memory of Marianne taking a picture of his Holiness The Pope that was propping something up. She put it on her knee and rolled up an enormous joint in the drawing room. The family did not notice but Mick and I did."

When they arrived back in London they were surprised to find a residual resentment still simmering among some of the public after the trial. Several taxi drivers refused to give them lifts from the airport. The mockery of Marianne had continued after the trial. *Private Eye* dubbed her 'Marijuana Faithfull'.

Members of the pop and rock aristocracy were keen to re-brand themselves as country gents and ladies during the late-1960s. Christopher Gibbs was considered a suitable arbiter of taste and accompanied Marianne and Mick as they visited various piles. Their search led to the aptly named Stargroves, a dilapidated mansion near Newbury in Berksire, with 10 bedrooms and set in 37 acres of parkland. The legal work took months to complete but Jagger finally secured the property for a knock-down price of £25,000, mainly because the previous owner, Sir Henry Carden, had let the 16th century manor house fall into disrepair. Marianne took direct control of most of the work. "She enjoyed it because she is very good at that sort of thing," said Gibbs. "She loves beautiful things and is more educated about them than Mick. She had a much more developed and yet delicate sense of what is beautiful. These things were new to Mick, outside his experience. She has natural taste and understanding. She is a very good maker of an exquisite nest, rather than a home. There is a sense of impermanence of what she has created; everything had to be instant – done in a jiffy – but it had to look not instant, it had to look old. She never quite finished things off."

Stargroves was used mainly for weekend breaks. The Who visited once and held an impromptu rehearsal. Marianne and Jagger sometimes roared around the grounds on motorcycles. They allowed a group of travellers to stay for several months. Among them was Sir Mark Palmer, a godson of the Queen (he was a page boy at the Coronation) who had denounced his wealth and status to dress in Druid clothes and live in a gypsy caravan. A handyman was employed to maintain the grounds and Marianne talked with him animatedly about her long-term plans to install herb gardens and a medieval maze. The schemes came to naught and Stargroves stood in the same apologetic state for the 10 years it was under Jagger's stewardship.

Before *Girl On A Motorcycle* Marianne had rejected several film offers, including playing opposite Dave Clark of The Dave Clark Five in the John Boorman-directed *Catch Us If You Can*. She told the producers in 1965 that she considered the part 'too poppy'. Barbara Ferris, a former model, stepped in to play Clark's girlfriend, Dinah. Marianne's screen debut came when she effectively played herself in Jean-Luc Godard's *Made In U.S.A*, a film version of the Richard Stark novel *The Juggler*, about a woman private detective, Paula Nelson (played by Anna Karina), searching for her lover's murderers in Atlantic City. Marianne sang 'As Tears Go By' and was billed 'the girl in the café'. The chief film critic of the *New York Times*, Anthony Oliver 'A.O.' Scott, saw a newly restored print of *Made in U.S.A.* at New York's independent Film Forum cinema in 2009 and wrote: 'It's far from a lost masterpiece, it is nonetheless a bright and jagged piece of the jigsaw puzzle of Mr. Godard's career. There is, for one thing, a pouting and lovely Marianne

Faithfull singing an *a capella* version of 'As Tears Go By'. There are skinny young men smoking and arguing. There are the bright pop colours of modernity juxtaposed with the weathered, handsome ordinariness of Old France, all of it beautifully photographed by Raoul Coutard. There are political speeches delivered via squawk box. And of course there is a maddening, liberating indifference to conventions of narrative coherence, psychological verisimilitude or emotional accessibility.'

Marianne's next role, as Josie in *I'll Never Forget What's 'isname*, released in December 1967, was more substantial. Directed by Michael Winner and starring Orson Welles and Oliver Reed, it was one of several attempts by the film industry to reflect the era's verve, colour and sense of rebellion. The long opening sequence is of Reed, bullish and mad-eyed, travelling to work with an axe over his shoulder. He plays Andrew Quint who is disillusioned with his job at an advertising agency and about to resign in extraordinary fashion. The commentary begins: 'This man is a success. He has a wife, two mistresses, an Alpha Romeo. And one day he decided to get rid of them all. What he wanted was the simple life... an explosive film from young director Michael Winner [he was 31] that cuts deep into the flesh of life today'. Quint finally arrives at work after passing the obligatory Mini cars, London landmarks and shimmying mini-skirts, and brings the axe down on his desk. As he searches for a greater meaning to life, a fixation particular to the 1960s, he lands a job with an ailing literary magazine. Between pondering existence, he fornicates with a procession of women, including Josie, in disused railway huts and houseboats.

In a real London flat that was so cramped Winner spent most of the time directing from a toilet seat, Marianne appeared nude in a bath, carefully positioning her arms and legs to conceal her breasts. After a minute or so where she argues with Quint, Josie next appears at the end of the film. Quint, tempted back to Jonathan Lute's (played by Orson Welles) slick agency, has his advert for the 'Hamayasha Super Eight' camera screened at an awards ceremony. The advert is an amalgamation of Quint's oddball life and views. A nuclear bomb explodes into the familiar mushroom cloud and the voice-over begins: "Everywhere you look it's history – the present is all you have." In the next scene Josie

(Marianne) bursts open two swing doors. "Get out of here you fucking bastard," she yells. The word 'fucking' is bleeped out (as the advert is supposedly intended for television) but the viewer is left with no doubt what lies behind the bleep. Although the word was not actually heard, Marianne had the distinction of being the first woman in a British film to use the profanity on screen.

"A part of a lifetime" was Marianne's response when asked by the press about her first major film role, in *Girl On A Motorcycle*. The film had begun life as a novel, *La Motocylette*, written by the French surrealist André Pieyre de Mandiargues. He was a friend of the motorcycle journalist Anke-Eve Goldmann, the inspiration for the main character, Rebecca. Goldmann was thought to be the first woman to ride a motorcycle in a one-piece leather racing suit, which she designed with the German manufacturing company Harro. The film was intended chiefly to introduce Alain Delon to the English-speaking market. Delon, at 32, had already secured fame in his home country of France through films such as *Is Paris Burning?* and *The Leopard* but had missed out on Hollywood because of his inability to learn English. At first he rejected the part in *Girl On A Motorcycle* because he did not approve of the original director and co-star. Jack Cardiff and Marianne Faithfull respectively were considered more suitable and he agreed to take on the role. The film was financed jointly by London's Mid Atlantic Film Holdings and Ares Productions of Paris and they agreed to give Marianne, as Rebecca, and Delon, as Daniel, equal billing. Marianne was aware the role would involve several nude scenes. "It's just an additional hazard, really," she said.

The trailer for *Girl On A Motorcycle* opened with the heavy revving of an engine before the voice-over began: 'Now you know the thrill of wrapping your legs around a tornado of pounding pistons like the girl on a motorcycle. She goes as far as she wants, as fast as she wants, straddling the potency of 100 wild horses, the girl on a motorcycle'. The film begins with Rebecca in bed, dreaming that she is standing on the back of a horse, galloping around a circus ring. The ringmaster, her lover, Daniel, begins to whip her, tearing away the motorcycle leathers. Rebecca's taut, upright stance on the horse's back and the obvious cuts to a stuntwoman suggest believability will be stretched during the rest of the film. The dream ends and she leaves the bed, reaching for her one-piece leather suit. She squeezes into it and delivers the first in a series of inane one-liners: "It's like skin, I'm like an animal."

As she speeds to Daniel's (without ever turning the handlebars), she shouts to the deserted early-morning streets: "Rebellion's the only thing that keeps you alive – why don't they rebel, especially the young?" Rebecca stops for petrol and as the nozzle glides into the tank, the camera lingers to emphasise the clumsy eroticism. She thinks of her husband, Raymond, left behind in their marital bed. "It's his bloody kindness that's killing me," she says to herself as memories of his gentle, affectionate ways provoke lunatic laughter. In a myriad of flashbacks her meetings with Daniel are related: he visits her father's bookshop, stares in Rebecca's direction and says: "I can't wait to get my hands on *that*." Daniel is a college lecturer whose 'cruel, arrogant, conceited and callous ways' are irresistible to Rebecca. He teaches her to sup a glass of kirsch in a single swig and introduces her to oversized black motorcycles – he rides a 750cc Norton Atlas while she has a Harley Davidson Elektra Glide. The motorcycles are a symbol of their sexuality. She caresses hers tenderly and snaps: "Take me to him, my black pimp." The dialogue is brimming with similarly trite lines. As Daniel unzips Rebecca's suit he whispers: "Your body is like a beautiful violin in a velvet case." Numerous takes were made of this scene because Marianne could not stop laughing. The predictable final scene has Rebecca supping too much kirsch and crashing her motorcycle into a truck. She flies through the air and smashes head-first through the windscreen of an oncoming car to certain death. The rider acting as a stunt double for Marianne throughout the film was Bill Ivy, a British Grand Prix champion. He was a small man, the same height as Marianne, and wore a blonde wig. He died a year later at the age of 26 after a crash in Germany.

The publicity leaflet sent to cinemas and the press about *Girl On A Motorcycle* outlined the story in hackneyed terms: 'Dawn is breaking over a small French town. By the side of her pyjama-clad schoolteacher husband, 19-year-old Rebecca (Marianne Faithfull) stirs, and then awakes. The morning calls and so do memories... memories of a lover, and a love, that six weeks of marriage have heightened to an irresistible urge.' It explains that she dons a 'clinging, black leather suit lined with white fur' and rides her 'black, gleaming American highway patrol-type motorcycle to her lover, Daniel'. On press adverts, the zip on the leather suit was pulled down to Marianne's waist but cropped so her head did not appear. Owners of motorcycle showrooms and garages were invited to apply for posters and stills from the film, showing Marianne and Delon astride a Norton motorcycle. Marianne, dressed in leathers, was featured on the cover of the reprint of Pieyre de Mandiargues' book, now retitled *The Girl On The Motorcycle*. In the United States the film title was changed to *Naked Under Leather*.

During filming Marianne smoked large quantities of hashish, which she quickly regretted because she felt it made her performance lacklustre and more accepting of the banal script. She claimed later that Delon had tried to 'pull' her. "When I turned him down he became sullen and difficult. He was such a pompous git," she said. She realised the film had little of the vitality of the novel and among her friends she referred to it as 'that awful film' and 'a piece of cheesecake'. On a more positive note she also pointed out that her appearance fee had been £20,000 for three months' work.

On its release in September 1968 a handful of reviewers detected some elegance in the interplay of Delon and Marianne but most were savage in their criticism. 'If you relish the prospect of Marianne Faithfull clad only in a skin-hugging black leather suit, riding a motorbike for hours on end around the European countryside, this is for you,' advised the *London Illustrated News*. The industry's main reference book, *Halliwell's Film Guide*, lists *Girl On A Motorcycle* as: 'An incredibly plot-less and ill-conceived piece of sub-porn claptrap, existing only as a long series of colour supplement photographs.'

Most of the filming had taken place in Zurich, Heidelberg and the South of France. Jagger visited Marianne regularly and sent roses every day. He was unaware that she had started an affair with an American photographer called Tony Kent who was living and working in Paris. Kent took pictures for most of Europe's leading style magazines, among them *Elle*, *Vogue* and *Paris Match*. He was official photographer to

Rainier III, Prince of Monaco and regularly took family portraits of the prince and his wife, Princess Grace (Kelly) with their three children. Marianne had visited his studio for a photo shoot. They smoked dope and began talking at length about magic. She left to board an airplane to Heidelberg. Kent dashed from the studio and joined her at Paris' Orly Airport. He flew with her and they embarked upon a 'wonderful romance'. She wrote in her autobiography: 'My relationship with Mick was completely public, and my love affairs were wonderful because they were private'. Kent went on to become an author of self-help books. He has a website that melds much of the idealism of the 1960s with modern-speak: 'The purpose of this site is to share with you many of the systems, philosophies and ideas that have helped me create a truly blessed lifestyle.'

In the four years since her recording debut, Marianne's image had changed spectacularly from prim and demure folk singer to sex symbol with a particularly liberal view on drug-taking and most allied counterculture issues. "She was made to do it, born to do it. It was duck to water stuff," said Christopher Gibbs. "She had lived this rather sheltered childhood with this strange, high-minded father, and I don't know what we can say about Eva. I don't think we understand middle European baronesses very well in this country. The things that turn them on are pretty unfamiliar territory to us. So there was this exotic Transylvania, Corinthia, Sacher-Masoch Count Dracula world, the Austro-Hungarian empire and refugees. Some of the books she read were by authors that ordinary English girls would not have read, like E.T.A. Hoffmann who wrote a book called *The Devil's Elixirs*. She was also well-read in the best ghost stories. She liked the historical occult, brink of magic stuff. She was perfectly capable of being quite commonsensical when it was absolutely necessary but she was extremely fanciful, imaginative and transparently gifted."

After completing *Girl On A Motorcycle*, Marianne and Jagger decided to take a holiday with Nicholas. They travelled first to Barbados where they were thinking of buying a house or even a small island. They viewed a few places, travelling in light aircraft, and moved on to Rio de Janeiro. They stayed in the hotel most of the day and in the evenings called at the best restaurants to drink champagne and eat caviar. They were told of a district called Bahia in the north-east of Brazil on the Atlantic coast and decided to visit. One evening, while stoned, they became caught up in a street festival and sensed hostility towards them from the wholly non-white gathering. Marianne felt the experience informed 'Sympathy For The Devil', especially its driving Samba beat. While in Bahia she read *The Naked Lunch* by William Burroughs and had a 'blinding flash' – she would become a junkie. 'It wouldn't be in that high-life way like Robert [Fraser], little lines on expensive mirrored tables, but in a real-life way: a junkie on the streets. This was to be my path', she wrote.

Back in England, Marianne began learning her lines for a role in the first production of Edward Bond's *Early Morning*, again at the Royal Court. The theatre, under the artistic direction of William Gaskill, then in his early 30s, seemed on a mission to confront and agitate, far beyond its self-image as a 'writers' theatre'. Several speculated that the casting of Marianne was a wily attempt to appeal to the younger generation and galvanise a revolt similar to the one that had so altered the music scene.

Early Morning was a lengthy play featuring 21 scenes using landmarks and characters from Victorian England and placing them in bizarre, surrealistic situations. So, Queen Victoria had a lesbian relationship with Florence Nightingale; the Royal Princes, Arthur and George, were Siamese twins; Benjamin Disraeli and Prince Albert plotted a coup and, finally, all the players fell from Beachy Head to end up in a heaven where they turned cannibalistic. Gaskill, a founding director of the National Theatre, assembled a cast that included Peter Eyre as Prince Arthur, Moira Redmond as Queen Victoria, Nigel Hawthorne as Prince Albert, Malcolm Tierney as Disraeli, Dennis Waterman as Len, and Marianne as Florence Nightingale.

Edwards Bond's previous play, *Saved*, staged at the Royal Court in 1965, had become a cause célèbre. It focused on a group of working-class youths drifting into barbarous mutual violence. One of the scenes featured a baby in a park being stoned to death while in a pram. Irving Wardle, writing in *The Times*, said the play amounted to 'a systematic degradation of the human animal' and Herbert Kretzmer of the *Daily*

Express wrote: 'From first to last, Edward Bond's play is concerned with sexual and physical violence.' The Theatre Regulation Act of 1843 had been invoked which required the script to be submitted for approval by the Lord Chamberlain's Office. Bond was asked to censor his work and omit the scene featuring the killing of the baby, but refused. The theatre also defied the censor in staging the production and was prepared to do the same again with *Early Morning*.

The bizarre plot of *Early Morning* has Queen Victoria trying the protagonist, Len, for eating a man who pushed in front of him while he was queuing to see the film *Policeman In Black Nylons*. Victoria rapes Florence Nightingale and as the coup begins she poisons and strangles Albert, and George is shot. William Gladstone joins the insurrection and Victoria and her sons are placed before a firing squad, but released when Gladstone dies. Although George has shot himself, Arthur continues to carry around the corpse of his conjoined twin. The conflict continues in heaven, where Victoria accuses Arthur of 'spoiling it for everyone'. He is eventually eaten but rises again into the air, unseen by the weeping Florence who had tried to save his head by hiding it under her skirt. The play ends with Victoria declaring 'there is no dirt in heaven' and Len asking his girlfriend, Joyce, to 'pass us that leg.'

The play opened and closed on the same day, Sunday, March 31, 1968. Undercover police and members of the vice squad attended and their presence influenced either the theatre manager or the theatre's 'committee' – both have been cited – to close down the production. The sole performance was staged on a 'club members' basis to enable it to fall outside formal jurisdiction. The audience entered the theatre by a side-door. Critics were invited. Harold Hobson of *The Sunday Times* wrote: 'It is like a nightmare dreamt by an overheated child whose head is a jumble of misunderstood fragments of what he has learnt from misguided elders about sex, religion, and the sort of history that is made up exclusively of palace intrigues, plots, murders and wars.' He objected to the third act where Queen Victoria, Prince Albert and their children ate human flesh in heaven, dubbing it 'unspeakably horrible'.

✳✳✳

By mid-1968 Marianne, principally through her non-musical projects and the Redlands bust, had firmly registered her singular brand of eccentricity. "People seem to have the idea of me being some kind of freaky character. I don't mind if they think of me as a nut, but I happen to feel passionately about certain things," she said. Her acceptance of risqué film and theatre roles was, she said, a deliberate attempt to cast off the virginal image she strongly disliked. "I think when you are very young, your emotional life and sensual life is very confused and she was kind of wanton," said Christopher Gibbs. "It was that feeling of physical generosity, feeling it very natural and easy to give yourself to people. It is a way to be loved and a way to be wounded. I don't think it is a common quality. It is based on purity and non-innocence too."

Marianne agreed to appear on *Personal Choice*, a BBC television programme billed as 'face to face interviews with notable cultural figures'. She answered questions put to her by the experienced broadcaster Michael Barrett with disarming honesty. On LSD she said: "If it wasn't meant to happen it wouldn't have been invented. I knew so many people that, before they took LSD, were such a drag and they took LSD and they really opened up. Drugs are the doors of perception. I mean, you don't go anywhere. You just see a crack like I'm looking at you." On marriage she said: "For some people marriage may be very groovy. For me, it wasn't. I don't think it is for many people either." She said she wanted to 'go into death, but it's very wrong'. When asked about her son, Nicholas, she said it would be good for him to make his own way in the world. The film was remarkable, profiling someone completely without artifice and apparently unaware of the mores and conventions of television. She slumped in her chair and raised her foot to her thigh, as if she were chatting at a party. When explaining the doors of perception she demonstrated a small hole by bringing together her forefinger and thumb and drawing it to her eye, much in the way of a child.

Chris Reynolds of the *Reading Standard*, the newspaper circulating in Marianne's hometown, was angered by her conduct on *Personal Choice* and the views she expressed. He wrote an 'Open Letter to Marianne', which read: 'But, really love, you talked absolute nonsense. About marriage and children. And about drugs. Especially drugs, this was a little boy [Nicholas] you were talking about, Marianne. A defenceless little child. I wonder if your mother, to whom you referred as living in a tiny terraced house in Reading, felt proud of you. I didn't. Grow up, Marianne, or shut up.' The tirade contained a phrase that was to recur throughout Marianne's life. He referred to her as 'a person most publicised for doing nothing'. This claim was patently unfounded at the time because her recording output was still fresh in the memory and she had begun a parallel acting career. All the same, such pieces were cumulatively reductive of Marianne's worth and for a long period reduced her to curio value.

Unknown to Reynolds and the viewers – for it would probably have incurred more opprobrium – Marianne had fallen pregnant. The news was kept from the media and there was little sign of her changing body shape when she attended the Stones' live comeback performance at the Empire Pool, Wembley, at the *NME*'s Poll Winners' Show on May 12, 1968.

The youth looked increasingly towards direct action during 1968. The optimistic spirit of the previous year was fading. Timothy Leary, the radical psychologist and writer, noted that 'the flowers had turned to seed'. There were skirmishes at colleges, including a sit-in at Jagger's former alma mater, the London School of Economics. In Paris, student activists, said to be 30,000 in number, fought for days with police and 1,000 people were injured. The biggest disturbance in Britain was at the anti-Vietnam War demonstration in March at Grosvenor Square where 90 police officers were hurt as the 25,000-strong crowd tried to storm the American Embassy. A year earlier, the square would have been filled with flower children making their point with homemade banners, tambourines and guitars. Idealism that had led to ideas such as the 'white bicycle' scheme in Oxford – where bicycles were painted white and left unlocked for anyone to use – were later scoffed at as bikes were stolen and immediately painted a different colour. Tom Keylock drove Jagger to the Grosvenor Square demonstration and picked him up 30 minutes later. The experience was said to have inspired The Rolling Stones song,

'Street Fighting Man', featured later that year on their album *Beggars Banquet*.

Amid this new hostility Marianne and Jagger announced that they were expecting a child. "It's real groovy," Jagger told reporters camped outside Cheyne Walk. "I'm very happy about Marianne having our baby. We'll probably have another three. But marriage? Can't see it happening. We just don't believe in it." Jagger secretly *did* want to marry but Marianne was reluctant to repeat the vows she had made and broken three years earlier.

On October 12, 1968 Jagger was invited to appear on a special edition of *Frost On Saturday* alongside Mary Whitehouse, the founder of the National Viewers' and Listeners' Association and spokeswoman for the Clean-Up TV pressure group, launched in 1964. Mary was to argue in favour of upholding Christian morals and decency, and Jagger to espouse the liberal views of the young generation. His high standing among the youth made him an ideal spokesman and he was further seen to be the epitome of the permissive age because he was 'living in sin' with a child on the way, conceived out of wedlock. They both made their points articulately and with reasonable humour but afterwards Marianne, as an implicated party in Jagger's stance, began receiving hate mail, including some suggesting she should kill herself. The Archbishop of Canterbury, Dr Michael Ramsey, asked his flock to say Intercessory Prayers [a petition to God on behalf of another] for Marianne.

After the Redlands bust and for a good while afterwards, the press set about Marianne without any dispensation for her relative youth (she was 21 in 1968) or her comparatively inconsequential standing – she was a pop singer and actress, not a politician or similar figure of authority. "The press behaved disgustingly towards her," said Chris O'Dell. "They tried to get to everyone in the family. They are an absolute disgrace to humanity. Sex, drugs and rock 'n' roll became an icon and Marianne became sacrificial to this end. She was a symbol for the general moral degeneracy. She could not control it very well. I think Marianne and myself were quite unworldly when we were young, late developers. We were from enclosed schools, protected from the real world. I just don't think she ever realised what was going to happen to her. We used to read the cuttings that came in from her agency and so much crap was written. I did not recognise the person in the press. It was a myth created by reporters. Half of the people they used to interview in the 60s were out of their trees anyway when they got their quotes."

Jagger and Marianne were delighted with the pregnancy despite having to fend off questions from the media about the morality of their situation. Friends said Jagger was uncharacteristically excited about impending fatherhood. At play with Nicholas, he entered the child's world exuberantly. "They were very happy. It seemed very tender and enjoyable. There were no sort of anxieties and miseries," said Christopher Gibbs. The pregnancy was troublesome, however, and Marianne suffered a great deal of discomfort and sickness. She took up residence in a rural mansion in Tuam, County Galway, with her mother, at a price of more than 100 guineas per week. It provided an escape from the media and granted her a period of solitude. Jagger visited regularly and on one occasion arrived with the Harley Street gynaecologist Dr Victor Bloom, who gave her a thorough examination and reported that everything appeared to be going well.

During the autumn of 1968, Jagger began his own acting career as the lead, Turner, in *Performance*, a film directed by Donald Cammell and Nicolas Roeg. Warner Brothers had invested almost £2 million in the story of a pop star on the run from members of his own protection gang. Marianne was initially cast as Turner's girlfriend but when she became pregnant, Anita Pallenberg accepted the role. In order to create the debauched mood needed to play Turner, Jagger reportedly smoked a drug called DMT, which, according to legend, condensed a 12-hour acid trip into 15 minutes.

Marianne had coached Jagger and told him to 'be Brian [Jones]' who, within the Stones' realm, had become a lost and often debauched figure. One scene in the film called for Pallenberg and Jagger to simulate sex and it was done with unusual zeal. Jagger's co-star, James Fox, confided to the cast that he had discovered them making love in the dressing room between takes. Jagger denied the fling. Marianne wrote later: 'The depth of his attachment to her [Keith Richards' to

Anita Pallenberg] was just flowing out of him. Very romantic, very consummate love. Which is why Anita and Mick's betrayal during *Performance* was so devastating to him.' Marianne was more forgiving of Jagger because of her own affair with Tony Kent and 'knew things weren't right between Mick and me'.

While Marianne was in Ireland, Jagger had Cheyne Walk decorated ready for the arrival of the baby. He invited the celebrated interior designer David Mlinaric to make recommendations and bought a huge Regency bed and bath dating from 1770. In mid-November Marianne returned to England. She was weak and feeling unwell and stayed at a nursing home in St. John's Wood, London. Jagger and the other members of The Rolling Stones sent her flowers, chocolate and fruit. On November 22, 1968, Marianne miscarried, two months short of the prospective birth date. She was too anaemic to come to full term. The baby, had she survived, would have been called Corrina, the name of an Ancient Greek poet from the 6th century BC and a track ('Corrina, Corrina') featured on *The Freewheelin' Bob Dylan* containing the apposite lyric: 'I got a bird that whistles, I got a bird that sings, but I ain't a-got Corrina, life don't mean a thing'. The couple's friend Yoko Ono had also miscarried a day earlier.

In the middle of this personal crisis, Jagger was heavily involved in preparing the Stones' expensive and calamitous extravaganza, *Rock'n'Roll Circus*. At a cost of £50,000, the Stones, with the help of Sanford Lieberson of the film production company Goodtimes Enterprises (which had produced *Performance)*, were organising a multi-media event that they planned to screen worldwide. They wanted to feature major rock stars with authentic circus attractions such as trapeze artists, plate spinners, fire eaters, midgets and rodeo horses. On December 11 and 12, 1968, more than 800 guests including John Lennon and Yoko Ono, The Who, Eric Clapton and Jethro Tull, were taken in chauffeured cars to television studios in Wembley. Everyone was asked to dress for the occasion, with 400 ponchos and hats supplied. Marianne, wearing a crepe Jean Harlow-style dress, was given a specific part, as were Anita Pallenberg and Yoko Ono, while the other Stones partners, Suki Potier

(Jones' new girlfriend), Astrid Lundstrom (Wyman's girlfriend) and Shirley Watts, were in the crowd scenes.

The event marked a return to singing for Marianne. She performed a confident version of 'Something Better' while sitting on the studio floor with the low-cut, flowing dress draped over her. The show evolved into a freestyle format and extended into the early hours of the following morning. When the footage was played back it was agreed it lacked energy and focus, and it was not made public, at least not at the time. A clip subsequently appeared in The Who's movie *The Kids Are Alright*, and on the BBC's special Stones programme *25 × 5* before it was finally released as a feature film in 1996.

Marianne, Jagger and Nicholas spent Christmas 1968 on a cruise from Lisbon to Rio de Janeiro, with Keith Richards and Anita Pallenberg. They had several weeks at sea and settled for a while on a deserted beach in Brazil. Back home in England, Eva Faithfull left Milman Road and moved into Yew Tree Cottage in Upper Basildon, near the hamlet of Aldworth in Berkshire. Her new home, bought for her by Jagger, was positioned among handsome chalk downs countryside between a series of small woods, each with quaint names – Green Wood, Knapps Wood, Paddle Hill Wood, Harley Hill Wood and Black Wood.

9

During a busy but problematical 1968, Marianne had neglected her singing career and Decca needed product to remind fans that music was her first calling. A compilation album sufficed perfectly and in February 1969, *The World Of Marianne Faithfull* was released, accompanied by the engaging single, 'Something Better'. Decca had embarked on a series of similar albums under the title of *The World of...* Almost every artist on its roster, with the notable exception of The Rolling Stones, was packaged in the collection, alongside genres of music such as *The World Of The Trumpet/Tijuana/Soul* etc. The aim was to introduce acts to a wider audience and the records were sold as budget items. In the United States the album was titled *Marianne Faithfull's Greatest Hits*. Her last American hit had come four years earlier so it was perhaps unsurprising it sold poorly, reaching 171 in the *Billboard* LP chart.

On her first visit to a recording studio in nearly two years, Marianne found the sweet timbre of her voice had altered slightly, replaced by a more raspy and husky tone that better suited a lower key range. She recorded the Goffin/King number 'Something Better' in the United States with a team of considerable talent. Jagger was in the control room producing with the help of Phil Spector's arranger, Jack Nitzsche, who often admonished Marianne for taking cocaine, telling her it was bad for her vocal cords. "Everyone in the band can get wrecked except the drummer and the singer," he told her. The distinctive slide guitar was laid down by Ry Cooder. Marianne was in the United States with the Stones who were mixing the record that became *Let It Bleed.*

Marianne decided to include a song on the B-side of 'Something Better' that Jagger had worked on with Keith Richards. She had heard them playing a sequence of chords on acoustic guitars and offered them a set of lyrics to a song she had titled 'Sister Morphine'. The words had been written while on holiday in Rome and were influenced by John Milton's pastoral elegy, *Lycidas*. 'Sister Morphine' was not autobiographical, although it was later mistaken as such ('I became a victim of my own song' – Marianne). The lyrics recounted the last moments in the life of a man who had been gravely injured in a car crash and was pleading for pain relief. Marianne had been listening to The Velvet Underground, particularly the drug-referencing tracks 'Sister Ray' and 'Waiting For The Man'. As the Stones had just released *Beggars Banquet* and had a surfeit of material, they agreed Marianne could feature the track on her single. In the studio Jagger played acoustic guitar with Charlie Watts on drums, Jack Nitzsche on piano and Ry Cooder, guitar. The song was a revelation and stood to effectively re-route Marianne's musical career. It opened with the line: 'Here I lie in my hospital bed' and the delivery was resolutely spare as she narrated the call for morphine: 'When are you coming round again, Oh I don't think I can wait that long'. The vocal, across five minutes and 33 seconds, was deep with feeling and for possibly the first time in her career, she had contributed to a piece of work she had helped create and believed in completely.

At first there was no reaction to the song at Decca, possibly because no one thought to locate the acetate and actually play the B-side. When, two days after the record's release, word filtered through to senior staff, the response was swift. Vans carrying the record to shops were ordered to turn back and the pressing plant switched off production immediately. A piqued Marianne demanded a meeting with the label manager but was given few material reasons why the record had been withdrawn, apart from that it dealt with drug taking and actually mentioned morphine. She told them it was a serious work, neither condoning nor glorifying the use of drugs. Jagger called on Sir Edward Lewis personally, to no avail. About 500 copies made it to record shops but the label's plan to reignite Marianne's career with the compilation album and single was scuppered by its own censorship.

Decca and Marianne parted company shortly after the row over 'Sister Morphine', causing her recording career to stall for more than six years. Few heard of the furore and the track remained largely unknown until The Rolling Stones – without any objection – included it on their album *Sticky Fingers* in April 1971, on which Marianne did not receive a songwriting credit. Keith Richards wrote to Allen Klein and made him aware that she had written the lyric. As royalty cheques began to arrive in the early 1970s, a time when Marianne was desperate for money to fund her drug addiction, there were two distressing ironies – that a song about drugs should finance her habit and that a piece of work so fulfilled could have sustained her creative career, had it been properly supported.

"If I'd have carried on after 'Sister Morphine' I would have come up with something interesting, but I didn't. I lost heart. I couldn't stand it and broke away," she told *Zigzag* magazine in 1980. The issue affected her profoundly on a professional and personal level. 'My relationship with Mick started to shatter,' she wrote. 'I was now caught up, against my will, in the gathering gloom of the late 1960s. I could see that the undisputed champion and winner of the rock 'n' roll stakes was going to be Mick. I could never compete. I would just have to accept my fate and be Mick's muse. The role of a muse is one of the acceptable ones for women, but it's terrible.' Marianne, incidentally, was not listed as a co-writer of 'Sister Morphine' until *Sticky Fingers* was re-mastered and re-released in 1994.

Marianne was offered the role of Ophelia in *Hamlet* playing opposite Nicol Williamson and with Gordon Jackson (Horatio), Anthony Hopkins (Claudius) and Judy Parfitt (Gertrude). Tony Richardson, the director, had seen Marianne in *Three Sisters* and thought her perfect for his robust version of the Shakespeare tragedy. He said of his take on Prince Hamlet: "He is not a conventional poet and scholar, but the anti-establishment dropout: rough, sensual, impulsive, voicing thoughts and desires as relevant today as in Shakespeare's own time." The play opened in February 1969 at the Roundhouse Theatre in Camden Town to good notices, mainly due to Williamson's granite performance in the title role. As Irma in *Three Sisters*, Marianne's force had been mildly incongruous but as Ophelia the intensity was essential. *Time* magazine's reviewer was impressed: 'Marianne Faithfull's Ophelia is remarkably affecting. She is ethereal, vulnerable, and in some strange way purer than the infancy of youth.' The performance of February 28, 1969, was filmed by Columbia Pictures and released several months later to the cinema, the first version shot in colour.

During the play's run, Marianne had an affair with Nicol Williamson whom she described as 'very mad and possessed'. They often made love in his dressing room before taking to the stage. Marianne felt this had been orchestrated by Tony Richardson who, typical of most directors, indulged in game-playing to bring energy and intrigue to performances.

The sexual constituent of Marianne and Jagger's relationship had faded by 1969 but this coincided with a period of promiscuity for Marianne. She had a fling with Prince Stanislaus Klossowski de Rola (known as Stash), the son of a Swiss aristocrat and an omnipresent dandy on the scene through the 1960s. He climbed the wisteria on the side of Cheyne Walk to reach the balcony, from where he made a grand entrance into the bedroom wearing a cape. "Well, that deserves a fuck," said Marianne. She was one of many to share a bed with the Prince. "The list of women that I loved and bedded who are somehow connected to rock is endless," he said. "And includes Joan Blackman [an actress who had lead roles in two Elvis Presley films], Tuesday Weld, Gretchen Burrell [wife of Gram Parsons], Phyllis Major [model and wife of Jackson Browne], Nico, Anita Pallenberg, Marianne Faithfull, Suki Potier and Linda Eastman. I do not want to brag, but sex, and lots of it with beautiful models, movie stars and groupie queens was a daily occurrence."

Marianne and Jagger were the subject of another drugs bust, on Wednesday May 29, 1969. They had finished their evening meal at Cheyne Walk when they heard a knock at the door. Detective Sergeant Robin Constable and five of his colleagues found a small quantity of cannabis in the premises. The next day more than 200 fans congregated outside Marlborough Street Magistrates Court and cheered Marianne and Jagger as they arrived separately. They were remanded for a month. Later on the same day Jagger told the press he was to play the role of Ned Kelly, the Australian criminal and folk hero, in a film. "I am taking this film very seriously," he said. "Kelly won't look anything like me. You wait and you'll see what I look like. I want to concentrate on being a character actor." He had been cast by Tony Richardson with Marianne playing his on-screen sister, Maggie. The symbolism of her part in *Ned Kelly* could not have been greater for Marianne. She was once more playing a subordinate role to Jagger and in a domain she had considered hers, where she had also served an apprenticeship of sorts.

Heroin began to play an increasing part in Marianne's life. Tony Sanchez, 'Spanish Tony', the main supplier of drugs to The Rolling Stones, would arrive with a jack of heroin for her during the intermission of *Hamlet*. Initially she smoked the drug, a practice known as 'chasing the dragon' where it is heated on tin foil and inhaled through a small tube. Within seconds the user has a 'rush', a feeling of excessive pleasure which subsides into a 'high' where a sense of calm detachment takes over. She was taught to inject heroin by a dealer – it is a more economic method because much of it is lost in thin vapour trails when heated. Marianne had two willing allies in Anita Pallenberg and Keith Richards. They too were developing habits, regularly alternating heroin with cocaine to increase the potency. Marianne began an affair with Sanchez to allow her greater access to drugs. She did this despite considering him 'low-life', 'loathsome' and 'a spiv'. She was also taking cocaine after first trying it at the Kensington flat of Christian Marquand, the French actor who had played opposite Brigitte Bardot in *And God Created Woman*. Six lines of cocaine had been laid out on a table and Marianne, unsure of the etiquette, sniffed them all. "There was a dissatisfaction that had to be filled, and it was being filled by coke," she said.

Christopher Gibbs detected signs of Marianne's disaffection when she was part of a small party that visited Bermingham House, an 18th century residence between Tuam and Dunmore in County Galway, Ireland, owned by one of the country's most famous horsewomen, Lady Molly Cusack Smith. Marianne was with Gibbs; the American girlfriend of Donald Cammel, Deborah Dixon; and Nicholas who woke Gibbs each morning, reciting the colours of the rainbow. "Things were already beginning to go wrong," said Gibbs. "Marianne was falling about a bit, taking too much of whatever she was taking. We went across in a little boat to the Aran Isles. We climbed about and went to this great fort on top. We then went to some holy well and Marianne threw her cigarette into it. It wasn't the sort of thing she ever did. She always had a great sense of place and sanctity but something was getting to her and she was beginning to get into a muddle. Obviously the drugs and her relationship with Jagger were interdependent but I think it was the drugs thing more. The pressures and anxieties of the affair and the availability of dope conspired to pull her down. She took refuge in drugs, I suppose, because she realised that the relationship wasn't progressing or fulfilling either of them like she dreamed it might."

One evening Marianne consulted the *I Ching* and was alarmed by the prediction it made for Brian Jones: death by water. She threw the coins again, with the same result. Within their circle, Marianne was presumed to be the most in touch with her spiritual side, a de facto swami. She persuaded Jagger to phone Jones who was staying at Redlands and check on his wellbeing. Jones was surprised to receive a cheery, solicitous call from Jagger from whom he had felt estranged for months. He invited him and Marianne to Redlands. Brian was there with Suki Potier ('Very beautiful but perfectly silly' – Marianne) and they cooked a meal. Jagger had taken a few mouthfuls when he announced: "I can't eat this shit, we'll have to go out." He and Marianne went out for a meal and when they came back found Jones in a furious mood. A row broke out between Jones and Jagger which led to a fistfight. They grappled and Jones fell into the shallow moat surrounding Redlands. Marianne assumed the prediction had been symbolic and the water element signified a fight, not a death.

On Monday, June 9, 1969 Brian Jones announced that he was leaving The Rolling Stones. "I no longer see eye to eye with the others over the discs we are cutting," he said. "We no longer communicate musically. The Stones' music is not to my taste any more. The only solution is to go our separate ways, but we shall remain friends. I love those fellows." While there was a strand of truth in his statement – he *did* prefer more experimental music to the band's increasing rock formula – there were a myriad of other reasons for his departure. He was of extremely poor health and drug-dependent, lacking the strength to tour. His convictions for drug offences meant that he was barred from entering the United States. Jagger and Richards had marginalised him within the group. Marianne believed they had a deliberate policy of undermining him with mockery and ridicule in the hope he would eventually leave. His replacement, Mick Taylor, who had previously played with Greg Lake [later of Emerson, Lake & Palmer] and toured with John Mayall's Bluesbreakers, had already rehearsed and recorded with the Stones before Jones' departure. Indeed, he was all set to play with them at a free concert in Hyde Park, scheduled for a month later.

Brian Jones was found unconscious at the bottom of the swimming pool at his home, Cotchford Farm, on Wednesday, July 2 1969. His new girlfriend, Anna Wohlin, from Sweden, discovered him at midnight and said he had a pulse when pulled out. He had decided to take a swim in hour or so earlier, complaining of being too hot. He was joined by Frank Thorogood, a builder friend of Tom Keylock who had been living on site while constructing a wall. "Brian had been drinking. He was a bit unsteady on his feet. He and Frank were in no condition to swim," said Janet Lawson, a friend of Thorogood's who had also spent the evening with them. Jones had drunk brandy, vodka and whisky and taken amphetamine tablets. Lawson had been so concerned that she followed them out to the pool. "Brian had trouble getting on the springboard," she said. "Frank helped him and he flopped into the water. The two were sluggish in the pool, but I gathered they could look after themselves." Thorogood left the pool to get a towel and cigarettes and soon afterwards they saw Jones at the bottom. Lawson, a nurse, pumped water from him and massaged his heart. He could not be revived. PC Albert Evans arrived at the farm at 12.10am and Jones was already dead. He was officially pronounced dead soon afterwards by a local doctor.

Dr Albert Sachs, consultant pathologist, carried out a post-mortem at Queen Victoria Hospital, East Grinstead. At the inquest held on Monday July 7 he said there was no evidence that death had resulted from an asthma attack – this was an early theory because the pollen count had been unusually high and Jones had used his inhaler often through the day. "For a man of his age, his heart was a bit larger than it should have been. It was fatty and flabby. His liver was twice the normal weight and in a state of fatty degeneration," said Dr Sachs. Jones' blood contained 140 milligrammes of alcohol [the legal limit for driving is 80 milligrammes of alcohol in 100 millilitres of blood]. The blood also contained a large quantity of drugs. "I came to the conclusion that the cause of death was drowning by immersion in fresh water, in association with which there was severe liver dysfunction because of the fatty condition and the ingestion of alcohol and drugs," said Dr Sachs. The coroner, Dr Angus Sommerville, recorded a verdict of death by misadventure.

Newspapers that had previously delighted in tales of Jones' debauchery – his many court appearances, the five children he failed to acknowledge and his admittance to numerous clinics – were curiously sympathetic. The *Daily Express* reminded readers that Jones had once been a 'sinless' baby and made his first public performance in the 'beautiful babies' section of the West Gloucestershire Women's Institute Annual Show. The quality press dealt with his death far more poetically, especially with the compelling imagery of the swimming pool, at the time a relatively new symbol of wealth and status in Britain. There was also the additional lyricism to be had from the location. Cotchford Farm near Hartfield in East Sussex had belonged previously to A.A. Milne and featured many relics of Winnie The Pooh. Milne had moved there in 1926, writing the books soon afterwards, and remained there until he died in 1956, aged 74. The farm was on the northern edge of Ashdown Forest, which became Hundred Acre Wood in the Pooh stories. The sundial commissioned by Milne's wife, Daphne, and decorated with the carved figures of Eeyore, Pooh and Piglet was still in the grounds and, nearby, the stream where Pooh and Christopher Robin (in real life Milne's son) first played Pooh-sticks. Jones loved these wistful, childhood associations and they had influenced him to buy the property for £35,000 just eight months before his death.

Well-known figures in the music industry were keen to mark the passing of Jones whose musical and sartorial style along with his rock 'n' roll demeanour (which he went a good way to conceiving) was a principal influence. Even before his death he had been the subject of songs, such as The Animals' *Monterey* ('His Majesty, Prince Jones, smiled as he moved among the crowd/Ten thousand electric guitars were groovin' real loud). On hearing of his death, Pete Townshend of The Who wrote an eight-line poem titled *A Normal Day For Brian, A Man Who Died Every Day*, which was printed in *The Times*. It opened: 'I used to play my guitar as a kid/Wishing that I could be like him.' Jim Morrison of The Doors wrote a freeform poem, *Ode To L.A. While Thinking Of Brian Jones, Deceased* containing the lines: 'You've left your Nothing, to compete with Silence. I hope you went out Smiling Like a child. Into the cool remnant of a dream'. While appearing on a television programme in the United States, Jimi Hendrix dedicated a song to Jones. Bill Wyman, the Stones' bass player, said of his band-mate: "He was probably a better natural musician than the rest of us put together. Brian was weak, had hang-ups and at times was a pain in the arse. But he named us, we were his idea. Without him our little blues outfit wouldn't have become the greatest rock 'n' roll band in the world." *Rolling Stone* magazine asked Mick Jagger in 1995 if he felt any guilt over Jones' death. "No, I don't really," he said. "I do feel that I behaved in a very childish way, but we were very young, and in some ways we picked on him. But, unfortunately, he made himself a target for it. He was very, very jealous, very difficult, very manipulative, and if you do that in this kind of a group of people, you get back as good as you give, to be honest. I wasn't understanding enough about his drug addiction. Things like LSD were all new. No one knew the harm. People thought cocaine was good for you." Keith Richards had once said to Jones, 'You'll never make 30, man' to which he replied, 'I know'.

Marianne was devastated by Jones' death. "Brian was a hopeless mess and they [Jagger and Richards] were just so cool," she told *Spin* magazine in 1987. "Brian really fucked himself up by letting himself get much, much, much too involved in drugs, even before Keith got like that. I always felt that Keith's way of reacting to Brian's death was to become Brian. But Keith is so strong, physically, that he didn't look as if he was disintegrating. Brian really did disintegrate." She could see her own potential demise if she remained within the same power-play in which Jones had been caught and if she showed the same fixation with drugs. Jones, much the same as Marianne, was highly intelligent (he had an IQ of 133 – the average is 100) and well-educated, but he did not have the guile or fortitude of Jagger and Richards, or his ex-girlfriend, Anita Pallenberg. Marianne and Jones had shared a close friendship because of their similar backgrounds and personalities. They both failed to distinguish boundaries and acted impulsively where those around them were more careful and calculated.

A ball was scheduled for the night after Jones' death at the home of Prince Rupert Ludwig Ferdinand zu Loewenstein-Wertheim-Freudenberg (better known as Prince Rupert Loewenstein or 'Rupie the groupie'), the financial advisor to Mick Jagger. Guests were asked to wear white and everyone did apart from Marianne who told friends that only black suited her mood. A marquee was put up in Prince Rupert's garden in Kensington and among the guests were Princess Margaret and Peter Sellers. The music was loud and more than 60 complaints were made to the police during the course of the evening. Bolstered by drugs and alcohol, Marianne was determined to see the party through because earlier in the day they had each agreed that they should carry on as normal. There was a far greater test of this resolve two days later when The Rolling Stones were due to appear at the free concert at Hyde Park.

Granada Television, known for its progressive outlook and high production values, had bought the rights to film the concert and produce an accompanying documentary. The morning of Saturday, July 5, 1969 began for Jagger with a television camera crew tracing his outline as he descended the steps at Cheyne Walk, followed by Marianne holding Nicholas. They travelled in a limousine on a circuitous route to the rendezvous of the Londonderry House Hotel in Park Lane, overlooking the park. In the car Nicholas asked Jagger: "What's Charlie [Watts] going to do?" He told him Charlie would give him a wave. Police estimated that 250,000 people were in the park as the Stones, lying down flat on mattresses, were ferried through the sun-soaked crowd in a green converted army ambulance late in the afternoon. Jagger, wearing a white smock, took to the stage and blew kisses while the band set up behind him. Holding a book in his hand he approached the microphone and shouted: "Allllriiiight". He continued, his sentences not fully formed because of nerves and a bout of laryngitis from which he had just recovered: "OK, now listen. Now will you just cool it, just for a minute because I really would like to say something for Brian. I'd really dig it if you will be with us with what I'm going to say... I hope you can just cool it just before we start. If you do, I'll really appreciate it... a few words about what I feel about Brian and I'm sure you do, and what we felt about him just dying when we didn't expect him to." There was still some shouting. "OK. Are you going to be quiet or not? OK," he said. He read a stanza from Shelley's *Adonais*, a pastoral elegy written in 1821, a few weeks after the death of John Keats. A hush enveloped the park as Jagger began: "Peace, peace! He is not dead, he doth not sleep. He hath awakened from the dream of life..." As he finished, 3,500 butterflies were released from cardboard boxes roughly shaken by roadies on the stage. The band started up the opening chords of the Johnny Winter song 'I'm Yours And I'm Hers', which was a favourite of Jones' at the time he died – the Stones never performed the track again.

Marianne, lost in a long white dress, was feeling unwell at the concert. She had hardly slept and was nauseous from the large amount of dope she had smoked. She was also anorexic and sickly from the effects of trying to come off heroin. The cameras panned across to her and Nicholas as they watched from the side of the stage. Nicholas spent part of the concert perched on Marianne's shoulders. The day before, she had received a petition for divorce from John Dunbar, citing Mick Jagger as a partner in adultery.

During the concert Marianne was unaware of a woman standing above the crowd on a specially built gantry with several others in a section known as a 'musicians' enclosure' – effectively a primitive VIP suite. She was the singer and actress Marsha Hunt, a 23-year-old American who had scored a minor chart hit two months earlier with the Dr John song 'Walk On Gilded Splinters'. She had also appeared in the first British stage version of *Hair* at the Shaftsbury Theatre in September 1968. Although she spoke only two lines of dialogue her photograph was used on the poster and playbill. After the Hyde Park concert Jagger left with Marsha, and Marianne and Nicholas returned to Cheyne Walk. 'And there was Marsha bursting out of her white buckskins. She was stunning,' wrote Marianne. 'If I'd been Mick in that situation I might have done exactly the same thing.' The two women met many years later and Marsha told Marianne how much Jagger had spoken about her and that it had been impossible for her [Marsha] to form a relationship with him while he was still in love with her. "I've tried then and since to understand why he came to me," said Marsha. "He must have had a selection to choose from. But he came like a golden eagle with a broken wing and I suppose he believed I had the willingness and capacity to bandage it up and help him to soar."

The day after the concert Jagger and Marianne had to catch a plane to Australia and begin filming *Ned Kelly*. The sunshine that had bathed the crowds in Hyde Park was superseded by a dank grey day and they travelled to the airport in heavy rain. They had strict orders to begin filming on Wednesday, July 9 as stated in their contract, with the possibility of legal action if they failed to show. This meant they had to miss Jones' funeral on Thursday July 10. A handful of reporters were at the airport and shouted across: "Mick, how do you feel about what happened to Brian?" "Devastated," he replied.

Several days before the flight Marianne had visited her doctor and told him she had developed a fear of flying. He prescribed Tuinals, a barbiturate sedative designed to alleviate acute insomnia, which was widely used as a recreational drug in the 1960s. The distinctive blue and red capsules had the street names 'Christmas trees', 'rainbows', 'beans' and 'jeebs'. The writer Ian Fleming occasionally had James Bond knocking back one these 'ruby and blue depth-charges' after a mission. Bond would then fall asleep 'poleaxed'. As Marianne was leaving the country for up to three months and needed help to sleep during the stay, the doctor gave her a prescription for 150 tablets. The journey, including lengthy stopovers, lasted 35 hours and Marianne spent most of it in a light sleep. By the time they landed in Sydney she had taken 15 tablets. The routine dose was one or two, taken 20 minutes before bedtime. The side effects of barbiturates – chiefly drowsiness, dizziness and confusion – were particularly strong when mixed with alcohol or other drugs. Marianne was desperate to sleep because she had stomach ache brought on by withdrawal from heroin, which she had promised Jagger she would eschew while in Australia. He had been apprehensive of her trying to carry heroin or LSD through customs.

Jagger and Marianne were detained at Sydney (Kingsford Smith) Airport for nearly 30 minutes and were the last of the airplane's passengers to walk into the terminal building. A throng of about 50 reporters besieged them. Hiding beneath a floppy brimmed hat and large sunglasses, Marianne clung tight to Jagger for fear of collapsing. "You seem a strange choice to play Ned Kelly, Mr Jagger, don't you agree?" asked the pressmen. Many Australians were angry that an Englishman was to play the part of their national folk hero. They were further peeved that this embodiment of Antipodean manliness was entrusted to someone who routinely wore 'dresses' and make-up – the Australian press had featured photographs of Jagger wearing the white smock at Hyde Park. "What sort of Ned Kelly are you going to play?" asked a newsman. "A violent one," growled Jagger. The antipathy towards Jagger had actually begun before he even arrived in the country. Acting unions and descendants of Kelly's family had objected to him taking the role. There had also been complaints about the filming taking place in New South Wales in preference to Victoria where the Kellys had lived. The day after their arrival, the Sydney newspapers would report every last detail of what Jagger was wearing, from the long white Isadora scarf to the high-heeled black boots. They also pointed out that he had been welcomed at the airport by 'only four fans'.

The couple was taken to the headquarters of Ajax Films in Neutral Bay, a harbourside suburb three miles north of Sydney. Jagger spent two hours being fitted with wigs he was to wear in the film. They then travelled to the nearby Chevron Hotel at Potts Point overlooking Sydney Harbour, with the intention of sleeping off their jet lag. A group of longhaired youths sat on the hotel steps strumming guitars and waved to them as they rushed past and booked into a suite on the thirteenth floor. Jagger climbed into bed and fell asleep within minutes. Marianne ordered a cup of hot drinking chocolate from room service, which was quickly provided. She was impatient to sleep and reached into her handbag for the bottle containing the Tuinals. She began taking one after the other, staring into the mirror as she did. She estimated that she took about 150 tablets. She thought she saw Brian Jones looking back at her and then she became Ophelia, both in front of the mirror and staring out of it as well. She rose to her feet, stumbled towards a window and looked down to the street below. She imagined she could see Jones waving to her. She tried to lever open the window but could not unhook it. She moved back across the room and into bed. Within seconds she dreamed of a place without a sun, clouds, temperature or darkness. Brian Jones came bounding through the greyness, as absolute as he had been ever been. "Oh, thank God you're here, Marianne." He began complaining that there was no Valium, no cannabis and none of his favourite pills. "But man, I can adjust. You tell Mick, I can adjust." Marianne looked at the surroundings and said later it reminded her of a picture by the French illustrator Edmund Dulac or a copper engraving depicting hell by Albrecht Dürer. This was the backdrop as she spoke animatedly with Jones. They moved along like skaters on ice, discussing hundreds of subjects in great detail. All the time, Jones said he was not sure if he were dead or not. They reached the edge of the Dürer landscape and he disappeared after telling Marianne he had to complete the remainder of the journey alone.

'COLLAPSE! DRUG SQUAD AT HOSPITAL' ran the headline in the *Sydney Daily Mirror*. The paper had little on which to base its story apart from the fact that two members of Sydney Police's Drug Squad,

Detective Barry Kennedy and Policewoman Shirley Morgan, had arrived to presumably interview Marianne Faithfull, a singer from England who had spoken openly on television of taking LSD and cannabis. Jagger, who had awoken soon after Marianne drifted into unconsciousness, told them. "I don't think she's overdosed. Marianne's very delicate and the air journey has exhausted her. Her condition doesn't seem serious, but they are checking her out to see if she will be all right."

An absurd rumour spread through Sydney that Marianne had disturbed Jagger while he was having sex with another woman in their hotel room and this had led her to take the overdose. Another outlandish version had Jagger administering the tablets – the police later asked Marianne: "Did you take them yourself or did someone force them down your throat?" Marianne was comatose when lifted into the ambulance and her stomach was pumped immediately to flush out any traces of tablets. The ambulance staff took the empty bottle that had contained Tuinals with them to St Vincent's Hospital in Sydney's Darlinghurst district. Doctors said that if all the missing tablets had been consumed and entered Marianne's bloodstream, it was enough to kill her three times over. As a natural response to the barbiturates poisoning, her body had fallen into a coma. The first news bulletin from the hospital was that Marianne had collapsed, 'possibly related to fatigue'.

During the early hours of Thursday July 10, 1969, the world became aware for the first time of the gravity of Marianne's situation. A spokesman told reporters camped on the hospital steps that her condition had worsened and was 'giving rise for concern'. By 2 p.m. that afternoon she was said to be 'stabilising' but a story circulated that she had suffered brain damage and would not recover to anything more than a shell of her former self. Meanwhile, on the other side of the world, in the small 900-year-old St Mary's Church in Cheltenham where Brian Jones had sung as a choirboy, the Rector of Cheltenham, Canon Hugh Evan Hopkins, was conducting his funeral. The Canon had no truck with sentimentality or discretion: "He [Brian] had little patience with authority, convention and tradition. In this he was typical of his generation who have come to see in the Stones an expression of their whole attitude to life. Much that this ancient church has stood for in 900 years seems totally irrelevant to them." The Canon closed the 15-minute ceremony by asking the congregation to think of Marianne and pray for her recovery.

Tom Keylock had principally organised the funeral and it was marked by grand gestures – a field strewn with flowers, a 14-car cortege, a flower arrangement spelling out 'Gates of Heaven' sent by The Rolling Stones and another in the shape of a guitar, from his parents and sister, Margaret. Fans swarmed to the hearse and the graveside. There were fears that, amid the pushing and shoving, someone might actually fall into the grave. Bill Wyman and Charlie Watts attended (Keith Richards was said to have 'studio commitments'). Jones was buried in a huge bronze casket supposedly sent by Bob Dylan. He was laid to rest in a powder blue jacket with his hair dyed and specially cut in his trademark 'bob'. The casket was buried unusually deep, thought to be 12 feet, to deter obsessive fans from trying to reach it. This fear was not without substance. Cotchford Farm later became a place of pilgrimage and 'souvenirs' were often sought. When Alastair Johns and his wife, Harriet, who owned the property for over 40 years after Jones' death, refurbished the pool, they sold the original tiles to fans for £100 each. They made £12,000. The first mutterings of a story that would circulate for many decades were heard at the funeral. There was a suggestion that foul play may have been involved in the death. No one was ever charged but it was a theory that, over the years, has drawn much speculation and coverage in newspaper articles, books and films.

Jagger spent a great deal of time at Marianne's bedside. On his way into the hospital a reporter asked: "What does she mean to you, Mick?" He answered: "She turns me on to lots of good things. She has led me into music, drama and literature which I haven't read before." A British journalist managed to enter the room where Marianne was lying. Hospital staff forcibly restrained Jagger as he went for him, fists clenched. On July 12 a freelance photographer, Peter Carrette, breached the hospital's security when he dressed as a doctor and took a photograph that was later beamed around the world. Challenged by a nurse, Carrette brushed her aside and, inches from Marianne's face, clicked away before rushing out of the intensive care ward.

The photograph appeared first on the front page of the *Sydney Daily Mirror* and showed Marianne lying on her side with her hair scraped from her face and tubes attached to her nose and mouth. The headline was 'SCOOP! MARIANNE IN COMA' and the copy read: 'This picture illustrates for the first time this week's terse bulletins from St Vincent's Hospital. The bulletins used words like 'mild concern', 'condition stabilising' and 'satisfactory tests', leaving the outside world uncertain about the 22-year-old star's condition.' Dr Ron Spencer, the acting medical superintendent at St Vincent's, said Carrette had shown 'a complete contempt for patient safety and the privacy of the individual'. Within days the picture was featured in newspapers throughout the world and was seen as a nadir in press intrusion. Mr Norman Travis, the editor-in-chief of Australia's Mirror Newspapers Ltd, said, "We purchased it as we believe any one of our competitors would have done if they had the same opportunity."

The picture marked Carrette's debut as Australia's first genuine paparazzo. He was the son of a Fleet Street printer who had emigrated to Australia purposely to become what he called a 'rock 'n' roll' photographer. There has been differing accounts as to how the picture of Marianne was secured. Carrette said in an interview with the *Sydney Morning Herald* in February, 2005: "I went in to try and get the picture one day. But I was wearing the wrong gown – a doctor's gown tied up at the back. When I got into a lift a couple of doctors asked me, 'What paper do you work for, then?' The older one said I had been watching too much *Dr Kildare* because doctors didn't wander round hospitals in operating gowns." Carrette was shown from the premises but, as he left, another doctor tipped him off. "He said 'You'll never find her because she's on the fourth floor in the other building and the best time not to find her is between 12.45 and 1pm, when the staff change.'" A couple of days later Carrette returned, dressed in an ordinary doctor's gown, took the picture and walked out.

Other versions of the story have Carrette working with a team. They paid a sister at the hospital (who was also a part-time model) to draw up a floor plan of the area where Marianne was being treated and supply them with light-readings. Carrette said this was 'total fucking fantasy, complete bullshit' and claimed he worked alone. He said he received £1,000 from a Briitish tabloid for the picture but an agency sold it on his behalf to other papers around the world. The agency netted $18,000 of which his share was $2,000. "I was ripped off shitless," he said. Down the years he revealed ambivalent feelings about the escapade. "It was a long time ago. It was not a clever thing to do," he said. "I'm not particularly proud of it. I was a stupid kid who needed a quid." At other times he said the picture helped forge his image as an audacious and resourceful operator and once referred to Marianne as 'a dirty little junkie'. He died of a heart attack in November 2010 in his aparment overlooking Bondi Beach, aged 63. He had married an English backpacker, Lisa Fillingham, in 1997, when she was 22 and he was 50. They separated in May 2004 due to his 'drinking and drug taking causing friction between them'.

The photograph garnered Marianne a great deal of sympathy. The overdose, coming so soon after Jones' death, showed the public that young and brash pop stars were a far greater danger to themselves than they were anyone else. A deluge of supportive phone calls was made to the hospital. Bouquets arrived from around the world. Cards and letters came in their hundreds. In England, the *Sunday Mirror* told its readers: 'All of them express the hope that the agony of a young girl caught up in the mad whirl of the pop world will soon be over.' The hospital spokesman revealed that the nurses were calling her 'their dear little Marianne'.

After nearly six days in a coma Marianne stirred and the first person she saw was Jagger. According to the *Sydney Morning Herald* her first words were: "Hello, I love you." Marianne, in a press interview in March 2011, refuted this and said they had been: "Wild horses couldn't drag me away." The track 'Wild Horses' was included on The Rolling Stones album *Sticky Fingers*, released two years later, but Jagger denied the link with Marianne. In the sleeve notes of the compilation album *Jump Back*, released in 1993, he wrote: 'Everyone always says this was written about Marianne but I don't think it was; that was all well over by then.'

Above: Marianne and Mick Jagger at the London Records 20th anniversary dinner at London's Savoy Hotel, 1966. *(Rex Features)*

Above: Jagger, Marianne and Brian Jones in 1967. *(Napier Russell)*

Andrew Oldham *(Music Sales)*

Gene Pitney *(Music Sales)*

Keith Richard *(Music Sales)*

Brian Jones *(Music Sales)*

Anita Pallenberg *(Rex Features)*

Barry Fantoni *(Michael Bennett)*

Christopher Gibbs *(Gibbs)*

Harley House, Jagger and Marianne's first home together. *(Music Sales)*

Left: Marianne as Irina in Chekhov's Three Sisters. *(Rex Features)*

Below: "Naked Girl At Stones Party"—The infamous headline. *(Rex Features)*

Above: Marianne and Jagger on their way to meet the Maharishi in Bangor, August 1967. *(Rex Features)*

Below: Redlands, Keith Richard's home near Chichester, the scene of the infamous 1967 drug bust. *(David Lolley)*

Scenes, including one with Oliver Reed, from
I'll Never Forget What's 'is Name.

(Philip Glassborow Collection)

Scenes, including one with Alain Delon, from *Girl On A Motorcycle*. *(Above, Philip Glassborow Collection)*

Above: Marianne and Jagger at work together in the studio, 1968. *(Gered Mankowitz)*

Below: Marianne and Jagger leaving Marlborough Street Court after being charged with possession of marijuana, June 1969. *(Rex Features)*

Jagger contacted Les Perrin, the Stones' publicist, and asked him to arrange a flight to Sydney for Eva Faithfull. "I am on an errand of mercy," Eva told the press. Jagger postponed a trip to Canberra where he was due to complete location filming, so he could be with Marianne. Eva travelled via the United States on a false passport to avoid detection by reporters. Eva's fears had been heightened by news stories in the British papers and on television where 'experts' had graphically explained the consequences of barbiturates overdose: 'Drugs interfere with the essential supplies in the blood to the brain. This leads to a loss of functioning power and the effects could be permanent,' warned the *Sunday Mirror*'s 'doctor'. Soon after arriving at Marianne's bedside, Eva requested a local priest to carry out an extreme unction (better known as anointing the sick) whereby sacramental oil is rubbed on to the body and a liturgy issued to prevent the patient losing 'Christian hope in God's justice, truth and salvation'.

At her mother's request, Marianne was transferred to Mount St Margaret Hospital in the Sydney suburb of Ryde, for after-care and convalescence. The hospital, an exclusive private clinic for the treatment of 'nervous disorders', was run by an order of nuns – the Sisters of the Little Company of Mary. The matron, Sister Isabel, assigned a psychiatrist to Marianne. Eva was given a room in one of the hospital's wings, delighted that Marianne was cared for by fellow Catholics. Marianne was ordered not to speak for two weeks while her throat healed (from where the various tubes had been inserted) and communicated with her mother by whispering and writing notes. By Monday July 28, Marianne's voice had returned and she agreed to the first interview since her overdose. She walked with Jagger and a journalist from the Australian *Daily Telegraph* in the hospital grounds, making the most of a sunny day in the middle of the Australian winter. "Tell everyone in Australia I love them and want to thank them for being so kind," she said.

Newspapers, in between articles extending compassion ('Sun Shines Again for Marianne' and 'Marianne Reported Cheerful' were two typical headlines), persevered with the line that the drugs taken by Marianne had been imported illegally. Detective Sergeant Cecil Abbott of the Sydney Drugs Squad finally interviewed Marianne. The police leaked the contents of his report on its way to Detective Superintendent Don Fergusson – the drugs had been legally prescribed in London, no case to answer.

On Wednesday August 6, nearly a month after admission to hospital, Marianne was well enough to leave. She left carrying a toy koala bear and a copy of the Australian *Women's Weekly* which featured a cover story of her recovery. A waiting reporter asked the question on everyone's mind: "Why did you do it, Marianne?" "It's private," she said. Many years later she was more forthcoming: "It was because of Brian's death. That's why I did it. I was going to punish Mick by killing myself."

She flew with her mother to join Jagger in Canberra where she planned to relax further, living at a ranch and riding horses in Bungendore, a tourist area in rural New South Wales. Meanwhile, Steve Mauger, a Liberal member of the New South Wales Legislative Assembly, representing the district of Monaro, accused the media of turning Marianne into a celebrity. He told the assembly: "By this unscrupulous use of the media they [presumably Jagger and Marianne] have hampered the efforts of the Police Drug Squad, the Department of Health, Members of Parliament and a number of organisations trying to combat the evils of drug taking in this State. Drug pushers could not buy better publicity." Others in Sydney and around the world felt he had missed the point – Marianne's ordeal had been a potent deposition *against* drug taking.

10

The filming for *Ned Kelly* continued but the project was dogged by bad luck. The cast and crew suffered illness through the 10 weeks of filming. Jagger was slightly injured by a backfiring pistol. Several costumes were destroyed by fire. Mark McManus, Jagger's co-star, who played the part of Joe Byrne, Kelly's closest ally, narrowly escaped serious injury when a horse-drawn cart in which he was riding overturned during filming. Marianne's part as Maggie, Ned's sister, was taken by the Irish-born actress Diana Craig, a 20-year-old who was a year into a course at NIDA (National Institute of Dramatic Arts) in Kensington, Sydney. The film, the seventh based on the life story of Kelly but the first shot in colour, opened to poor reviews. Many ridiculed Jagger's accent, which veered from Irish to Cockney to Australian, although no one was really sure how a second-generation Irish-Australian spoke in the mid-19th century. They also felt his build was too slight and his manner too shifty. Kelly had previously been depicted as burly and straight-talking. The film cost A$2,500,000 to make but grossed only A$800,000. Jagger and the director, Tony Richardson, as good as disowned it afterwards. They did not attend the London premiere and Jagger said he had never watched it back in its entirety.

In the evenings, after filming, Jagger often rang 'Miss Fuzzy', the term of endearment he used for Marsha Hunt. She had seen the headlines and news bulletins emanating from St Vincent's and expected he would be too pre-occupied to get in touch. Jagger, however, needed to talk. "His letters and phone calls during his absence strengthened our friendship which was more sensitive and delicate than I had expected," she said. "He wrote laughing, sad, pensive, deep, observant, touching letters to me." One, sent to her flat in Endsleigh Court near Euston Station, began: 'I feel with you something so unsung that there is no need to sing it' and continued, describing the Australian outback: 'The early morning mist turns red and violent then hard and warm'. He closed by thanking Marsha for being 'so nice to an evil old man like me'. Another was written on Sunday July 20 1969, hours after Apollo 11 had landed on the moon and the astronauts walked on its surface. Jagger dated it: 'Sunday the Moon'. Marsha sold 10 of the letters in an auction at Sotherby's in December 2012, claiming she was 'broke'.

Before returning to England, Marianne visited a psychiatrist in Switzerland, paid for by Jagger who covered all her various expenses during this period. While she was there she heard that Kenneth Anger had sent most of her friends a telegram warning: 'Watch out, Marianne radioactive. Returning to these shores.' After a brief stay in England she headed to Los Angeles where the Stones were finishing *Let It Bleed*. She was still, in her own words, 'chipping' at heroin but had not developed a major habit. Jagger asked Phil Kaufman, Gram Parsons' roadie, to meet Marianne at the airport and 'get her back into shape'. Over a few days she drank fruit juice, took vitamins, swallowed Percodans (aspirin-based painkillers) and had plenty of massages. She joined the Stones' party and made a series of trips into the Joshua Tree National Park where they took mescaline and wandered around late at night. They climbed up rocks and lit a fire under a full moon. Marianne heard an 'unearthly' sound and turned to Gram Parsons. "Why, Marianne, don't you know that's just a little old coyote," he said.

On one occasion, after finishing a day's recording, Marianne and Jagger were alone at the house they were renting. Marianne was in the bedroom and Jagger entered, putting his head on her knees like a child. 'I felt great empathy for him but I wasn't in love with him any more,' wrote Marianne. 'And really nor was he with me. He was trying to hold on to me. I could see how much he loved me, and it broke my heart.' Jagger had taken other lovers and was still in regular contact with Marsha Hunt but spent a lot of time talking with them about Marianne, who knew of his infidelities.

On November 7, 1969, the Stones began their first tour for two years, at the State University in Fort Collins, Colorado. The tour, for which $1 million worth of tickets had been sold for 23 concerts held mainly in arenas, was to last until early December. Jagger had been on the road almost a week when some news about Marianne filtered through, hours before the band were due to take the stage at the Moody Coliseum in Dallas, Texas. He had expected to hear of a collapse or drugs bust but according to newspaper reports in the British press she had left him and moved into an apartment in Rome with a new lover, Mario Schifano, a 35-year-old artist known as 'Italy's Andy Warhol'.

Schifano had previously been a boyfriend of Anita Pallenberg. She contacted Marianne and asked whether he could stay with her while he was in London. "Anita was probably thinking, 'poor Marianne, so lonely and in need of a good fuck'. So Mario stayed at Cheyne Walk and, needless to say, we had sex," she said. When asked by the press about Schifano, Marianne apparently oozed: "He's my Prince Charming." At the same time reporters were also quizzing Jagger. He was asked at a press conference before a show in Alabama about his state of mind, whether he 'was any more satisfied now'? He answered cryptically that he was, 'financially dissatisfied, sexually satisfied and philosophically trying'. During the tour Jagger's sexual needs had been catered for by the élite of the groupie class, among them Miss Mercy (Mercy Fontenot) and Miss Pamela (Pamela Ann Miller, later Pamela Des Barres) who reportedly introduced him to strawberry-flavoured douches. Beneath the pretence of indifference to the news about Marianne, Jagger was hurt and distressed. He had been ringing her most nights while on tour.

The *Daily Mail* tracked down Marianne to Old Rome, the renaissance district comprising piazzas and tightly packed streets, where she, Nicholas and a nanny called Helen were staying with Schifano. The journalist found them in a 'squalid' flat where the log fire did not light properly and cardboard boxes were scattered around alongside mattresses placed haphazardly in various rooms. Nicholas played on the wooden staircase that led to the living quarters. Schifano, tall, thin and shoeless, wound Marianne's hair around his long fingers and kissed it. The interview was a tirade by Marianne against her home country: "The people in Britain imagine they have some form of right to me. They must realise I am not their property and what I say, do, or think is absolutely no business of theirs. I love Mario. I am happy with him. But this is all very delicate and a girl's private affairs have to be seen with some compassion. There is a curiosity about me. People's real interest in me is morbid, the girl who tried to commit suicide. They never see a woman with body and soul with private difficulties. They will never let such a person be. I am happy. I am absolutely penniless. I am going to start from scratch. People can help me by just forgetting me."

Born in Libya in 1934, Schifano, the son of a wealthy and cultured family, had moved to Rome as a young child. Early in his career he worked with his father as a restorer of artwork, which led to him taking up painting. He was a contributor, with Andy Warhol and Roy Lichtenstein, to 'The International Exhibition of New Realists' show at New York's Sidney Janis Gallery – a major supporter of Jackson Pollock, Willem de Kooning, Mark Rothko and Josef Albers among many others – in 1962. Schifano, in typical 1960s fashion, worked across several mediums. He developed a series known as 'Passaggio TV' [Passage TV] where he manipulated Polaroid photographs he had taken of the images shown on numerous television screens piled up in his studio based in Trastevere, the artists' quarter of Rome. Only a few weeks before meeting Marianne, Schifano had released an album, *Dedicato A*, credited to Le Stelle Di Mario Schifano. He had recruited four musicians, including the American avant-garde composer Peter Hartman, and 'conducted' them through several cacophonous pieces, influenced by The Velvet Underground, with one track filling a whole side of the album. "Mario was a great painter and an even greater cocaine freak," said Marianne. "I could have loved this man but the deck was stacked against us."

Schifano had struggled most of his life with a drug habit that earned him the nickname in Italy of 'Maledetto' (The Cursed One). Despite his addiction, he remained prolific and achieved a certain fame and notoriety in mainland Europe. He often worked with stencils and spray cans, and critics have plotted a link between his work and contemporary artists such as Banksy and Blek le Rat. "He was an all round no-good arty type," said Christopher Gibbs. "Marianne and he were two crazy waifs hanging out with each other." Marianne believed she had fallen for him because he had been a 'great love' of Anita's and she wanted to make a similar connection. They had only been together a few weeks in Italy when Nicholas, who said he was missing Jagger, took a fur coat given to Marianne by Mario and put it on an electric fire to watch it burn. 'After that, it hit me that I had to think completely about Nicholas,' wrote Marianne. 'He loved Mick, and my betrayal of Mick was terrible for him'. The next day they headed back to England to spend Christmas at Yew Tree Cottage with Eva.

Over in the United States, Jagger was soon to become embroiled in a tragedy that more than reflected his personal turmoil. On December 6, in a windswept, smoky amphitheatre, the 1960s was metaphorically brought to its knees. Having been refused permission to stage a free concert in San Francisco's Golden Gate Park, The Rolling Stones had instead rearranged the concert at the Altamont Speedway near Livermore, an hour's drive east from San Francisco. Throughout the tour there had been complaints that ticket prices, ranging from $4.50 to $8 each, were too high. The band responded by tagging on an extra concert with free entry for up to 300,000 people. The Hells Angels were invited to attend in a semi-formal capacity, though there was disagreement as to the extent of their agreed involvement – whether they were expected to merely 'guard' the stage (which was only one metre high) and equipment or 'police' the event. Their 'fee' was reportedly $500 of free beer.

Throughout the day, when Santana, The Flying Burrito Brothers, Jefferson Airplane and Crosby, Stills, Nash & Young each performed, the atmosphere had gradually worsened. The Hells Angels became drunk on the free beer while the crowd, some of whom had taken LSD and amphetamines, had grown restless. Dealers had set up trestle tables around the festival site selling acid tabs for $1 each. A motorcycle was supposedly knocked over which further antagonised the Angels. Fights broke out and, in fear of being set upon, the Angels armed themselves with pool cues, motorcycle chains and cans of beer. An Angel knocked unconscious Marty Balin, singer with Jefferson Airplane, during the band's set. Balin had left the stage to intervene when the Angels set upon a fan with sticks. Denise Kaufman, guitarist with the all-girl San Franciso band, The Ace Of Cups, suffered a fractured skull when a beer bottle thrown from the crowd hit her. She was six months pregnant. The Grateful Dead, who were billed as main support to the Stones, refused to play and left the venue. It had been on their recommendation that the Hells Angels were brought in – they had been used previously at Dead concerts, which had passed off peaceably.

The Rolling Stones were made aware immediately of the hostile mood. Mick Jagger was punched in the face as he ran from the helicopter to his trailer. His assailant shouted at him: "I hate you, I hate you." It was nightfall when the band opened with 'Jumpin' Jack Flash'. "What I remember is that as the darkness fell, the danger seemed to increase," said photographer Eamon McCabe. "The drama was always going to be the Stones. Mick going through his Satanic stage. But when the violence started erupting all around him, he suddenly seemed so small and vulnerable." During their third song, 'Sympathy For The Devil', a fight broke out in front of the stage. Men and women, some of them naked and disorientated after taking LSD, were beaten to the ground. Photographers trying to record the violence were also beaten, their cameras smashed into the soil. Jagger appealed for calm and after a lengthy pause they restarted the song. As they broke into 'Under My Thumb', an 18-year-old black youth wearing a lime green suit was attacked. An Angel, Alan Passaro, stabbed Meredith Hunter five times in his upper body. He was then kicked and stamped upon by other Angels. Hunter had pulled a gun from his pocket but as he lay dying he told Passaro: 'I wasn't going to shoot you'. Passaro was later charged with murder but acquitted on the grounds of self-defence after the jury saw film of the incident – footage was being shot for inclusion in a documentary about the tour called *Gimme Shelter*. During the remainder of the concert Jagger pleaded constantly for 'cool' (as many of the other performers had done throughout the day) but, blinded by stage lights, he was aware of little apart from the white-hot tension. After a much-interrupted performance the band and a few fortunate associates were plucked to safety by a helicopter.

Afterwards the Stones were heavily criticised for putting on a concert where they had largely ignored the essential considerations of lighting, toilets, car parking, medical provision, security and the suitability of the location (Eamon McCabe, the English photographer who was studying film in Los Angeles at the time, arrived at the venue early in the day and said even then it felt to be 'a strange and ominous place'.) "Woodstock and Altamont seem like bookends to the great social experiment of the late-1960s. But, really, they weren't," said Joe McDonald of Country Joe & the Fish who had attended both festivals [Country Joe & the Fish appeared at Woodstock]. "Altamont went wrong for practical reasons – a bad site, bad organisation, greed, arrogance, stupidity."

On returning to England, Jagger phoned Marianne regularly and asked her to resume their relationship. She was convinced they should split and repeatedly turned him down. He arrived at Yew Tree Cottage where, according to Marianne, 'there were a lot of operatic scenes between Mick and Mario'. Eventually Jagger spent the night in bed with Marianne, and Schifano slept on the coach. Schifano left in the morning and Jagger was said to be 'very pleased with himself'.

The next time Marianne and Jagger were sighted together in public was at Marlborough Street Magistrates Court on Monday January 26, 1970. The drugs charges against them had been postponed several times to accommodate their nomadic lifestyle. Magistrates were told that on the arrival of Detective Sergeant Robin Constable at Cheyne Walk, Jagger instructed Marianne not to answer the door and shouted: "They are after the weed." Jagger's distinguished QC, Michael Havers, had warned beforehand that he was to make grave allegations about the police. He said Constable had showed Jagger white powder sprinkled on silver paper to which Jagger exclaimed: "You bastard. You have planted me with heroin." Jagger was then told, he claimed, that if he gave £1,000 to Constable he would be repaid in kind for his co-operation. The magistrates did not believe this story and Jagger was fined £200 and told to pay costs of £52 10s. Marianne, whose role had been stressed as being 'between secondary and nil', was acquitted. Jagger's claims were later investigated by Detective Chief Inspector William Wilson of Scotland Yard. 'Michael Jagger is an intelligent young man, and doubtless is on the fringe, if not embroiled in the world of users of dangerous drugs,' reported Wilson. 'Mr Constable is a hard-working and competent police officer. Basically it comes down to one man's word against another's.' As a side issue, he reported of Marianne: 'I would not be prepared to place any reliance at all on her'.

Marianne and Jagger's relationship continued to deteriorate. They rarely had sex, in fact it had not been a regular feature of their relationship since their first six months together. 'I'm not that interested in sex, and I've noticed that this upsets men,' wrote Marianne. 'They want women to think about sex a lot, and always be wanting it.' She did not share Jagger's newfound enthusiasm to mix in the highest social circles. David Lord Brooke, the Eighth Earl of Warwick, invited them to dinner at Warwick Castle. "I didn't care a flying fuck about him," said Marianne. "He was a raging bore. It was an insufferably stuffy evening and I soon found myself swooning from boredom." Marianne took five Mandrax tablets and passed out in the soup. Jagger had to carry her upstairs. "Mick has always been good with the afflicted," said Christopher Gibbs. "He's very gentle and takes a lot of trouble with them. I've seen him looking after Keith and Brian whenever they were in a mess, which was quite often."

Despite heroin often making her ill and causing her to break out in spots, Marianne gradually developed a habit. She sometimes returned to those feelings that had overtaken her in Sydney. One day she was drawn towards the edge of the River Thames, much the same as Ophelia in *Hamlet,* and resisted the temptation only at the last minute. On another occasion, Jagger returned to Cheyne Walk and found her prostrate in the bath. He immediately suspected another suicide attempt but she had taken just a small number of sleeping tablets. Word of Marianne's condition spread. Ahmet Ertegun, the founder and president of Atlantic Records with whom Jagger was especially close, visited their flat. The Rolling Stones had set up their own record label, which was to fall under the auspices of Atlantic. Marianne overheard their conversation. Ertegun told Jagger, 'She could jeopardise everything' and warned him: 'I've seen a lot of heartbreak with junkies. It wrecks the lives of everybody around them. It's a bottomless pit, and she'll drag you into it unless you let her go'. She felt Prince Rupert Lowenstein was also advising Jagger to end the relationship. He had recommended that the band relocate to France to avoid extortionate British taxes and had singled out Marianne as someone who 'wasn't a team player'. Marianne told Jagger she did not want to move with him to France. Jagger hired a private plane to view property along the Côte d'Azur and invited Marsha Hunt to accompany him.

In the spring of 1970 Marianne moved to live with her mother in the timbered cottage in Aldworth. Jagger recognised that this would mean she was cared for by Eva and was away from the London drugs scene. Marsha briefly moved into the flat in Cheyne Walk. "I got the feeling that he missed family life, the child Nicholas, and the dog more than the woman," she said. Jagger had a loose arrangement with Hunt and had a series of one-night stands, often at Stargroves. He had a fling with Suki Potier, a former girlfriend of Brian Jones, and spent several weeks in the company of the Californian model Catherine James. Friends sensed he was filling in time before reconciliation with Marianne. He visited her at the cottage and put a tape into the deck. As the opening bars rang out, he knelt in front of Marianne, clasping her hands: 'I watched you suffer a dull aching pain/ Now you've decided to show me the same'. When 'Wild Horses' had finished Marianne held Jagger and cried. She said later that she was not crying because she wanted to get back with him, but for what their relationship might have been. 'Mick was helpless. He didn't know what to do,' she wrote. 'It was a big bother to him that I was that way, and I hate being a bother. I'd rather just go off and be a bother by myself'. She had detected a narcissistic element in Jagger's love for her. In her beauty he saw his own reflection and it elevated his self-image. She resolved to undertake 'a systematic, cold-blooded self-desecration'.

Marianne rallied a little during the spring of 1970 and was cast as the female lead, Anne Torel, playing opposite Ian Ogilvy (Alban Torel) in a BBC production of the Somerset Maugham short story *Door Of Opportunity*. In the 50-minute play, which was broadcast in June 1971, Torel receives news of a violent uprising by immigrant Chinese workers on a plantation in Malaya where he is a divisional officer of the local council. One of Torel's English friends is killed and his bereaved family in danger. Torel has a moral dilemma, whether to risk his life by visiting the plantation or stay with his own family. Marianne performed satisfactorily in her television debut and soon afterwards was offered the part of Desdemona in Jack Good's *Catch My Soul*, a rock musical based loosely on *Othello* which was due to open in Manchester and move to London (The Roundhouse and then the Prince of Wales Theatre) before touring the UK. She met Good and was offered the part on a provisional basis. She retired to Birmingham's Midland Hotel where she was spending the night. The next day, the *Birmingham Evening Mail* broke the news that Marianne had 'overdosed'. She had taken two sleeping tablets but collapsed after leaving the bed. She lost her role in the production, her place taken firstly by Angharad Rees and then, Sharon Gurney. Another with a part in the musical was P.P. Arnold playing, with appropriate irony, a character called Bianca. Marianne was later offered a role in the Jacobean comedy *Women Beware Women* by Thomas Middleton, but 'fell ill' before rehearsals began.

On a flight between Belfast and London, Marianne suffered an anxiety attack and fell unconscious. She was taken to Hillingdon Hospital in Middlesex on landing but the precise details of the cause of illness were not revealed. There were reports that she had also 'fallen ill' during the reading of a script for a play and fluffed her lines. Gossip columns said she had missed out on a part in a film directed by Roman Polanski [probably *Macbeth*] after attending the audition stoned. She was resolute about her desire to act and was proud that her passport listed her as an actor and not an 'actress'. "In my mind an actress is an unreal person – all jewels, furs and boyfriends and with no real dedication to the theatre," she told the London *Evening Standard* in 1970. "I have always been fighting to be recognised by acting people as a real, serious actor and not some sort of pop singing freak who happens to be given parts. I can act and I know it and I have been praised by critics for work on stage, on television and in films, yet there are still people who will not take me seriously, and that hurts."

During one of her frequent visits to Ireland with Jagger, Marianne had met Lord Patrick Rossmore, whom she referred to as 'delightful'. She met him again, this time on her own, and after just three weeks together they announced their engagement. Ireland's heavy land-rates had forced Rossmore and his mother to sell the family home and most if its contents eight years earlier and they were living in a gamekeeper's cottage in the grounds of their former residence, Mangapp Manor in County Monaghan. Rossmore, a former Etonian, was working as an architectural photographer and had earlier served as a second lieutenant in the Somerset Light Infantry. Aged 43, he was three years short of double Marianne's age. The English press described him as a 'shy, retiring bachelor peer'. His only previous appearance in the national press had been in June 1962 when the *Daily Express* mocked his folly of selling an 18th century German marquetry cabinet for £205 which was valued two months later at £6,000. "Paddy is an incredibly sweet, charming guy," said Christopher Gibbs. "He is a very gentle, sensitive man, one of those men who knows a lot about birds, flowers, fishing and poetry. He is very perceptive and tender with people. He was like Marianne's cavalier. I don't think she had ever come across a man so driven by compassion."

Marianne and Rossmore shared a passion for William Blake. He presented her with a copy of *Songs Of Innocence And Of Experience*, an illustrated collection of 45 Blake poems, and they discussed his work endlessly. Within days of becoming a couple, Rossmore introduced Marianne to his 87-year-old mother at a dinner party. "Marianne is one of the loveliest girls I have ever seen. I am delighted about the engagement," Lady Rossmore told reporters. Lord Rossmore was photographed at Dublin Airport bidding farewell to Marianne, his arm positioned protectively over her shoulders. Tall, gaunt and with his dark hair positioned into a perfect side parting, he was the antithesis of Mick Jagger. Pressmen met Marianne as she left the airport in London. "What does Mick Jagger think of it all?" they asked. "I don't really care," she snapped.

Jagger hurried to Aldworth to uncover the truth behind the headlines. He spent three hours with Marianne and Eva, who was also being briefed about Rossmore for the first time. Jagger emerged, smiling, and blew a kiss to the journalists gathered around the cottage. "Her engagement is simply beautiful, man," he said. Jagger continued to send Marianne letters, including one written on Sunday 16 August, 1970. It began: 'Dearest Marianne, I woke up this morning and had you in my mind so I thought I would just talk to you a little. I haven't seen or heard of you much lately and wondered how you were?' He wrote a little of the band's plans and then closed: 'I have no idea where you are in your mind nor should I expect to but I hope there are green fields and flowers where you walk. I'm sure Nicholas is having a good time. Please throw him in the air for me. Marlon [Keith Richards' and Anita Pallenberg's son] is now 1 and walks and is bright but will inevitably have an Oedipus complex don't you think! If you find time please drop me a line or telephone before I go away at the end of August as I would love to hear from you. You will always be precious in my thoughts. As ever, Mick.' The letter was sold in 2010 via the New Jersey auction house Robert Edwards Auctions and fetched £3,600.

Henrietta Moraes, who had been a model for Francis Bacon and lover of Lucian Freud, was a close friend of Marianne's and, similar to others within their circle, was surprised at the affair with Rossmore. "I think he was mad about her and just really fell in love with her and she went off with him," she said. "It always seemed highly unlikely. I think she was quite sick at the time. They did a lot of driving about Ireland banging on chemists' doors. Poor Paddy didn't have a clue what it was all about – he did not know anything about smack, so what could he do?" Marianne said later that her affair with Rossmore was a way to extricate herself from Jagger. "I used Paddy, but I figured he was a grown-up and knew the score," she said. He initially knew nothing of her drug habits – she was attempting to curb her heroin use by substituting it for barbiturates and alcohol. Rossmore paid for her to see a Harley Street specialist who, twice a week at a cost of £80 per visit, injected Marianne with Valium, which was a highly unusual approach to treating people with a heroin problem.

There were two final episodes of Jagger and Marianne's affair to be played out. One of his last gifts had been a ranch mink coat. After a trip abroad she tried to pass through customs in England while wearing it. Officers did not believe Marianne's story that her mother had paid the duty and court proceedings were instigated. There were several adjournments until on June 29, 1970, Marianne appeared at Uxbridge Magistrates Court on charges of attempting to evade customs duty and making a false declaration. She was fined £500 and told she must pay a further £850 if she wanted the coat back: £344 duty and £506 to cover its current market value. She told the court the coat could go to public auction and apologised to the bench. "I am sorry. I am really humiliated," she said. "I didn't take this seriously. It has brought me only bad luck." While she was with Rossmore, Jagger had written and phoned Marianne, asking to meet. She relented and agreed to see him at Cheyne Walk. She was drinking heavily and her weight had increased from seven stones to 10. 'He took one look at me – a look of utter horror – and sort of gasped 'Who is this chick?' she wrote in *Faithfull*.

Nik Cohn, one of a number of writers absorbed by the Marianne story, tracked her down in the autumn of 1970 and spent an afternoon in her company at Aldworth. Soon after moving there a group of skinheads had called to welcome the new arrival. They shouted through the windows that she was a 'dirty slag' and 'slut'. When Cohn met her she was overweight and appeared exhausted. Her face was swollen due to influenza, she explained. Dogs were barking. Nicholas, now five years old, was competing with them for attention. She developed a headache. The rain lashed down on the cottage and during the course of the interview, she answered in monosyllables, negatives and diversions. "I look after my family, I am the breadwinner now," she said. "I cook and do the housework and go for walks, and I have a few friends in the village. I see them quite often. I am an avid TV watcher, it's all there is to do." They went for a walk, through puddles and sodden grass around Aldworth. "I want to be a good actress, really good," she told Cohn.

The affair with Lord Rossmore barely lasted a year. They had remained living with their mothers and saw each other for occasional weekends or holidays only, including one in Ibiza. Marianne said later that she had been a 'zombie' through most of her time with Rossmore. He turned his experience with her into a positive force when he established the Coolmine Therapeutic Centre in 1973, a voluntary body concerned with the treatment of addicts in Dublin. At first it was a low-key service but grew in the 1980s to include a residential facility for 100 recovering addicts based near Navan in Co. Meath. After splitting from Marianne, Rossmore appeared only once more in the British press, when a terrorist group, the South Armagh Republican Action Force, burned down his £300,000 cottage in 1980.

The headline wrote itself: 'Marianne Wasn't Faithful'. On October 30, 1970, Marianne attended a civil court in London for the divorce proceedings to annul her marriage to John Dunbar. During the 13-minute hearing she did not deny allegations of adultery with Jagger. Dunbar also admitted adultery without naming anyone specifically. The divorce was granted to him, a largely cosmetic ruling but one that apportioned principal responsibility to Marianne. She sat, as the newspapers noted, in a 'wet-look maxi coat' while lawyers appealed for a waiving of the usual year's waiting period for the divorce to become final. The Judge, Sir Roger Ormrod, was told Marianne was 'quite anxious' to remarry. He refused and snapped: "I don't think this case is substantially different from any other." Newspapers speculated about the man Marianne was quite anxious to marry. They were aware that her relationships with Lord Rossmore and Mario Schifano had come to an end. Sir Ormrod granted custody of Nicholas to both parents with Eva Faithfull having responsibility for his care and control.

Kenneth Anger re-emerged into Marianne's life and asked her to play Lilith in his film *Lucifer Rising*. Although Anger was to take liberties with various sacred texts, Lilith, in Jewish mythology, was thought to derive from a class of female demons. She declined to eat from the Tree of Knowledge and so did not learn to differentiate right from wrong. Anger had started work on the film six years earlier, hiring Bobby Beausoleil, a 20-year-old musician from Santa Barbara, to act and compose the soundtrack. Filming was suspended in 1967 because Anger claimed footage had been stolen by Beausoleil – others said Anger had simply spent all the money earmarked for the film. Beausoleil was unavailable when filming recommenced. A member of the Charles Manson 'family', he stabbed to death one of their associates, Gary Hinman. He contributed the soundtrack from his prison cell. *Lucifer Rising* was completed with funds from the National Film Finance Corporation of Great Britain, prompting controversy about state funding of a 'devil film'. Anger also received financial assistance from Germany's Hamburg 1 Television Company and the United States' National Endowment for the Arts.

Mick Jagger was asked to play Lucifer but declined. His younger brother of four years, Chris, took on the role instead. The cast was flown to Egypt and within a day Jagger was on the plane back to London after he had ridiculed Anger on the set. Marianne was pleased because she found Chris Jagger to be 'an incredible loudmouth and smart-arse bully'. With a certain degree of inevitability, Anger became Lucifer. Donald Cammell played Osiris and Jimmy Page of Led Zeppelin was featured for a few seconds, playing a bearded man holding an Egyptian stele [slab of stone or wood used to mark burial sites] while staring at a picture of Aleister Crowley. Anger filmed Marianne daubed in fake blood crawling around Arab graveyards at sunrise. He felt her sickly state brought on by heroin added to her performance. Billed cryptically as a 'presentation of Anita Pallenberg', Anger explained: "It is a film about the love generation, the birthday party of the Aquarian Age showing actual ceremonies to make Lucifer rise. Lucifer is the light god, not the devil – the Rebel Angel behind what's happening in the world today. His message is that the key of life is disobedience. Isis (Nature) wakes. Osiris (Death) answers. Lilith (Destroyer) climbs to the place of Sacrifice. The Magus activates the circle and Lucifer – Bringer of Light – breaks through." There was no dialogue during the 28 minutes of film, instead Anger created a well shot if unsettling assembly of colour-saturated images. "It was a hazy experience. I felt like I was playing with fire and I'm glad I got out safely," Marianne told *Melody Maker* in September 1987. "I have no interest in diabolism myself, thank God. Kenneth was always trying to get me into that ship but for once I was completely clear and assertive, and despite the fact that I love and respect him there was no way he could persuade me to get into Satanism."

Lucifer Rising was not completed until 1981 and did not receive an official widescale release. It appeared mainly at art-house cinemas and later had cult appeal to the video and DVD market. Mikita Brottman, author of *Moonchild: The Films Of Kenneth Anger*, wrote: 'The montage of hermetic symbols becomes first dreamlike, then menacing; centuries of mystical thought are distilled into a series of voyeuristic fantasies, a kinky psychodrama backed by the carnival strains of a maleficent calliope. Anger intended *Lucifer Rising* to stand as a form of ritual marking the death of the old religions like Judaism and Christianity, and the ascension of the more nihilistic age of Lucifer." Tony Rayns, writing in the *Monthly Film Bulletin*, commented: '*Lucifer Rising* burns on a slower fuse than his earlier work: it strikes a balance between Eisensteinian montage (the relation of one image to another) and an interest in the 'spiritual' essence of individual images." Among these images were shots of a swimming tiger, nude dancers, UFOs, Stonehenge, baby crocodiles emerging from an egg, Tarot cards, waves on the sea, wood nymphs etc – all set to a stop-start organ soundtrack not dissimilar to Pink Floyd.

Marianne learned of Jagger's marriage to Bianca Perez-Mora Macios on Wednesday, May 12, 1971 when she was on her way home from London after seeing the doctor who administered her Valium. She saw from her taxi window a newspaper billboard that read: 'Mick and Bianca Wed in France'. Jagger had met the 24-year-old daughter of a successful Nicaraguan import-export merchant in September 1971 after a Rolling Stones concert in France. She was four months pregnant when they married. On reaching Paddington Station, Marianne did not catch her usual train to Goring-on-Thames but called at the station bar where she began to drink heavily. The mixture of alcohol and Valium made her drowsy but she managed to stagger to an Indian restaurant in Praed Street, immediately outside the station. She ordered a curry but slumped into her food soon after it arrived. The owner called the police and she was taken to the newly opened Paddington Green Police Station with its 16 subterranean cells, which were later used to hold high-risk terrorist suspects. Marianne was kept in a cell and told to 'sleep it off'.

The next morning she was asked to sign the visitors' book as a mark of her celebrity status. She was picked up by Chris O'Dell and driven to Yew Tree Cottage. A week later she appeared at Marylebone Magistrates Court and was fined £15 for being drunk.

Heroin became part of Marianne's daily life. She became listless around the house, infantilised by her mother's hectoring. She was determined to become a street addict, a character drawn from *The Naked Lunch*, seduced by squalid glamour. She left the cottage and began living with various friends in London where she had easy access to drugs. The first she called upon was Pamela Mayall, wife of John Mayall. Pamela had four young children living at home with her and accommodating Marianne's habit was difficult. Dirty needles were left around and she often shot up at the house. At a dinner party Marianne returned from the toilet with her dress tucked inside her knickers. Pamela left Marianne alone one day at the house. When she returned she found her asleep in the bath. Water was cascading down the stairs. In trying to pull her out, Pamela fell backwards and knocked herself unconscious. She came round 20 minutes later and the structure of the house had been seriously damaged by the water.

Marianne befriended a dealer called Gypsy who had a small flat over a restaurant in St Anne's Court, between Wardour Street and Dean Street in Soho. She was still wearing designer clothes bought from her previous life – hand-made boots and dresses, now growing tatty. Her regular haunt was a wall left partially standing after a building had been struck by a bomb many years earlier. She quickly became a member of London's underworld. "I really think now that it was a very good experience, because I was completely anonymous. It was exactly what I needed after the Mick Jagger thing, and so much attention and no privacy," she told *The Independent* in May 1990. "Just losing myself on the streets of London was great, having no address and telephone number. The people I met on the street didn't care about my fame, those values didn't mean a shit there. It was really good for me. It did what it was meant to do... pulled me back together as a real person. It was something I needed to do." She found compassion among street people. One time she overdosed on Pethidine which had been stolen in a raid on a chemist shop. She was kept on her feet and walked around until she came to again. She was offered places in squats or would wake on the street to find that someone had put a coat over her. The staff at a nearby Chinese restaurant washed her only set of clothes in their washing machine, wrapping her in a blanket as she waited for them to dry. She lost weight and fell below seven stones.

She met up with a friend from Reading, Anthony Howell, a dancer with the Royal Ballet. "I was with a hugely tall and fit Californian with a blond moustache," he said. "Competitively cool with each other, they decided to shoot up. It was such a ceremony – warming a spoon and finding a vein. The Californian giant immediately conked out. But completely! It didn't seem to affect Marianne very much. I sat there, with a slightly fixed smile, wondering if he was going to die. Luckily not. But I became even more wary. Friends on H became bug-eyed and desperate. Friends dropping acid, well – I'd say they just seemed to lose their edge, cease being as active in their fields as they had been. After a while, I tended to avoid those I knew who had a habit, and that included Marianne."

The exact content of the heroin procured on the streets was unknown, but it was seldom more than 50 per cent pure (in New York at the same time it was often under 10 per cent). It was usually thinned with talcum powder, bicarbonate of soda or brick dust. Most of the heroin filtering through to London's streets was from south east Asia and came as two types, 'rice' and 'elephant'. The 'rice' was light coloured and granular while the 'elephant' was a mild brown colour and more potent. It received its nickname because of the elephant illustration on the bags supplied to dealers. Heroin addiction, at this scale and street level, was a relatively new phenomenon in Britain in the early 1970s and the medical profession was unsure how it should be tackled. A handful of medics took the view that heroin was an acceptable way to alleviate the pain of everyday life and readily dispensed the drug. Dr John Petro, a Polish GP who had emigrated to England in 1916 and worked with Alexander Fleming, visited tube stations handing out prescriptions for heroin to addicts. Known as 'The Junkies' Friend', he appeared on the

David Frost Show talking about his radical approach to a rising problem. Dr Petro was later struck off the Medical Register when he began prescribing Methedrine, which was not at the time regulated under the Dangerous Drugs Act. He continued to tend the conditions of addicts around the Piccadilly Circus area for many years on a voluntary basis.

The only friend from her former life to visit Marianne regularly was the polymath Brion Gysin, a friend of William Burroughs who was said to have invented the 'cut up' technique of writing. 'He was very sweet to me,' wrote Marianne. 'He didn't care whether I was with Mick Jagger or the man in the moon'. The Scottish novelist Alexander Trocchi, himself a long-standing heroin addict, introduced Marianne to a doctor working at Bexley Hospital in south-east London, a former mental asylum. Marianne was signed up to an NHS programme whereby she was prescribed heroin 'jacks', white pills which were dissolved in water and injected into the body. Marianne would call every day at John Bell and Croyden chemists in Wigmore Street for her 24 jacks of heroin, which Trocchi administered on her behalf at his house in Observatory Gardens, Kensington. The rest of the day was spent in a dream-like trance back on the wall, of which Marianne spoke and wrote a great deal over the years. Some of her friends were sceptical about the veracity of her recollections whether she actually 'lived' on the streets. "Marianne always had her mother to go to – it's only an hour from London," said a close friend. "She had no reasons to be on the streets. That's not to say she didn't go through some pretty poverty-stricken times. She is a tremendously resilient person. I know for a fact that she did not have any handouts from her parents."

11

On a rare trip to see a friend from what Marianne called her 'former life' she visited Talitha Getty, the wife of the oil heir and philanthropist John Paul Getty Jr. Talitha had played small parts in several films during the 1960s and the Gettys had been friends of Marianne and Jagger. Their wealth, style and youth made them archetypal members of 'swinging' London. Keith Richards said 'they had the best and finest opium'. The fashion designer Yves Saint Laurent labelled them 'the beautiful and damned' – borrowing the epithet from the title of F. Scott Fitzgerald's novel.

Marianne met Talitha's lover, a French aristocrat called Count Jean de Breteuil whose parents had owned French-language newspapers published in North Africa. He and Marianne had an instant attraction. "What I liked about him was that he had one yellow and one green eye," she said. "And a lot of dope. It was all about drugs and sex." The count had ingratiated himself with Keith Richards after arriving with a plentiful supply of heroin at Nellcote, the mansion in the south of France where The Rolling Stones were recording *Exile On Main Street*. Richards and Pallenberg were so grateful that they offered him their flat at Cheyne Walk for his use when in London.

Marianne stayed with de Breteuil for several months. In July 1971 they travelled to Paris for a weekend break. They were staying at L'Hotel in the heart of the West Bank when de Breteuil received a call from Pamela Courson, the girlfriend of Jim Morrison of The Doors. He left immediately, ignoring Marianne's request that she go with him – she was keen to meet Morrison. Marianne took a handful of Tuinals but was woken by de Breteuil in the early hours. He was agitated and hit her before insisting they pack immediately and head for Morocco where Marianne could meet his mother. Marianne learned that Morrison had overdosed on heroin supplied by de Breteuil. "Jean saw himself as the dealer to the stars," she said. "Had he lived [he died of a heroin overdose later that year], he might have turned into a human being. He was with me because I'd been involved with Mick Jagger, he was obsessed with all that."

After Morrison's death on July 3, 1971 at the age of 27, stories circulated speculating on Marianne's involvement. Some had her at Morrison's rented apartment at 17 Rue Beautreillis when he died, others that she had discovered the body or supplied the heroin (or both). She has denied any connection whatsoever, beyond accompanying Breteuil to Paris that weekend and has marked down the conjecture as her 'role in mythology'.

Marianne's relationship with her mother had by now broken down and they no longer spoke to one another. She visited Yew Tree Cottage occasionally to bathe and make a meal but left without speaking to Eva. One day after taking a quantity of cocaine Marianne began cutting her face with a razor blade. She was set on destroying her beauty, which she held largely responsible for ruining her life.

News of Marianne's deterioration reached Dunbar and he became worried about the well-being of Nicholas, now six years old. On March 10, 1972, Dunbar drove down the snaking B4009 to Aldworth to remove Nicholas from a household that he believed was causing him psychological harm. His efforts were thwarted by the type of episode drawn from the pages of a Thomas Hardy novel. By his agitated tone during a brief telephone conversation, Eva was wary. She 'hired' a local man to guard Nicholas on the three-mile journey to and from school at Compton. Dunbar's attempt to abduct Nicholas ended when a group of villagers surrounded his car and refused to budge until he was returned to his grandmother. Several mothers from the nearby Glebe estate joined the protest as they returned from leaving their children at nearby schools. Dunbar tried to make his point but had little chance as the community stood firm. The police were called and Dunbar was advised to return to London for his own safety. "Marianne and her mum are very popular in the village. Nicholas is a very nice child and we just wanted to help," a 'local mum' told the *Reading Evening Post*. The next day Dunbar began court proceedings to claim custody of Nicholas.

At the court hearing, Dunbar, his parents, Bob and Tatiana, and friends of both Marianne and Dunbar, said that Marianne was not fit to look after Nicholas. "Marianne was out to lunch at this point and lots of mud was slung about in court. It was awful," said Dunbar. Marianne considered it 'wicked and hypocritical' of Dunbar because he also had a drug habit, albeit 'small maintenance'. She was also angry that Dunbar's parents had questioned Eva's suitability to look after him. "It was true Eva was becoming a bit unbalanced by then," said Marianne. "She loved Nicholas so much. But it should never have come to Eva having Nicholas."

Marianne felt Dunbar was bitter because Jagger had effectively been Nicholas' father for four years, although the boy had still seen Dunbar occasionally over the period. "I know there is a sort of law that lays down what a mother is, but I don't know if it's that important to recognise it always," she told the writer Jenny Fabian in 1981. "Different people do things different ways, and it really hasn't been bad for him. He's fine. It's John who's been like the mother. I've been something else. It's a difficult area, children, and I don't know if we are liberated regarding it all."

Eva Faithfull was devastated by the court decision and shortly afterwards took an overdose of liquid morphine. The narcotic had been prescribed for Eva's own mother many years earlier and she had kept it. A friend of Eva's claimed to have received a 'psychic message' and drove to the cottage in the early hours. She found Eva collapsed on the floor with a series of notes left for friends and family. When she awoke in hospital Eva was furious with her friend and told her she had wanted to die. 'I hate to admit it, I honestly hadn't given a thought to what effect my behaviour might have on her,' wrote Marianne. 'That's the trouble with selfishness of this kind, the drug kind.'

The Royal Lyceum Theatre Company offered Marianne a leading role in its production of the 17th century comedy of manners *Le Misanthrope* by Molière. She was to play Célimène, the much-pursued flirt who rejoices in pointing out the flaws of others behind their backs. Rehearsals were going to schedule when Marianne became ill again. The official line given to the media for two separate hospital admissions was, firstly, a 'boil that required lancing' and then a twisted ankle. Days after the 'ankle' injury, the press was informed that a doctor had ordered her to pull out of the production completely.

Another offer of work came from an old ally, Mike Leander, who tracked her down to the wall in Soho. She told him she had no permanent place to live and he helped set her up in a flat in Russell Square, Bloomsbury. Leander had a production contract with Bell Records (now part of Sony). "It was during one of her bad spells and I said, 'Come on, let's have another try'. We went in with just a folk group," he said. "Her voice had not gone but it had changed – dropped an octave. It had what I thought was very sexy – a sort of smoky, whisky, country voice which I tried to get on to tape." Marianne made a token effort to quit heroin before returning to the studio with Leander. She checked into a private clinic but stayed for just a day and a half. She had arranged for someone to smuggle in heroin. She later claimed that this had angered a male nurse who punched her in the mouth, causing her to lose two front teeth.

In the studio she recorded a version of 'It's All Over Now Baby Blue', the Bob Dylan song that had been a hit for her idol, Joan Baez, in the autumn of 1965. The hierarchy at Bell was enthused and commissioned an album. "I don't know what she was still doing, whether it was heroin or coke or whatever she did, but she was perfectly well behaved with me," said Leander. "She was punctual but did not look great. I knew she was having a bad time and I think it helped her emotionally to get working. It kicked her off again."

184

Marianne had been listening to the Cat Stevens album *Tea For The Tillerman*, and both she and Leander shared a love of Paul and Linda McCartney's album, *Ram*. James Taylor, Melanie and Janis Ian were also influencing their musical ideas as they began recording, pitching Marianne against a stark acoustic backing. She covered songs by Bob Dylan, George Harrison, Tim Hardin, Cat Stevens, James Taylor, Joni Mitchell and others. When Leander delivered the completed album, the mood had changed significantly at Bell. "They had gone off the whole idea. These things happen. I was very pissed off about it," he said. "It had taken a couple of months and we had done a lot of work on it. I think there was a lot of negative interest in her and some of it may have rubbed off on Bell Records. By the time I delivered the master tapes nobody liked it, I don't know why."

The album had the provisional title of *Rich Kid Blues*, named after the opening track written by Terry Reid, a protégé of the record producer Mickie Most and early collaborator with Graham Nash of The Hollies. Marianne was scathing for many years about the record, which was not formally released until 1985. "My voice is so weak. I can barely listen to it. It's the voice of somebody incredibly high, probably on the edge of death," she said. She later viewed it – similar to many critics – as the missing link between her former folk persona and the more abrasive, direct material that followed. Leander fared much better with a project he undertook simultaneously with the Marianne album. Paul Raven, a long-time failure while signed to Decca, was repackaged as Gary Glitter and, with Leander co-writing and producing, had the first of 12 Top Ten hits in June 1972, 'Rock And Roll Parts One And Two'.

Barry Fantoni had not seen Marianne for more than four years when he met her in unusual circumstances while playing for the *Private Eye* cricket team in a match at Aldworth. Marianne had been walking through the village when she recognised Fantoni on the cricket pitch. "I suddenly saw this blonde figure in a long dress. It was like something out of a Benjamin Britten opera. She was wearing a white dress and just came on to the pitch to give me a hug," he said. He ushered her to the boundary and afterwards they met in the pavilion. Beads of sweat were

185

breaking out on her face. He realised immediately that she was unwell. "She had obviously taken a terrific pounding. Her body looked like it had been dropped from an aeroplane, but it came through that she had a strong presence and personality. I could see she had been through a hell of a fight and her eyes told me that she knew I had recognised the fact," he said.

Marianne had another chance meeting as she walked down the King's Road in Chelsea. She had just visited a friend who owned a shop selling Moroccan carpets. He was concluding a cocaine deal and sent her away with a quantity of dope. As she passed Granny Takes A Trip Marianne met Mick Jagger. They held hands and stared into each other's eyes. Jagger asked the manager of Granny Takes A Trip if they could have use of an upstairs room. Without speaking, they made love and then went their separate ways. Marianne did not view it as a particularly loving experience but more 'like an exercise of power, or perhaps property rights'.

In the midst of her drug addiction, Marianne was able to rouse herself on an intermittent basis at least. She appeared once more alongside Nicol Williamson, in the James Leo Herlihy (famous for *Midnight Cowboy*) one-act play, *Terrible Jim Fitch*, which was broadcast as part of the BBC's 'Thirty-Minute Theatre' series. Marianne played 'Lonesome Sally' who had to remain 'speechless and inert' while Williamson, in the title role as the petty thief on the run, soliloquised from his motel room. Marianne was also cast opposite Britt Ekland in a BBC version of the short two-hander by August Stringberg, *The Stronger* – another play with minimal dialogue.

For more than a year, taking in most of 1971 and the early part of 1972, Marianne was without a regular partner. In the few newspaper interviews she did, she expressed the joys of being single. In the spring of 1972, however, she began a relationship with Oliver Musker whom she had met while he worked as an assistant at Christopher Gibbs' antique shop. "She was always coming into the shop," said Musker. "She claimed to be living on the streets but I don't think she was really. She was a junkie and was at the stage where she realised something had to be done about it. She looked all right. She was always a bit pale anyway." Musker went on to play a pivotal role in Marianne's life. "It was Oliver who hauled me back. Without him I wouldn't be alive today," she said.

Marianne booked once more into Bexley Hospital with a new-found determination to quit heroin. Musker accompanied her to the clinic with Eva and saw a trail of beer bottles leading to its door. "It was a mental hospital for alcoholics and drug addicts. The alcoholics thought they were better than the addicts," he said. In an attempt to avoid press sleuths, Marianne booked in as Gabrielle von Crontall. She was weaned off heroin on a very gradual basis, a grain per day over a three month period. Musker sometimes considered these reductions tokenistic and suspected many of the patients, including Marianne, relished the free, clean and constant supply of heroin, which came without the worries of street dealing – perpetual hustling, price haggling, the non-arrival of a dealer or police harassment. Musker visited three times a week, usually taking a train with Eva. "A lot of people did not like her mother but I regarded her as a very good friend. I used to go and see her occasionally. She was a very practical woman," he said.

The press was soon aware of Marianne's admittance and Dr James Wilson, one of the hospital's consultants, issued a statement. He described her addiction as a 'tragedy' but stressed that she was 'determined to be cured'. Marianne spoke later in a press interview of her reasons for entering the hospital: "You mustn't give anyone the impression that heroin is a good thing. It's totally ghastly. You start by thinking: 'Who am I hurting? Only myself', but you are hurting all the people who love you. I had lost Nicholas. I was going to lose everyone else. The first real step I took was to get myself registered. That's the most important step a junkie ever takes. Before that, buying it takes up your whole life, but once it's admitted, the secret is out."

The doctors at Bexley, some of whom Marianne believed did not expect her to quit, warned that it would take up to six years for her to be properly well again. Marianne's plight became symbolic for the other patients at the clinic. Musker felt some of them did not want their star patient to leave clean and would resort to subterfuge to stop her, almost as if her failure excused their own. "I once or twice saw people behaving very shiftily with her cigarettes. She was determined to stay clean, but not determined enough as it turned out later." Marianne left Bexley requiring one jack of heroin per day. She and Musker spoke often of a holiday in Bali they would take when she left hospital. "She was going to get better. I had faith in her. It had all taken a lot longer than we thought for her to become clean," he said.

The issue of the *Daily Mirror* of Wednesday, October 4, 1972, carried a front page photograph of Marianne and Musker sitting on a park bench. The accompanying piece read: 'Radiant and in love again, the star who beat heroin sits in a park with the new man in her life.' The interview was an attempt by Marianne to announce to the acting profession that she was once more available for hire. Musker was unaccustomed to dealing with the press but learned fast. "They bug you quite a lot if they get a bee in their bonnet. Marianne is a joy to interview because she always gives them a good quote. I think everything one says looks ridiculous in print," he said

One evening after returning from Bexley, Marianne collapsed and was taken to St Stephen's Hospital in Fulham Road, Chelsea. Musker assumed one of the nurses had rung the newspapers because a posse of pressmen was outside the entrance to their flat. "We couldn't go home – there was even a mad vicar who had come along to save her life. I suppose it was quite amusing in a way," he said. The dealers still phoned but Marianne declined their offers of a rendezvous on a street corner or in a pub. "They were a real pain in the arse, on the phone all the time," said Musker. "I just wouldn't let them in the flat. She was doing a TV show once and two fans came along with a handful of Mandrax. They thought they were being kind to her but of course they weren't."

Early in 1973 Marianne was offered a leading role in the British film *Ghost Story*. The film was supposedly set in rural southern England but was actually shot in India, which flushed scenes with an unusual amount of light. The actors, among them Penelope Keith, Murray Melvin and Anthony Bate, agreed to accept 'deferred payment' which meant they did not receive a full fee until the film attracted the necessary finance. "Marianne accepted it because they gave us both tickets to India and we wanted to travel through the country," said Musker. They stayed at the prestigious Taj Mahal Palace Hotel in Mumbai. "When she came out of Bexley we said we would go away for the weekend to Venice but we thought it was a bit boring so we went to Bali and then India," he said.

The film was directed by Stephen Weeks who had made *I, Monster* two years earlier, a version of the *Dr Jekyll And Mr Hyde* story starring Peter Cushing and Christopher Lee. *Ghost Story*, about a group of college friends spending a weekend together at a country house, was stylistically a Hammer production in all but name. Marianne, as Sophy Kwyker, played a girl who escapes from an asylum to murder her cruel brother. It was the only film appearance of Vivian MacKerrell on whom the character Withnail was based in the 1987 film, *Withnail and I*. In the United States *Ghost Story* was re-titled, *Madhouse Mansion*. A marked improvement on *Girl On A Motorcycle* and considerably more mainstream than *Lucifer Rising*, it was a flawed but atmospheric thriller that marked a creditable return to acting for Marianne.

An incident in India, remembered and interpreted differently by both parties, became a portent for Marianne and Musker's relationship. In her autobiography, Marianne recalled Musker becoming 'increasingly testy' on a train journey between Bangalore and Delhi. She was reading E.M. Forster's *Howard's End* but Musker, who she said 'loved gossip', wanted to chat. 'Any withdrawal into one's self he considered an act of hostility. Oliver is sweet but a savage, really, very grand but completely uneducated,' she wrote. He snatched the book from her and threw it from the train window. In his account Musker said she was reading a different E.M. Forster novel, *A Passage To India*, and was 'becoming' the central lead character (presumably Adela Quested, the young British schoolmistress visiting India). "It was so annoying that I ripped it up and threw it in a waste paper bin," he said. On a more harmonious note, while in India they walked in the Kullu Valley at the foothills of the Himalayas with Robert Fraser, a friend of Musker's from Eton, who was living there with his mother, Cynthia. "It was beyond therapy, it was overwhelming. It was one of the best times of my life," said Marianne.

On her return to England, Marianne was invited to team up with David Bowie for a television spectacular, *The 1980 Floor Show* (which had futuristic connotations at the time), hosted at London's celebrated Marquee Club. The other guests were The Troggs and Carmen, an American band relocated to England that fused rock with flamenco. Bowie, now established as a major solo performer, was to revive his Ziggy Stardust persona for one last time in a performance screened across the United States by the NBC network as part of its *Midnight Special* series of rock programmes. It was recorded over three days on October 18, 19 and 20, 1973, and the audience comprised transvestites, gays and colourful figures drawn from Bowie's entourage and fan club. Marianne and Bowie sang a version of Sonny and Cher's 'I Got You Babe' to close the show. Her voice was raspy and she missed many of the notes but as a visual spectacle – at Bowie's request she wore a nun's habit complete with cowl while he was adorned in glitter and feathers as the 'Angel of Death' – the duo were compelling. Earlier in the show, which has never been broadcast in Britain, Marianne sang 'As Tears Go By' and a version of Noël Coward's 'Twentieth Century Blues'.

Marianne and Musker regularly visited David Bowie to spend evenings with him and his wife, Angie. One night after they had been drinking, Bowie began flirting with Marianne. They went into the corridor and Marianne unzipped his trousers and attempted to give him a blow job. Bowie was afraid they might be caught by Musker who, Marianne said, 'had this Gestapo vibe to him'. She told Bowie he need not be anxious, Musker would not have been upset and, had he discovered them, 'would have laughed'.

Musker was more usually considerate and supportive but at times he found Marianne infuriating and would rage. "She was very keen on Oliver to begin with, but then he became rather a bully and I don't think she liked that very much," said Henrietta Moraes. "She never liked anyone interfering in her professional life and Oliver tried to do just that. He was behaving as if he were her manager or something and she has always been absolutely private about that and quite determined to run her own life."

The various film and musical projects through 1972 and 1973 had improved Marianne's finances and she returned to London's fashionable retail haunts. "She was always broke," said Musker. "She is one of those people who never saves anything. I always thought it was her money and she could do what she wanted with it. Sometimes I did think she spent unnecessary amounts. It was irritating. I remember she once bought a pearl choker when she was completely broke – I hope she's still got it."

She bought herself a new wardrobe, much of it from Yves St Laurent. She was wearing an Yves St Laurent summer dress when she met the fêted American photographer Robert Mapplethorpe at a party held at Catherine Guinness' house in London. He shot her leaning awkwardly, sitting on the banister of a stairwell and it became another in a portfolio of relatively famous pictures of Marianne. "He was a really interesting guy and a very fashionable guy in London at the time," she said. "Oliver's the reason why I was dressing so sexily. And, of course, it was a party! It was a very happy time of my life. The photograph shows very clearly that I wasn't on drugs and hadn't been for a long time. I look so healthy in this picture. It's almost a society picture, which Robert didn't really do. Robert put me into the pose. Behind the staircase was a long drop. What I find interesting about the photograph is the modesty of the crossed legs and the abandon of the open arms. It's almost like there are two different bodies in this picture." The trademark blonde hair, now darkening to ochre, was cut shorter by society hairdresser Ricci Burns. The long hair had been an unmistakable badge of the young, pop star Marianne. By having it cut she was stressing her commitment to acting – it made her a more versatile prospect and reduced the risk of typecasting.

Marianne accepted another challenging role, appearing at the Hampstead Theatre which was housed in a large portable cabin and known for its innovative output. She played opposite Denholm Elliott in *Mad Dog*, a play written by the author Nicholas Salaman. The director was Patrick Garland, famous for a documentary he made in 1964 about Philip Larkin, *Down Cemetery Road*. He had earlier cast Marianne in *The Stronger*, a play he adapted for television. The photo-shoot to promote *Mad Dog* took place in a park close to the theatre in Swiss Cottage. Pictured alongside Elliott, who was 50 at the time, Marianne leaned against various trees with most of the buttons on her blouse undone. The play opened its short run in August 1973 to generally positive reviews and marked a relatively low-key return for Marianne.

Theatre roles were offered regularly and Marianne's next moved her back to familiar controversial territory. In 1965 when the Royal Court Theatre staged John Osborne's *A Patriot For Me* it was forced once more to change from a public theatre to a private members' club. The play had been deemed 'sexually transgressive' and denied a licence by the Lord Chamberlain's Office. Eight years later, in November 1973, *A Patriot For Me* was staged at the Palace Theatre, Watford, standing incongruously between shorts runs of *HMS Pinafore* and *Aladdin*. Marianne was cast as Countess Sophia Delyanoff in the true story of Alfred Redl, a Jewish homosexual in the Austro-Hungarian intelligence service of the 1890s. The final scene – the one that had most troubled the censor – was the 'Drag Ball' in which members of the upper tiers of Viennese society appeared in drag. The American novelist Mary McCarthy famously said of the play: "Its chief merit is to provide work for a number of homosexual actors, or normal actors who can pass as homosexual." Incidentally, two members of the cast at Watford went on to have leading parts in *Coronation Street* – John Savident (Fred Elliott) and David Nielson (Roy Cropper).

Marianne's next role was unexpected and has been largely written out of formal biographies. In December 1973 she signed up to play Alice in a pantomime production of *Alice In Wonderland* at the Theatre Royal, Brighton. She was due to appear alongside an impressive cast of players, which was customary before the arrival of television soap stars and celebrities into this theatrical realm. The formidable Peggy Mount was to be her principal co-star, alongside show business veterans Julian Orchard, Desmond Walter-Ellis, Raymond Francis and Dennis Ramsden. The ensemble was completed by Broadway regular American actor Kenneth Nelson and the ballet dancer Anton Dolin. On Friday December 14, after two weeks of rehearsal, it was announced that Marianne had pulled out of the panto and her place taken by local actress Jane Hayward. The *Brighton Evening Argus* reported that the decision had been reached following a 'talk' with the producer, Duncan Weldon, who was at the time married to another famous British female singer, Helen Shapiro. The official line was that Marianne felt 'she could not do the role justice and concentrate on two parts simultaneously' [the other being Sophia Delyanoff in *A Patriot For Me*].

She returned to the theatre in February 1974 when she was cast as Miranda Grey in the stage version of John Fowles' 1963 novel, *The Collector*. The story centres on Frederick Clegg, played by Simon Williams, who works as a clerk in a city hall. He collects butterflies and is obsessed with Miranda, a middle-class art student. He drugs her with chloroform and imprisons her in a remote house in the countryside. The novel had been turned into a film nine years earlier with Terence Stamp in the lead role. Simon Williams had starred in the hugely popular television series *Upstairs Downstairs*, playing the roguish son of the 'upstairs' household, Major James Bellamy.

During the days preceding the opening night, newspapers carried gossip about Marianne, although little of it was about the forthcoming production. A few weeks earlier she had revealed (although 'confirmed' might have been more apposite) that she had 'slept' with three members of The Rolling Stones. It soured the publicity calls for *The Collector* and as she posed for photographs with Simon Williams, talk was still of the Stones. 'Me And My Big Mouth' was the headline in the *Daily Express*, a heading drawn from Marianne's reply when asked why she had divulged the shenanigans with the Stones. Most of the gathered reporters failed to appreciate the irony when she commented: "Everything I do is inconsequential and unimportant. I flutter about and do nothing. That's what I am. I don't take life seriously. I just want to have a good time." The theatre's publicists needed a strong news angle and cajoled Marianne and Musker to announce their 'engagement'. "We went along with it. We had not really thought about it," said Musker. "I had not told my mother about what we were doing and she sent me a ring that had been in the family for years as an engagement present."

The play opened at the Wyvern Theatre, Swindon, on February 11, 1974 and ran for a week before moving to St Martin's Theatre in the West End where it failed to receive the critical acclaim needed to establish a long run. The *Daily Mirror's* reviewer, Arthur Thirkell, dubbed it a 'contrived, often clumsy, lightweight play'. Many had expected Marianne to disappoint but Thirkell took the opposite view:

'The play serves as little more than an extended audition in which Miss Faithfull clearly shows she has a talent ready for more convincing roles.'

The weighty role as half of a cast of two in *The Collector* drained Marianne and she became unsettled. She suspected that her name was being used chiefly to attract publicity and sell tickets. Directors were continually casting her as wan or tragic figures. The other actors were civil with her but she did not feel complete acceptance. After *The Collector* she decided to take a break and reconsider her professional career. "I think she is an excellent actress. The main reason she stopped was that she was offered crummy parts," said Musker. "The pay was pathetic as well; £50 a week – Marianne cannot operate like that. It was costing me £100 a week to keep her in work and eventually I said 'no more'. She was disillusioned because of the parts she was offered. It was not an exciting period for the British theatre in the mid-1970s and she did not want to be in things like *Confessions Of A Window Cleaner*. She had her standards." Theatre companies were also aware of Marianne's drug habit. "She had a history of being a junkie and it was one of the reasons she couldn't get work. It is difficult to get insurance for them and they are seen as unreliable. There are millions of actresses out there who are reliable and not junkies, so obviously they will get chosen," said Musker.

On Monday July 15, 1974 a journalist from the *Daily Express* spoke to the couple at a party held to celebrate 'Mama' Cass Elliott's opening night at the London Palladium. They revealed that a wedding date had been set for the autumn. "It will take place when the leaves turn brown – it suits our mood perfectly," said Marianne. Just two weeks later, Elliott died of heart failure at the age of 32.

Marianne and Musker flitted to several different flats in Chelsea. The only link with her former life as a pop star was the occasional fan letter that found its way through their letterbox. "She did not play her early records. I think she thought they were a bit of a joke to be honest. I don't think she found her style until she did *Broken English*," he said. "She used to get the regulation amount of love letters from prisons. She did not read many of the fan letters. I think I read more than she did. Most of the time we just lived as a normal couple. There were other people far more hedonistic than we were. Marianne did not like parties all that much. Some other person could party for 24 hours a day but no one notices it, but when Marianne does everyone knows about it. She has amazing powers of recuperation."

Friends advised Marianne to marry Musker but she knew instinctively that the marriage would not have worked. "I was lucky to have a nice man like Oliver who was in love with me and wanted to look after me, but I knew I was never going to fit into his aristocratic circle and he would regret marrying me sooner or later," she said. Musker later left England to set up Imperial Furniture Co. Pvt Ltd in Delhi, India, a bespoke furniture-making business. "I don't think we seriously considered marriage," he said. "We have still kept in touch and I am very fond of her. When we split up it was dramatic for about a minute but it was then amicable. We both agreed it was the time to finish."

12

Despite doubts over continuing her acting career, Marianne found an offer to appear in her mother's home city of Vienna irresistible. She was cast early in 1975 to play the lead role of Myrtle Ravenstock in the peculiar Tennessee Williams play *Kingdom Of Earth* [later re-titled *The Seven Descents Of Myrtle*]. The production was being staged by Vienna's English Theatre in its neo-baroque 250-seat auditorium on a picturesque cobbled side-street in the city. Established in 1960 by the Austrian director Franz Schafranek, the company had a reputation for attracting world-famous actors and casting them in intelligent, modern dramas. As Myrtle, Marianne was a former showgirl and occasional prostitute newly married to Lot, an impotent transvestite suffering from tuberculosis. They return to his ramshackle family home by a swollen river where Lot's half-brother, Chicken, begins to fall in love with Myrtle.

After just three performances, however, Marianne fell ill with peritonitis and had to be taken to hospital. Ruth Brinkmann, the American actress and wife of Schafranek, took her place. On the first evening she performed while cradling the script in her arms but by the second night she had learned all the lines. Marianne, meanwhile, decided while in hospital that she no longer wished to act. "I was doing a play I didn't like and I suddenly decided I hated the theatre, loathed the actors, and if this was supposed to be Great Art, I'd rather get back to recording and do something I enjoyed," she told *Creem* magazine in June, 1978.

Marianne made a gradual return to drug taking. Musker was no longer by her side encouraging her to stop and she began using heroin on a regular basis. She had not heard from her close friend Madeleine D'Arcy, for a few days and decided to call at her flat in Maida Vale. Madeleine had been a girlfriend of Tony Sanchez, accompanying him to France when he visited The Rolling Stones. Marianne took two male friends, both drug dealers, with her to the flat and after knocking several times, they broke down the door. Madeleine, aged 27, was dead on the bed, bruised and bloody, wearing a long gown. The two men left immediately and Marianne remained with the body for five hours before police arrived. "I was disgusted by the drug culture that night. I flushed everything down the lavatory in complete revulsion," she said. The inquest heard she had taken an excessive amount of methadone. The coroner, Dr Gavin Thurston, recorded a verdict of 'death due to drug overdose'. Marianne later channelled her feelings about her friend into 'Lady Madeleine', her first self-written song since 'Sister Morphine'.

In view of her evident disdain for the acting profession, friends were surprised in August 1975 when Marianne accepted a demanding acting role in a touring production taking up the best part of three months, embracing more than 70 performances. She was to play the lead role of Lizzie Curry in *The Rainmaker*, visiting 13 theatres, most with a capacity of about 400, at out-of-the-way places such as St Annes-on-Sea, Billingham and Wilmslow, where the play would run in blocks of six days. Written by N. Richard Nash, the play is set in an American drought-hit rural town in the West during the Depression. It tells the story of a pivotal hot summer day in the life of Lizzie Curry who keeps house for her father and two brothers on the family cattle ranch. A charming confidence trickster named Starbuck arrives and promises to bring rain in exchange for $100. His arrival sets off a series of events that causes Lizzie to see herself differently.

The production opened at the Richmond Theatre on September 8 to good reviews. Marianne appeared opposite Peter Gilmore, famous for playing James Onedin in the television series *The Onedin Line*. Marianne had successfully completed almost 50 performances when disaster struck on Monday November 3, 1975. The play was due to open at the Grand Theatre, Swansea. The venue, with a capacity of 1,000, was half full when the audience was told of a delay. Another announcement followed – Marianne Faithfull had 'failed to turn up'. As an act of conciliation, the cast went front-of-house to sign autographs. John Chilvers, the theatre manager, told the press afterwards that he was 'disgusted' and considered it unprofessional that an understudy had not travelled with the touring group. Audience members received refunds. As they left the building they saw Marianne arriving. She told them she had caught the wrong train from London. She asked whether she could apologise the following night but Chilvers vetoed the idea. He said the audience comprised a different set of people, so it was a worthless gesture.

Curiously, ticket sales for further shows were boosted as punters were intrigued to see whether Marianne would appear or not. As she took the stage the next night, there was a spontaneous round of applause. Despite the fiasco in Swansea, Marianne had shown a high level of commitment, as she pointed out to the press after the show's last performance in Wolverhampton on December 6: "I've done it. It's the first time I've been on the road like this. People said, 'She'll never last'. The fact that I got through means a lot to me." And on the non-appearance in South Wales, she said: "I missed my train, that's all!"

A return to music for Marianne was thwarted initially by a lack of interest from record companies. She had talks with Warner Bros but it declined to offer a deal because it had signed Emmylou Harris who was 'too similar' to Marianne. "They were terribly sweet. They said they had Emmylou Harris coming up. Well, I could understand that. What they were really thinking was: 'Poor thing, we must be nice to her or she'll go off and kill herself'," said Marianne. Tony Calder, Marianne's former manager, had been appointed CEO at NEMS Records and he signed her to the label. "I didn't know what I wanted to do, didn't know who I wanted to work with. I just wanted to start very quietly just to get the feel of it all, and for that NEMS was perfect," she told *Dark Star* magazine in 1979. "They gave me the contract partly out of pity, partly out of my name and partly out of the possibility that I may just, you know, they couldn't actually rule out that I might do quite well."

NEMS handled the European publishing of several American songwriters, among them Allen Reynolds who wrote for a string of country artists including Don Williams, Waylon Jennings and Crystal Gayle, and was later to produce most of the multi-million selling albums by Garth Brooks. When Calder heard Reynolds' song 'Dreaming My Dreams' [often listed as 'Dreamin' My Dreams' or 'Dreaming My Dreams For You'] he thought it perfect for Marianne. To best suit her lower singing register, she approached it in the style of a 'country and western Marlene Dietrich'.

In a long flowing green dress and with her hair hot-brushed back from her face, Marianne unveiled her new image for the first time when she appeared on the short-lived children's television programme *Supersonic* in September 1975. The song was released as a single to indifference throughout the world, apart from Ireland. It entered the Irish charts at number four on March 11, 1976 and made its way to number one for a week, replacing Sailor's 'A Glass Of Champagne' before being superseded by Tina Charles' 'I Love To Love'. The eight-week stay in the Irish Top 20 was principally down to the respected and influential broadcaster Pat Kelly, of RTÉ 1, who championed the record on his morning radio programme. "Getting into the charts was a kind of forgiveness," said Marianne. "We don't care what you did, we like it anyway. I don't know whether it's the church in Ireland or the drinking, but these people do know how to forgive."

The success in Ireland prompted NEMS to commission an album which, Marianne decided, would further explore country music, but with an element of Celtic and English folk roots. She had been listening to Hank Williams and songs recorded in the 1920s and 1930s by country's first major star, the yodeller Jimmie Rodgers. Five different producers worked on the record – Bill Landis, Bob Potter, Derek Wadsworth, John Worth and Mike Leander – and this inevitably gave it an uneven feel. Among the country-tinged songs, she covered Jackie DeShannon's 'Vanilla O'Lay' – 'an absolutely absurd pop jingle' according to

Marianne. She later said she had fallen for 'a typical Tony Calder scam'. She felt his priority was not the album itself but what he saw as a chance to showcase the various songwriters represented by NEMS, which led to such a hotchpotch of material. By far the most accomplished song on the album was the heartfelt 'Lady Madeleine' ('And Spanish Tony don't know what to do, he's missing you'), which laid the trail to Marianne's comeback proper a year later. It was the only track written by Marianne, who was helped with the musical arrangement by producer Bill Landis.

Dreaming My Dreams was released with little promotion, to a lukewarm reception. The response of Tony Mitchell writing in *New Musical Express* was typical: 'My advice to anyone who expected this to be a really spirited comeback brimming with new ideas is: forget it'. Down the years, Marianne has often reasserted that her aim was true: "I'm still not ashamed of my motives for making the record," she said. "It was a fascinating idea to try and do an English country album and if I had met an interesting producer then I feel sure that people would have picked up on it. We could have done a great album. It was terrible timing, quite a while before the country boom, no independent radio or anything, but I think we could have hit the country thing in such a weird way." The album was removed from sale a year after release. "They had no plan and no style at NEMS," said Marianne. "It was the most helpless, hapless record company you could imagine."

NEMS took two songs written by Allen Reynolds from the album and released them together as a single. 'All I Wanna Do In Life', an eccentric hybrid of country and calypso which he had co-written with Nashville's Sandy Mason Theoret, was notionally the A-side although the more traditional 'Wrong Road Again' received most airplay. Again, it charted in Ireland only, reaching number 11 on June 30, 1976. It left the charts two weeks later, marking Marianne's last ever appearance in the Irish singles chart.

Marianne decided to form a touring band to maximise her popularity in Ireland. Among the musicians set to audition was Ben Brierley. He called to see her but she was sitting at a large table eating a meal with friends. He felt awkward and shouted from the hall that he would return another time. On his next visit he strummed an acoustic guitar and they sang together The Everly Brothers' 'When Will I Be Loved'. "We did fantastic harmonies together," he said. "I thought, 'She's nice', but I wasn't bowled over by her, impressed or anything. I just wanted a gig, and we were musically compatible." Marianne liked him instantly. "He looked pale and interesting in that leather-jacketed, drug-addicted way," she said.

Before they had time to rehearse more songs, Brierley was stricken with a potentially fatal strain of hepatitis, an illness to which addicts are prone. While he was recovering in hospital he received a postcard from Marianne. "It said that she wanted to meet me, blah, blah. I think she fancied me!" He left hospital and moved into a friend's flat in Fulham where Marianne visited. In the space of three days they became lovers. "She slept on the sofa for a couple of nights. I suppose it was rather sweet. She wasn't going out with anybody at the time," he said.

Brierley was brought up in Reddish and West Gorton, working-class suburbs of Manchester. Although his name was Ian, he became known as Ben at an early age, possibly – he thinks – named after the 19th century Manchester writer Ben Brierley. His parents separated when he was young and he lived with his father, a works manager. He took up the guitar at school and was determined to enter the music business. "The industrial scene was still quite big then and most people in Manchester went into engineering. I didn't fucking want to be an engineer and I wasn't going to work in a factory. I left school without any qualifications. I just wanted to be in music," he said. While in Manchester he played in the beat group Tomorrow's Children, who had made their live debut at Reddish Vale School in December 1967 when Brierley was 15 years old. He played his last gig with them in June 1968.

Within weeks of moving to London in 1971, Brierley joined a group called Streak, newly signed to A&M Records for an advance of £10,000. They had been formed in New York by Alan Merrill and Jake Hooker but had relocated to Britain. "It was a massive advance at the time and basically we just spent it and had a good time," said Brierley. "We went to New York and bought lots of equipment, clothes, and all the usual pop star things. We were quite reckless really but when you are 21 and someone gives you a cheque like that, I don't know what they expect you to do with it." The band's debut single, on which Brierley played bass, was 'Gonna Have A Good Time', an assured rocking number similar in style to the New York Dolls. The group split, though later evolved, without Brierley, into the teen-marketed glam band The Arrows, who had three hits in Britain and their own television series on Granada TV.

Marianne moved into Brierley's flat and lived on the £100 per week she received from NEMS, most of which was spent on drugs. During the early 1970s, Brierley, much the same as Marianne, had progressed through 'musicians' drugs' such as dope, speed and cocaine, to heroin. At the time there were no government-sponsored media campaigns [these followed in the early 1980s] warning of the dangers of heroin. Public awareness was low and knowledge of the users' vocabulary – terms such as smack, horse, skag, H, junkie, fix, gear, high, cranked, score, digging, mainlining and rush – almost nil. Heroin was still a clandestine drug with a dubious chic, too expensive for the masses but a toxic secret for the few. "I thought it was normal to take drugs," said Brierley. "Everybody did it. I thought people were weird if they didn't use them."

A year into the habit, Brierley had contracted septicaemia and fell into a coma which caused him to be hospitalised. This often happened with addicts – the process of administering the drug into the body was a point of risk, as much as the substance itself. Blood clots could form near the insertion area and travel to the brain, cutting off oxygen supplies, or a dirty needle might introduce poisonous bacteria into the body. The large radial vein in the forearm was used mainly, with a tie put around the upper arm to make the veins swell and protrude through the skin. Scar tissue formed after time and veins often 'collapsed' which meant addicts had to inject via the large femoral vein in the groin or the jugular, or smaller veins in their ankles, hands and fingers. Women addicts have been known to insert needles into their breasts as an alternative to their forearms.

Both Marianne and Brierley were heavy users of heroin, if not addicts. They set up home in Lots Road, a rundown part of Chelsea. The squat belonged to an astrologer and beneath posters depicting astrological patterns, a mattress was the only item of furniture. The toilet was outside and did not work properly. There was no electricity or hot water. "It was an absolute shit-hole, just a dirty basement," said Brierley. "If they wanted to do a documentary on squats, it would be the perfect place." They had two cassette tapes, one of reggae music and the other, Lou Reed's *Berlin* album – a tragic rock 'opera' about a doomed couple, featuring drug use, depression, physical abuse and suicide. "We had no money, not a penny, but we were actually having a nice time together," he said. "We were very happy and very much in love. I must have been thick or something. She is quite a big name, but she was just Marianne to me. We would sometimes go out and meet some famous pop star who knew her and I would realise she was quite a famous person."

The squat was strewn with Brierley's guitar collection and he fell in and out of various bands. He earned a little money giving bass guitar lessons. Stuart Goddard, later to become Adam Ant, was one of his pupils. Their tape collection expanded and they played music constantly at the squat – James Brown, Otis Redding, Bessie Smith and Janis Joplin. Marianne was still mining country music through Waylon Jennings, Hank Williams and Willie Nelson. "Ben and I had two things in common: music and sex," she said. "It was the most passionate relationship of my life and, naturally, the one that caused me the most pain."

Brierley was soon made aware of the drawbacks of an association with Marianne Faithfull. At its crudest, it was the odd shout of "Where's the Mars bar then, Marianne?" but there were weightier issues. "Not to be unkind, but Marianne was a has-been pop star when I first knew her and the most famous thing she was known by was of being a junkie and Mick Jagger's girlfriend," he said. "She will never shake the thing about Jagger, just like I'll never shake the thing about being connected to Marianne Faithfull. I think time magnifies it. It's all that 60s legend crap. I find it a big yawn, personally."

Newspapers sporadically descended upon them, usually hunting down a new angle on the Jagger story. "They would ask me the size of his dick and all that stuff. I would tell them I didn't know, because I never asked Marianne about Jagger anyway," he said. They awoke one morning to find a newspaper photographer standing at their window. Brierley hurled a shoe at him. He was sometimes offered money for the 'inside' story of Marianne, which he has resisted.

Brierley could hardly compete with the living legend of Jagger but an optimistic few, including Eva Faithfull, felt he should at least try. "Eva was a bit of a showbiz mum," he said. "She used to show me pictures of Jagger and look at me knowingly as if to say, 'This is what you should be doing, Ben. Why aren't you a star like this?' I think her mother liked me but thought I was a hopeless case, a ne'er do well." Brierley twice met Jagger – at a fashion show hosted by Ossie Clark, where Brierley was put off by Jagger's feigned heavy south London accent, and at the Electric Lady Studios in New York. Jagger had called to see Marianne and spent time chatting to Brierley. They later sang together at a piano.

A new movement began stirring in London's more run-down, intimate clubs during the end of 1975 and beginning of 1976. Bands were wearing their hair shorter, speeding up the music and showing disdain for intricate arrangements and virtuoso playing. The lyrics were focused and heartfelt – they were singing their lives. The term 'punk' had first been used to describe garage bands in the United States during the late-1960s and became the catch-all phrase for the new movement on both sides of the Atlantic. Ben Brierley, the same as thousands of other struggling musicians, fixed his hair spiky with sugar, pinned button badges to the lapel of his leather jacket and began wearing narrow trousers and baseball boots. He did not subscribe particularly to the anti-musicianship of punk but valued the energy and the sweeping away of musical pomposity. He was soon mixing and playing music with figures that would form the hierarchy of this new scene.

Brierley's new focus made for a strained home life where he felt Marianne's shadow was cast large over his own dreams. She even managed the unlikely feat of securing a finger-hold on the punk movement. The *Sunday People* informed its readers on September 18, 1977: 'Marianne To Star In A Punk Movie'. The piece began: 'One of the world's most controversial stars of the Sixties has new shocks up her sleeve…' The director of the film about The Sex Pistols, *Who Killed Bambi?*, was to be Russ Meyer, best known for madcap soft-porn movies such as *Beyond The Valley Of The Dolls* (one of Marianne's 'favourite films in the world') and his fixation with voluptuous women – one critic wrote that he viewed the female body as a 'tit transportation device'. In the film Marianne was to play the mother of Sid Vicious, viewed at the time as Britain's most obnoxious citizen and someone with whom Marianne shared a drugs dealer. The role involved a sex scene where she would 'romp naked' with her 'son', Sid. "The lads are all old mates of mine, so it'll be fun," she told the papers. Marianne had an instinctive understanding of punk. "I knew Johnny Rotten. He liked me," she told *Mojo* in 2005. "He always liked older women! I knew Malcolm [McLaren]. I knew a lot of people in that world. The essence of the punk thing was anyone can go and do it if they want to, and you don't have to be incredibly rich and grand, you can just do it."

Who Killed Bambi? was abandoned just a couple of days into shooting. The financier, 20th Century Fox, was reportedly shocked by the script and pulled out. The film was originally titled *Anarchy In The UK* and was intended as a punk riposte to The Beatles' *A Hard Day's Night*. The famous American film critic and long-time Meyer cohort, Roger Ebert, had scripted it with assistance from Malcolm McLaren. Two years later, McLaren revived the idea and made *The Great Rock 'N' Roll Swindle* with Julien Temple as director. Marianne teased the press: "It would have been a very controversial film and I'd have got a lot of nasty letters saying, 'You dirty little bitch – we all thought you'd reformed and you haven't'. And, of course, I have as far as drug taking is concerned. But basically, I suppose I'm still a dirty little girl. I like to shock people. Not as much as I once did, but it still appeals to me."

Occasionally, Brierley and Marianne humoured reporters, with inevitable results. He began using the stage name Ben E. Ficial, but when a *Sun* reporter called to see them, he fibbed that he was called Tommy Trouble. 'Marianne's Got Tommy Trouble' ran the heading. In between his musical ventures Brierley worked as a 'dustman', according to Marianne. "Ben collects then flogs the stuff the council won't handle," she told *Zigzag* in December, 1979.

Brierley was in a pub in the King's Road one day when he met the songwriter Tim Hardin. A contemporary of Greenwich Village folk writers such as Phil Ochs, Tom Paxton and Paul Simon, Hardin spoke enthusiastically about plans to revisit his better days, the mid-1960s, when he had written forceful pop/folk numbers such as 'If I Were A Carpenter' and 'Reason To Believe', the standard Marianne and many others had covered. He returned to the squat with Brierley who was keen for him to write a song for Marianne. Hardin agreed to do so, in exchange for being allowed to stay with them for a while. Marianne found him 'self-pitying' and as 'irritating as hell'. Whenever she asked if he wanted a drink, he responded: 'three Southern Comforts with pills, please.' Hardin was heavily addicted, taking regular heroin and cocaine cocktails, and was unable to concentrate for more than a few seconds. He promised to finish the song he was working on, called 'Brain Drain' (in truth all he had was a title), if he was in a sunnier climate. So, Brierley, Hardin and Brierley's friend, John Porter, formerly a bass player with The Gas Board – the band that became Roxy Music – and later producer of The Smiths, travelled to Antigua. They achieved little of note although Brierley completed 'Brain Drain', albeit on his own because Hardin was so incoherent he could barely speak.

In dire need of money, Marianne and Brierley approached NEMS with the idea that they form a band to tour Europe. They were given an advance and had six weeks to assemble a backing group. Brierley was to play bass although he was previously reluctant to collaborate musically with Marianne. "I honestly didn't want to be in her shadow, I did not want to be known as Marianne Faithfull's sidekick," he said. One of the first to audition was Barry Reynolds, a guitar player who was to remain by Marianne's side for most of the rest of her career. "The minute I met him I knew he was a great musician and someone I could work with," she said.

Reynolds was born in Bolton, Lancashire, and had been part of a vibrant music scene in north-west England, playing with groups such as Ivan's Meads and The Measles in the mid-1960s. He was a member of The Sponge, signed to a management deal with Kennedy Street Enterprises, which secured them a record contract with Nova Records, a label launched by Decca to promote progressive music. The Sponge had previously been the resident band at the Jokers Wild club at the Atlantis Resort, Nassau, in the Bahamas and this location inspired a name change to Pacific Drift. The album, *Feelin' Fine*, was released in January 1970 and described by *Disc & Music Echo* as 'a sound somewhere between the Small Faces and Jethro Tull'. Reynolds had written or co-written 13 of the songs, several of which had been influenced by William Blake, one of Marianne's favourite writers. The album was met with public indifference and in September 1970 Reynolds joined the blues outfit Blodwyn Pig. He spent two years with them before moving to the United States. Back in England, he was looking for a new musical project when he walked into the rehearsal studio in Chelsea where Marianne was conducting auditions.

The tour was focused mainly in Holland and began at the Paradiso Club in Amsterdam where Marianne was support to Southside Johnny & the Asbury Jukes, a band with strong links to Bruce Springsteen. A press reception was held at a hotel in the afternoon before the show and Marianne began drinking brandy. By the time of the concert she was very drunk. While the band played the introduction to their cover of The Velvet Underground's 'Sweet Jane' she watched from the wings, missing several cues to take the microphone. When she eventually stirred, she tripped over cables trailing across the stage and fell flat on her face. After the concert Brierley was furious and berated her. She told him: "Ben, you don't understand. It's all theatrics."

During Marianne's absence from live performance, the mood and attitude to music had altered drastically. The audience did not want practised perfection or a conventional 'show'. It demanded honesty, the true-to-life version of a performer. Marianne, with her raw, thrown-together music and erratic vocals, epitomised the spirit of punk. She was, at 31, a little older than most of her contemporaries on the scene but looked younger than her years and had the apposite mixture of insouciance and snarl, especially when in drink.

Marianne argued often with Brierley while on tour. She acknowledged that he was a good songwriter but a 'useless' bass player who was 'just about good enough for a punk band'. He was, in fact, playing in various punk-inspired groups. He was a member of The Blood Poets who quickly evolved into the Front. Andrew Lipka, a former bouncer/bar man at the punk venue the Roxy Club in Neal Street, Covent Garden, had formed the group. Lipka adopted the stage name of Drew Blood and with Brierley on bass (listed on the sleeve as Tommy Trouble) they released a single on a label – called 'The Label' – run by Dave Goodman, the Sex Pistols' early live sound engineer and producer of their demos. Also playing on the record was John Porter and Bryson Graham, formerly the drummer with Spooky Tooth. The single, 'System'/ 'Queens Mafia', was released in February 1978 wrapped in an archetypal montage picture sleeve. The music within was similar punk orthodoxy – fast, raw and with shouty vocals on an anti-establishment theme: 'Working for government trash/ making some fat man's cash/ Spending your time going out of your mind/ where in the world are you gonna find time?' Curiously, three musicians who played with the Front were to each have relationships with famous women. Lipka had a three-year affair with Angie Bowie, ex-wife of David Bowie, during which time they had a daughter, Stacia; John Porter married Keith Richards' former girlfriend, Linda Keith; and, of course, Brierley was with Marianne.

The squat in Lots Road became one of several gathering points dotted around London for members of the burgeoning scene. "Ben put me in touch with musicians again, with people who thought musically and played all the time," said Marianne. "This was just what I needed." Brierley became friends with Greg Van Cook, a guitarist living with future Police drummer, Stewart Copeland. Van Cook had co-written the punk classic 'Fuck Off' with Wayne [later Jayne] County, and invited Brierley to join him in a new line-up of The Vibrators. The group, fronted by Ian 'Knox' Carnochan, had been in the first wave of punk, forming in March 1976. They had recorded a session for John Peel in October 1976 and supported Iggy Pop in March 1977 on his British tour. Their single 'Automatic Lover' reached 35 in the chart and earned them an appearance on *Top Of The Pops*. Carnochan explained the appeal of both Brierley and Van Cook: "The line-up before they joined felt too 'safe'. It didn't have a danger kinda feel, so Eddie [John

'Eddie' Edwards, the band's drummer] and I sacked them and got Ben on bass and Greg on guitar. They were actually *very* dangerous – good players but too out of control! We played Dingwalls one night and the manager was going on about what a terrible gig it was. I think they were a bit drunk."

Off stage, the new line-up blended well. "We all thought Ben was quite a nice bloke," said Edwards. "He chats a bit. Marianne always seemed a natural person. She's got a bit of a posh voice but when you get used to it, she's easy to talk to." The band was aware of Brierley's heroin use but he was committed and went missing on only a few occasions. Six months after Brierley had joined, Carnochan mentioned possibly making a solo album and this precipitated the group splitting up. They closed with a farewell concert at The Marquee at the end of 1978 although the original line-up re-formed in 1982. "Every time Ben got a band together, something would happen where it would be fucked," said Marianne. "He didn't get along with people."

The two chart hits in Ireland generated sufficient interest for Marianne to undertake a tour of the country. The first date was in the civic splendour of the Isaac Butt Memorial Hall in the small town of Ballybofey, County Donegal. Tony Wilson of *Sounds* was one of only a handful of writers to attend the concert. He remarked on her nervousness and the 'dry, cracked vocals' but concluded: 'Once she's settled into her tour there will be a lot more confidence in her performance'. Henrietta Moraes was invited by Marianne to join the tour party. "It was hard to get her on to the stage," she said. "We had to shove her on and her voice was pretty hopeless at the time. Everyone over there adored her, it didn't seem to matter what she did. They just saw her as this little convent girl. She was taking too much smack. It is something I never took because it makes you feel so ill. I had to get her up, make sure she was at places on time, and make her laugh. There was no way she could organise herself at the time or look after herself."

The tour criss-crossed the country and was undertaken on a small budget. Nerves and friendships frayed and arguments broke out, usually about payment. Venues were often packed but the fees sometimes less than £300. Most nights they stayed at Castletown House, the pile in Celbridge, County Kildare, owned by Marianne's old friend Desmond Guinness. It was run-down, with no electricity and a leaking roof. Marianne was in no state to resolve the petty disagreements and one night, exasperated after a row, she took a handful of pills and spent the show crawling around the stage on her hands and knees. The band were apprehensive of playing in Belfast and Marianne had to guarantee them £200 each – what she termed 'danger money' – before they agreed to play. The band eventually mutinied and Brierley flew over to Dublin with a few musician pals to complete the remaining dates on the tour.

Money was needed by Marianne to continue with her music and a close friend of hers and Brierley, Isabella Dulaney, loaned her £3,000. Dulaney was known to everyone as 'Missy' as she came from Mississippi in the United States. "Missy gave Marianne a hell of a lot of support," said Brierley. "She was financing rehearsals and she found a flat for me and Marianne. I think she had got the money from her parents, who were quite rich. She never got a penny back. Marianne had the money, but she never gave it back. Marianne is not very good at giving credit to people. She likes taking all the credit herself, and Missy is a classic case. Marianne is quite ruthless and very, very ambitious when it comes to her career." Marianne did not mention Dulaney in her two autobiographies but she was thanked on her next album.

Barry Fantoni met Marianne by chance at the bohemian Chelsea Arts Club where she was enjoying a drink with Brierley. She was in a cheerful mood, throwing her arms around Brierley and kissing him without self-consciousness. "Ben looked a bit of a rogue but you could tell Marianne really liked him," said Fantoni. Despite the apparent amiability, Brierley was sometimes uneasy outside his own circle of friends. He came into contact with John Dunbar through Marianne's meetings with Nicholas and disliked his manner. "Dunbar used to get on my nerves a bit," he said. "I got the impression that John Dunbar thinks that everybody else is stupid. He has never seemed to get it together since Marianne left him. Personally, I quite like him but I always thought he was laughing at me, and other people as well. He is a hippy. He's got the social security well sussed. He's got the John Lennon glasses and everything.You know:'Let's have a spliff, man.' He still says 'man'. I remember Nicholas saying to me that you'd have thought his first word was 'man' and not 'mam' when he was a baby."

Nicholas was approaching his teenage years when Marianne met Brierley and it took a while for them to bond. Brierley gave him guitar lessons and felt he shared a little of his father's condescending nature. "I think I was an embarrassment to him. It was certainly very difficult to get on with him at the start," said Brierley. While Marianne was relatively academic, Brierley was street-wise. "I think she likes people to think she is an intellectual. I used to find her skipping a few chapters of Proust and pretending to have read the lot. I think she *is* very clever but I think she has pretensions to be an intellectual. She convinced me a few times that she knew what she was talking about! She used to say to me 'You mustn't say that word, or use such a phrase, because it is very working-class'. She was quite proud of having blue blood in her veins and was not averse to talking about her background."

Marianne felt ready once more to face a London audience and two shows were booked in the autumn of 1978, at The Music Machine in Mornington Crescent and Dingwalls, Camden Lock. As part of the low-key promotion Marianne was featured in 'My Weekend' in the London *Evening Standard*. She revealed: "On Sunday mornings I like to go to the Tate. I wander around the modern bit, obviously the Turners, but I also like the surrealists." Fans had no real idea what to expect at the shows. They had read of her relationship with a punk called Tommy Trouble and gossip column dispatches of her spotted at gigs by newcomers such as the reggae band Merger and NEMS-signed punks, The Boys.

The set was short, comprising nine songs. They opened once more with 'Sweet Jane' and ran through similar bluesy numbers such as the Marsha Hunt hit 'I Walk On Gilded Splinters' and Nick Lowe's 'Music For Money'. The only link with Marianne's back catalogue was a dirge-like run-through of 'As Tears Go By' where Barry Reynolds sang the opening lines in a monotone. They played several new songs that would be honed later for the *Broken English* album. The concerts left the music press bemused. James Parade of the *New Musical Express* admitted that he had attended 'not sure whether to expect punk, new, old, boring old farts, an act, or what', but decided it 'was 'all rather disappointing, anyway'. Ian Birch of *Melody Maker* was one of the first to discern a new image and musical style that was to become Marianne's trademark. In her studded leather choker and Lana Turner-styled wraparound, he dubbed her 'the elegantly ravaged outsider' and remarked that she appeared to be moving in the 'Edith Piaf direction'.

The relationship between Marianne and Brierley was volatile and, for the first time in her life, Marianne said she often felt 'searing jealousy'. "He was a gorgeous guy," she said. "And dreadful women were always coming on to him. It was absolute torment." On his part, Brierley felt secure and they decided to marry. "We used to make each other laugh," he said. "And that was a strong part of our relationship. It never entered my head that she would want anyone else but me. When her mum mentioned marriage, I thought, 'Why not?'."

The couple posed briefly for pictures outside Chelsea Register Office on Friday June 8, 1979 – Brierley, 27, dark haired, a black suit, a cigarette hanging limply from his right hand and Marianne, 32, fair, in a wide brimmed hat, silk dress, sandals with ankle straps, one arm linked to her new husband and the other gripping a small bunch of flowers. "Ben is a very good fellow. I expect to be with him for the rest of my life," she told the *Daily Mirror*. Among the wedding guests was Johnny Rotten, happy to bow to convention in a suit.

13

The wind blew fiercely across the racecourse at Newbury, Berkshire. Mark Miller Mundy searched for his friends, peering into hoods pulled tightly around faces. He came across a small hunched figure in a long fur coat. He identified the woman as Marianne Faithfull and discovered that she had travelled to the point-to-point horse-racing meeting in search of the same people as himself, so they immediately had mutual friends. "I gave her a lift home to her mother's," he said. "There were a lot of country and western tapes in my car and we got talking and found that we both had a love for it. In those days, there weren't a lot of people who had heard of country and western, let alone knew much about it. It turned out later that apparently Marianne had nothing on under the fur coat!"

Miller Mundy, a graduate of Oxford University, had made a late entrance into the music business after befriending his neighbour, Steve Winwood. The multi-instrumentalist who first emerged as the teenage star of the Spencer Davis Group was establishing himself as a solo performer after the final split from Traffic in 1975. "Island Records could not persuade him to work but I had an idea about doing some tracks and he said he wanted to get involved and help," said Miller Mundy. "I wouldn't say I played a very great role in his life but I think I was just the catalyst to get him moving. I think my enthusiasm triggered him off."

Through his work with Winwood, Miller Mundy was introduced to Island Records' founder and chairman, Chris Blackwell, who gave him a brief to 'find new talent'. Miller Mundy kept in touch with Marianne and went to see her play at The Music Machine. He was impressed by a song she performed called 'Why D'Ya Do It'. "It was so obviously brilliant," he said. "It was so powerful. Remember, it was the punk era. There was a lot of anger, a lot of passion coming out of music, but most of it was misdirected. It had no real cohesion, a lot of it was pseudo-anarchic – it was spouting forth. But 'Why D'Ya Do It' was really pertinent, strong, powerful, vicious, and obviously very sincere. The band played it very well and Marianne sang it with an enormous amount of feeling."

'Why D'Ya Do It' was originally a poem written by the old Etonian, Heathcote Williams, who had dated Jean Shrimpton. He was a polymath working across several mediums – poetry, journalism, painting, sculpture, magic, play-writing, street art and, later, conservationism – who in 1988 published the feted book-length poem *Whale Nation*. He had first performed 'Why D'Ya Do It' at a reading in Amsterdam in 1968. An outpouring of crude sexual jealousy, it contained numerous expletives and crystallised exactly how Marianne felt, especially about Brierley. "It just expressed all my anger, rage and fury for everything for the last 15 years," Marianne told *Dark Star* in 1979. "I only understood sexual jealousy like that three years ago. The song came to represent all my anger, which is why the voice is so powerful and the whole thing is so powerful."

Williams was aware that the poem suited a musical context and had earmarked it for Mick Jagger or Tina Turner. Marianne used all her guile to ensure it became her song. She visited Williams and told him: "I would die to sing these lyrics, Heathcote." She resorted to high drama when he reiterated that they might better suit Tina Turner. Marianne began laughing uncontrollably and told him: "Hell will freeze over before Tina would do a song like this. Let me do it and I will nail it, darling. You don't need a black singer to authenticate this. It's the real thing already." It took four hours for Marianne to wrestle from him what she called her 'Rosetta Stone'. "He didn't have a clue, he sold the publishing outright, he was a complete innocent," she said.

Ben Brierley had heard the song evolve over many months and had a different perspective. "I think there was a lot of unnecessary hoo-ha about it," he said. "I thought it was funny, not particularly profound. It is a poem about sexual jealousy but if you knew Heathcote Williams you would laugh because he is a very funny guy; very intelligent. Avant garde is French for bullshit, John Lennon said that, and I agree."

Miller Mundy was determined to commit the song to tape but was aware of the disillusionment in the band. "They had fallen out. They hadn't had much sleep in Ireland and had earned virtually nothing," he said. "There was a huge row and they were pissed off and said they did not want to play together again. I knew at this point that it was really important that whatever happened, we had to get them back together again because they had to put down 'Why D'Ya Do It'. To me, it seemed that if the band had disappeared and Marianne had gone her own way, there was a good chance it would be heard by no one apart from the people who went to those few gigs." Miller Mundy felt Brierley played a vital role. "Ben was very influential in getting Marianne to act with integrity. He was like her conscience. She is given to flights of intellectual fantasy. She has got quite heavy pretensions but Ben was a contribution to her honesty. There were no frills on her at that time. She was very honest, very direct," he said.

At first Miller Mundy wanted to augment the line-up with stellar players, mentioning Keith Richards and the legendary reggae rhythm section of Robbie Shakespeare and Sly Dunbar. Marianne cut short his reverie: "We fucking will not!" she told him. "We will use the band, *my* band." The 'band' comprised Marianne, Barry Reynolds, Joe Mavety (guitar), Steve York (bass) and Terry Stannard (drums). Miller Mundy volunteered to pay the recording costs of the demo, with himself as producer, booking them into Matrix Studios, a former dairy in Little Russell Street, Bloomsbury, where bands recorded in windowless, underground rooms. It was the studio of choice for many on the punk and new wave scene, among them Adam and the Ants, Gary Numan and XTC. After recording the vocals for 'Why D'Ya Do It' Marianne slumped exhausted to the floor. Miller Mundy was aghast at the power emitted from such a small frame. "The song was there before we even started the overdubs, it was so strong. When Marianne had finished, there was static electricity coming off the walls," he said.

Miller Mundy wanted the session to provide at least enough material for a single, so they recorded another song, 'Broken English'. Brierley had spoken to Marianne many times of a desire to write a song about the Baader-Meinhof Gang [aka Red Army Faction], the left-wing German terrorist group. It had been particularly active through 1977, killing several police officers, the director of the Dresdner Bank, Jürgen Ponto and the federal prosecutor-general, Siegfried Buback. "I beat Ben to it," said Marianne. She claimed to identify with Ulrike Meinhof, the former journalist who had co-founded the terrorist cell and was found hanged in prison in 1976. "The same blocked emotions that turn some people into junkies turn others into terrorists," she said. Marianne had picked up the phrase 'broken English' when she watched a Russian film on television with English subtitles.

The two songs were taken into Island by Miller Mundy and played to Chris Blackwell. "He liked it straight away and said, 'What do you want?' He more or less gave us a carte blanche, or should I say, he gave *me* one," said Miller Mundy. "I went back to the band and said: 'You're on'. Blackwell wasn't frightened of her. He has handled some tricky people in the past. Marianne had a willingness to get out there and play." Brierley was drawn to the project, though he wanted to concentrate on his own work. He sat in at many sessions at Matrix during the six months of recording, often playing guitar and singing. "Miller Mundy had an unfortunate attitude to musicians. I mean, really he should have been in the army," said Brierley. "He knew nothing about music except that he liked it. He was very good but he used to rub musicians up the wrong way. He used to make Marianne cry. He was a bully, and I didn't like him for that." Marianne was similarly forthright about Miller Mundy. "He turned out to be disappointing as a producer as well as a flaming arsehole," she said. She credited the engineer, Bob Potter, with shaping much of the sound.

After three weeks of recording backing tracks, Miller Mundy suggested Steve Winwood might provide an extra dynamic. Winwood had known Marianne for more than 15 years. They had first met as teenagers at various television studios as they waited to promote their new singles – Winwood had joined the Spencer Davis Group at the age of 14. Shortly after the London showcase concerts, Winwood had seen Marianne perform a one-off concert in his home city of Birmingham and been astonished by the power and tension she created. His own career had lost momentum under the onslaught of punk. "Steve went on to play a major part in the album," said Miller Mundy. "The thing about Steve is that if he thinks the music is good and honest, he'll play with anybody. He liked Marianne and was full of admiration for her as an artist." Marianne welcomed Winwood to the sessions on the condition that she could 'sit on his head' to ensure he did not 'over sweeten, over electrify or over synth' the sound.

Steve Winwood spent four days proffering a variety of sounds on the keyboards and synthesizers at Matrix. He was given instructions such as 'make it schizophrenic' on 'The Ballad Of Lucy Jordan'. "He gave the tracks character, their mood. It is hard to translate some of the work he did but some of it was genius," said Miller Mundy. "There was some really inspired playing from the whole band and singing from Marianne and I have not heard an LP like it, by anyone else, before or since." A much less successful addition was Bob Mothersbaugh, lead guitarist with Devo. Miller Mundy had seen him perform in concert and was impressed by the way he chopped at his guitar to layer disjointed lead patterns. Marianne later said his contribution was 'pitiful' and was delighted when her regular guitarist, Barry Reynolds, 'nailed it in one take'.

Marianne drank heavily during the recording and was inebriated when she performed the final take of 'The Ballad Of Lucy Jordan' and John Lennon's 'Working Class Hero'. Her drunkenness added to the naked force but it meant a few lines had to be dropped into the mix afterwards to disguise the odd slurred word. "Once the guide vocals were done we did not see her very much. She was not very interested in the mechanics of over-dubbing," said Miller Mundy. "She'd come in every now and again. She did not care whether we put a harmony vocal on the track or anything else. She'd already put a hell of a lot of feeling into the lyrics and just wanted the tracks to sound real. She trusted us. She was an old hand and knew we were working with the top guys." Indeed, the band comprised several seasoned musicians, each dating back to the Beat group movement of the 1960s, which had indirectly spawned Marianne. Steve York had played with Manfred Mann, Vinegar Joe and Eric Clapton; Joe Mavety, a Canadian, had played with Roxy Music, Dr Hook and Joe Cocker; and Terry Stannard had co-founded the 10-piece Kokomo, a much-touted British soul band of experienced personnel who released three albums in the 1970s and who helped Bob Dylan record his 1975 album, *Desire*, although only one track featuring them appeared on the finished record.

The album *Broken English* took six months to record and when it was delivered to Chris Blackwell he felt the promise of the earlier demo tape had been realised. He guaranteed that the label would give the record its full support. Blackwell was aware that Marianne needed to be re-branded to suit her new sound and commissioned a series of photographers, among them David Bailey, Barry Lategan and Clive Arrowsmith, to produce a shot suitable for the cover. They each failed to supply a definitive image so a session was booked with Dennis Morris, Island's art director and himself a respected photographer. "Marianne said 'Do you know who I am? This will make you' and suggested we had a drink," he said. They called at a pub near Notting Hill tube station where Morris was the only black man. "She announced, loud enough for the entire room to hear: 'I am not some cheap hooker, you know – it is going to cost you at least £200.'" They moved on to an Italian restaurant where, after eating their meals, Marianne pushed over the table and told Morris: 'Don't pay, the food was terrible.' Back at the studio, loaded with a carrier bag full of wine and cigarettes bought from an off licence, Marianne emerged from the dressing room and, according to Morris, asked him: "Do you want to fuck me?" Morris said 'no' and she responded: "You'll be the first." She then proceeded to roll around the floor. "I had listened to her album and had a setting in my head, which was quite simple: just an armchair and two lights," he said. "I wanted to capture her husky, evocative voice. If you look at the picture used for the cover, it was actually one frame. It was never posed. She was smoking a cigarette and I caught the moment." Asked by the

Daily Mail in June, 2010, whether they made love after the session, Morris said: "I made my excuses and left. I've regretted it ever since."

Controversy was anticipated over 'Why D'Ya Do It' and it quickly arrived. EMI, the company that pressed and distributed Island's product, refused to handle the master tapes. Island removed the song from its position as the opening number on the album but even relegated to the closing track, EMI refused to budge. Blackwell negotiated with several other companies and found an alternative pressing and distribution network. "People seem to think we recorded it deliberately to cause a stir," said Marianne. "To cause a sensation, make people buy the record because it's a dirty song. And that really pisses me off because it had nothing to do with it. Those things may be there, and I'm glad if it does have that effect, but that's just a bit of luck."

By the late 1970s public opinion had warmed considerably to Marianne. Many erroneously saw her as the rejected figure in the Jagger affair, a misconception furthered by the attempted suicide. The innumerable drugs busts and drunken episodes invoked sympathy as much as they did the censure of old. Two newspapers representing opposite strands of British culture gave positive early notices to *Broken English*. *The Sun* ran a feature by Nina Myskow headlined 'Jagger's Bird Bounces Back' while in *The Guardian*, Robin Denselow profiled 'a singer who found fame first, talent later' in a feature titled: 'Forever Faithfull, back in the groove'.

Rob Partridge, Island's head of press, had been briefed on the importance of *Broken English* and how it should be presented to the media. "I did not want her fossilised in the 60s as some kind of museum curio when she was making the most important music in her career," he said. "She was hitting a very new audience. Some of the journalists aged about 23 and 24 had not heard her earlier stuff." He arranged interviews principally with the broadsheets. "The tabloids were invariably obsessed with the Jagger connection and I tried to steer them clear of her. They still think, after all these years, that there is some story involving Jagger and her that hasn't been heard. I wanted to establish a critical consensus for the album because we knew it was an LP of consequence. Chris [Blackwell] did not work on a day-to-day basis at the label but he was very involved in *Broken English* and was enormously proud of the record. The budget was fairly substantial," said Partridge.

Broken English was released on Friday, November 2, 1979. Many years later, Marianne explained its magnitude to *Mojo* magazine. "I gave myself permission to make a record that I'd wanted to make for a long time. I thought I was going to die, that this was going to be my last chance. That is the thing about *Broken English*, it's this sense, this energy, that 'Fucking hell, before I die I'm going to show you bastards who I am.' That's what it is. It has a lot of attitude. And of course that's why I can never do that again. I can't repeat *Broken English*. Because I actually realised, obviously I'm going to die but not yet."

The album contained just eight songs, running to under 38 minutes, and included two cover versions, 'The Ballad Of Lucy Jordan' and 'Working Class Hero'. Shel Silverstein, the multi-talented poet, playwright, musician and children's author, had written 'The Ballad Of Lucy Jordan'. He was a regular supplier of songs for Dr Hook & the Medicine Show and they had released it as a single in 1974. Lee Hazlewood had also included it on his album of 1975, *20th Century Lee*. Marianne said she identified strongly with the character, Lucy Jordan. "She is me if my life had taken a different turn," she said. "If I'd become Mrs Gene Pitney, for instance, and ended up in a big, empty house in Connecticut. It's a song of identification with women who are trapped in that life and the true private horror of the 'good life', the one women are meant to aspire to."

'Working Class Hero' was drawn from John Lennon's first post-Beatles album of 1970, *John Lennon/Plastic Ono Band*, and seemed an odd song for Marianne to choose. "I sent John a copy, I never got a reply, and then he was shot [December 8, 1980]," she said. "He didn't really have very long to reply, did he? But he did listen to it and he told Yoko that he really loved it. And every time I see Yoko she never ever fails to tell me how much John really loved it. There were people who said to me, 'How dare you do this song, you're not working-class.' But it's not about that. It goes beyond that. I have every right to sing that song. I would say our lives were pretty parallel, me and John. I didn't actually have as many tragedies in my childhood as he did, but John got exactly what I was doing." She also viewed the song as a tribute to friends she defined as 'working class heroes' – Mick Jagger, Keith Richards, Iggy Pop and David Bowie.

'Brain Drain' was the song written by Ben Brierley with help from Tim Hardin, although Brierley was registered as sole songwriter. Hardin was in no fit state to notice at the time and died in December 1980 of a heroin overdose. Marianne thought Brierley's behaviour over this issue was 'really dreadful' and 'typical of his small-time, hustling mentality'. She acknowledged his generosity, however, in allowing her to record the track. "I just take what's offered and move on. I don't think twice," she said. "I suppose my way of repaying him was to buy him expensive guitars and clothes." 'Witches Song' [on records it has also been listed as 'Witche's Song' and 'Witches' Song'] was Marianne's 'sisterhood' number, heavily influenced by her mother's experiences and personality. "Eva had a very light, loving side and its ominous twin, a very dark side indeed," she said. 'Guilt', a track written by Barry Reynolds, had a choppy, engineered feel not dissimilar to Steely Dan but with a gentle twist to the lyrical hookline of 'Like a curious child, just give me more, more, more'. "Barry is a recovering Catholic," said Marianne. "I identified with 'Guilt' immediately. It's my mantra and I knew whereof it came."

Although peppered with guitar solos 'What's The Hurry?' was typical of the techno-punk finding favour in the music press and played regularly on John Peel's seminal late-night radio programme. 'Why D'Ya Do It' polarised opinion. It was a work of high art, a shard of the finest polemic feminism to some, while others saw it as absurd sixth-form shock-rock. Charles Shaar Murray of the *NME* fell into the latter category. 'It is the album's grand failure. A torrent of cusswords and sexual/scatological extremism, it seems to have been included for no good reason other than to bait the *Sunday Express* into one of those orgasms of outraged decency so beloved by connoisseurs of the ludicrous and grotesque,' he wrote. Murray, perhaps Britain's most influential music journalist at the time, was not impressed with the rest of the album either. 'Records like this serve absolutely no purpose except voyeurism and a cheap *frisson*,' he wrote. 'Junk is not a useful metaphor for any aspect of the lives of non-users, and I'd prefer to save my sympathy for people whose suffering is not self-inflicted. Marianne Faithfull has only followed in the footsteps of other professional victim-type artists: she has made a record which is little more than a collection of symptoms. She has pasted sequins on her scars and charged admission for customers to come and gawk at them.'

Initially *Broken English* did not sell particularly well in Britain. In fact, its highest ever chart position was number 57 but it sold steadily during the year of release and thereafter. Island had a bona fide word-of-mouth hit album, an accomplishment beyond mere shock value or curiosity over the extraordinary re-positioning of a famous name. The record succeeded because it had three essential elements – the songs were strong and melodic, they coalesced as a body of work and it was considered authentic, both in terms of lyrical content and for the time it was released. Another important factor was that it sold well to women, which few albums and artists achieve. Before *Broken English* Marianne was considered quintessentially English (despite her multi-ethnic background) but it broke her into new markets that would service the rest of her career. The album went Top 10 in Austria, France, New Zealand, Sweden and West Germany and also charted in Australia, Canada and Holland. In France, where it sold more than 270,000 copies, it was the sixth best-selling album of the year and it also went Gold [250,000 plus copies] in West Germany. In the United States it reached number 82 in the *Billboard* chart, evidence of an album and artist balanced between cult and popular status.

'The Ballad Of Lucy Jordan' was released as a single and took Marianne back into the British charts for the first time in 12 years when it reached number 48. It performed better elsewhere, reaching number two in Austria, five in Germany and Switzerland, and 18 in Australia. While it was not an authentic chart 'hit', the song became an Everywoman anthem ('At the age of 37, she realised she'd never ride through Paris in a sports car with the warm wind in her air'), reaching out to middle-aged women [which 37 was considered in the 1970s] sensing life and their dreams had passed them by as they succumbed to motherhood and routine. The song was used in the soundtrack for the Swedish black comedy *Montenegro* (1981), which had a storyline seemingly based on the song's theme and featured a family with the surname Jordan. More famously, the song was also included in *Thelma & Louise* (1991), the Ridley Scott film starring Susan Sarandon and Geena Davis, which was again about women looking to escape a mundane existence. 'The Ballad of Lucy Jordan' has remained popular since release and the official video has been viewed over 1.5 million times on YouTube.

During interviews to promote *Broken English*, Marianne continued, in solemn tones, to place the record in the wider context of her life. "I think if I hadn't made it I would have either gone insane or cut my throat – it was that intense. I hadn't been thinking that way for years and years, but I can now see that my hunger to do something worthwhile was incredible," she told *Penthouse*. She fluctuated between confidence, optimism, nervousness and neurosis when speaking about the record. "To be frank, I always knew I was something quite extraordinary. It was as if I had a lot of potential but would never fulfil it. I blew it on purpose or had no confidence," she told *The Guardian*'s Robin Denselow. Minutes later, the bravado evaporated. "Am I very paranoid? Oh yeah – can't you sense that? Why? Because of everything that has happened. It's taken me 10 years to really get back into the business. It wasn't getting ripped off that matters, it was just that I never got the opportunity to do anything any good or work with people any good. They saw me as something they might be able to make a bit of money on, but never as someone who had anything to say."

The film director Derek Jarman was asked to make a film to accompany three tracks from *Broken English*, 'Witches Song', 'The Ballad Of Lucy Jordan' and 'Broken English'. Jarman had established himself with *Jubilee*, the film featuring luminaries from the British punk scene. The brief from Island Records was unusually liberal and the film owed little to conventional pop videos made at the time, or since. The only link between the continuous music – the songs segued into each other – was footage of Marianne walking through London, wearing a short mini-skirt and high heels. Jarman used a cut-up technique, blending images much in the style of Kenneth Anger – a man with a paper bag over his head, people holding hands around a fire, a nuclear bomb exploding, soldiers marching, buildings burning and shots of Hitler delivering a speech. During the filming Marianne and Jarman became friends and he asked her to contribute a version of the Scottish folk song 'The Skye Boat Song' to his film of 1987, *The Last Of England*.

The critical response to *Broken English* was positive in the United States and Marianne was keen to maximise its impact. Debra Rae Cohen of *Rolling Stone* stumbled upon her in defiant mood. Marianne had been labelled a 'survivor' in several British newspaper pieces and she disliked its patronising connotations. "I'm so, so strong. People have no clue," she told Cohen. "Oh I know, they all think I'm a victim – or a survivor. I hate that, I hate the word. A survivor of what? The Titanic? It's not just that I'm a survivor, I'm so much more than that." Warner Bros handled the album in the United States and had noted its consistently strong sales. The word from the label's hierarchy was that it was looking to excessively promote a female artist and the two favourites to acquire this backing were Marianne or Chrissie Hynde with her band, The Pretenders.

Marianne was booked to appear on the prestigious television show *Saturday Night Live*, at the time the principal influence on American mainstream culture with a weekly audience of 30 million viewers. "After years of poverty and struggle it was a magical trip for Ben and me," she said. "For the first time in my life I was on the verge of being accepted for who I was, and it made me extremely apprehensive." Chris Blackwell realised the importance of the appearance and contacted an old friend, Mim Scala, and asked him to effectively chaperone Marianne. Scala, the grandson of an Italian immigrant, had been an agent in the early 1960s, representing both actors and musicians, among them Cat Stevens and Richard Harris. He had hit the hippy trail for several years, painting and recording ethnic music in Morocco, Spain and Sri Lanka, before becoming, in 1972, Island's head of promotions. "At this time, Marianne was, by her own admission, a naughty girl," said Scala. "Her capacity for abuse was well-known. My first job was to see that rehearsals happened and that Marianne was healthy. This meant no drink or drugs. She was a wonderful mix of lady and tramp. My main task was to spoil her fun and freeze out any bad company."

A limousine was waiting for Marianne at JFK Airport driven by a chauffeur who routinely worked for the comedian and heavy drugs user John Belushi. The driver offered Marianne 'supplies' but Mim told him his services were not required. Booked into New York's prestigious Berkshire Place Hotel in Midtown Manhattan, Marianne was in the lobby when the elevator doors opened to reveal Anita Pallenberg. According to Scala, the pair 'fell into each other's arms screaming and shrieking like Macbeth's witches on Prozac'. They went up to the penthouse suite but were interrupted by Scala 'before too much damage was done'. The rehearsals went well at the NBC studio and Scala phoned Blackwell in Jamaica to tell him Marianne was on good form.

The next day, Marianne went missing three hours before she was due to appear live on the programme. Scala tracked her down to a toilet where she was sitting at a stall with a bottle of brandy between her knees. She had also taken procaine, an anaesthetic used at the time by dentists. "Apparently it freezes the top of your head, leaving you feeling blissed out like you're suspended in a great block of ice," said Scala. Marianne revealed later that one of her backing singers 'who loathed me on sight' had sourced the drug for her, supplying it as a substitute for cocaine. While she was sleeping it off, Mick Jagger called at the hotel to wish her well. Scala refused to let him see her. "I couldn't tell him that she was unconscious on a bed from too much brandy and procaine," he said. "I know she would not want her first meeting with him in ages to be like this. So I stuck to my guns."

Mark Miller Mundy had also travelled to New York, to oversee the sound and liaise with Warner's staff. He was peeved to hear Scala informing everyone that he was Marianne's 'manager' and in this assumed role had agreed that she would appear at the Mudd Club in downtown Manhattan, a punk venue renowned for its 'sheer kinkiness' and boasting gender-neutral toilets. "Scala came along against my will," said Miller Mundy. "He had somehow managed to persuade Chris to pay for his ticket. He's an old hippy. He thought when we were in America it was the 60s all over again – you had to get fucked if you possibly could and you had to take as many drugs as possible. To Marianne it was an excuse to party. She was having a high old time." Scala had agreed that Marianne would appear at the Mudd Club directly after *Saturday Night Live* but the band had only rehearsed three songs, the number required by the television company. When Miller Mundy said they should pull the concert, Scala said he had already received the fee. Marianne had taken exception to Miller Mundy's manner throughout the trip. "He had taken on the role of personal tormentor and papal representative of snotty, authoritarian patriarchy. I had been told what a complete piece of shit I was and I was beginning to believe it," she said.

The procaine affected Marianne's voice and she struggled to talk, let alone sing. A masseuse was summoned to the dressing room to help her relax. Meanwhile, outside the studios a line of stretch limousines belonging to directors of Warner's ringed the entrance like a circle of wagon trains. The red light went on and the cameras were set. Chevy Chase, a *Saturday Night Live* regular, introduced Marianne. Her hair tousled and wearing a tight top and jeans, she took hold of the microphone ready to perform 'Broken English'. "When I opened my mouth to sing, a strange strangled whisper came out. I had lost my voice. It was a moment of true horror," she said. Miller Mundy reached for the dials on the mixing desk. "I turned the echo up but it was still a complete disaster," he said. "It was really important but her voice had gone because she had been up all fucking night, the day before. She blew it. There was not a single car outside before she finished. Her voice was like a gargle, a kind of croak." The singing became even more fractured by 'Guilt', especially during the opening section where almost every other word failed to leave Marianne's lips.

The performance was the subject of great legend but since it pre-dated universal home recording, it was, for many years, heard about but largely unseen. In December 2010, however, a Marianne Faithfull fan, Melissa Jimenez, posted the footage on YouTube with the caveat: 'I'm not doing Marianne any favours by uploading this in bad quality. But if you were curious as I was to see this infamous performance and what all the fuss was about…here it is.' Most viewers posting comments on the site were surprised it had been remembered so negatively. Indeed, while her voice *did* break up, the performance was strong and confident and the musicianship first-rate. As an artist caught at the vanguard of punk and new wave, she was setting a precedent for a raw and edgy style of delivery that soon became routine. "She got through it fantastically," said Mim Scala. "But we all knew she was a bit shaky. On the other hand she always looked vulnerable when she performed."

Anita Pallenberg was in the dressing room at the television studio, exhilarated by Marianne's performance. She insisted she go through with the concert at the Mudd Club to fulfil her destiny as a 'punk diva'. "What you must do now is go all the way," she told Marianne. "Forget about those fucking record company idiots with their fucking golf carts and their hot tubs." She promised Marianne that when she sang 'Sister Morphine' she would shoot up in the toilets and become her 'angel from hell'. On the drive to the club the streets were clogged with traffic and Marianne had to take an elevator to the top of a building and make her way across the Manhattan skyline to gain access to the venue. Word had travelled through New York's underworld about her appearance and the city's hardcore alternative set made the pilgrimage. "There's no good going on about old troupers and all that. That's all very well, but it's a load of shit," Marianne told *Rolling Stone*. "The point is that you've given your word. You've got to do it, even if you can't sing a fucking note. And lo and behold, I couldn't."

As she took the stage a member of the audience passed her a bottle and she gulped down most of the unknown contents before starting. Marianne kept upright by holding on to one of the pillars on the stage. Her voice was frail and barely audible. Miller Mundy was so angry that he left after the first song 'in a fury like a splenetic rat' – according to Marianne. Mim Scala considered the concert one of the most thrilling rock 'n' roll events of his life but Miller Mundy referred to it later as a 'total disaster'. The reviewer from *Rolling Stone* wrote that it was 'bare and scary, like nails scraping across a floor'.

Ben Brierley was in contact with Marianne by telephone throughout the fateful day. "It is just not true that she was out of her head. She was scared," he said. "It was psychosomatic and she lost her voice and that's not bullshit. If it were, I'd say so, because she was out of her head on a number of occasions. Miller Mundy had a lot to do with it. He'd say things to her like: 'Either you do this gig really well, or your whole career is blown'. It used to freak her out."

Miller Mundy was exasperated because, as he saw it, she had used the New York trip as a chance to party and hang out with old friends rather than regenerate her career. He disagreed wholeheartedly with Scala that it formed a perverse but significant rock 'n' roll episode (a view he felt Scala was bound to hold as he had orchestrated, or at least sanctioned, most of the chaos). "She has always blamed Jagger, the fact that he arrived just as she was about to go on. I don't think it is true exactly. She should never have been allowed to go on the trip in the first place," said Miller Mundy.

On the flight home Miller Mundy chatted with Marianne. Appropriately, Scala was positioned between them, asleep in his seat. "I have a theory about Marianne," said Miller Mundy. "And that is that in a way she is terrified of succeeding. With *Broken English* she had an opportunity to really make something of what she had always promised. There is something deep inside Marianne. She has a fear of success. She can cope with failure far more easily." He asked her repeatedly why she had not applied herself. She shrugged her shoulders and said she did not have an answer. Just two days before the *Saturday Night Live* appearance, Marianne had told a reporter from a New York magazine: "I want commercial success and I want recognition from my peers. I have a great need for that. I've just been mocked for years, and it gets to you."

The album earned Marianne critical respect but served only to make her relationship with Brierley more lopsided. She repeatedly asked him to join her band but he felt the only way to establish himself as an equal partner was to become a success himself. "It was very difficult after *Broken English* took off because I found myself with nothing to do for a period of time," he said. "Marianne was very much in the spotlight and I did begin to feel a bit of a prick, but I think anyone would have done in that situation."

In the *New Musical Express* Marianne was asked her favourite poets and among a list that also included Keats, Shelley and Burroughs, she included the name 'Ben Brierley'. "I'm very keen that Ben has great success. It's difficult if one of you is bigger than the other; the only really good relationship is reasonably equal," she told a magazine in 1981. At other times she was less supportive and conceded that after *Broken English* she treated Brierley 'absolutely ruthlessly'. She would later draw a parallel between Brierley and how she had felt in her relationship with Mick Jagger. 'I treated Ben much the same way Mick had treated me, and eventually Ben came to perceive me as an oppressor who had more money, more power and more control than he did, and he absolutely hated me for that,' she wrote in *Faithfull*.

Decca, now trading as London Records, had noted the increase in Marianne's public profile and moved swiftly, gathering 14 songs recorded during the mid-1960s and issuing them as the compilation *As Tears Go By* in February 1981. More than 10 years after the event, the label decided the world was ready for Marianne's version of 'Sister Morphine', but it stood out incongruously among the pleasant folk songs. Island Records gave permission for Decca to use a shot of Marianne it had commissioned from the American photographer Sheila Rock for the cover of *As Tears Go By*. Marianne was pictured crouching on stairs, the nails on her fingers bitten down to stumps and a tattoo of a swallow visible on her hand. It was a clear attempt to frame the new, street-smart version of Marianne – an image wholly incompatible with the music on the record – but it missed the subtlety and shading of Island's branding, which was to serve Marianne well for many years.

Mark Miller Mundy was in the unofficial position of acting as Marianne's manager but the situation changed when two others began vying for the job. Brierley introduced Marianne to Tony Secunda, described by *NME* writer Nick Jones as 'a Svengali figure who bridged the gulf between the old-style Tin Pan Alley music biz people and the hippie underground', and elsewhere as a 'dark, brooding and somewhat menacing figure'. Public school-educated, he first managed The Moody Blues, signing them to Decca in 1965, before taking on The Move. He was famous for engineering publicity stunts which included goading The Move's singer, Carl Wayne, into using an axe on stage to smash up television sets and kitting the band out as gangsters. His notoriety reached its peak when 2,000 postcards depicting a nude caricature of the then-Prime Minister, Harold Wilson, reclining in a bath, were mailed out, ostensibly to promote The Move's single 'Flowers In The Rain', released in August 1967. The card suggested an inappropriate relationship between Wilson and his private secretary, Marcia Williams. The band, completely unaware of Secunda's scam, was sued and the High Court ruled that all royalties – today thought to exceed several million – were to be redirected to charities in perpetuity, chiefly the Spastics Society. Marianne's other potential manager was Alan Seifert who had formerly represented Elkie Brooks, whom several members of Marianne's band had backed previously. He had parted company with Brooks a few months earlier and was seeking new artists to manage, particularly female singers. He also acted as an agent for the actors Sarah Miles and Vanessa Redgrave, while managing Toyah Wilcox, Lynsey de Paul and Hazel O'Connor. Marianne met Seifert and provisionally agreed to sign with him, but on the day she was to confirm the deal at his Chelsea office, she settled for Secunda instead.

Tony Secunda hardly needed to amplify Marianne's notorious image which meant that the field in which he specialised was largely superfluous. The main priority was contractual intricacies with Island and similar administrative tasks to which Secunda did not fully apply himself. Within three months, Marianne was regretting not taking on Seifert, whose style was less prolific but more thorough. Seifert's persistence worked and after a courtesy call to check on Marianne, he was installed as her new manager. The short period with Secunda was not without its eccentricities, which endeared him to Marianne's circle. "He was great, a lunatic," said Miller Mundy. "On one occasion Marianne told me to give him £3,000 in cash. I had to go to my bank, draw out £3,000 in £20 notes and hand them to him on the floor of the bank. We walked out together past Trafalgar Square and he said, 'The funny thing about people is that they don't like money'. I laughed. He took up a wad of money and pulled off about 40 notes. He walked up to two students and said, 'Here, take it'. They both looked at about £700 in cash and neither of them would take it. He put it back in his pocket and walked off leaving these wretches with their jaws drooping." Marianne, who called Secunda 'a wonderful madman manager of the old school', had few dealings with him afterwards but they reunited in the late 1980s when she asked him to act as an agent for her book *Faithfull*, for which he set up a deal with the publisher, Michael Joseph.

Seifert discovered that many of the customary dealings between artist and record company had not taken place, not least because Marianne's drug taking and drinking had meant she was in no fit state to converse with Island's staff. He tried to develop stronger links with the label but this was difficult because he did not have a strong relationship with Blackwell. Marianne later referred to Seifert as 'a draggy, middle-class pop music person' and clearly viewed him as the antithesis of Secunda. He arranged for her and Brierley to move to Battersea, away from the junkies and dealers who preferred to operate on the other side of the River Thames. "Seifert couldn't see the point of Ben at all. People thought of Ben as a ligger, a liability," said Marianne.

When Brierley recorded with Marianne it had to be kept secret because he was not considered sufficiently competent as a musician. Occasionally Marianne was booked on flights by Island in first-class seats while Brierley was in economy. "Ben just went down, down, down and there was no honourable way for him to deal with it," said Marianne. "And I didn't lift a finger to help. The only way out for Ben was to leave. But leaving, because of the drug dependency, was a long way off." Seifert quickly grew accustomed to Marianne's presumptuous nature. She borrowed incessantly and manipulated those around her, often by playing them off against one other. Seifert's office became a clearing house as drugs dealers called to pick up the cash Marianne had earlier promised them. On her visits to Jamaica, Blackwell had been amazed by Marianne's ability to appropriate cash and ganja from dreads.

Marianne appointed a personal assistant when an American fan, Kate Hyman, called at her door and said she wanted to work for her. To test her mettle Marianne gave her a reading list comprising several titans of French literature and asked her to report back. Over the course of 10 days Kate made her way through Gustave Flaubert's *Madame Bovary*; Honoré de Balzac's *Cousine Bette*; Stendhal's *The Red And The Black* and Choderlos de Laclos's *Dangerous Liaisons*. Kate was put on a small wage by Island who – according to Marianne – wanted her to act as a 'spy' and report back on the shenanigans within the camp. Marianne was herself waged by Island and it was Kate's job to collect £400 each Friday on her behalf. By Saturday afternoon most of this had been spent, chiefly on cocaine and heroin. It formed a valuable entrée into the music business for Kate – she was to forge a long career and is today senior vice-president of Creative at BMG Chrysalis US, working on Broadway, New York.

Alan Seifert's allegiance to his client was tested routinely. Marianne sometimes called during the night, asking him to source sleeping tablets. He often took his phone off the hook to avoid these intrusive calls. When he quizzed her about the enchantment of drugs she embarked on a rambling chronicle about it being an intellectual decision to live on the edge, rather like a sociologist (a role her father had encouraged her to consider) carrying out participant observation. Her copious intake led to several regrettable scenes. When she was due to visit Seifert's office his personal assistant was instructed to clear papers from desks. Marianne would bound in carrying a bottle of wine and invariably spill the contents or knock the bottle to the floor after forgetting where she had left it. The heroin had affected her co-ordination and made her liable to bump into chairs or tables. Another habit was to fall asleep with a lit cigarette in her hand. She set fire to beds three times on promotional visits to Europe and whenever Seifert was with her he refused to sleep in the hotel room above her because of the obvious danger.

Marianne's imperious manner did not falter, whatever her circumstances. She would arrive in a foreign country with her belongings in a Sainsbury's plastic shopping bag and immediately ring Island's satellite office covering that particular territory. "Hello, Marianne Faithfull here. You must send me six pairs of tights and a quantity of fresh make-up. Please invoice the London office. Thank you." On a promotional trip to Paris, she wore the same tracksuit day and night and appeared before television cameras wearing it. Her seductive charm often impelled people to drive around during the early hours trying to find an off-licence willing to open and provide her with a bottle of vodka. As well as the drugs bills that Seifert had to cover, he also paid a weekly allowance to Eva Faithfull of £50. She would send him invoices for the food she had bought for Marianne's cat.

14

Broken English finally established Marianne Faithfull as a talent in her own right but caused her previous albums to be viewed largely as frivolous works made by someone manipulated by others or lacking direction. So, *Broken English* was virtually a début record and following it was inevitably going to be problematic. There was far less time for the music to ferment and because *Broken English* was such a strong musical statement it would inevitably reduce the impact of the follow-up, regardless of its quality. Also, as Marianne had spent so long promoting *Broken English* it did not leave much time for writing, rehearsal and the crucial interplay with the band.

Chris Blackwell advanced Marianne 'a ton of money' against the next album but it was all quickly spent on clothes and drugs. Another tranche was due on delivery of a batch of new songs but the day before they were due, nothing had been written. A bottle of brandy was procured and Marianne and the band sat around her kitchen recording directly on to a home recorder. Within a couple of hours they had three songs – 'Intrigue', 'In The End' and another where Marianne read aloud a piece from *Dangerous Liaisons*. The next day Kate Hyman played the tracks to Chris Blackwell and, as promised, he passed her a cheque for Marianne. Later that same day, however, he rang Marianne and told her he hated the songs because they were 'so down' and 'plain depressing'. She guessed he had wanted another *Broken English* – 'more anger, rage, lots of female ranting and invective'. "But I had moved on," she said. "I had done the rage-and-lust bit and now I wanted to explore a different set of emotions: tenderness, intrigue, betrayal, claustrophobia."

Marianne's new standing meant that she no longer had to record in budget studios and the initial work on the album that became *Dangerous Acquaintances* took place at one of the country's most prestigious facilities, the Chipping Norton Recording Studios in the Cotswold Hills, Oxfordshire. A meal was provided each night at exactly the same time and the band's girlfriends were invited to stay in the adjoining cottages. Drugs, mainly barbiturates and cocaine, were ferried to the studio on a regular basis from London. Kate Hyman, who was trusted with the keys to the mini-bar in Seifert's office, was asked to liberate several cases of vodka which the party consumed at Chipping Norton while trying to summon lyrics. The atmosphere was so homely that Marianne had even taken along her cat, Herod. He went missing one night and Marianne became convinced he had taken her soul. They had to find him immediately. She and Kate walked the dew-covered fields around the studio until they thought they heard him shout her name through the darkness [it was actually Barry Reynolds who had climbed a tree]. "Everyone was going crackers in the country," said Marianne. "The band soon became lonely and morose. Ben was jealous and unhappy, and I was going out of my fucking mind."

In a bid to alleviate the boredom Marianne began visiting various friends who lived in the rough vicinity of Chipping Norton. On a whim, she decided to look up Princess Margaret who she had heard was staying with mutual friends in Gloucester. The taxi fare was £100 one-way but, incredibly, she was granted an audience with the princess. Marianne was poured a gin and tonic and they chatted for a while by an open fire. They discussed Rudolf Nureyev and Shakespeare and Margaret gossiped about 'my sister, the Queen'.

The band were well-fed and pampered but there was a degree of friction. Barry Reynolds was still in the band but a new rhythm section had been installed of Calvin 'Fuzzy' Samuel on bass and Bruce Rowland on drums. Both were experienced and highly accomplished musicians. Rowland had been a member of The Grease Band and Fairport

Convention and Antigua-born Samuel had played with a host of top names including Eddy Grant, Stephen Stills, Rita Coolidge and Crosby, Stills, Nash & Young. He was given the nickname Fuzzy because he was one of the first bassists to play through a fuzz box. There were intimations that Rowland's stylish but light playing did not furnish songs with the necessary drive. Arguments also developed about songwriting credits, one of rock's perpetual battlegrounds. "Everyone was hard up for cash," said Miller Mundy. "There had been all these great reviews for *Broken English* but the money was taking ages to come through. We'd had this huge success but we were all broke and everyone was going crazy. All this shit was going down and I began to feel the new songs were not as strong. The melodies were not as powerful and everyone took the attitude of 'Well, you did it before, see if you can do it again, boy'."

The instructions from Miller Mundy grew increasingly bizarre and confused the band. At one point he asked them to make a section of music 'sound like lemmings falling into the sea'. According to Marianne he began taking excessive quantities of Valium. He locked himself in a room and stayed there for several days, emerging only to fire the group, one by one. "After driving the band to the brink of insanity he proceeded to fall to pieces himself," said Marianne. Exasperated, Miller Mundy decided on radical action and re-hired the old band, including Steve Winwood, and booked them into Matrix again. The tapes of the sessions at Chipping Norton were shelved at a cost of £9,000. The switch in location and personnel was not the panacea everyone anticipated. "It is the only time I have been in a studio with Winwood and it hasn't worked," said Miller Mundy. "He was very negative about the sessions and the band were bickering in an unreasonable way. I tried, somewhat foolishly, to follow the same path, and it never works. We were under a lot of pressure to follow up the record. There was new staff at the record company and Blackwell was never around."

After three weeks at Matrix, backing tracks had not been committed to tape and there were doubts whether the record would ever be made. "Island should have let us stop and take a breather for six months. We were under too much pressure. In the end, I don't think the record should have been released," said Miller Mundy. Progress was made slowly but as the recording reached its final stages, Miller Mundy was hit by a personal tragedy when his father died just days before the mixing. His relationship with Marianne had deteriorated to such a degree that he said he would no longer work with her after completing the album. Marianne became suspicious that he was holding back money. She ordered an audit of the accounts at a personal cost of nearly £1,000 and discovered there had been no impropriety. A few weeks before the release of *Dangerous Acquaintances* Miller Mundy was challenged by Brierley who claimed Marianne was owed £30,000. Miller Mundy felt Marianne was sometimes too willing to listen to members of her entourage who were often ill-informed or trying to pull favours from her for themselves.

Dangerous Acquaintances was released in September 1981 to, at best, lukewarm reviews. The new wave snap of *Broken English* was eschewed in favour of stop-start dance beats, impeccably played but missing both verve and focus. Marianne's voice was more controlled than before and songs such as 'So Sad' conjured an engaging melancholy. Marianne wrote the lyrics to all but two of the nine tracks and, as the record contained no cover versions, it was a more sustained personal statement than *Broken English*. The album, destined to be compared to its incendiary predecessor, fell short ultimately because the songs were not as melodic or original. Marianne's throaty register (dubbed 'a posh, parched, cocaine-clogged rasp' by the *NME*) was now familiar and her status as – in her words – 'the raging virago of pop' already established, so there was less curiosity about the record. Cynthia Rose, writing in the *NME*, distilled the general reaction: 'Gone are the angry, churning undercurrents and thick bubbling synthesizer with which Stevie Winwood gave depth and mystery to the title track on *Broken English*. Enter in its place something approaching the thin, tricksy, tinny vaudeville which props up Grace Jones.' In sales terms, it was a disappointment. It reached the Top 10 in France, Sweden and New Zealand but only made 45 in the UK and 104 in the United States.

Police made regular visits to Marianne and Brierley's flat in Danvers Road, Chelsea, and their vigilance was often rewarded. Marianne estimated that they were being raided at least once a month. In the summer of 1981, while shops were looted and cars burned elsewhere in London in the infamous riots, devoted Metropolitan cops were looking through Marianne's linen basket and finding small quantities of heroin and cannabis. She pleaded not guilty to possessing 15 milligrams of heroin when she appeared at Snaresbrook Crown Court in London. She said the drug had been left there by a friend who had stayed at the flat while she was away. She was found guilty in November, 1981, fined £100 and told to pay £200 towards the prosecution costs. "The police were convinced that Ben and I were, at the very least, running a cocaine ring," she said. "They were looking for a pulp-fiction character, a hippy spider lady, the Mastermind of the Chelsea Drug Set. And that was meant to be me!"

Marianne was using cocaine heavily but Seifert was more concerned about her use of heroin. She never mentioned her habit to him directly but he was aware she was an addict. He booked a place for her at a health club in Hampshire. Marianne checked in but was soon on the phone to her dealer friends in London who were happy to spend a day away from their regular patch. Her heavy drugs use made live appearances unlikely and she played just one British concert in 1982, appearing at the Dominion Theatre in Tottenham Court Road on Tuesday, June 8. It was her first performance in London for three years and she was tense. She exited the stage frequently (to knowing cheers from the audience), presumably to top up her intake of substance. Johnny Waller, reviewing the show for *Sounds*, attacked the 'faltering, curiously amateurish, fledgling stage-craft' but conceded that Marianne's mixture of 'charisma and mythology' produced 'intermittent rapture'. More than 2,000 fans had packed into the venue and another reviewer noted: 'It was rather like gatecrashing a stranger's party'. At the front of the throng was the photographer David Corio, who captured several iconic images of Marianne holding the microphone and smoking, staring into the middle distance. "Marianne looked almost transparently pale on the enormous dark Dominion stage," said Corio. "Her chain-smoking all through the gig and her wailing voice were totally at odds with her delicate appearance and girlish white blouse."

Above: At Island Studios, London, 1983. *(Adrian Boot)*

Right: Marianne with Oliver Musker, October 1972.

(Syndication International)

Left: Marianne backstage at St Martin's Theatre, London, after a performance of *The Collector*, March 1974.

(Michael Ackermann Collection)

Above: Ben Brierley.

Left and below: Marianne in 1975. *(Adrian Boot)*

Above: Marianne in the mid-seventies. *(Rex Features)*

Above: Marianne with guitarist/co-writer Barry Reynolds. *(Rex Features)*

Above: Appearing on French television, 1982. *(Rex Features)*

Above: Performing at Dingwall's, London, 1978. *(Barry Plummer)*

Left: Marianne in New York, before her appearance on *Saturday Night Live*, and, below, with Anita Pallenberg, 1980.

(Ebet Roberts/Rex Features)

Island Records publicity shots for *Broken English* (left) and *Dangerous Acquaintances* (below).

(Dennis Morris/ Clive Arrowsmith)

Above: Marianne in costume for her appearance in Roger Waters' *The Wall* concert in Berlin, 1990. *(Rex Features)*

Right: Chris Blackwell, head of Island Records.
(Adrian Boot)

Marianne on stage in 1990. "Even in disgrace, she was always a lady." *(Ebet Roberts)*

Marianne and Bono, at
the Tivoli Theatre,
Dublin, February, 1990.
(Irish Independent Newspapers)

Marianne was convinced that her caterwauling persona on *Broken English* had led to her receiving special attention by the police. She left London to spend time with a friend, Richard Booth, a pioneering bookseller who had helped established Hay-on-Wye as 'the town of books'. While she was there, helping Booth unpack books and stock shelves, a news story broke that LSD was being manufactured in Wales. Soon afterwards police visited Booth's three-storey emporium containing hundreds of thousands of books. "The police put together my presence near Wales and an LSD factory there, and I became the Acid Queen of Wales!" said Marianne. "Just amazing. They thought Richard and I were shipping out mountains of acid."

Two news stories running consecutively on television in the summer of 1982 had a profound effect on Marianne. The first was a report of Pope John Paul II holding an open-air Mass at Wembley Stadium on Saturday May 29, 1982 and the other, an update of the number of casualties in the Falklands War, Britain's conflict with Argentina that lasted from April 2, 1982 to June 14, 1982. "I was getting to the end of my tolerance with England. I just thought, 'I've got to get out of here, I can't bear to stay in this country a minute longer'," she said.

Soon afterwards Marianne moved with Brierley to New York, renting an apartment in Manhattan on East 18th Street, between Second and Third Avenues, a few streets from Stuyvesant Square, famous for its collection of English Elm trees. They were both heavily addicted, using mainly heroin and cocaine. "The thing with Ben staggered on," said Marianne. "I didn't expect love from him. In the world of drug addiction love is not one of the coins that you deal in." She conceded that Brierley effectively became her 'minder'. "It becomes caretaking rather than love," she said. The various court cases meant they often had to travel back to England. Late in the summer of 1982 she invited Nicholas, now 17, to spend time with them. She collected him from the airport in a limousine and offered him a line of cocaine as they travelled to Manhattan. He declined. Back at the apartment she roused herself to cook dinner each evening but was otherwise camped in front of the television 'out of it all the time'. She had quickly absorbed herself in the New York drugs scene and referred later to this period as 'endlessly painful, mortifying and deadly'.

Brierley began an affair with Cristina Monet-Palaci, a singer signed as 'Cristina' to ZE Records. The label had been set up by Cristina's husband, Michael Zilkha, the British-born former Westminster School pupil whose father, Selim, was the founder of Mothercare, and his mother, a Lebanese oil heiress. Zilkha had met his future wife when they both contributed theatre reviews to the *Village Voice*. Cristina was a drop-out from Harvard University, the daughter of a French psychoanalyst father and an American novelist and playwright mother. "Ben fucked Cristina and broke my heart. It was horrible and humiliating," said Marianne. Cristina was 12 years younger than Marianne, who once caught them together at the apartment. "New York is a small village, everyone knew about the affair except me," she said. She surmised that Cristina had sought out Brierley to further her career. "He probably told her he was the key to my success, my Svengali, and that he could do for her what he had done for me. She even went so far as to cover 'Why D'Ya Do It' [if this was the case, it was never recorded]," she said.

Cristina had entered Brierley and Marianne's orbit because ZE Records was licensed throughout the world by Island Records. Chris Blackwell was a close friend of Anna Wintour, the famous fashion editor, who, at the time, was the girlfriend of Michael Esteban, the co-founder of ZE with Zilkha. Cristina had worked early in her career with John Cale, formerly of The Velvet Underground, and her well-received eponymous debut album (later re-titled *Doll In The Box*) released in 1980 was produced by August Darnell of Kid Creole & the Coconuts (who were also signed to ZE).

Blackwell often spoke of the 'family' nature of his label and encouraged musicians to work together on specific projects. Barry Reynolds, for instance, had been seconded to work with Grace Jones, Black Uhuru and Joe Cocker at various times, which intermittently left Marianne without the most vital member of her musical team. So, several of Marianne's backing group, including Brierley, had been asked to help Cristina on her second album, which became *Sleep It Off*. Reynolds contributed music to the track 'The Lie Of Love' and co-wrote 'What's

A Girl To Do' with Cristina and the album's producer, Don Was. Ben Brierley received songwriting credits on 'Rage And Fascination' (along with Cristina and another Marianne collaborator, Joe Mavety) and 'He Dines Out On Death' (with lyrics by Cristina). Another song co-written by Brierley, the quirky 'Deb Behind Bars', surfaced in 2004 when the album was re-released with six bonus tracks. Interestingly, also included on the album was 'The Ballad Of Immoral Earnings' composed by Bertolt Brecht and Kurt Weill, who would later feature heavily in Marianne's canon. Indeed, parallels were often drawn between Marianne and Cristina. Chris Connelly of *Rolling Stone* described *Sleep It Off* as: 'A grimly hilarious gavotte through the upscale decadence of the titled apocalypso with an effect somewhere between Marianne Faithfull and the Flying Lizards but with music more enjoyable than either'. The album failed to chart and Cristina retired from music soon afterwards to return to writing.

Both Brierley and Marianne knew their marriage was nearing the end but found it difficult to separate. "I've always had a problem extricating myself from relationships," said Marianne. "I never know how to let go in any remotely normal way. I simply get as high as possible." Music, once more, formed succour and Marianne travelled to the Compass Point Studios in Nassau, Bahamas, to work on her next album. The studio had been set up five years earlier by Blackwell as a musical hub for artists signed to Island. A core of musicians had quickly melded to become the 'in-house' team of players on many Island releases. Known as the Compass Point All Stars, they included Sly Dunbar (drums), Robbie Shakespeare (bass), Mikey Chung (guitar), Uziah 'Sticky' Thompson (percussion), Barry Reynolds (guitar), Wally Badarou (keyboards) and Tyrone Downie (keyboards). Blackwell himself often produced, with support from engineer Alex Sadkin. "I wanted a Jamaican rhythm section with an edgy mid-range and a brilliant synth player. And I got what I wanted, fortunately," said Blackwell.

Wally Badarou, the Benin-born musician who had worked extensively with Level 42 and was regarded as one of the world's finest session players, was asked by Blackwell to co-produce Marianne's next record, with Barry Reynolds and the experienced sound engineer Harvey

244

Goldberg, who had worked with Sparks, The Ramones and Soft Cell. While she was in Nassau, Marianne's relationship with Reynolds exceeded a professional arrangement and in *Faithfull* she revealed they had 'become quite close' which was probably a euphemism for an affair. "Then Ben turned up," she said. "Nothing was ever said or discussed, but he knew. To Ben that was justification for divorce – he's very old fashioned in that way, a real Manchester working-class lad under all that punk veneer."

The royalties accrued by *Broken English* finally came through and Marianne received a cheque from Island for £90,000, a substantial amount for the early-1980s. She spent the money 'in no time at all' on clothes and drugs, its arrival coinciding with a particularly heavy period of drug use. She was flitting between New York and the Caribbean, taking great quantities of cocaine. While in New York she developed a psychosis that creatures were living and crawling beneath her skin. In a bid to release them she cut her face with a razor but after making the small incision a friend saw the blood trickling down and threw a jug of cold water over her. Marianne contacted Chris Blackwell and, the very next day, he arranged for her to fly to Jamaica where she stayed for six months. While she was there Brierley became implicated in a serious drugs case and was deported back to England.

The team that set about recording Marianne's third Island album was much changed from the one that had sparked the initial inspiration for *Broken English*. Apart from Marianne and Brierley – who was at different times either at the heart of the group or its periphery – only Terry Stannard and Barry Reynolds remained. The Detroit-born bassist Fernando Saunders (later a collaborator with Lou Reed) was drafted in on bass, with Mikey Chung on guitar. Chung was a stalwart of the Jamaican reggae scene and had played with, among many others, Lee Perry, Peter Tosh and Sly and Robbie. The rhythm section was complemented by percussionist Raphael DeJesus, an American of Puerto Rican origin who was making his debut on a major label record but would later play with Duran Duran and Talking Heads. Reynolds had established himself as Marianne's musical conduit and wrote or co-wrote four of the eight songs on *A Child's Adventure*.

The opening track, 'Times Square', written wholly by Reynolds, is a musician's soliloquy on the familiar theme of loneliness among the bustle of a city, contemplating that either alcohol or Jesus Christ could bring solace. 'The Blue Millionaire' contains the rhythmical footprint of the Compass Point All Stars and Marianne is almost indiscernible from Grace Jones as she sing-speaks through the track. 'Falling From Grace', co-written by Brierley, opens with an uplifting keyboard riff provided by Badarou – a feature of most of the album's tracks – and it is a catchy, insistent song with a clear autobiographical thrust: 'Falling from grace, falling from grace, Lord you have a pretty face'. She complains of 'feeling haunted' and screams, 'Don't put it in the paper – please don't.' 'Morning Come' is a fine ballad where Marianne shows she can still coerce the strands of ragged vocal cords back to impeccable tuning.

'Ashes In My Hand', one of Marianne's favourite songs on the album, is an anti-celebration of reaching 'a zen plateau of negativity', singing of a 'happiness that feels like pain'. 'Running For Our Lives' boasts another fine keyboard riff played by Badarou, and veers into clear pop territory with a simple arrangement and a strong, brisk chorus. The album closes a little flat with 'Ireland' and 'She's Got A Problem'. 'Ireland' is a sentimental commemoration and the stereotypes flow unabashed from her pen: the wind, the sea, the greenery, the people who laugh and drink. 'She's Got A Problem' was written by Brierley assisted by Caroline Blackwood, the writer, socialite and ex-wife of Lucian Freud.

The accomplished playing on *A Child's Adventure*, the superb recording facilities and production, and a return to a more traditional songwriting approach (certainly compared to *Broken English*) sugar-coated what Marianne referred to as 'my most anguished record'. Her feelings probably related more to other elements of her life at the time of recording – the break-up of her marriage, the drugs torpor – because it sounded a good deal less anguished than *Broken English* and lacked a comparable lyrical bite.

A Child's Adventure was released in March 1983. Marianne's 10th album and her third in four years, it marked the end of the most sustained creative period of her life. In many ways her initial three albums on Island could be seen as a series: the raw opening statement of

Broken English; the considered, thoughtful experimentation of *Dangerous Acquaintances*; and finally, the arrival of a muscular, confident sound by *A Child's Adventure*. The evolution generated by the itchiness of punk had led Marianne to a distinctive brand of urban folk, everyday tales, mainly sad, set against the backdrop of skyscrapers and nightclubs.

'Running For Our Lives' was released as a single with an accompanying video. Based on a customary boy-girl romance, it featured Marianne and her screen lover meeting at a railway station and then spending the day together in the city – eating at a restaurant, walking the streets and then dancing into the evening. While she was in Paris, Marianne met a 'good-looking boy' she refers to only as Jean-Pierre in *Faithfull*. He visited her later in New York and they went together to the Danceteria, the celebrated new wave nightclub across six floors with a video lounge. Marianne began dancing with others, laughing and flirting, and when they returned to the flat Jean-Pierre 'became insanely jealous and had a fit'. He cut his wrist with a razor blade. Marianne took a $10 bill from her purse and wrote a note which she told him to show to the taxi driver: 'Take me to Bellvue Hospital' [the oldest public hospital in the United States, known principally for its emergency department and psychiatric facilities]. She said later that she was 'profoundly ashamed' of how she had behaved.

The promotions department at Island tried to minimise the effect of Marianne's dearth of live appearances by setting up a good number of press interviews. Early in 1983 she was interviewed by future Mick Jagger biographer Philip Norman of *The Sunday Times*. She was as quotable as she had been in previous decades, telling Norman of a remark made to her by a fellow member of the Chelsea Arts Club. She had been speaking about a forthcoming photographic session in West Berlin when he proffered: "How appropriate, you and Berlin have so much in common. Armies have passed through you both!" The quote was the lead-in to Norman's lengthy piece, in which she laughed off the comment, adding: "It was a bit strong, don't you think? Armies have passed through us both! I made him modify it in my case to a platoon."

Marianne grumbled that even with two 'highly regarded albums' to her credit, she did not rate as high in promotional terms as her manager's other main female client, the 'shock-headed' Toyah [Wilcox]. "I know this country still bears me a grudge," she said. "People think I betrayed them in some way. I know they think of me as a rich, spoilt kid who doesn't really have to work. In fact, Ben and I are nearly skint at the moment. I do want to make it again, and I know I deserve to. There's a foreign part of me that still rather likes to be thought of as a gifted amateur. But what I am is a highly trained professional, brought up by another highly trained professional [her mother, Eva]."

A few months later Marianne had a new resolve to tour. She had pondered on the next record release and decided on a new method of working. Instead of pulling together an essentially ad hoc group of musicians and merging them in the studio, she wanted to develop the sound through a spell on the road. She contacted Steve Winwood and he suggested she use members of his band who had just finished playing with him during the summer of 1983 promoting his album *Talking Back To The Night*, also released by Island. The rhythm section was drummer JT Lewis and bassist Fernando Saunders, with Geoffrey Chung (the brother of Mikey) on keyboards. Marianne invited her old friend Joe Mavety to play guitar and he agreed to join her on her first ever complete tour of North America.

Delayed flights and poor organisation hit the rehearsal schedule and instead of spending a week in New York learning the tracks, the band met for the first time just two days before the opening show in Boston. The early concerts were extremely raw and the whole tour received little promotion, with few on-the-road luxuries. The sound crew travelled on the same bus as the band and the musicians carried their own instruments. Word had filtered through to Marianne's increasingly hardcore following and, with just a few posters advertising the fact, Marianne appeared at the Ritz in New York before more than 1,500 fans. The band had settled reasonably well and was soon performing for up to 90 minutes, drawing material from all three Island albums. They covered 'Because The Night', the Bruce Springsteen song that had been a hit for Patti Smith, and were augmented in New York by Brierley who played on an unrecorded number called 'Scoring With Elvis'. Jim Bessman, writing in *Billboard*, noted that the performance 'could have stood some tightening' but conceded that the audience was 'uniformly pleased and seemed genuinely attached to this most unique artist'.

Most of the venues had a capacity of just a few hundred which meant many were over-subscribed. They played five shows in Canada, including one at Fryfogle's in London, Ontario, where fans queued outside for six hours to ensure they were admitted. One of the final concerts was at Scorgies in Rochester, New York, on Saturday, October 1, where she was struck by nerves a few minutes before she was due on stage. The band had started 'Broken English' and Marianne was making her way towards the stage when she suddenly ran into the toilets to hide. The club owner, Don Scorgie, had to tempt her out with cries of 'Marianne, we're over here'. The show was particularly intense and featured Marianne rolling across the stage, knocking over drinks. Afterwards she invited fans on to the tour bus where she smoked two joints and a cigarette simultaneously, holding them between the fingers of one hand.

Marianne was consuming a bottle of Jack Daniel's a day but kept the heroin use out of view of the tour party. If she were taking it, most guessed it was an occasional indulgence, much like her use of cocaine. The three and a half week tour took in several day-long drives and tension inevitably led to disagreements. A searing wave of feedback had pierced most of her performance at a cramped concert hall in Houston and after the show Marianne was incandescent. She summoned the tour manager, Ivan Clarke, who protested that the poor, under-powered equipment, a cramped stage and a small concert hall with tinny acoustics were to blame. Marianne retorted that the planning should have been more thorough and 'dismissed' Clarke. He was later reinstated. Marianne suffered a sore throat but the band was impressed by her ability to raise her voice from an off-stage whisper to a hearty croak and cackle when a microphone was placed in her hand.

As well as a creative bookend, *A Child's Adventure* also marked the end of Marianne's marriage to Ben Brierley. "It was a lack of communication," he said. "We just didn't seem to like each other any more. It got very, very nasty and more than a bit unpleasant. I had a girlfriend. I was very jealous after *Broken English* took off because I found myself with nothing to do for a period." As they became increasingly estranged from one other, their conversations were usually on the telephone, especially as Marianne's workload increased. "It was all very petty. I think we were trying to hurt each other," he said. "I felt bitter about things. I felt rejected and badly hurt. I'm not saying I was blameless because I did a lot of things to her that were pretty nasty as well. It was always 'You've hurt me, so I'll hurt you'."

Marianne gave Brierley an ultimatum when she asked him to accompany her on one of her regular holidays in Jamaica. "She sent me a letter and said either I joined her in Jamaica or it was all over, so I didn't go. So that was my answer. She sent back the wedding ring in very dramatic style, so I threw it out of the window. Actually I gave it to a friend of ours, Henrietta Moraes, and she threw it out of the window. When we split up she didn't have anyone else. She was in Jamaica so she might have had some black man for all I know, but I didn't know about him at the time," said Brierley.

Moraes had watched the couple fall apart and saw heroin as the major factor as much as the difference in personalities. "Marianne was taking so much smack. People are just not very fanciable when they are like that. Ben was taking a lot of drugs too but he wasn't taking it like she was – he wasn't covered in spots." The inexpensive but symbolic ring that Brierley had slipped on Marianne's finger six years earlier fell amid the shrubbery at the bottom of the flat they were sharing at 222 East 18th Street, New York. It was not until 1986, however, that their marriage was finally annulled in a formal granting of divorce. Brierley later embarked on a six-month heroin withdrawal programme at a clinic in Weston-super-Mare. "I had to get sorted out because I was at the stage where heroin wasn't working for me any more. I got clean and wanted to start a new life," he said.

Visits to England were infrequent for Marianne in the mid-1980s as she took up semi-permanent residence in the United States. During one stay at her mother's she became involved in a comical episode at a snooker match. 'BOOZE SNOOKERED ME ADMITS MARIANNE' was the headline in *The Sun* in February 1984. A bottle of Jack Daniel's had warmed up Marianne after a day out in Reading. In the evening she found herself at the town's Hexagon Centre where a snooker match was in progress. She backed the volatile Irishman, Alex Higgins, in a match against John Virgo. After meeting Higgins at the interval, she began shouting encouragement each time he potted a ball. Marianne's behaviour worsened and she fell down stairs beside her seat. She was ejected from the theatre. "The whole lot are too damned stuffy," she told reporters. "They ought to stop taking themselves so seriously and let their hair down. They ought to let me promote the game. I'd be a great ambassador for them. I might even behave."

Staff at Island were hopeful that living in the United States might galvanise Marianne on an artistic level but she was soon lost to addiction. Henrietta Moraes was summoned by Marianne, with Chris Blackwell's blessing, to watch over her, but even she, accustomed to Marianne's excess, was perturbed. "It was hopeless," she said. "She would disappear for days with her pusher who lived on the West Side. She was taking loads of drugs and came out in the most frightful spots and I got really worried. I was supposed to be looking after her but she couldn't get enough smack. I thought she was going to get terribly ill. I did not think I could help her. It appeared to be quite wilful. When I say she was covered in spots, I mean sores. They were horrible but she just kept on doing it." Henrietta realised she could not dissuade her from taking heroin so resolved to merely care for her as best she could. "I don't think it is much good bullying anyone. I've always thought that if you suggest that they should do it, they don't. I'm inclined to think it is a pattern that people get into and that they have to hit the bottom if they are going to get better. I don't think I was particularly helpful. She was very headstrong. There was nothing anyone could do. If she wanted it, she would get it."

Henrietta Moraes spent almost three months in New York with Marianne while she was at her worst. As well as the heroin, Marianne was taking large amounts of cocaine. She usually visited her dealer friend, a woman known as 'Frin', and shot up at her flat. The plentiful supply of heroin in New York was a major influence on the escalation of Marianne's usage. She had quickly established a network of dealers ready to accept a glamorous customer into their circle. Henrietta felt she understood why her friend was tempted by heroin. "Taking smack is a way of avoiding pain, isn't it? So I suppose she had a lot of pain when she was young. I think she thought she was a bit of a misfit – an only child, no father to speak of – that's what I think."

Marianne's communication with her home country was often vitriolic and she bitterly conveyed her dislike of England from across the Atlantic. "I hate London and I hate England," she told an English newspaper in June 1985. Her future plans were hazy but news filtered through that she was writing the first draft of an autobiography with the working title of *So Bad, So Good, So Far*. Publishers were reported to have offered advances running to six figure sums. One newspaper carried a story quoting £500,000 if she guaranteed to the publisher that she would linger on the period of her life with Jagger. Henrietta contacted Chris Blackwell and told him of Marianne's desperation. He suggested a short spell in Jamaica to take her away from the New York pushers. Marianne flew out with Dickie Jobson, a close friend of Blackwell's, and Henrietta joined her a week later. "Marianne did a sort of cold turkey and when I met up with her again she was fine. There was a lot of rum around and she smoked quite a lot," she said.

Back in New York, Marianne began a relationship with a musician called Hilly Michaels. He had played as a drummer with Sparks since the mid-1970s and quickly established himself as one of New York's finest session players, appearing on records by Dan Hartman, Ellen Foley, the Hunter/Ronson Band and John Mellencamp. In 1979 Michaels had secured a major $1 million deal with Warner Bros and was launched as a quirky, post-punk figure, replete with permed hair, aviator glasses and tight jeans. Roy Thomas-Baker, famous for his work with Queen, produced his debut single, 'Calling All Girls' – 'I got lots of money, I got lots of time, found myself a penthouse, filled it up with bubbly wine'. Their relationship coincided with a period of heavy drugs use by Marianne and it is recalled sourly in *Faithfull*: 'Every day I woke up with such loathing, self-loathing and self-disgust. I hated my situation. I hated this man I was next to. I hated everything; but most of all I hated myself,' she wrote.

At Christmas 1985 they decided to call on Anita Pallenberg who was living in Westbury, Long Island, in a house that had formerly belonged to Bing Crosby. Anita was out and they had to crawl through a window to get in. Anita turned up a few hours later looking 'very large and wobbly' and stole Marianne's drugs, locking herself in a bathroom and refusing to come out. She asked Marianne about Michaels: 'What are you doing with a creep like this?' Indeed, Marianne felt Michaels was interested in her chiefly to advance his career. He had spent the Warner Bros money and developed his own drugs habit. 'Of all the creeps I've lived with, Hilly was the worst. It was such a perverse situation, one of those grisly dependent relationships, all connected to drugs and sex. He looked like Dracula,' she wrote.

Marianne began writing songs with Michaels, laying them on to tape with Mike Thorne who had been an A&R manager at EMI Records before working as a producer with post-punk bands such as Wire and Soft Cell. Marianne was freebasing [taking heroin in its pure state] and using speedballs [heroin mixed with cocaine or morphine] and in her dope-sick state realised she did not like the music she was recording. Initially she blamed Thorne but later conceded that this was a mindset she had held for most producers since working with Andrew Oldham, considering them manipulative and bullying. "But Mike Thorne wasn't like this at all," she said. "He was very straight and even a bit like a machine, actually."

In her confused, depressed state, she thought of a way of not making the record – killing herself. She moved through the house collecting up the heroin, most of it a highly potent compressed Chinese variety, heated it up on a spoon, and shot it into her vein. She began to feel unwell immediately and, at that very moment, realised she did not really want to die. She began looking for some cocaine, feeling it might neutralise the heroin, but her co-ordination failed. She smashed down on to her face, fracturing her jaw in several places. She managed to crawl upstairs to Michaels who was himself almost comatose from drugs. He got off the bed and they walked along the street for some time until Marianne began to feel better.

The jaw was fixed in position with wire to aid recovery and Marianne's heart was checked and found to be fine. As soon as she was feeling reasonably well again she resumed her drug-taking. She made the decision, however, to leave Michaels. She contacted Thorne and he arranged for her to stay at the famous bohemian hotel the Gramercy Park, at the bottom of Lexington Avenue where it meets 21st Street. The album they had worked on was abandoned, though Marianne rued that one song, 'Park Avenue', with lyrics about her relationship with Mick Jagger, was never released. "Hilly was a good songwriter, I'll give him that," she said. "The song is a very proficient, crafted sort of thing."

A member of Island's A&R team visited Marianne at the hotel. She wanted to discuss plans for the forthcoming album but everywhere she looked she saw drugs or drugs paraphernalia. Marianne knew this would be reported back to Chris Blackwell. "I became very peaceful," said Marianne. "I just sat in my room knowing everything was going to be taken care of." In November 1985 she was admitted to the Hazelden Clinic in Minneapolis. Founded in 1949 at a lakeside farmhouse in Minnesota, the clinic was one of the world's largest and most respected treatment centres for addiction and alcoholism. On admission, Marianne, knowing what to expect, asked for 10 blankets and covered herself on a bed. She lay there in 'hardcore detox' for a week, shaking and sweating.

Addicts, while in recovery, often re-direct their passion and commitment on to one another, and Marianne followed the classic pattern. Howard Tose was a manic depressive and multi-addicted. He twitched, trembled, stuttered and was unable to focus his eyes. Marianne found him irresistible. "He was the most damaged person I had ever met, and I liked him immediately because of that," she said. While Marianne thrived at the centre, Tose did not progress and after six weeks, discharged himself. Soon afterwards Marianne left too and boarded a plane to Tose's home city of Boston, Massachusetts. She drank five brandies on the flight and when she met Tose at the airport she noticed he was 'a bit wobbly'. They moved in together to an apartment on the 36th floor of a building overlooking Boston harbour. Tose spent most of the time curled up in the foetal position in bed. Marianne also became ill when her jaw started to swell. A wisdom tooth had been removed at Hazelden but they had chipped off a piece of bone which became infected. A surgeon wired her jaw shut again with pins which meant she could barely speak.

Tose managed to stir himself and found work at a photographic lab even though, according to Marianne, he was 'very, very ill'. Aside from the brandies on the plane, Marianne had gone six weeks without alcohol or drugs. She realised though that she would not be able to stay clean while she was with Tose. She decided they would have to separate. On their last night together, in April 1986, she had what she later described as 'the most amazing experiences of my adult sex life' and felt Tose 'pour his whole being' into her. The next morning she spoke to him in the sitting room, as he sat naked on the sofa. She told him she loved him but thought they should live on their own for a while. She told him to admit himself to a hospital and get well. After she had finished speaking his 'heart jumped out of his body' – by this she meant a section of muscle suddenly protruded in the centre of his chest. Marianne went into the kitchen to make tea and Tose entered the bedroom, ostensibly to get ready for work. After a while Marianne realised she had not heard the front door close and began searching for him around the apartment. The bedroom window was open and, looking down, she saw a red shape on the sidewalk that she realised was Tose's body.

After his death Marianne drew close to Tose's mother and sister, as they comforted each other. Tose had told Marianne of the many unkind episodes involving his family, which he regretted. Marianne tried to relate these feelings of contrition to his mother. "I realised from going to Howie's funeral – you never comprehend the havoc you wreak on the lives of the family and everyone around you," said Marianne. "I had no idea of the pain that everyone goes through when somebody commits suicide. I had never even thought of it. And I'd tried the same thing myself. Twice. It never occurred to me what a horrible thing it is to do to other people."

The death had a profound effect on Marianne. She suffered nightmares and bouts of tremendous guilt. She had hallucinations where she would see waves of blood. She fell under the care of McLean Hospital, the renowned psychiatric hospital in Belmont, Massachusetts. At one point she asked her psychiatrist, Dr Jack Bergman, whether she was insane.

He told her she was going through a series of delayed reactions and experiencing them properly for the first time because her drugged state had previously inured her to mental pain. He advised her to read the Sigmund Freud essay *Mourning And Melancholia*, published in 1917, in which he writes that mourning and melancholia share a cause, namely the loss of a love object, but while mourning is considered normal, melancholia is seen as pathological. Marianne found the paper illuminating and relevant to her own situation.

Marianne and Tose had made nebulous plans to move into a house together in Cambridge, Massachusetts, when they were both well and free of drugs and drink. Loyal to the dream, Marianne made the move, albeit with three others – her mother, Eva; her sponsor from Narcotics Anonymous, Deb; and a new boyfriend, who was also called Howard and a recovering heroin addict. Eva was drinking heavily, usually half a bottle of bourbon a day. She was reluctant to embrace the new, sober Marianne and complained that she had become 'very serious and dour' – like her father.

Although her jaw was still wired, Marianne travelled across the state in July 1986 to Mansfield, 30 miles south of Boston, to see Bob Dylan and Tom Petty & The Heartbreakers perform at the Great Woods Center for the Performing Arts. She met Dylan backstage and he asked her why her face was encased in metal and what had happened to her since they had last met. She told him the full story, ending with how she was clean of drugs and about to start life anew. He responded with a grunt roughly formed into words: "What? You? Nah!"

15

By the autumn of 1986 Marianne wanted to return to making music, though she was in 'too much pain' to write lyrics. She spoke to Chris Blackwell and another Island artist, Tom Waits – with whom she had developed a friendship largely conducted over the phone – and between them they engineered a plan for her next album. "I wanted to take the classic jazz and blues love songs of loss and yearning, and filter them through the devastation I was feeling about Howie's death, a sort of exorcism," she said. At first Waits had wanted to form a group of songs based on the characters who inhabited Storyville, a suburb of New Orleans which, between 1897 and 1917, was designated an official red light district based on a model used at ports in northern Germany and Holland. 'Blue' books were published containing information for visitors including descriptions of brothels, prices, services offered and the 'stock' [type of women] at each house. "In Tom's view of it, I would be bawling out raunchy songs in a pair of fishnet stockings and a suspender belt," said Marianne. "Much as I'd love to believe that sexpot image, I don't really see myself as an unrepentant hooker belting out blues from the bordello."

In the midst of her heroin dependency, Marianne had recorded 'Ballad Of The Soldier's Wife' with Chris Spedding for an album of Kurt Weill songs put together by producer Hal Willner, called *Lost In The Stars: The Music Of Kurt Weill.* Sting, Todd Rundgren, Lou Reed

257

and Tom Waits had also contributed tracks to the album released by A&M. At a similar time Marianne also put down 'Trouble In Mind' with composer Mark Isham, the theme song of the neo-noir film of the same name starring Kris Kristofferson as a police officer released from jail after serving time for murder. The song, written by jazz pianist Richard M Jones, was a slow eight-bar blues standard, first recorded in 1924. Marianne found that these tracks, recorded on a one-off basis, suited her mood, voice and age – she was about to turn 40 – and she wanted to do more of the same.

Hal Willner was considered the perfect collaborator on the nascent album project. Although only in his late twenties, the Philadelphia-born producer was an expert in classic pre-Second World War music. Before compiling the tribute to Weill he had assembled albums dedicated to the Italian film composer Nino Rota and the jazz pianist and composer Thelonius Monk. Over several weekends Willner visited Marianne's home in Cambridge and played her scores of records from his collection by the likes of Billie Holiday, Memphis Minnie [Lizzie Douglas], Mildred Bailey and Dinah Washington. "We listened to about 400 songs. She would wander around, listening all the time. Each weekend we would find 10 songs we would want to record," he said. About 20 songs were selected and acclaimed jazz guitarist Bill Frisell and pianist Mac Rebennack (better known as Dr John) were asked to help Marianne demo the material. The other musicians playing with them were Fernando Saunders on bass, JT Lewis, drums, and lead guitar was played by Robert Quine who had recently worked with Tom Waits and Scritti Politti.

Chris Blackwell had requested a 'beautiful tragic album of melancholy ballads' and Marianne was determined to deliver. "In the process of singing other people's material I stumbled across the fact that I'm not a bad interpretative singer," she said. The songs she and Willner chose were personalised by Marianne projecting on to them scenes from her own life. They began recording in October 1986 and within a few weeks had enough material to fill two albums. 'Strange Weather' was chosen as the title track. It had been written for Marianne by Tom Waits with help from his songwriter wife, Kathleen Brennan. During a lengthy telephone conversation Marianne had recounted to Waits the tale of meeting and then losing Howard Tose and he channelled it into the song.

A fleeting guitar piece by Bill Frisell called 'Stranger Intro' opens the album before Marianne sets a mood of reflection and sorrow with 'Boulevard Of Broken Dreams' from the 1934 film *Moulin Rouge*, set in Paris, in which it was sung by former silent films star and five-times married Constance Bennett. The short a cappella version of Huddie Ledbetter's 'I Ain' Goin' Down To The Well No More' is appropriately stark and direct. 'Yesterdays', a song featured originally in *Roberta*, the Jerome Kern and Otto Harbach musical of 1933 and long associated with Billie Holiday, is reclaimed as her own by Marianne: 'Golden days, olden days. Days of mad romance and love.' The texture is handsome and Willner marries the instruments to perfection. Frisell's guitar playing on the spiritual 'Sign Of Judgement' is surprisingly lively and Marianne has a knowing lilt in her vocal. 'Hello Stranger', written by Doc Pomus and Mac Rebennack, is musically interesting but misses the lyrical poundage of the rest of the record. 'Penthouse Serenade' is Broadway camp and Marianne's throaty delivery serves it well.

'As Tears Go By' would at first seem an unusual number to include among a collection of refined, romantic and classic songs. The critical observer might detect a strategic move by Marianne and Island – a signpost to the past included to make more palatable a new oeuvre of music. The song, as Marianne said many times, had been extremely world-weary for a young girl to sing, where its narrator had journeyed to 'the evening of the day'. Over the years the lyrics had fermented into rich prose and taken on a visionary element. "Forty is the age to sing it, not 17," she told the writer Rory O'Connor of *Vogue* in 1987. The new version was slowed down and sung an octave lower. Jazz composer Michael Gibbs arranged the strings and, many years after the event, the song at last made good sense.

The theme of isolation was explored on 'A Stranger On Earth', a song co-written by Sid Feller who was for many years Ray Charles' arranger. It contained the line pertinent to Marianne: 'Someday when I prove my worth, I won't be a stranger on earth'. The slow pacing of the album falls a little flat on both the blues standard 'Love Life And Money' and Bob Dylan's 'I'll Keep It With Mine', a song which both Judy Collins and Nico had already visited with more success.

Strange Weather, released in July 1987, was dedicated 'with love and thanks' to Howard Tose and warmly received by critics. The reviewer in *Spin* wrote: 'It's like a weather map, beautifully overcast with a lot of highs and lows. It's a depressing album, but wonderfully so, like a Leonard Cohen record or an Ingmar Bergman film.' *Time* compared her voice to 'Lotte Lenya [the wife of Kurt Weill] serenading from a sidecar' and praised her for using an 'eerie, ragged, shattered voice to instil gutter sophistication into fey songs that were normally the reserve of chanteuses that played hotel lounges off-season'. In Britain the reaction was similarly favourable. *Melody Maker* announced that Marianne had 'At last fulfilled her potential and shed her risqué reputation'. Q said it was an album of great songs 'interpreted with profound feeling – a triumph of talent over adversity' and *New Musical Express* – 'played in the right mood and at the right hour (preferably a small one), this music could give the blue angel wings once more'. The album sold moderately well over a period of time, charting in four countries – Sweden (number 32), Austria (48), Canada (71) and Britain (78).

At Island the album was viewed as similarly groundbreaking to *Broken English*. "I think most people think she is capable of coming out with classic albums and *Strange Weather* was a really great record, even though it was very sombre," said Rob Partridge. "She is a very strong woman who has obviously been through it." Once more, whether through serendipity or design, Marianne found herself ahead of her time. Albums of cover versions, often themed, would later become a staple of the music industry. Marianne and Willner had chosen the songs judiciously and this, coupled with the album's tasteful packaging, served to forge yet another branding. If the Marianne of the 1960s was sappy and the punk-driven late-1970s version slightly forced, this was a much better fit. The 'edge' had not dissipated but was merely given more potency by the introspection of the music and lyric and Marianne's use of vocal dynamics – the whisper, the near-croak, the soft anger. Perhaps most importantly it was an image, a look, a stance, an artistic way-of-being, within which she could age with grace.

The space between *A Child's Adventure* and *Strange Weather* was filled by two compilation albums. *Summer Nights*, released by Decca in March 1984, was another collection of early folk based numbers, not dissimilar to the *As Tears Go By* LP of 1981. *Rich Kid Blues* on Castle Communications, a company that specialised in leasing tracks from record companies and re-packaging them as compilation albums, was a more interesting project. Castle had taken control of the master tapes Marianne had worked on with Mike Leander in the early 1970s and had used the tracks to form a double album with practically the whole of the *Faithless* album. The song 'I'm Not Lisa' from *Faithless* was the only one missing, replaced by 'Fairytale Hero'. The switch was probably prompted by the inclusion of a cover of Cat Stevens' 'Sad Lisa' from his *Tea For The Tillerman* album of 1970 and the presumption that two songs about Lisa might be excessive.

The 12-song collection supervised by Leander was actually a much stronger and defined set than the one it preceded by several years on the *Faithless* album. Leander, with his typically meticulous approach, had coached Marianne into several fine vocal performances. The strongest track was 'Sad Lisa' where Marianne sang impeccably against a twanging acoustic guitar. Although recorded at a time when Marianne was heavily reliant on drugs, the record had a light, appealing touch. The album's packaging did not match the music within. On the cover Marianne sits uneasily against a wall, gripping her thigh and a glass of drink. Her skin is blotchy. *Rich Kid Blues* was billed as part of a 'collector series' but contained no sleeve notes or technical details, such as when the songs were recorded, who played on them, the composers or even producers – all information that a 'collector' might reasonably expect to be included in such a package.

Throughout 1987 Marianne was plagued by letters from the immigration authorities questioning her right to reside in the United States. The threat of a deportation order was especially distressing because Nicholas, now 22, had been accepted to study Planetary Sciences at Harvard University, close to where Marianne was living in Cambridge, a home found for her by Chris Blackwell. Her old friend, the beat writer Allen Ginsberg, invited her to hold seminars on lyric writing at the Buddhist-inspired Naropa Institute in Boulder, Colorado, but it did not constitute a legitimate job and validate her status as an American resident. Finally, after months of wrangling, the authorities had their way and Marianne was given a month's notice to leave the United States. An immigration officer accompanied her from her home to the airport.

She moved to County Kildare, back in the Ireland she had sung about and praised unconditionally to friends. "I've always had a good relationship with Ireland. The people make me laugh," she told the *Dublin Evening Herald* in February 1990. "I don't have illusions about it. I don't live there because it's all so wonderful. It's because I like it. It's small so it's sort of manageable. I like the people. They're kind of private too, which is nice. I suppose they're kind of shy. Reserved in a nice way." Marianne's friends had a surprise when she arrived in Ireland with her third husband. Unknown to either her father or close friends, Marianne had met and quickly fallen in love with another former addict, Giorgio della Terza, while in the United States. They married before few had even met della Terza and the first time most were introduced was when Marianne invited them to their cottage in Ireland. Rob Partridge was one of a handful to meet della Terza in the States and during a dinner party he found him to be 'pleasant company'.

Marianne had met della Terza at a Narcotics Anonymous meeting. "He was good-looking, intelligent and urbane and made me laugh," she said. Della Terza was the son of Dante della Terza, a leading academic who had taught at several Italian universities before moving to the University of California and then, in 1962, to Harvard where he was professor of romance languages and literatures, emeritus. He was considered one of the world's foremost scholars of Dante. Giorgio, who claimed to be an actor and writer, would quote Dante to Marianne and she found this 'irresistible'. They married and moved together to Shell Cottage, a folly based in the 1,000-acre grounds of Carton House in County Kildare, adorned with shells, crystals, sea urchins, sea weed, birds' eggs and other marine flotsam and jetsam. The centrepiece was a dome lined with thousands of tropical shells of every size. Emily FitzGerald (nee, Lennox, 1731-1814), the great granddaughter of Charles II, had painstakingly decorated the cottage. She had married James FitzGerald, the 20th Earl of Kildare, at the age of 15. They had 19 children and Emily had three more to her second husband, William Ogilvie, who had been her children's tutor.

Della Terza had plans to write at the cottage which was set in gardens designed by Capability Brown and included a small lake and an Egyptian obelisk. "I once wrote a song called 'Perfect Stranger' which is about relationships and about what I wanted and eventually found," Marianne told *Elle* in July 1990. "In fact, I did find a perfect stranger and we fell in love and got married. So he's not a stranger any more, and he's also by no means perfect – because you can only be perfect when you're a stranger. But he's the loveliest thing that's ever happened to me."

Henrietta Moraes was one of the first to visit them at the cottage. "It is very pretty and very, very romantic. It is in the grounds of a house and is a bit of a folly, really," she said. "It is said that Queen Victoria once took her lunch there. While I was there I never saw Giorgio doing any work. He appeared to be living off her, put it like that. He looked a bit like Ben Brierley oddly enough, but not so good looking."

After some deliberation at Island an idea surfaced that Marianne's back catalogue should be repackaged, not with another tawdry compilation album but in a contemporary, live setting. She would sing the songs that had made her famous but in the style that had brought her so much recent acclaim (and, coincidentally, the one that now best suited her lower octave voice). The Church of St Ann and the Holy Trinity, a building designed in a Gothic Revival style and opened in 1847 in New York's Brooklyn Heights, was chosen as the venue where Marianne would record two 90-minute performances. The shows themselves would provide a strong news story but would also be recorded to form her next album and video release.

The concerts were held on the weekend of November 25 and 26, 1989, with Hal Willner again producing. They were condensed on to a single album, *Blazing Away*, released in May 1990. Several songs recorded at the concerts had to be omitted because of a shortage of space, among them 'Conversation On A Bar Stool', a song written especially for Marianne by Bono and The Edge of U2, another Island recording act. 'Tower Of Song' by Leonard Cohen was also left out, as was a new song, 'Human Evil' written by Marianne and Barry Reynolds. The 13 songs that did make the record represented an eclectic set. Songs such as 'Les Prisons Du Roy', the cover of the Edith Piaf original, and 'Strange Weather' reaffirmed her new style. She plundered *Broken English* heavily for the title track; 'Why D'Ya Do It'; 'The Ballad of Lucy Jordan'; 'Working Class Hero' (replete with more than a little jazz-inspired doodling); and 'Guilt'. 'As Tears Go By' and 'Sister Morphine', the two Marianne staples, made expected appearances. As well as the title track and 'When I Find My Life' (both written by Reynolds), 'Times Square' was included and the traditional 'She Moved Through The Fair'.

Critical opinion was divided on *Blazing Away*. The *Daily Mail*, a newspaper that had often held a jaundiced view of Marianne, said her voice was 'irritating' and concluded that the record was a work of 'almost superhuman self-absorption'. As the album was aimed chiefly at the relatively new but fast-expanding CD market, *Q* magazine's review was particularly important in Britain. David Hepworth took several paragraphs to make a similar point as the *Mail* but in more sympathetic tones. 'Some may find they've heard this saga once too often,' was his parting shot. David Quantick in *New Musical Express* concentrated on the music rather than the legend: 'Faithfull's strengths are as an interpretive singer; given a good tune to scrape the guts out of she can work wonders. Not here, though.' Only *Melody Maker* welcomed it unequivocally. Chris Roberts dubbed it: 'An outstanding document of everything that was ever intriguing about Marianne Faithfull's personal, twisted vision.'

As a warm-up for concerts later in the year, Marianne appeared at the Tivoli Theatre in Francis Street, Dublin, a former cinema with a capacity of 1,000. She played three consecutive nights in February 1990. Flanked by an audience on three sides, she gave an insight into her new album with a short but powerful set lasting 40 minutes. U2's Bono was in the first night crowd and was photographed afterwards with Marianne.

A single British performance was arranged to promote the album, at London's Dominion Theatre on Tuesday May 15. As always, Marianne's imminent arrival in town (for the first time in eight years) prompted press interest. In keeping with Island's policy of placing Marianne at the high-end of the media, interviews were conducted chiefly with the quality press. She was asked to fill in a questionnaire by the *Sunday Correspondent.* Her answers were suitably erudite. Her favourite painters were: Francis Bacon, Joseph Turner, Nicholas Dunbar [her son], Diego Velázquez, Willem de Kooning, Robert Motherwell and Georges Braque. And her favourite writers, Emile Zola, D.T. Suzuki, Stendhal, William Burroughs, Robert Lowell, William Carlos Williams, Salman Rushdie, Giorgio della Terza, David Mamet, William Shakespeare and Oscar Wilde.

The interview with the *Daily Telegraph*'s Cassandra Jardine was particularly spiky. Jardine quickly noticed Marianne's self-regarding air and commented that she could not issue a sentence of more than five words without using 'I'. On learning that Marianne had settled in Ireland, Jardine remarked facetiously that she had not realised Ireland was 'full of exiles from the Sixties'. Marianne turned upon the interviewer and 'hissed and presented her profile like an outraged duchess'.

The show at the Dominion Theatre was not as solemn as many expected after listening to the album, and won almost universal praise. The audience was spared the musical jams that punctuated the record mainly because Marianne's only accompaniment was guitarist Barry Reynolds. She began the evening by introducing her 'backing band' from New York. "Actually, he's from Manchester. But when we play in New York I say he's from Manchester and people are impressed, so I thought that now we are in England you would be more impressed if I said he was from New York." The directness of a microphone, voice, guitar and her charisma held the audience from the opening strains of 'Falling From Grace' to, 16 songs later, the closing 'She Moved Through The Fair'. The reviews were possibly better than at any other time in her career: 'A powerful affirmation of artistic health' – Adam Sweeting,

The Guardian; 'Her qualities as a singer and her grip on the public's curiosity remain undiminished by time' – David Cheal, *Daily Telegraph*; and, 'An evening of bliss with too few lows to be counted' – Dele Fadele, *New Musical Express.*

Three weeks later, on Monday June 4, 1990, Marianne performed 'The Ballad Of Lucy Jordan' on BBC television's *Wogan* programme, a chat show hosted by Terry Wogan that drew an audience of 10 million viewers. Marianne, wearing pastel-coloured summer clothes, spoke candidly, covering old themes such as Jagger, the 'summer of love' and her issues with drugs. Asked specifically about Jagger, she said any feelings of bitterness had now subsided and 'the embers were dead'. In living rooms across Britain her radiance and pleasant manner were noted and, the next day, people were commenting on how well their prodigal daughter was looking. Glynn Faithfull taped the interview and watched it several times with fatherly pride.

Marianne was among scores of performers invited to take part in Roger Waters' live version of the Pink Floyd album *The Wall*, filmed as a television spectacular and held on the former no-man's land between Potsdamer Platz and the Brandenberg Gate in Berlin – the Berlin Wall had tumbled eight months previously. Marianne appeared towards the end of the show on Saturday July 21 in 'The Trial' scene with Tim Curry, Thomas Dolby, Ute Lemper and Albert Finney. As the jury passed judgement on the main character, Marianne, as his 'mother', screams: 'Come to mother, baby, let me hold you in my arms'.

Concerts were scheduled throughout the winter of 1990 and Marianne mentioned in several interviews that it formed her heaviest workload since starting out back in 1964. By November she had reached Vancouver in Canada and ecstatic audiences had become a routine feature. Caroline Longford in the magazine *Disorder* wrote: 'Some yahoos scattered in the audience were so psyched they wouldn't let her take a breath without assuming the song was over. This led to wild and premature clapping, stamping, and yip yip yipping. I can't say I recall having heard such loud and enthusiastic appeals for encores in my life.' In San Francisco, Marianne appeared before an enthusiastic packed house – including many gay men – at Slim's Club owned by Boz Scaggs. Reviewer Gina Arnold, of the *San Francisco Chronicle*, explored the same theme: 'Faithfull could have been extremely bad and the audience would have cheered her, in the curiously slavish, half-pitying, half-admiring manner that fans of ex-junkies use when lauding their heroes.' Nick Coleman, in London's *Time Out*, was more specific about Marianne's fan base and described it as a 'clucking posse of hagiographical camp-followers'.

Support for Marianne among the gay community was first noted in the early-1980s, principally in the United States. While Marianne's music contained few direct lyrical references or expressions of support for the gay sector, her prevailing belief in tolerance and general non-judgmental attitude gave her iconic status. They could also relate to the persecution and ridicule Marianne had endured, and admire her self-belief.

Eva Faithfull died in May 1990, aged 80. Marianne was on tour in Australia when John Dunbar rang with the news. She returned to England immediately and visited the funeral home to view Eva lying in her coffin. "She looked so beautiful. Her face almost looked carved," she said. Marianne, assisted by Jane, the wife of Chris O'Dell, picked rosemary and May blossom from Eva's garden and placed them on the body. Eva was buried in the circular churchyard at the 800-year-old St Mary's in Aldworth, which also contained the ashes of Laurence Binyon, famous for the remembrance poem *For The Fallen*.

Healthy and free of drugs, Marianne was able to enjoy a richer social life. While on a trip to Los Angeles in February 1991 she was invited by the fashion photographer Steven Meisel to visit Madonna with him. Meisel, known for his work for *Vogue* was collaborating with Madonna on the book *Sex*. "She had a gym in her bathroom and a very impressive collection of paintings," said Marianne. As they walked around the house, Madonna was wearing only lingerie. Marianne noticed a magazine rack in the kitchen and each one featured Madonna on the cover.

They moved on together to the Ahmanson Theatre where Rupert Everett was starring as Nicky Lancaster, the drug-addicted society wastrel in Noël Coward's *The Vortex*. Afterwards they visited a gay club where Madonna asked Marianne to join her on the dance floor. "She dances incredibly, doing proper steps as if she's on stage," said Marianne. "I felt very odd, to me it was like something out of Moliere."

Marianne's personal life suffered another setback in 1991 when her marriage to Giorgio della Terza broke down. "I think he went off with another girlfriend. No, I don't think he went off, I think Marianne just found out that he had a girlfriend," said Henrietta Moraes. Marianne had sensed she and della Terza were drifting apart while she was on the road. "Life for him at Shell Cottage was like a house arrest," she said. "He was a junk food addict who loved the bright lights, and here he was stuck in the middle of nowhere." She pondered later on whether della Terza had properly understood her. "Giorgio had a very skewed image of me. He thought of me, until he'd almost lost me, in terms of blonde hair and big tits." While she was at Shell Cottage, Marianne had found a love letter, written in an 'incredibly drippy and illiterate style', sent to della Terza by a girlfriend. Marianne realised that this woman was someone she had asked 'to help me get my looks together'. "She took me to a stylist who promptly cut off all my hair and dyed it grey!" said Marianne.

Marianne remained uncharacteristically embittered about della Terza. In an interview with Chrissy Iley in 2011 she said: "A lot of my boyfriends were really nice. There was only one – and that's the American I married [Giorgio della Terza] – who was not. I met him in an AA meeting, the bastard. I never talk about him." Iley noted that 'her eyes seem to whirl with anger at even the thought of him'. Henrietta Moraes felt Marianne's attitude to men revealed a seldom-acknowledged pragmatic aspect of her personality. "I think she is very old fashioned in the way that she thinks she's got to have a man, and to be married to them. Maybe there's a bit of the father figure tied up in it. She wants to do the wife bit, but she wants a career as well and I don't think men like that much. I think she has to decide what she wants. The problem is that it is very lonely without a partner. During the time she was with Giorgio she was learning to be sort of quiet and have ordinary people to dinner and things like that. People who have known her for a long time are very fond of her. She is very affectionate and has got great charm and is very funny. She's a bit thick, you know, and clever. You can be both at the same time."

Marianne was still grieving over Eva's death when she agreed to play the role of Pirate Jenny in a production of *The Threepenny Opera* at the Gate Theatre, Dublin. "I cried all the way through rehearsals," she said. "I'd come home and see my mother's face everywhere – in the stars, the water, the trees and the moon." Set in Victorian England, *The Threepenny Opera*, written by Bertolt Brecht and Kurt Weill in 1928, focuses on the dealings of Macheath (Mackie), an anti-hero of the underworld. Marianne, as Jenny, is a lowly maid and prostitute working at a 'crummy hotel' who dreams of pirates from *The Black Freighter* ransacking the town ('This whole frickin' place will be down to the ground, only this cheap hotel standing up safe and sound') and taking her away with them. She has given Mackie, her former lover, shelter from the police but is jealous of his wife, Polly Peachum. Eventually, she tips off the police, who catch Mackie and take him to his hanging. Her song ['Pirate Jenny'] – perhaps the best-known in the production after 'Mack The Knife' – suggests that she relishes the idea of having Mackie's fate in her hands.

The Threepenny Opera, with a new translation by director Frank McGuinness, opened on Tuesday, July 9, 1991. Marianne was sent a bouquet of flowers by Mick Jagger and his new wife, Jerry Hall, with a note reading: 'Break a leg!' The musical, which ran until Saturday, September 14, received positive reviews, especially Marianne's performance. "I became respectable overnight," she said. "Journalists to whom all these years I'd been a series of caricatures, all of a sudden came to the conclusion that there was a point to this person, that I was more than a Mars bar story."

During the production's run Marianne was invited by the snooker player Alex Higgins to spend a night with him. They had enjoyed a 'wild night' together a few years before – when Marianne was so inebriated she could barely recall it – and he wanted the same again. She was anxious that their tryst did not make the papers, especially now she felt she was being taken seriously by the media. She agreed on condition that he met her at the theatre at 11.30p.m. and they booked into a hotel, where she would spend two hours with him before returning home. She briefed Higgins in the taxi on how to behave at the hotel to ensure their anonymity but he completely ignored her request. As he approached the check-in desk, he shouted to her: 'Don't worry, Faithfull, I'll call you Vicki, not Marianne!'

Marianne was invited to narrate a new film version of *The Turn Of The Screw* in 1992 (it had been filmed originally in 1961 as *The Innocents*). Patsy Kensit played the lead role of Jenny, with Julian Sands as Mr Cooper, in the Henry James story of a young woman hired by a wealthy but sinister man to tutor his two children at the family's isolated estate. Marianne's role in *When Pigs Fly* a year later was more substantial. She played opposite Alfred Molina in the dark comedy directed by Sara Driver, who had produced two early films for Jim Jarmusch. Marianne, as 'Lily', was a wife who returned to haunt the husband who had killed her. She had to dye her hair black for the part. "It's a great idea," she told the *Chicago Tribune*. "It will free me from this thing of being a busty blonde, which has always been a pain in the neck, in a way. I guess I'll change the colour back after the film because I've got used to being a blonde, but I'm still waiting to have some fun." The film was scored by Joe Strummer and received the 'Best of Festival' feature award at the 1994 Long Island Film Festival.

The fashion photographer and occasional film-maker Bruce Weber invited Marianne in 1993 to appear in *Nice Girls Don't Stay For Breakfast*, a documentary he was making about the film legend Robert Mitchum – dubbed 'the soul of film noir' by critic Roger Ebert. Marianne was an admirer of *Let's Get Lost*, a film Weber had made five years earlier about the jazz musician Chet Baker. She recorded two duets with Mitchum at the Capital Records studios in Los Angeles but was unclear on why Weber had thought to involve her in the project. "I suspect the real reason I was there was to help Bruce pull the personal stuff out of Mitchum, which I never could have done even if I'd wanted to," said Marianne. "Hell would freeze over before Bob Mitchum was going to bare his soul, he's from the old school." An example of this was caught on camera. Weber asked Mitchum how he felt when he was arrested for smoking pot [as he had been in August, 1948]. Mitchum responded: 'Who gives a fuck what I felt like?'

During filming Mitchum made a pass at Marianne but it was rebuffed. They had spent an evening together with Weber at the restaurant at the fashionable Chateau Marmont Hotel on Sunset Boulevard, Los Angeles. Mitchum had sunk a few vodka Martinis and was telling stories of old Hollywood. Marianne was wearing a short black skirt, high heels and a low-cut top. As they left the restaurant Mitchum leant back, took Marianne in his arms and gave her what she referred to later as a 'classic screen kiss'. In the car Mitchum wanted to take it 'a bit further' but Marianne responded by giving him a 'little cuff'. "Maybe that's one of the reasons I've become so cool in my old age [she was only 46 at the time and Mitchum, 75], and sort of reserved," she said. "I don't know what it would take to get me into bed now. And it's not Catholicism, really – it's just too much trouble."

Nice Girls Don't Stay For Breakfast has yet to be completed. Weber has revisited the film intermittently over the years and there were thwarted plans for a release in 2007. Excerpts were shown in 2010 at the Hamptons International Film Festival held in New York. It is narrated by Dr John and features interviews with Mitchum, his brother John, and friends and family. When it is finally released there are plans for an accompanying book of still photography and a soundtrack which will, of course, feature Marianne.

Marianne became a grandmother in 1993 when Carole Jahme, the wife of Nicholas, gave birth to Oscar, named after Oscar Wilde. "Oscar looks just like me and is therefore the best thing ever," said Marianne. Carole, a former model and actress, was a fitting addition to the extended Faithfull family tree. She began her working life as a member of Gerry

Cottle's Circus where she worked on the trapeze and tightrope, and did clowning and acrobatics. She is an expert on the work of Charles Darwin and manages to synthesize Darwinian Theory into most of her creative ventures which include stand-up comedy, a column for *The Guardian* newspaper and a documentary made for Channel Four about Michael Jackson and his pet chimpanzee, Bubbles.

16

Rumours circulated over many years that Marianne was working on an autobiography. Cynics scoffed that she would not be able to recall a good portion of her life and there were stories of advances being secured and then returned as she found more interesting ways to spend her time. She chose David Dalton to work with her on the book, though their precise roles and individual contributions to the whole have never been divulged.

Dalton was a founding editor of *Rolling Stone* where he considered himself a 'rock evangelist'. "Rock was the very plasma that held the counterculture together. Everything was plugged into it, everything I cared about, anyway. It was the Pentecostal flame that would bring the New Jerusalem into existence," he said. Between 1968 and 1971 he penned cover stories on global stars such as Little Richard, James Brown and Elvis Presley. Along with fellow *Rolling Stone* writer David Felton, he won the prestigious Columbia School Of Journalism Award in 1970 for an interview with Charles Manson. ('It was a scary awakening for me to find out that not every long-haired, dope-smoking freak was a peace-and-love hippie.') Before working with Marianne he had authored biographies on The Rolling Stones and Jim Morrison and afterwards wrote books on Sid Vicious, Grateful Dead and Meat Loaf.

Although born in London, Dalton was raised in British Columbia on the east coast of Canada. He was asked by Steven Ward of the website

RockCritics.Com about his approach to writing biographies. "It's more like fiction," he said. "Basically you conceive of your subject as a character, and, being rock stars, rock dogs, etc., they already have well-established personae – masks through which they speak. Then you write their stories as if you were writing a first-person novel. You dilute your subject into a literary solution, so to speak, and get high on them. Afterwards one has to have one's brain rewired." Of Marianne, he said: "She fused the myth of the decadent Romantic poet with the jaded, hipster rock star in one seamless persona that was so potent it almost killed her (a number of times). I love Marianne. She's an aristocratic Beatnik. In other words, a hip, literate, post-degenerate rock star who has become the curator of her persona and voice."

Faithfull was published in 1994 by Michael Joseph, an imprint of the Penguin Group, to almost universal praise. Dalton and Marianne marshalled the facts and anecdotes well and placed the narrative within its greater cultural context. The authorial voice was presumably close to the actual as Marianne flitted between compassionate and dismissive, sensitive and harsh, pretentious and humble. "The book has given me pride in myself, faith in myself again. I needed it," she said. Paul Jones, writing in *The Independent*, was one of the few left disappointed: 'This is not an entertaining read. In fact, it's a while since I enjoyed a book as little as this one. It is quite absorbing, though, in a tabloid sort of way – sensational and, on its subject's own admission, unreliable. Much of the book is ripe for inclusion in Pseuds' Corner. When Bob Dylan turned up in London, 'the Zeitgeist streamed through him like electricity... my existential hero... Jangling Rimbaud of rock... I was somehow absorbing by osmosis buried layers of meaning. I knew there was more to this than me sitting at the feet of the master, absorbing the arcana of Bob.'

Marianne sent a copy to Glynn Faithfull at Braziers and received a letter back that she would frame and treasure for the rest of her life. It was sent on Wednesday August 3, 1994, and Glynn wrote: 'I only now realised how difficult your life has been. I didn't know and I'm sorry, darling.' He acknowledged that she was the child of 'a strange wartime marriage of two rather difficult people'. In closing, he congratulated her on being 'such a nice and mature person'. By reading the book Glynn had learned properly for the first time of Marianne's feelings, especially during her growing up years, where, according to Marianne, she and Eva were 'two lost souls shuffling about the house in a fog of rage and desperation'. Glynn's final years at Braziers had not been happy. "It was a nightmare!" said Marianne. "My dear stepmother – who really helped me to get my place back at the family table – became ill with leukaemia. She had to go into hospital and they kicked him out of the commune. I mean, he did run it as if it were an autocracy, but it was a commune and they voted on it. He and my stepmother died within four weeks of each other."

The letter precipitated a new closeness for Marianne and Glynn Faithfull. "He was the great unrequited love of my life," she told Will Self of the *Independent On Sunday* in 1999. "But when he was dying I was able to ask him questions – and he answered them. He told me about some of the things he'd seen in the war and it was clear that he'd been terribly traumatised. He came back a committed pan-European, determined to help prevent it happening again." Glynn was disappointed that he had been considered tight-fisted and began taking Marianne out for lunches at country pubs near Ipsden, encouraging her to eat well. Over the years the food at Braziers had been a source of complaint for Marianne. "My father belonged to a commune and the food was ghastly," she told *The Guardian* in 2011. "My idea of food hell is the salad cream they'd pour all over bits of lettuce, cucumber and tomato. It was just disgusting." Glynn told her about his war service with MI6 – the secret agency that was not formally acknowledged until 1994 – which provided foreign intelligence to the Government. He revealed for the first time that he was part of the team charged with debriefing Heinrich Himmler, the highest-ranking SS officer.

An invitation to record a duet with the Senegalese musician Ismaël Lô in 1994 instigated great change in Marianne's life, both professional and personal. Philippe Constantin, who had set up Virgin France in the late-1970s with Patrick Zelnick and had discovered Angélique Kidjo and Mory Kanté, asked Marianne to sing 'Without Blame' with Lô. The polemical lyrics had been written by Roger Waters, formerly of

Pink Floyd: 'Burn your boardwalk basement trade, feel the flame, feel the curve of the sun, your living flesh reeks of compromise, babe...' Constantin, described by Virgin founder, Sir Richard Branson, as 'a wild ragged individual, on and off heroin, but with excellent musical taste' was at the time President of Mango Records, Island's World Music subsidiary label, based in Paris. The duet with Lô worked surprisingly well and their voices, although dissimilar, blended powerfully. The song remained unreleased until February 1997 when it appeared on Lô's compilation album, *Jammu Africa*. Constantin died before its release. He contracted a virus, thought to be malaria, while sourcing new artists in Africa and died at his Bordeaux home in January 1996, aged 51.

While Marianne was working on the track she was introduced by Constantin to a man with whom he shared an office, François Ravard. Constantin and Ravard had known each other for many years. While he worked at Pathé Marconi EMI, Constantin had signed Téléphone, who were managed by Ravard. Marianne and Ravard dated and a loving relationship developed that was to be the most long-lasting of her life. He became her manager and remained so after they separated romantically 14 years later, overseeing a tremendously sustained and creative period of her career.

Ravard was 36 when he met Marianne, nine years the younger. A vastly experienced operator in both the music and film industry, as a student at the Lycée Edgar-Poe, a private secondary school in Paris, he had befriended the guitarist Olivier Caudron, who introduced him to another guitar player, Jean-Louis Aubert. The three of them moved into an apartment in Avenue Fremiet, adjacent to the River Seine in Paris, which effectively became the epicentre of the French punk scene. Aubert formed Téléphone with Louis Bertignac (guitar), Corine Marienneau (bass) and Richard Kolinka (drums) while Caudron (better known as Olive) played in Diesel and, later, Lili Drop. Ravard became manager of Téléphone and was behind early ruses such as the impromptu gigs at the American Centre in Paris in November 1976 and another at the Paris Metro in March 1977. He negotiated a deal for Téléphone with Pathé Marconi EMI although he was only 19-years-old at the time. He was an excellent networker, calling on record producers

Glyn Johns, Martin Rushent and Bob Ezrin and others including the fashion photographer Jean-Baptiste Mondino and the renowned album sleeve photographer Lynn Goldsmith. Téléphone's self-titled debut album, recorded in London and released in 1977, was a collection of speeded up rhythm and blues tracks given a punk snarl with titles such as 'Flipper', 'In Your Bed' and 'On The Road'.

Téléphone were successful across mainland Europe. Their second album, *Crache Ton Venin* [*Spit Your Venom*], sold 600,000 copies. In June 1982 they opened for The Rolling Stones at their concert at the racecourse in Auteuil, Paris. Ravard branched out and set up the publishing company Téléphone Music, and was one of the first to invest in video promos made by directors such as Julien Temple. Téléphone split in 1986 and Ravard joined Artmedia, one of France's leading high-end arts agencies representing actors, scriptwriters, composers and film directors. He was one of a team of agents with his own mini-roster comprising his old friend from Téléphone, Jean-Louis Aubert; the pop group Les Rita Mitsouko; the composer and music video director Laurent Boutonnat; and the film actress Marie Trintignant. In 1987 he left the agency and formed R Films, producing three feature films – the quirky *Divine Child* (1989) about a six-year-old on a madcap road trip; *Stan The Flasher* (1990), directed by Serge Gainsbourg, about a former teacher recalling the private lessons he had given to girls in his younger days; and *The Shambles* (1991) which focused on the estrangement of a marrried couple.

Faithfull galvanised interest from production companies keen to craft the film of the book of the life. Initially the film went into development with Dreyfuss/James, a company headed by film actor Richard Dreyfuss and Hollywood production veteran Judith James. It was announced later that the project had been taken up instead by Hell's Kitchen International, the production company co-owned by the Irish film director Jim Sheridan, a six-time Academy Award nominee, famous for *My Left Foot, In The Name Of The Father* and *In America*. Reports leaked of various actors set to play leading roles. Michelle Pfeiffer, Uma Thurman or Cate Blanchett were favourites to play Marianne. Willem Dafoe was to be Jagger and –

apparently at Marianne's' request – Daniel Day-Lewis was to be Keith Richards. When asked whether she would appear in the film herself, Marianne responded: "No! It's an artistic venture, a serious art form, not some dotty old biopic. It's got to be done in its own way, which is why I'm so pleased Sheridan's got it." The screenwriter, Dolores Rice, who had worked with Sheridan before on *The Whole Of The Moon*, funded by the Irish Film Board, was asked to work on the screenplay.

Relations between Marianne and the team involved in the film project turned sour, however, and led to it being abandoned. The details remained unclear but it would appear that another scriptwriter, Simon Carmody, became involved (despite it remaining on Rice's formal CV as a sole piece of work) and Marianne objected to the 'mythologising' [her words] of her life story. During an interview with Joe Jackson of the *Irish Independent* she raged: "One of the reasons I've pulled back from my time in Ireland is because I was so appalled by Carmody's script, it was dis-gust-ing. Un-f***ing-believable. People may think it was based on my book. It was not, and I have taken back the copyright so the film cannot be made." François Ravard was also present at the interview and added: "I read a copy I got from Hollywood and I discover what a piece of sh*t it is, saying Marianne is a bad singer, a drug addict, a prostitute." Marianne interjected: "A prostitute! And there is even a scene where my son sees me going off with a punter. It says, 'Draw back to seven-year-old Nick,' which is totally made up. And Sheridan will make that movie over my dead f***ing body. No way will it be made."

Both Jim Sheridan and Simon Carmody were dumbfounded by Marianne's comments and defended themselves in the *Irish Independent*. Sheridan denied there was such a scene in the film. "On the contrary, there is a scene where you see her down and out on the streets but she says, 'I never resorted to prostitution.' I would never do anything to harm Marianne, and in fact I gave her back the copyright." Simon Carmody added: "I really can't remember a scene like that. Marianne was never a hooker, and I love her and am a huge admirer of her work. Like Jim, I wouldn't do anything to hurt or upset her." Marianne contacted her friend, the actress Carrie Fisher, to discuss the issue. "I didn't realise they could do that – that they could just buy a book title and then make it all up. Carrie did try to explain it to me, and I've eventually gotten it. What she said was amazing, really. She said, 'You know, you may think that your story has been degraded enough' – which I do think – 'but there are people who will want to degrade you more.'"

Acting roles were offered to Marianne consistently and she maintained a parallel career across several decades. In 1994 she played the small part of 'Bev' in *Shopping*, a film about a group of British teenagers indulging in joyriding and ram-raiding. It was notable for being the first major leading role for Jude Law who was 22 at the time. A critical and box office disappointment, *Shopping* was voted the eighth worst British movie of all time on an online poll run by Virgin Media in 2013. The judges deemed it: 'A style-over-substance flick that deserves to be deposited in a large landfill site and left to rot for eternity. Unless anyone really likes watching Jude Law and Sadie Frost poncing around and trying to look cool while going on a ram-raiding spree.' The 'winner' of the poll was *Spice World*, which narrowly beat the Ken Russell-directed *The Lair Of The White Worm*.

Through the late 1980s and early 1990s the reliance on Weill/Brecht material, cover versions and songs revisited from Marianne's own back catalogue was becoming formulaic. Both Island and Marianne felt a radical new approach was due. Marianne told Island's A&R manager, Kevin Patrick, that she wanted to make a soundtrack to her 'mental film'. Patrick immediately suggested that Angelo Badalamenti would make the perfect collaborator. The Brooklyn-born composer had won great acclaim for his scores featured in *Blue Velvet*, *Twin Peaks* and *Wild At Heart*, among others.

Marianne pursued Badalamenti 'like an elusive animal' until he agreed to co-write and produce an album with her. "My musical world is a little bit dark, a little bit off-centre," he said. "I think of it as tragically beautiful. That is how I would describe what I love best: tragically beautiful." His style was to compose fragmentary instrumental pieces to complement specific scenes. At first Marianne was frustrated because he took the same approach to songwriting, telling her constantly, 'We need more fragments'. They eventually shaped 10 short songs and recorded them at New York's Excalibur Sound and National/Edison studios.

The album was released in March 1995 and titled *A Secret Life*. It opened with 'Prologue' where Marianne read an extract from Dante's *The Divine Comedy* and closed with 'Epilogue' featuring an extract from Shakespeare's *The Tempest*. In between, Marianne's voice sat exquisitely across Badalamenti's electro-classical arrangements, especially on 'Love In The Afternoon' and 'She'. *A Secret Life* was created in a completely different way than any of her other records, by musicians and a recording team with whom she was initially unfamiliar. While the voice remained, of course, everything else was changed and the record formed a cool breeze across her musical canon.

Marianne was invited to appear on the long-running BBC Radio Four programme *Desert Island Discs* on Sunday May 28, 1995. The presenter, Sue Lawley, led Marianne through the customary set-pieces of her life – her family background; how her pop career began; the relationship with Mick Jagger; The Rolling Stones; the Redlands bust; the overdose; living on the streets; drug addiction; her survivor status; her fondness for Ireland and her love of the music of Kurt Weill. Despite supposedly celebrating her life, it seemed Sue Lawley (and presumably the production team) saw Marianne as an agent from whom to gather information on Mick Jagger (Was he stingy? Is he bisexual?) and The Rolling Stones – a strategy Marianne had encountered many times down the years.

Her Desert Island Discs were: 1. Jimi Hendrix – 'Hey Joe' ("I knew Jimi, he was a wonderful man"); 2. Ensemble Modern – 'Berlin Im Licht' ("When I was growing up there were a couple of Brecht/Weill songs on a 78rpm record in the house. I think they were my mother's. This is a Kurt Weill song. I've put it in because of my parents"); 3. Cast of *Gigi* – 'The Night They Invented Champagne' ("I went to see *Gigi* with my mother when I was 12 or 13 and it made a very deep impression on me and I used it as my life model and I still believe in all that"); 4. Bob Dylan – 'Highway 61 Revisited' ("One of my all-time favourites. I couldn't live without it"); 5. Traffic – 'Dear Mr. Fantasy'

("This is a picture of what it was like and this really is our life and how it felt"); 6. The Rolling Stones – 'Gimme Shelter' (Marianne did not comment); 7. Bob Marley – 'Small Axe' ("This really represented the 70s for me, the bit I really hold. The music that meant more than anything to me was Jamaican, reggae. It has a great spiritual charge"); 8. Claudio Monteverdi – 'L'Orfeo' ("I thought my dad would like this. I want to play it for my dad"). She chose Daniel Defoe's *Robinson Crusoe* as her book and her luxury was paper and a pen with an attached magnifying glass from Asprey's [the long-established New Bond Street company].

Marianne put in what many consider to be one of her finest screen acting performances in *Moondance*, a film shot in Luggala in County Wicklow, Ireland, chiefly on land owned by the wealthy arts patron Garech Browne. The film focuses on Patrick (played by Ian Shaw) and Dominic (Ruaidhri Conroy), two brothers living an unusually independent life on a dilapidated country estate. Their lives are changed when Anya (Julia Brendler) comes to stay and they battle for her affection. Marianne played the boys' mother, an anthropologist who returns from a trip to proffer great wisdom. "I play someone who knows the answer and is very wise," she said. "One step above a ghost – similar, but more substantial!" Marianne contributed a version of Van Morrison's 'Madame George' to the film, played over the closing credits. The song, drawn from Morrison's classic album *Astral Weeks*, was also included on the tribute album *No Prima Donna: The Songs Of Van Morrison*. It was recorded at Dublin's Windmill Lane Studios in Ringsend where Marianne met up with Morrison whom she considered one of her 'dearest friends'. "He's like a mentor, really, Van," she said. 'I tell him about my personal problems and he gives me advice. It's like having a hotline to God, but Van's better because he's here."

An uncanny capacity of knowing with whom to associate was reinforced in 1996 when Marianne agreed to record with Oxbow. Founded in 1988 in San Francisco and playing music variously termed 'noise rock' or 'avant rock' but also touching on jazz and classical, their debut album was

Fuckfest. By their fourth album, *Serenade In Red,* produced by Steve Albini (formerly of Big Black, Rapeman and Shellac), they were considered one of the United States' most formidable and uncompromising independent bands. Oxbow's frontman, Eugene S. Robinson, had become obsessed with Marianne's *Strange Weather* album. "I had been a fan back in the late 1970s but *Strange Weather* put the hook in me," he said. "I maybe listened to it 300 times in a row and decided in full-on crazy guy fashion that I needed to have her sing on the next Oxbow record. So I wrote to her management and curiously they responded. But US immigration screwed us over and prevented her from getting in to the States, so we relocated the recording to Windmill Lane Studios in Dublin."

Robinson flew to Ireland with fellow band member Niko Wenner and sound engineer Gibbs Chapman. They made the journey despite being unable to contact Marianne in the days preceding the planned recording. "We had no idea if she was going to show but had to do what was expected of us and hope for the best," said Robinson. "In any case, we get to Dublin and head over to the studio. Eventually she showed up with her manager, François, in tow. He had failed to pay her phone bill, so hence no phone. She was a grand dame really, which was great. But we were really tense about getting this recorded because we're broke and going all-in on this. So while we figured to start right away, she was not feeling it and said she would return the next day. We took photos, chewed the shit, she disappeared with François." When Marianne arrived the next day she said it was too cold in the studio. "She sent her runner out, a guy who sang for some band called The Golden Horde [Simon Carmody was singer with The Golden Horde, signed to U2's Mother Records], which I misheard as The Golden Whore, to score some weed I believe," said Robinson. "It made me nervous as I was envisioning our next-to-last-day literally going up in smoke. But Marianne buckled down and started to sing."

At first it was planned that Robinson and Marianne would lay down their parts at the same time, side-by-side in the sound booth. They were recording a cover of the Willie Dixon song 'Insane Asylum'. Marianne was unaware that Robinson was noted for – as one reviewer described it – 'howling in a high-pitched, anguished voice somewhere between

Robert Plant and Birthday Party-era Nick Cave'. "We go into the room together and gather around the microphone," said Robinson. "I weighed 245 pounds at the time – obviously a barbell boy. But I knew she had not heard or listened to our band really so when giant me started screaming the first verse I could see her tense up. We stopped the song and she said, 'You know, I'll let you go first and then I'll come back in.' She left, returned after I finished and absolutely slayed the song. Sitting around after, she asked us how long we were staying and we said we had to get back to California. She asked why and we said that we had day jobs and she turned to François, stomped her foot on the ground and said, 'François! 'I want a DAY JOB!' We all laughed. She was wonderful."

Oxbow invited Marianne to the mix in the United States but their e-mails remained unanswered. 'Insane Asylum' was the closing track on their album *Serenade In Red*. While Robinson screamed and hollered, Marianne provided the more traditional counterpoint as she sang: 'I went out to the insane asylum/ I found my baby out there/ I said please come back to me…' Marianne also added a piece of narration to another track on the album, 'Over'. She did not request a fee for her contribution and nebulous plans to draw up a contract did not materialise. The next time Robinson heard of Marianne was when it was announced that she had recorded with Metallica, later in 1996. "We watched with great interest a Metallica interview when they were asked where they got the idea to use Marianne for vocals," said Robinson. "And they kind of choked and paused and then mumbled something about it being their manager's idea. In any case, working with Marianne was a high-water experience for me."

Marianne revealed later that she had actually been approached by Metallica in a similar way to the Oxbow project. "Lars [Ulrich, drummer] literally rang me up, and they came over and we did the song," she said. "I don't really like singing with other people, but I made an exception for Metallica. They're a really good working band, they know what they're doing. James [Hetfield, singer] was nothing like how I imagined, which is the raison d'etre of my life. They're all nice boys, good to their mums and their wives."

Marianne sang on the Metallica track 'The Memory Remains', which opened their seventh album, *ReLoad*. Although her contribution was relatively slight – a section of 'la, la, la's' judiciously placed and sounding discernibly 'Marianne' – the song hugely increased her profile. It was the main single from the album, released in November 1997, and made number 26 in the United States and 13 in Britain. The band, with Marianne, performed it on the December 6, 1997 edition of *Saturday Night Live*. She also appeared in the video accompanying the single, where the band played on a large, suspended platform making full and continuous rotations as if on an enormous swing. Marianne was filmed wearing a ringmaster's uniform, turning the crank of a street organ. The video, directed by the documentary-maker Paul Andresen, was filmed at Van Nuys Airport in the San Fernando Valley, Los Angeles, at a reported cost of £400,000.

Despite the excursions into different styles of music, both on *A Secret Life* and in her choice of side-projects, Marianne reverted to type – with one notable administrative change – through 1996 as she planned another album of dark cabaret and torch song material. "I think I must have the Weimar Republic in my DNA," she said. "That night world of intellectual cabarets – Kurt Weill and Bertolt Brecht – and Neue Sachlichkeit [the New Objectivity] painters – George Gosz and Otto Dix – which fell asleep in my mother and woke up in me." Although it received little media attention and was barely acknowledged by Marianne in press interviews, her next album was due to be released by RCA Victor. She had spent almost two decades with Island Records and had been an integral part of the extended family formed by its founder, Chris Blackwell. The parting appeared amicable with no ill-will expressed by either party. In later years they would work together repackaging existing material in various collections and formats. On its part, RCA Victor was trying to reposition itself as a boutique label of credible artists and had signed Morrissey, The Strokes and Foo Fighters within the space of a few years.

Marianne accepted a small part in the British film *Crimetime* in 1996, a thriller starring Stephen Baldwin, Pete Postlethwaite and Sadie Frost.

During an early scene shot in a nightclub, Marianne is on camera briefly singing 'She', the song she had written with Angelo Badalamenti from *A Secret Life*. The film's screenwriter, Brendan Somers, had lobbied personally for Marianne to be featured. "It was me that suggested Marianne's inclusion in the film. I had heard *Broken English* and was so impressed by it that I begged the director to listen to it. He did and Marianne was approached. The start is the best bit of the film." *Crimetime* was relatively well funded – at least for a British production – with a £4.3 million budget, but it received a disappointing response. The reviewer at *Film 4* website commented: 'Despite a decent cast and the odd stylistic flourish this psychodrama is dragged down by histrionic plotting, clunky talk and a general sense of confusion over what it wants to be.' Somers said later that the film had not turned out as planned. "My script was basically intended as a comic slasher movie but it ended up far too grainy and arty. Steve Baldwin was not well-cast but Pete Postlethwaite was wonderful," he said.

The idea to record a live album based predominantly on Weill's music arose after Marianne performed at the Brooklyn Academy of Music in New York. The set had focused on material by the German composer Paul Hindemith, George Gershwin and Brecht/Weill, and led to a series of concerts titled *An Evening In The Weimar Republic With Marianne Faithfull*. The New Morning jazz and blues club in Rue des Petites-Ecuries, Paris, was hired and Marianne ran through her set accompanied by the pianist and composer Paul Trueblood, a stalwart of Broadway and New York's cabaret scene. The Colombian-born musician Chuchow Mercham, who had relocated to England in the 1970s, played acoustic bass on some tracks.

The album of the concert was *20th Century Blues*, released in January 1997. It contained 15 songs, nine written or co-written by Weill and the rest drawn mainly from films and musicals of the 1920s and 1930s. The title track was the Noël Coward song Marianne had covered originally in 1974. The pairing of Marianne's world-weary voice with the polished but occasionally playful accompaniment from Trueblood worked well.

The year-long tour to promote the album began inauspiciously when Marianne suffered an injury at one of the first shows. She had just finished the opening number, 'Alabama Song', and after looking up to a spotlight (signifying the moon of the lyric), she fell from the stage and injured her back. She fractured her coccyx and had to complete the show and the rest of the tour in a great deal of pain. At all her concerts afterwards she insisted that the crew marked out a white line a foot or so from the edge of the stage. On July 5, 1997 she appeared at the Spectrum de Montreal as part of the city's international jazz festival. At this point her back had improved and she was wearing high heels again, complementing her two-piece pin-striped suit. The performance was recorded and later released as a DVD, *Marianne Faithfull Sings Kurt Weill*.

20th Century Blues was a precursor to Marianne taking on a greater challenge in the ouvre – *The Seven Deadly Sins*. The short satirical 'ballet chante' [sung ballet] lasting 35 minutes was composed across seven scenes by Kurt Weill to a libretto by Bertolt Brecht in 1933. The production was a joint commission from the Russian poet and dancer Boris Evgenievich Kochno and the Anglo-American arts patron Edward James (whose former home, West Dean House, Marianne had visited with The Rolling Stones' entourage on the day of the Redlands bust, three decades earlier). It was the last major collaboration between Weill and Brecht who had earlier fallen out over royalties due from *The Threepenny Opera*. At first Weill resented that Brecht wanted to turn his new creation into 'the *Communist Manifesto* set to music'. Indeed, Jean Cocteau was originally asked to be Weill's collaborator but turned him down.

The Seven Deadly Sins was translated into English by WH Auden and his life-long friend and occasional lover, the American poet and librettist Chester Kallman. The first performance had been a two-week run at the Théatre des Champs-Elysées in Paris opening on June 7, 1933. Weill had fled Germany three months earlier to escape the growing scourge of Nazism. The lead roles, both variants of the character 'Anna', were played by two Vienna-born women who looked very similar to one another – Lotte Lenya (Weill's wife, from whom he was separated at the time but would later remarry) and Tilly Losch, the wife of Edward

James, whose casting was a condition of his providing funding. The production moved to the Savoy Theatre in London that same month under the title *Anna-Anna*, before it was revived under its original title in the 1950s.

The executors of Weill's estate, a body made up of 20 trustees, were known to protect his work 'like the three-headed Cerberus guarding the gates of hell', according to Jackie Fletcher, reviewer for the *British Theatre Guide*. Marianne decided on direct action and visited the Kurt Weill Foundation For Music at 7 East 20th Street, off Broadway, New York. "I had to go there with Jason Osborn, my first conductor, and show them I wasn't some sort of bimbo, some idiot, and that I really understood what it was about and was prepared to go the whole way. The Weill Foundation won't let you perform it unless you use a 59-piece orchestra," said Marianne.

After featuring *The Seven Deadly Sins* as a stand-alone section of her concerts for more than a year, Marianne mooted the idea of recording it as an individual piece of work. Dennis Russell Davies, the Ohio-born conductor and pianist who had replaced Marianne's original collaborator, Jason Osborn, said he thought it was a 'great' idea. The Konzerthaus Theatre in Vienna, home of the Vienna Symphony Orchestra, was hired in June 1997 specifically for Marianne to make a live recording of *The Seven Daily Sins*.

During rehearsals Marianne received news from England that her father, Glynn, had died. She fell into a state of what she later called 'suspended time' and spent many hours walking the streets of Vienna with Ravard. On the night of the concert a doctor was on stand-by ready to administer a shot of Valium if required. She did not call on him and ran faultlessly through the seven 'sins' – sloth, pride, wrath, gluttony, lust, covetousness and envy – across pieces relating the story of Anna I (who sings) and Anna II (who dances), two facets of one personality. At the behest of her family, she/they travel to seven different American cities to make money to build a house on the banks of the Mississippi. In each city, she/they encounter a different deadly sin and Anna I (the practical side) rebukes Anna II (the artistic side) for engaging in sinful behaviour which hinders the accumulation of wealth. After each sin is repented in turn, they return to their new house. "The lyrics are deeply ironic," said Marianne. "The entire libretto is in the form of a looking-glass morality. What he's done [Brecht] is take the seven deadly sins and turn them on their head – they're the seven deadly virtues."

At the concert the musical accompaniment was provided by the Vienna Radio Symphony Orchestra, for whom Davies was the chief conductor from 1996 to 2002. Four additional Weill/Brecht songs were recorded to provide enough material for the CD album released by BMG Classics – 'The Ballad Of Sexual Dependency' and 'Pirate Jenny' from *The Threepenny Opera*; 'Bilbao Song' from the musical comedy *Happy End* and 'Alabama Song' from the opera *Rise And Fall Of The City Of Mahagonny*. *"The Seven Deadly Sins* is my favourite record," said Marianne. "It has very personal resonances for me." She was the fifteenth singer to record the piece and was inevitably compared to her predecessors, Lotte Lenya especially. Lotte had lowered the original pitch register by a fourth in the 1950s but Marianne's was a full octave lower.

The album was given a low-key release by RCA Victor and despite Marianne's professed fondness – which may have been based on personal sentiment – it was viewed as having limited appeal, predominantly aimed at torch song devotees. Andrew Oldham, the man who had galvanised her recording career more than 30 years earlier, had a typically arch view of her new modus operandi. In his gonzo-style memoir, *2Stoned*, he wrote: 'Every other decade, it seems, a bunch of air-rarefied muso exiles from mainstream revive Weill's Weimar forebodings. This newfound lust for Weill's dark melodies and intricate arrangements by ex-junkies and vegetarians is as inviting as a summer season stuck on a pier with Matt Monro crooning 'Monday Monday'.' Oldham was to revise his opinion a few years later after seeing Marianne in concert.

Marianne left Vienna immediately after the concert to return to England for her father's funeral. She took with her a cassette recording of 'The Last Post' made by the orchestra's trumpet player, specifically to play at the wake. During the last two years of his life Marianne had noted a marked change in her father. He had been admitted to hospital and at one point there was a slight delay in administering oxygen, which Marianne felt affected his emotions. "My father's moods shifted radically from the controlled, stiff-upper-lip Englishman he had been, to a sentimental man unable to keep his feelings under control," she said. He told her he had always cared deeply but had hidden it. "It was then that I realised that he had always loved me," she said. Towards the end Glynn Faithfull could remember little that had occurred after 1957, so failed to recognise his second wife and the children from that marriage. He asked Marianne. "Who are these people?" She told him she had no idea. "It's the worst thing I've ever done in my life," she said. "But I had felt left out all those years, felt they had usurped me in my father's affections."

As the century drew to a close Marianne sanctioned two projects that presented an overview of her life and career. *A Perfect Stranger: The Island Anthology* was released in October 1998 and formed a two-disc set of 35 songs chronicling her years with Island Records. Five previously unreleased tracks were included – a cover of John Lennon's 'Isolation'; 'Conversation On A Bar Stool' which Marianne had co-written with Bono; 'A Waste Of Time' written by Marianne with Steve Winwood; 'Gloomy Sunday', the song written by the Hungarian composer Rezso Seress and made famous by Billie Holiday; and 'A Perfect Stranger' written for Marianne by Tom Waits and Kathleen Brennan.

During the round of interviews to promote *A Perfect Stranger* Marianne was asked by journalist Barney Hoskyns if she was afraid of 'falling back into her old life' and was disintegration still a temptation? "My dear," she answered, "the next disintegration I reach is *death*! I don't want to take heroin, and therefore I don't. I don't want to take anything that's going to damage my brain or my emotional responses or my spirit. That's why it would be such a wise thing to stop making all these things so forbidden. Because if they weren't, people could assess whether they really wanted to take this stuff or not."

A year later, a well-assembled DVD of Marianne's life story, *Dreaming My Dreams*, was released with film footage dating back to 1964. The habitually camera-shy John Dunbar was among those featured. Where Marianne had previously been reluctant to make public her story and perhaps relished the intrigue, she had seen it commandeered by others and so decided to take full ownership. Although far from the biopic so often mooted, *Dreaming My Dreams* was a thorough documentary overseen and packaged by Marianne and Ravard. In effect, it formed a pre-emptive strike against producers, researchers, television or film companies planning the same or a similar project.

17

By the end of the 1990s Marianne considered herself to be, in her own words, 'well-marinated in the Brecht/Weill canon' and resolved to change musical direction. Her next album, *Vagabond Ways,* released in April 1999, was similarly slow paced and the vocals again sung predominantly in a low register, but it marked a subtle move into more contemporary music. Instead of covering songs written largely by composers of her parents' generation, she chose those by songwriters of her own – Elton John and Bernie Taupin, Roger Waters and Leonard Cohen among them. She also returned to songwriting, contributing lyrics to five of the 10 songs on the record.

Her status as a seasoned and credible artist was confirmed when one of the most acclaimed production teams in the world, Daniel Lanois and Mark Howard, agreed to work on the album. The pair, both Canadian, had worked together or individually since 1986 on albums by scores of respected, top-selling artists including R.E.M., Peter Gabriel, Iggy Pop and Neil Young. Lanois was most famous for his work with U2, which included co-producing, with Brian Eno, *The Joshua Tree* in 1987, which topped the charts in 20 countries and sold more than 25 million copies. Lanois and Howard had worked together on Bob Dylan's albums *Oh Mercy* in 1989 and *Time Out Of Mind* in 1997. "Bob has had a great influence, right to this day," said Marianne. "I see him quite often. It was Bob who told me to go to Mark Howard. He actually said to me – I was so proud – 'You know, Marianne, people like us with funny voices, you have to be very careful who you let produce you.'"

The album was recorded at the Teatro, a studio Lanois and Howard had installed at a former cinema in the run-down Hispanic quarter of Oxnard, Los Angeles. The cinema had closed in 1993 after 80 years of showing Spanish-language films. In between vocal takes Marianne would wander around the 10,000 sq ft building, replete with old movie posters of risqué Mexican comedies. Howard did most of the production on the album while Lanois co-wrote with Marianne. They did three songs together – 'Marathon Kiss' (on which Emmylou Harris contributed backing vocals), 'Great Expectations' and 'After The Ceasefire', which was based on a poem written by Marianne's good friend, the theatre director Frank McGuinness. "Dan and I wrote some songs together – beautiful stuff," said Marianne. "I'm not particularly fond of what he does with U2 but I love his own records." Marianne's long-term musical ally, Barry Reynolds, returned to co-write three songs with her: 'File It Under Fun From The Past', 'Electra' and 'Wilder Shores Of Love'.

Much of the album was autobiographical or featured material with a personal resonance for Marianne. She considered 'Incarceration Of A Flower Child', written by Roger Waters in 1968 but never presented to Pink Floyd, as 'having so many reverberations about the 60s, the end of the 60s and the consequences'. The lyric reads: 'Laying on the living-room floor on those Indian tapestry cushions you made, thinking of calling our first born Jasmine or Jade' before leading to the prescient: 'It's gonna get cold in the 1970s'. The release of *Vagabond Ways* was as much acknowledged as reviewed in the press, with few notices of great acclaim or criticism. The response of Kristin Sage Rockermann, writing for the leading musical website *Pitchfork* [18 million visitors per year], was typical: 'The album is darker and grittier than most major-label adult-contemporary albums, so it might interest your parents – if only to make them feel young and pure in comparison to Faithfull's thousand years.' In the review she referred to Marianne as 'a mummified Courtney Love'.

Despite having only minimal impact in sales terms, *Vagabond Ways* began a new phase of Marianne's career. "I was emerging from my cocoon," she said. "I'm very one-pointed. It was my first record back in my own genre. I felt I had to make a bit of a statement. A Mariannifesto!" Indeed, there had been a suggestion before recording began that Marianne should remain true to her course and work on an album of Jacques Brel songs. "I didn't want to be put on some old-standards assembly line, so that's why *Vagabond Ways* turned out to be so defiant," she said.

While ostensibly promoting the album, Marianne found herself meandering to more personal subjects when she took lunch at the Ivy restaurant in Covent Garden with Will Self from the *Independent On Sunday*. Self, like Marianne, a recovering heroin addict, wrote that he was 'utterly seduced' by her. In one of the few pieces to eschew the routine clichés of the Marianne story, Self wrote contemplatively of his subject and the prose and the protagonist sparkled. The most telling and insightful paragraph read: 'If I'd met Marianne twenty years ago I'm sure we'd have been talking highs and lows the way druggies do; but this being 1999 we talk recovery: the virtues of twelve-step programmes, vitamins, therapy, acupuncture, friends, isolation and routine. Yet even while discussing these most mature of considerations, there's a mercurial, capricious character about Marianne that won't go away. Intimacy and immediacy – the dramatic synergy so slickly and falsely imparted by narcotics – are qualities that she has written into her character the way "Brighton" is through rock.'

Marianne was among a host of performers invited to appear at a charity concert held in memory of Linda McCartney at the Royal Albert Hall, London, in April 1999. Among those performing at 'Here, There and Everywhere: A Concert For Linda' to raise money for animal rights causes were Paul McCartney, George Michael, Elvis Costello, Chrissie Hynde and Sinead O'Connor. "I didn't know her well, but she made my friend [Paul McCartney] very happy, that's the main thing," said Marianne. "Paul and Linda were living their own life, you didn't see them at parties or things. When I was really fucked up they were so kind, not overly understanding but on my side. She was a decent woman, really."

Marianne performed 'As Tears Go By' with Johnny Marr, formerly of The Smiths, among the backing musicians. Marr was already familiar with Marianne's back catalogue. At early rehearsals The Smiths had run through versions of 'Summer Nights' and 'The Sha-La-La Song'. The first record ever bought by Morrissey – at, he claimed, the age of six – was Marianne's single 'Come And Stay With Me'. Marianne returned the compliment by telling *Clash* magazine in April, 2011 how she would most like to spend her last night on earth: 'I'd go to a club and see a good band. I think I'd like to see The Smiths. I'd take everybody with me.'

A rare appearance on British television of Marianne performing (rather than as a chat show guest) came in June 1999 when she appeared as part of the BBC's coverage of the Glastonbury Festival. Her main performance at the festival was not broadcast but Marianne appeared in the on-site studio laid out within a marquee and sang the track 'Vagabond Ways' accompanied by Barry Reynolds on guitar and Fernando Saunders on bass. Marianne had chosen the perfect song to fortify her rebellious image, with its opening lines: 'Oh, doctor please, oh, doctor please, I drink and I take drugs. I love sex and I move around a lot. I had my first baby at fourteen'. She had written the song with her old friend, the socialite jeweller David Courts.

In September 1999 a year-long programme of events celebrating Beck's art collaborations with his grandfather, Al Hansen, came to a close at The Roxy in New York City with a series of 'happenings'. Marianne was invited to play and backed by Barry Reynolds on guitar she performed 'Working Class Hero', 'Why D'Ya Do It' and a version of Leonard Cohen's 'Tower Of Song'. Among the audience were Yoko Ono, Gwyneth Paltrow, Lou Reed, Laurie Anderson and Kate Moss. Beck was described by *The Observer* at the time as 'a magnet for every pop-culture swank in *fin de millennium* America'. "I did it because I wanted to meet Beck," said Marianne. "I thought he was great, really sweet. It was very interesting for me to see him in context, it sort of explained exactly how he is. And one day we might work together... or not [they did]."

✳✳✳

Joe Jackson, the English singer/songwriter who had relocated to the United States, invited Marianne to guest on his album *Night And Day II* in the autumn of 1999. He was revisiting a theme first explored on his album of 1982, *Night And Day*, which featured a collection of songs about New York as seen by different characters. Jackson wanted the follow-up to have a darker feel and carry a more cynical narrative. Marianne sang on 'Love Got Lost' which, at almost seven miniutes long, formed the record's centrepiece.

The century closed auspiciously for Marianne when her peers voted her the 25th 'Greatest Woman in Rock And Roll'. The poll, which carried votes from 'today's top music artists', was conducted by the television music channel VH1. The only British female performers ahead of Marianne were Annie Lennox and Dusty Springfield. She finished ahead of legends such as Joan Baez, Carly Simon, Diana Ross, Björk and Kate Bush. The high ranking was remarkable because Marianne's profile was relatively small – her last Top 40 hit had been almost 35 years earlier – and by virtue of being alive she had not been subject to posthumous career mythologising or retrospective overviews. The top three female performers, incidentally, were judged to be Aretha Franklin, Tina Turner and Janis Joplin.

While celebrating the momentous New Year's Eve of 1999, watching fireworks light up the London skyline, Marianne formulated plans for her next creative move. She was at a party held at a house on the River Thames owned by Dan Macmillan, the 35-year-old publishing heir (to £200 million) and great-grandson of the former Prime Minister Harold Macmillan. Marianne and Ravard had become friends with Macmillan through their mutual friend, the model Kate Moss. As the new century began, Marianne announced to Ravard that she wanted to 'stop writing songs about the past' and 'change everything'. They began to make a list of potential collaborators with the decree: 'No old warhorses'. They wanted to work with younger musicians who would help reinvent Marianne once more.

Marianne found her back catalogue visited by an unlikely figure in April 2000. Andi Sex Gang (Andrew Hayward), previously of the British goth band Sex Gang Children, released an album called *Faithfull Covers: A Tribute To Marianne Faithfull*. Released on the independent label Dressed To Kill, it was a comprehensive 12-song trawl through Marianne's canon including early material such as 'This Little Bird' and 'Tomorrow's Calling'. Although *Melody Maker* described it as 'Classics lovingly massacred in sparse electro-grumble style', it was actually a respectful tribute with most songs loyal to the originals and suiting Sexgang's epicene voice.

Before she could begin work on her next album Marianne had a busy touring schedule to promote *Vagabond Ways*. By September 2000 she reached New York where she appeared at the Sylvia and Danny Kaye Playhouse at Hunter College, part of the City University of New York. Her backing group included two musicians who had played extensively with Tom Waits – jazz bassist Greg Cohen and slide guitar specialist Smokey Hormel, who had toured Beck's *Odelay* album four years earlier. They were joined on stage in New York by Evan Dando, formerly of The Lemonheads. He played guitar on 'As Tears Go By' and 'Sister Morphine'.

Ann Powers of the *New York Times* attended and described Marianne as being 'in full rocker mode in a filmy flowered shirt with a plunging neckline, trousers and moppy hair. Her salty mood may have been enhanced by the support of a tight, inspiring band.' She concluded her review: 'Ms. Faithfull has sometimes been overwhelmed by the melodrama her music generates, but this evening she had fun with it, flaunting the jaded humour that lifts her out of the fray.'

Among the audience were fashion designer Calvin Klein; the comedienne Sandra Bernhard; the author Fran Lebowitz; and Marianne's former manager Andrew Oldham. In his memoir, *2Stoned*, Oldham appeared to have changed his mind about Marianne's appeal: 'The audience is happy to experience this actual re-creation of a near-death experience; many a Ma squeezes Pa Kettle's hand as Sonny nods off and the sensible walking shoe brigade heave ecstatically as identities are fused before them. It's a great trick, the splicing of Vaudevillian chicanery mesced with opiated recall for the stalls. If this is what she is leaving us with I can tell that backstage is going to be fun.'

✳ ✳ ✳

The author JK Rowling chose Marianne's track 'Guilt' from *Broken English* when she appeared on *Desert Island Discs* on Sunday, November 5, 2000. "I just love this song and it's an emotion I'm familiar with," she said.

Gregory Corso, the Beat poet, contacted Marianne at Christmas 2000 and invited her to visit him at his daughter's house in Minnesota. Corso was in the advanced stages of prostate cancer and, aware that he was dying, wanted Marianne to bring Hal Willner with her to record his voice and have Marianne reciting his poetry. Willner had already undertaken similar spoken word projects with Allen Ginsberg, William Burroughs and the 'poetry activist', Bob Holman. He had also set musical backing to the prose of Edgar Allan Poe.

Early in the new year of 2001 they worked for four days with Corso who sometimes had to break off to take morphine, administered by his daughter, Sheri Langerman, a nurse. Corso died two weeks later at the age of 70. His ashes were laid in the 'English Cemetery' [Cimitero acattolico, the Protestant Cemetery] in Rome, close to the graves of Keats and Shelley. *Die On Me*, the CD of 15 of his poems, read by Marianne and himself, was released in 2002. Willner added strings and Laurie Anderson provided backing vocals.

Marianne was back before the wider British public when she appeared in the hugely popular television sitcom *Absolutely Fabulous*, in an episode titled 'Donkey' shown on Friday, September 21, 2001. She played 'God' opposite Anita Pallenberg, the 'devil'. The episode featured Edina Monsoon (played by Jennifer Saunders), the heavy-drinking, drug-taking PR agent who had taken to bed in despair of her latest diet.

'The Ballad Of Lucy Jordan' played in the background while Marianne, dressed completely in white, and punk-themed Anita circled the bed discussing what would be best for Edina. The scene closed with the God and the Devil deciding to head to the pub and they left arm-in-arm. Marianne was reprising the role of God she had first played in an episode, 'The Last Shout', broadcast on Wednesday, November 6, 1996. Edina had a near-death experience while skiing and Marianne informed her it was not yet her time to enter heaven. The song 'We Got To Get Out Of This Place', performed by Marianne, was played during the scene. For this episode, Marianne, accompanied by P.P. Arnold, also sang the programme's theme tune, 'This Wheel's On Fire', written by Bob Dylan and Rick Danko, formerly of The Band.

While in a restaurant in Paris, Marianne caught sight of the film director Patrice Chéreau. She told him how much she had enjoyed his film *La Reine Margot* [the 1994 film based on the Alexandre Dumas historical novel of the same name]. She asked if she could have a part in his next film and he agreed, though he told her it would be as a down-at-heel, middle-aged woman. "The first time I saw it, it was a shock. But I would jump off a cliff for Patrice," said Marianne. "I don't know why, but I really fell in love with him." She revealed later that she based her character on Linda Moss, the mother of Kate Moss, and a former barmaid. The film was *Intimacy*, drawn from a novel of the same name by British author Hanif Kureishi, and focuses on Jay, played by Mark Rylance, a failed musician who leaves his family and embarks on a sexual relationship with Claire (Kerry Fox). At first he cares little about her but discovers she has a husband (Timothy Spall) and a son. He ends the relationship because he is reminded of his own sons. They meet for a final time and have sex with an intimacy that has been missing during the previous illicit sessions. "One of the loveliest things about *Intimacy* was the quite graphic nude scenes," said Marianne. "They looked like Lucian Freud paintings."

During the promotion for *Intimacy* Marianne agreed to an interview with Lynn Barber, the acerbic writer known in press circles as 'the demon Barber'. The resultant piece was irresistible reading but spared no mercy for Marianne, François Ravard and their alleged pretensions. The showdown began with Barber arriving at the studio of the photographer David Bailey, where she found Marianne 'trussed like a chicken in Vivienne Westwood with her boobs hanging out'. She described Ravard as 'a Frenchman who looks like Woody Allen but without his suavity and charm'. The session was over-running and Barber was asked to return later. When she did, she saw Marianne 'in a black mac and fishnet tights, sprawling with her legs wide apart, her black satin crotch glinting between her scrawny 55-year-old thighs, doing sex kitten moves at the camera. Oh please, stop! I want to cry – this is sadism, this is misogyny, this is cruelty to grandmothers'.

When the photo session was finally over Marianne apparently insisted on a limousine to ferry the party just 50 yards down the street to an Italian restaurant. 'No sooner have we been ushered into a private room downstairs,' wrote Barber, 'than Marianne is muttering, "What do you have to do to get a drink around here?" Order it, seems the obvious answer, but that's too simple – François has to order it for her.' Barber wrote that Marianne was rude to the waiter before turning to her and 'suddenly flicking the switch marked Charm and bathing me in its glow'. Marianne told her it had been 'a long day', not knowing that Barber was aware she had not woken up until 1pm – just six hours earlier. During the formal interview Barber covered a wide range of topics which frustrated Ravard who wanted to focus on the film. He eventually lost his patience: 'François explodes behind me,' wrote Barber. "I knew it! I knew this would happen! It's always the same – this is going to be the last time, Marianne." "Why don't you join us, François?" I say, thinking I'd rather have him in sight than shouting over my shoulder, but Marianne says quickly, "Oh, you don't want that!"'

As they drank their coffee at the end of the meal, Barber asked Marianne about Ravard: 'Darling François!' she exclaims, 'I'm sorry he's a bit grumpy – he's had so much of it. He's been my manager for seven years.' 'Well, I find him very difficult,' I tell her. 'Yes,' she says, 'but that's partly his job.' François then 'loomed over' Barber and – according to her – began shouting: 'Are you talking of me? I hate this fucking tabloid paper. Sex and drugs and all that. I just allowed this interview for Patrice [Chereau], because Marianne loves Patrice. If I could put it back, I will.' Marianne supposedly then 'hissed' at a publicist in attendance [probably from the film company] and yelled: 'You let him get drunk, you fool.' Ravard took the bill and slammed it down in front of Barber, raging: 'You will see the piece, it will just be sex and drugs, always the same shit. Trust me, for seven years I am telling you the truth.' Barber closed with a salvo of sleights: Marianne hadn't written 'a word' of her autobiography; *Broken English* was her only 'good' album and she was an actress with just 'one or two' good films to her name. She also claimed to discern where the power resided in Marianne's relationship with Ravard: 'I don't for a minute believe in their nice cop-nasty cop routine. If François is bad, she's bad too – in fact, maybe worse: she chose him, after all,' she wrote.

At the close of 2001 Lynn Barber was chosen by the British Press Association as 'Interviewer of the Year' and her article on Marianne published in *The Observer* was cited as 'one of the journalistic highlights of the year'. The feature became infamous and Barber was asked about it whenever *she* was interviewed. She told Matthew Lewin of the *Camden New Journal* in November 2010: "Yes, she [Marianne] was disappointing. She was so diva-ish and she kept me waiting for five hours, and just everything was horrible. She would probably scratch my eyes out if she saw me again."

The piece *did* affect Marianne and she referred to it during an interview with Joe Jackson of the *Irish Independent* who had asked about her relationship with Ravard. "Sorry Joe, I have decided never to talk about that," she replied. "Ever since I did an interview a couple of years ago with Lynn Barber, who wrote a really nasty piece about us... I was nasty to Barber, too, I guess." She proceeded to tell Jackson about it, all the same: "We were talking about self-loathing earlier," she said. "Well, I don't hate myself any more but I am terribly hard on myself. And, actually, at the moment I do hate myself for being overweight. Then again, François does give me the kind of approval I'd like to have gotten when I was younger. He also tells me the truth. Like when I am being a monster. And I can be. Sometimes I say to François, 'I see myself as Jesus' little sunbeam,' but I know I'm more of a monster."

The enigmatic Christian Leigh (C.S. Leigh) cast Marianne in his film *Far From China* in 2001. She starred as 'Helen' alongside Aurélia Thiérrée, Lambert Wilson, Antoine Chappey and Steven Mackintosh. In the early 1980s, Leigh, then a teenager, had been a feted fashion designer before becoming a curator of art exhibitions and then making films [seven from 1998 to 2012, all self-written]. He was known for his 'cut and run' approach, often leaving behind disgruntled actors and financers, and reappearing later – usually with a slightly altered version of his name – to start anew, utilising his considerable powers of charm and persuasion. *Far From China*, with a soundtrack by Suede, was premiered in June 2001 and the few that saw it claimed it to be fragmentary and surreal, in the style of David Lynch. There was uncertainty about whether it appeared at cinemas. It has yet to be released on DVD.

As Marianne and Ravard worked through their list of potential contributors to the next album the response was wholly positive. Two of the first they contacted were Alex James and Damon Albarn of Blur and they were keen to become involved. Marianne was invited to a concert by Smashing Pumpkins and thought they were 'absolutely fucking wonderful'. She told Billy Corgan how impressed she had been and he too offered to help with the record.

A few years earlier Marianne had met Jarvis Cocker of Pulp in the corridor of a television studio. A long admirer of what she called his 'great, witty, quirky kitchen-sink' lyrics, she had put a proposition to him on the spot: 'If I give you a title, can you write me a song?' He responded with an enigmatic 'maybe'. Two years later, a cassette arrived through the post to Marianne from Cocker containing the track, 'Sliding Through Life On Charm'.

The final personality drawn from a musical generation akin to her son's age was Beck, with whom Marianne had been in regular touch over the years. They had an accord between them not to dicuss religion – Beck was a Scientologist. "I don't approve of that at all," said Marianne. "But it simply never came up between us; it was never mentioned. And it didn't have to be, just as my awful past-life didn't. We worked really well together, me and Beck. Lovely boy."

The musical elite of the late 1990s/early 2000s wanted to co-operate with Marianne because she was perceived as authentic. She had not diluted her image by, say, hosting television dating programmes or advertising women's clothes, as several of her peers had done. Also, her idiosyncratic musical output and long period of drugs use (with its associated affimation of personal freedom) had granted her a renegade cachet. She was perhaps the sole British female singer of her generation who could bring 'cool' to a record or concert appearance, whether as a guest or if she had put out the invitation herself. Musicians were very particular about who they would co-operate with and lend their name to, and which projects they undertook. No matter the easy-going, accessible image they might proffer publically – they were almost always shrewd, discerning, careful: their (artistic) life depended on it.

Kissin Time, released in February 2002 on Hut Records (a subsidary of Virgin Records), formed the major change of direction to which Marianne aspired although it had a schizophrenic element that was almost inevitable considering the melding of such dispirate talent. The songs themselves each had their own appeal and strength but did not fall together as a conjoined whole. The various collaborators clearly had a different take on Marianne's voice. Across 10 tracks it was sometimes high in the mix, sometimes blended with other voices, occasionally spoken, harsh in places, subdued and almost-sweet in others. On most songs it was easy to plot the musical partner because Marianne sounded grafted on to what was identifiably their usual material or style. The three songs contributed by Beck – 'Sex With Strangers', 'Like Being Born' and 'Nobody's Fault' – were stop-offs from his own career output, the first vaguely cut-up and electro as if from *Midnite Vultures* and the latter two with a gentle folk lilt, akin to *Sea Change*. 'Sliding Through Life On Charm' was Pulp without the essential baritone oddball musings of Cocker. The most accomplished track was the sublime 'Wherever I Go', co-written by Marianne and Billy Corgan. "That's Billy trying to sit down and write me a hit," she said.

The reviews for *Kissin Time* were generally positive, though existing prejudices or preferences for the contributing musicans tended to feature strongly. The review in *The Guardian*, the British newspaper forming by far the largest constituency of potential record-buyers for Marianne, was especially important. Its reviewer, Alex Petridis, wrote: 'While more innately talented 1960s survivors have slipped into slick complacency, Faithfull has few laurels to rest on, and throughout the album, she never sounds less then heartfelt. "I never, ever tried too hard," she admits on "Sliding Through Life On Charm". That's about as close to an It Girl philosophy as you can get. The irony is that on *Kissin Time*, Faithfull sounds as if she is trying much harder than most of her peers.' In the United States, *Pitchfork* was impressed. Brent DiCrescenzo wrote: '*Kissin Time* stands as Faithfull's best work since *Broken English*, and achieves such a feat without taking clichéd "mature" detours into pop standards or orchestral arrangements. Here's hope that the model carries over to people like Jagger and McCartney. Aging rock stars take note: succumb to humbleness and work with others.'

Marianne later took a critical view of *Kissin Time*. She told Sylvie Simmons of *Mojo* in 2005: "It was an experiment which didn't really work, but it had some fabulous songs and fabulous people. Too many people, probably. Not everything I do works as well as I like, but every record I make I really truly try to make the best possible Marianne Faithfull record ever, and pretty often I do." It also emerged retrospectively that Marianne was unhappy with how the record had been promoted. Hut had tried to 'cross-collateralise' sales by marketing it to both Marianne's existing fanbase and fans of the other featured artists – standard record company practice. "They sold it as an album of duets," Marianne told *Word* magazine in June 2007. "They were just using those other artists with all the horrible stickers on and everything. And it didn't sell any more as a result. I realised: don't go there again."

Requests to endorse or advertise products were made to Marianne on a regular basis but habitually turned down. In 2002, the San Francisco-based fashion retailer Gap asked her to appear in a television advert. Gap had a long history of embracing artistic and cultural figures to lend its product credibility and chic. Famed mavericks such as Joni Mitchell and William Burroughs had obliged in the past, alongside contemporary actors and singers such as Madonna, Mary J Blige, Scarlett Johansson and Ashton Kutcher.

Marianne shared the 30-second advert with the actress, fashion designer and singer-songwriter Taryn Manning, who had appeared in the film *Crazy/Beautiful* a year earlier and was working at the time on *8 Mile*, starring Eminem. Marianne and Taryn sang a version of The Staple Singers' 'I'll Take You There' which had been a number one for

Stax Records in the United States in February 1972. The advert was specifically for Gap Stretch Jeans and closed with Marianne announcing to camera: 'For every generation'. Since they were both dressed alike in denim, danced similarly and had blonde hair, the mother-daughter dynamic was obvious. Marianne was 55 and Taryn, 23.

As a long-time admirer of William Burroughs, Marianne found the offer of a major role in a revival of a theatrical production of one of his later works irresistible. She was cast as Pegleg, an incarnation of the devil, in *The Black Rider: The Casting Of The Magic Bullets*. She had seen the original version when it premiered at the Thalia Theatre in Hamburg in March 1991. "I thought it was one of the most fascinating bits of theatre I had ever seen," she said. "It had everything – ancestor worship, magic, a love story, sound and movement. William saw it on its first night. It was very lucky that it was staged when he was still around [he died in August 1997, aged 83]. "I knew William in the 1960s, but I hardly ever spoke to him. I was just a little girl and was shy. Then, years later, in the mid-1980s, I was invited by Allen Ginsberg to sing at the Kansas Poetry Festival."

Marianne performed six songs at the festival accompanied by Fernando Saunders on bass. "That was the moment William believed I was really good – he didn't know before then," she said. "I think he thought I was just a chick. We started to talk and became very good friends. I was a big fan of his books and read them all when they came out. I read *Naked Lunch* when I was very young and thought it was telling people to go out and get high. I've just re-read it, though, and realised it's the opposite. It's an anti-drug book. They think he was about that one thing, but he went much further than that. What he did in his personal life and what he is as an artist are quite different."

The Black Rider: The Casting Of The Magic Bullets was a collaboration between the theatre director Robert Wilson and Tom Waits. Burroughs had based the book on a German folk tale called called *Der Freischütz* [*The Marksman*] which had previously been made into an opera. In the story Wilhelm, a clerk, falls in love with a huntsman's daughter. In order to marry, he has to prove his worth as a hunter and gain her father's approval. As a 'man of pen and ink' he is a poor shot until he is offered magic bullets by the devil, Pegleg, who tells him that the bullets will always have a sure shot apart from one which will remain under Pegleg's control. Wilhelm accepts the Faustian pact and on the day of the wedding strikes his beloved dead. The story contained strong autobiographical elements from Burroughs' own life. He accidentally shot dead his wife, Joan, in September 1951, supposedly in a drunken attempt to recreate the William Tell legend as he fired at a tumbler of water on her head.

The production opened in May 2004 at London's Barbican Arts Centre. It was principally the vision of its director, Robert Wilson, best known for producing Philip Glass' operas such as *Einstein On The Beach* and described by the *New York Times* as a 'towering figure in the world of experimental theatre'. "It was the first time I've worked with Wilson and it was a completely new theatrical language for me," said Marianne. "It's not naturalistic, it's unnaturalistic – all about space and how you use it. It's like being in the middle of a whirlwind."

The veteran theatre reviewer Michael Billington of *The Guardian* praised the production and Marianne in particular: 'It is a richly allusive, if over-extended, evening. Wilson's images embrace everything from medieval woodcuts to Matisse trees and Picasso doves. Waits's score, exuberantly conducted by Bent Clausen, nods towards the blues, Kurt Weill and even Jewish klezmer music. And the performers achieve the right degree of knowing stylisation. Faithfull may not be the sylph-like figure one remembers from the 1960s but her pigtailed, red-suited Pegleg has a growling authority.' After a three-week run at the Barbican, the show moved in September to the American Conservatory Theatre in San Francisco where it ran for a further six weeks.

Marianne appeared in the French film *Nord-Plage* [*North Beach*] in 2004, directed by José Hayot. The low-budget film was a portrait of the North Beach area of Martinique, the island in the Caribbean known as an 'overseas region' of France, situated between Dominica, St. Lucia and Barbados. The leading role of Oselia was played by the French-Belgian singer Viktor Lazlo [birthname: Sonia Droner – she took her stage name from the character in *Casablanca*]. The plot for *Nord-Plage*, with

305

a screenplay by the Martinique-born author Patrick Chamoiseau, was based on a true story. A group of inhabitants were evicted for their own 'safety' from the beach which is overhung by a steep cliff face. José Hayot was also from Martinique – his family had lived there for three centuries.

The policy of embracing contemporary talent was followed again on Marianne's next album, *Before The Poison*. It was released in January 2005 by the French label Naïve Records, a company set up in 1997 by Patrick Zelnick, a good friend of Ravard and the co-founder of Virgin France in the late 1970s. All but two of the songs on the album were contributed by PJ Harvey and Nick Cave, two artists who had been lovers briefly in the mid-1990s. In an interview with Marianne, the writer Sylvie Simmons, of *Mojo*, said she was fascinated by this link. "They didn't speak to each other," said Marianne. "They were with me. One is one thing and one is the other and I am the connection. With Polly I was in the studio for around 10 days and then later on I was in the studio for about five days with Nick and the Bad Seeds. Nick didn't even hear the Polly stuff – I gave it to him but I don't think he listened. The only area that was difficult was that they didn't want to be seen in competition with each other. Polly came to me and we worked in Paris. Only a woman would do that. All my life when I've worked with men I've had to do the travelling. They've got more ego."

Polly Harvey had attended one of Marianne's concerts in New York and told her afterwards that they should write together. Marianne had met Nick Cave at a fashion show in London. "I came cap in hand to her and said 'Could I write a song for you?' and she said 'Yes, darling' and that was that, really," said Cave. "I'm a sucker for a plaintive voice and there is something about Marianne's that is unique and intoxicating. I was a side man and could relax and it was a pleasure to do it in that respect. I didn't carry the burden of having to be the singer." Marianne said of Cave: "He's very serious but playful, which is lovely and he's much better looking in real life than in pictures."

The album was more focused than *Kissin Time* and contained material that better complemented Marianne's voice, while leading it to softer ranges not visited for many years. "I wanted the record to be as absolutely straight ahead as possible," said Marianne. "It is reportage, life seen from my perspective."

'Crazy Love', a piano-led ballad written by Cave and Marianne, and 'Last Song' with music by Damon Albarn were by far the best tracks, each boasting strong melodic hooks. Marianne said she considered PJ Harvey 'a brilliant, prolific, shape-shifting singer-songwriter'. "One of our jokes," said Marianne. "Me and Polly, was, 'Who is in fact the queen of doom and gloom?' Polly says 'Me'. And I say, 'Pipsqueak, you don't know anything about doom and gloom yet'. The way to make your life OK is to bring it into the work." Unfortunately, of the five songs co-written by Harvey, only 'No Child Of Mine' saw her move out of the familiar choppy, stop-start atonal style of her own output.

Before The Poison was acclaimed in the press. David Peschek of *The Guardian* was impressed: '*Before The Poison* is Faithfull's most stylistically cohesive album for some time. If the whole thing seems somewhat slight on first listen, the simple, intimately world-weary authority of Faithfull's delivery gives the songs a stealthy power, like bruises which only show their full colour a few days after the blows have fallen.' *Q* said the album was Marianne's 'worthiest addition yet to her legendary status'. In the United States *Pitchfork*'s Stephen M. Deusner also gave it a good review: 'Faithfull imbues every song and every word on *Before The Poison* with the weight of experience, as if age has granted her almost oracular powers. This may not be a perfect album, but it is affecting and haunting'.

18

Casting agents had become aware of Marianne's 'clean' status and allied reliability through the 2000s and she was offered substantial parts. Sofia Coppola, the daughter of famed film director Francis Ford Coppola, asked Marianne to play Empress Maria Theresa in *Marie Antoinette*, the story of a 14-year-old Austrian princess sent to marry the future king of France, Louis XVI. Sofia had earlier won plaudits in her own right for *The Virgin Suicides* (1999) and *Lost in Translation* (2003) for which she won the Academy Award for Best Original Screenplay. Kirsten Dunst starred in the title role of Marie Antoinette, the beautiful but naïve daughter of Empress Maria Theresa (Marianne) who sends a series of letters to the court of Versailles, instructing Marie on her mission. The part had special resonance for Marianne because her mother, Eva (Baroness Erisso), was from Vienna and had roots in the Hapsburg Dynasty, much the same as Empress Maria Theresa. Marianne said later that she based her part on Eva and described the film as 'sexy candy, pop daydream confections with sherbet colours and American accents'.

Sofia Coppola was indifferent to historical accuracy and in the French newspaper *Le Figaro* an academic and historian specialising in cinema history, Jean Tulard, dubbed the film 'Versailles in Hollywood sauce' and said it 'dazzled with a deployment of wigs, fans and pastries, a symphony of colours which all mask some gross errors.' Leah Rozen

309

of *People* magazine wrote: 'Her [Coppola's] historical biopic plays like a pop video, with Kirsten Dunst as the doomed 18th century French queen acting like a teenage flibbertigibbet intent on being the leader of the cool kids' club'. The British film magazine *Empire* continued the theme: 'Giving the finger to period-drama conventions, Coppola re-spins Marie's young life as an exuberant teen flick full of cliques, bitchery and gossip, as Marie pops pastries, vogues around Versailles and generally parties like it's 1779.' Coppola countered: "It is not a lesson of history. It is an interpretation documented, but carried by my desire for covering the subject differently."

During filming Marianne was overweight from taking cortisone after suffering two bouts of bronchitis. Sofia Coppola said to her: "Well, Marianne. You *are* rather buxom, but don't worry, it'll work as *period* buxom." *The Guardian* gave Marianne's performance grudging praise, Alex von Tunzelmann writing: 'Back in Austria, her mother Maria Theresa (Marianne Faithfull, who, believe it or not, gives one of the film's most credible performances) gets antsy. Until Marie-Antoinette stumps up an heir, her position at court is vulnerable. Cue lots of embarrassing bedroom scenes.'

The most important issue for Marianne was that she had been granted a significant role (though she was heard as much as seen because she had to narrate her letters to Marie) in a mainstream, global film – it played in 859 cinemas in the United States alone and grossed almost $61 million worldwide. One of its poorest box office performances was in Britain where it took under £2 million.

Inevitably a handful of critics said Marianne's inclusion in the film was due to her 'name' but this was to overlook a slew of allegedly nepotistic castings including Coppola's cousin, Jason Schwartzman, the son of actress Talia Shire and producer Jack Schwartzman; Asia Argento, the daughter of Italian horror director Dario Argento; Mary Nighy, the daughter of British actor, Bill Nighy; Katrine Boorman, the daughter of British director John Boorman; Danny Huston, the son of American director John Huston and the grandson of character actor Walter Huston; and Io Bottoms, who played a lady-in-waiting, the daughter of actor Sam Bottoms.

Marianne on the lawn outside her 19th C. cottage in County Waterford, Ireland 1994. *(Ken Goff/Time Life Pictures)*

French singer-songwriter Serge Gainsbourg with Marianne Faithfull in New York, September 1985.
(Jerome Minet/Kipa/Corbis)

Marianne with her son Nicholas, 1994.
(Richard Young/Rex Features)

Courtney Love and Marianne on *Later With Jools Holland*, May 1995. *(Andre Csillag/Rex Features)*

Marianne with Mick Jagger at Ronnie Wood's 50th Birthday Party in London, 1997. *(Richard Young/Rex Features)*

Marianne with Kate Moss, 1997.
(Richard Young/Rex Features)

Anita Pallenberg and Marianne backstage at the
Barbican Concert, London, 2002. *(Richard Young/Rex Features)*

Marianne with Sophie Dahl at London Fashion Week, 1997. *(Richard Young/Rex Features)*

Keith Richards hugs Marianne at the Rainbow Room in New York, 1996. *(Corbis)*

Johnny Marr and Marianne perform at the Linda McCartney Memorial Concert at the Royal Albert Hall, London, 1999. *(Richard Young/Rex Features)*

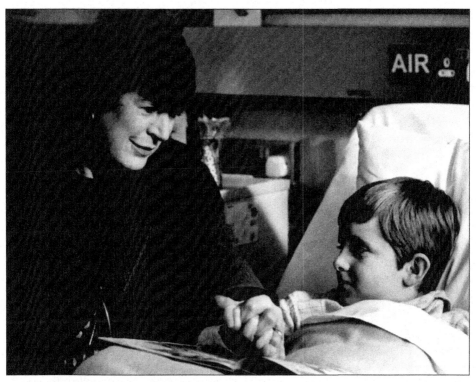

Marianne in the film *Irina Palm*, 2007. *(Everett Collection/Rex Features)*

Marianne Faithfull, Claudia Cardinale, Monica Bellucci and Angela Missoni at the Women's World Awards 2009 in Vienna, Austria. *(Willi Schneider/Rex Features)*

Marianne, Ryan Adams and Rufus Wainwright at the opening night of R.I.P. Paintings, a gallery showing artwork by Ryan Adams. *(James Lance/Corbis)*

Marianne performs 'The Seven Deadly Sins' at the Auditorium Parco della Musica, Sala Santa Cecilia, Rome, Italy, April 2009. *(Enrica Scalfari/Rex Features)*

Marianne and Lionel Bart at the Ivor Novello Awards, London 1986. *(Ilpo Musto/Rex Features)*

Marianne performing in Barcelona at Primavera Sound, May 2012. *(Simone Cecchetti/Corbis)*

Marianne at The Music of The Rolling Stones: Hot Rocks 1964-1971, Carnegie Hall, New York City, March 2012. *(Bobby Bank/WireImage)*

Marianne landed the first lead role of her film career when she was cast as Irina Palm in the film of the same name. The tragi-comedy was directed by Sam Garbarski, a former director of television commercials and short films, and drew on funding from several European countries. As 'Maggie', Marianne is a plain 50-year-old widow [Marianne was actually 59] who needs money to pay for her sick grandson, Olly, to travel to Australia for the specialised medical treatment he requires. While walking through Soho, Maggie sees a poster in a window at Sexy World – 'Hostess Wanted'. She applies, gets the job and has to masturbate men who insert their penis through a hole in a wall. "I didn't really know if I could take on the part of Maggie," said Marianne. "And when I saw the film for the first time, there were two things I realised: one of them was that I could carry a film and the other one is that there's not one minute that it is Marianne Faithfull. I *am* Maggie."

Perhaps unsurprisingly, a film with such a bizarre and unlikely plot was largely devoured by the critics, especially in Britain. Peter Bradshaw of *The Guardian* wrote: 'This is a gobsmackingly awful British film – awful in the way that somehow only British films can be: our TV drama, of whatever quality, is never as creaky, naive, badly written and flatulent as this. Marianne Faithfull gives a somnambulist performance as the ordinary-yet-gutsy provincial British lady whose grandson is supposedly suffering from a potentially fatal disease. The last hope is to get him to Australia for a specialist cure. The NHS won't stump up for the airfare: so how will they raise the cash? Through a series of plot quirks charitably described as 'implausible', desperate Marianne finds herself employed in a quaintly imagined sex club in London's red-light district, sitting in a dark booth providing hand-relief to punters who stick their manhoods through a glory-hole. They never see the plain old gran jerking them off, and it turns out her soft, regularly moisturised palms have given her the magic touch. As she poignantly reflects on her grandson's condition, and her own situation, Faithfull says: "He's dying. I'm wanking. It's a mess." It certainly is.'

Philip French of *The Observer* was similarly unimpressed: 'It's a truly ludicrous film, almost a laugh a line, that sets out to be the *Mrs Warren's Profession* [a George Bernard Shaw play of 1893 about a brothel owner] of our time, but turns out to be *Cranford* meets *Confessions of a Manual Worker.*' Marianne's performance was singled out for harsh criticism by Paul Hurley in a review which ran across several entertainment websites: 'Worst of all though is Faithfull's performance which derives from the startled rabbit school of acting. If there was a UK razzie ceremony she would be odds-on for the Worst Actress prize. Her wanking widow has only one expression and a monotonous, stilted delivery and quite how she passed the audition is a mystery.' Kat Brown in *Empire* was less damning: 'Faithfull is too sexy to be a convincing dowd, and the dramatic scenes cry out for Blethyn's [Brenda Blethyn, the actress] assured, er, hand. But it's still rather sweet. While some scenes test credulity – when mum reveals she's gone into sex work to save your child, the least you can do is say thank you – there's a heartwarming quality that softens the hardcore setting.'

Nicholas Barber, film critic of the *Independent On Sunday*, was so 'inspired' by *Irina Palm* that he set up a web campaign for an award called the 'Irina Palm d'Or'. "There was a run of awful British films in the first half of 2008," he said. "Films that no one saw if they weren't a critic – *Dangerous Parking*, *Freebird*, *Lady Godiva* ... they weren't just run-of-the-mill bad, they were so wrongheaded you couldn't quite believe what you were seeing. It was such a bizarre phenomenon, we started joking that we should award a prize to the worst of them all. Then when *Irina Palm* came out in June, it was obvious what that trophy should be called: the Irina Palm d'Or."

Barber said the judges were looking for amateurish acting, painful dialogue and bad camerawork. "We're looking for shoddiness across the board – the lot," he said. "It helps if the concept is so perverse that you want to scream, 'Why?' It's really a way of keeping your sanity when you're suffering through a truly excruciating British film. Instead of just wishing it would end, you start to think, 'Ooh, I wonder if this is worth an Irina.'"

The film was better received in the United States where critics viewed it as quirky and quintessentially British. A.O. Scott of the *New York Times* was typical: 'It might be the work of a German-born Belgian director, but it belongs to a sturdy and very British genre: the naughty-

312

granny comedy, in which an older woman is liberated and rejuvenated by an excursion into vice.' Scott was much more complimentary of Marianne's performance: 'Without showiness or actorly straining – but with a faint aura of rock'n'roll sexual glamour still hovering around her – Ms. Faithfull explores a full and fascinating range of emotion. Maggie is weary and timid at first, bruised by grief and by a sense of diminished prospects. To see her recover her toughness and humour is moving and satisfying despite the dubious narrative machinery that enables her rebirth. *Irina Palm* is, for the most part, a phony trifle, but at its heart, somehow, is a real and fascinating person.'

Despite the panning given to the film by the British press – one journalist claimed it made just £582 at the box office on its first week – it was not the disaster they predicted, either financially or with the public. It earned more than $10 million worldwide and won several nominations – the Golden Bear for the Best Movie of 2007 at the Berlin International Film Festival; Miki Manojlovic as the Best European Actor of 2007 by the European Film Academy and Marianne as Best Actress in the European Film Awards (she was beaten by Helen Mirren in the lead role of *The Queen*). Across newspaper blogs there was a backlash to critics such as Nicholas Barber and Peter Bradshaw. Most of those posting comments accepted that *Irina Palm* was flawed but said they detected an 'anti-British' stance among the broadsheet newspapers and the sniffy, indulgent tones of the 'Irina Palm d'Or' were criticised.

The next film undertaken by Marianne was the antithesis of *Irina Palm*. Her part in *Paris je t'aime* [*Paris, I Love You*] was minuscule by comparison at just one minute, 20 seconds on screen and five spoken lines, but the film received widespread critical acclaim and, for Marianne, credibility by association. The two-hour film starred an ensemble cast of actors appearing in 18 shorts, each made by a different director and set in a particular arrondissement [district] of Paris. Marianne appeared as a customer in 'Le Marais' [the name of a district in Paris containing many buildings of historic and architectural importance] directed by Gus Van Sant, famous for *My Own Private Idaho*, *Good Will Hunting* and *Milk*. In 'Le Marais' the young man accompanying Marianne to the print works

313

at the back of an art shop, possibly her son, is attracted to a handsome worker. He tries to explain that he believes the man to be his soul-mate, not realising that the man cannot understand him because he speaks barely any French.

Marianne was one of 42 famous musicians who contributed to the *Rough Guide Book Of Playlists* in 2007. She was asked to pick 10 tracks by 'the most iconic artists of the 20th Century'. Interestingly, she did not choose any of the songs included in her Desert Island Discs or any by artists born after her own generation. Only one of the artists featured, John Lennon, was British. The playlist comprised: Bob Dylan – 'One More Cup Of Coffee'; Otis Redding – 'Pain In My Heart'; Bob Marley – 'Redemption Song'; Aretha Franklin – 'Chain Of Fools; Billie Holiday – 'Fine And Mellow'; Iggy Pop – 'Lust For Life'; John Lennon – 'Mother'; Leonard Cohen – 'Then We Take Manhattan'; Elvis Presley – 'That's All Right'; and Johnny Cash – 'Delia's Gone'.

During a routine self-examination – the kind made abstractedly while washing or dressing – Marianne discovered something untoward. 'I found a lump,' she wrote in her book *Memories, Dreams & Reflections.* 'Just a little lump. It practically takes your breath away. Followed by a whirlwind of emotions: fear, of course, but also resignation, curiosity, anger, and even, yes, a strange elation (in a when-you-got-nothing-you-have-nothing-to-lose way).' She booked a mammogram which revealed that she had an early form of cancer in her right breast. The lump she had found was benign but a patch of tissue beneath it was not. "I went to a really great doctor and he saw something that somebody else might have missed," she said. "It was actually pre-cancer, so I was incredibly lucky. I was very scared and it really frightened me. It's different today but I grew up in a world where if you got cancer you were finished, that's it. A million thoughts went through my mind. I want to keep living my life, I want to see my grandchildren grow up, I want to be there for my friends, I want to be able to love and to work." Ravard was so upset that he went on a four-day drinking binge but, according to Marianne, afterwards he was 'an absolute star'.

Marianne had suffered occasional but serious health problems in the few years before 2006. She collapsed on stage in Milan in 2004 from 'nervous exhaustion' and fell into a coma with an acute kidney infection after attending the Cannes Film Festival for the premiere of *Marie Antoinette* in May, 2006. She believed the illness was exacerbated by the large amount of sleeping tablets she had been taking. She also suffered hepatitis C which had been diagnosed in 1996, a disease that was largely without symptoms but often caused long-term damage to the liver. "I'm absolutely sure it's all down to my old bad ways, but that was a long time ago," Marianne told the *Mail On Sunday* when discussing the hepatitis. "I immediately underwent treatment for six months, having injections of Interferon and another drug, which wasn't a lot of fun because it causes terrible exhaustion, but I got through it. I took the diagnosis on board and changed my life accordingly. The worst thing you can do is drink alcohol, so I don't drink any more [she was fibbing, though she had cut down significantly]. I don't do drugs. I eat well. I smoke occasionally [her smoking has always been heavy] but I fully expect to give up at some point. I meditate. I work out a bit with a personal trainer. It's a real blessing that I was able to do that early enough."

At first, despite the diagnosis of cancer, Marianne wanted to complete the planned two-month world tour which was due to begin in Paris on October 7. She asked her consultant whether delaying the operation would have any effect. He told her cancer cells were spreading 'even as they spoke' and she should have surgery immediately: the tour was cancelled. She underwent the operation on Wednesday October 11, 2006 at the Institut Gustave-Roussy in Paris, the world-renowned private cancer clinic where Kylie Minogue was also treated. Owing to the tumour being caught at such an early stage, no further treatment was necessary. While she was having the lumpectomy she also had a lift and a small reduction in the size of her breasts. "I might as well make the best of it, that's what I said to myself," she said.

While she was recovering from the operation, Marianne received a call at the clinic in the early hours of the morning. "Ello Marian, darling. How are you?' said the voice. "He didn't say who he was, he didn't need to," Marianne told the *Daily Mail*. "No one else in the world calls me Marian, as in Maid Marian. It could only be Mick Jagger and I knew it was him right away. He asked me how I was and I told him I was fine and getting through it. We spoke for a while, like musicians do. I knew he was on a world tour and asked him where he was. He said somewhere like Miami. I asked how his voice was holding up. He didn't say much but I could sense his famous shoulders shrugging at the other end. All the time I was thinking, this is so kind. He hadn't called me for 35 years and here he was on the phone, making sure I was OK. I didn't expect him to contact me and I was extremely touched that he'd made the effort to call. He's a good man. He loves me and I love him. The fact that our relationship ended in 1970 doesn't matter. If you love someone, you love each other for ever. It never stops. I found out later that Mick had phoned around agents and all my friends to get my number in the clinic. He went to a lot of trouble. That's a classy guy."

Other former lovers were similarly solicitous. Ben Brierley offered her a holiday home; Oliver Musker phoned from India; Keith Richards sent her get well faxes complete with drawings of pirates; John Dunbar sent a card and Jeremy Clyde (of Chad and Jeremy) – one of her first ever lovers – sent her a note which began 'I read the news today, oh boy...' Others to get in touch and offer support included Chris Blackwell, David Courts, Yoko Ono, Marsha Hunt, Roger Waters, the fashion designer John Galliano, and the famous chef Daniel de la Falaise.

After the operation Marianne spent her days either in the garden of their apartment in Paris or strolling through the Tuileries Garden, the famous park sandwiched between the Louvre Museum and the Place de la Concorde. In February 2007 Marianne visited her 'favourite place on the planet' when she booked into Jakes Hotel at Treasure Beach on Jamaica's south coast. She was there to also mourn the death, at 70, of the hotel's owner, Perry Henzell, who directed and co-wrote the legendary 1972 film *The Harder They Come*, starring reggae star Jimmy Cliff. Henzell had died three months earlier. "I went there to help his widow, Sally, and her son Jason get over their bereavement and to come to terms myself with the fact that my very good friend was not here any more," said Marianne. "Before he died I had a wonderful phone call from Sally and Perry asking me to visit to help my recovery. Perry died like I would like to die – in his sleep lying in bed. He chose his time beautifully. His cancer was about to become unbearably painful." She was fully recovered and free of cancer by Christmas, 2006. "I was very lucky. I had very good doctors. My partner was wonderful. My friends were really wonderful. My family ... it all kicks in."

The cancer scare led Marianne to reassess her life and relationships with friends and family. "It does wonders for the bitterness one feels about the past," she said. "In fact, it's gone! One of the more interesting consequences is how connected I feel to people. I've been talking to my half-sister, Hazel, again, and we had not been close in recent years." She visited Nicholas and got to know his new wife, Teresa. "During his first marriage, things were fraught between us – I lost him. He had such a hard time of it when he was little. He was taken away from me. We need to use the time we've got left together," she said.

Nicholas had chosen a lifestyle the antithesis of his parents'. He trained as a physicist at Manchester, Cambridge and Harvard universities before becoming a financial journalist. He was technical editor of *Risk* magazine from 1998 to 2009 where, in 2005, he launched *Life & Pensions*, a sister publication to *Risk* aimed at the insurance and pensions industry. He published his first book, *Inventing Money: The Story Of Long-Term Capital Management And The Legends Behind It* (John Wiley & Sons) in November 2000 and this was followed in July 2011 with *The Devil's Derivatives: The Untold Story Of The Slick Traders And Hapless Regulators Who Almost Blew Up Wall Street... And Are Ready To Do It Again* (Harvard Business School Press). In 2011 he joined the financial data company Bloomberg and launched the *Bloomberg Risk Newsletter*. He has appeared on the American television documentary series *Frontline* and as a specialist guest on BBC's *Newsnight*. "He's such a cool son, he's perfect for me," Marianne told Chrissy Iley of *The Telegraph* in March 2011. "I don't know if he'd suit any other mother but he's very free thinking. How did this happen to me, how did I get a child like this? He's very much like my father."

Down the years Marianne had rarely spoken of Nicholas in public but she was candid during a meeting with Evelyn McDonnell of *Interview* magazine, the publication founded by Andy Warhol said to be the 'Crystal Ball Of Pop'. Evelyn asked Marianne about her relationship with Nicholas. "It's really, really good. I go and stay with him," said Marianne. "Neither of us ever thought we'd get this kind of relationship. But we do." Was there 'stuff they had to work through'? "Oh, yeah," responded Marianne. "And, you know, I did a lot of therapy. In fact, I'm still in therapy. I didn't do any for quite a long time and now I've gone back. But it was time, in fact, that mattered. He loves my work, too. And I'm very proud of him. He's a writer. Of all the things that could happen, my son became an incredible expert on high finance. You know? And he wrote one book which is really very, very good. I've read it. And I don't understand a thing about high finance. Now he's writing another one about the crash and the whole thing going on. It will be very interesting. He's very, very clever."

In *Memories, Dreams & Reflections*, Marianne referred to her relationship with Nicholas as 'somewhat fraught'. She also wrote that Eva 'took over completely' when Nicholas was a child, 'We had huge rows. I would say, '*I'm* the mother, not you. Take a back seat; he's *my* son!' But she couldn't. She had no idea that I could ever function as an adult,' she wrote. In 2007 Marianne told Jenny Johnston of the *Daily Mail*: "When Nicholas was taken away I thought: 'Fuck this, may as well become a junkie. No reason not to, now.'" She said she was proud Nicholas had carved out a 'quiet, mainstream life'. "He's never done drugs, never been interested in that sort of life," she said. "Maybe it was because he was turned off it by watching me and his father go through it. I saw him last night. He came to talk to me about some trouble with his ex-wife. I actually do feel like I am his mother now." Johnston pointed out that this was an 'odd thing' to say. "It took me an awfully long time before I felt like a mother, until Nicholas was in his early twenties," she responded. "Luckily, I was able to rebuild that relationship. All I will say is we got through it together, and we are fine now. I am his mum. I love him, and more importantly he loves me."

Marianne and Ravard divided their domestic life between a flat in Paris, close to the Champs-Elysee, and a house in County Waterford, Ireland. "It's a lovely mix," said Marianne. "Lovely Ireland, bit scruffy, and all that. And, of course, Paris is a very nice place to be for a lady of a certain age! The French, they don't wipe you away. You're still somebody. You still exist." She had left Shell Cottage several years earlier, though the circumstances of her departure were unclear. The *Daily Mirror* ran a story that £5,000 of damage had been caused after a 'bash' which had been attended by, among others, the manager of U2, Paul McGuinness, the author J.P. Donleavy and the brewery heir Desmond Guinness. A stained glass window was broken, an antique table damaged and shells were broken off the outside of the house. Marianne denied that the landlord had forced her out. "I gave it up because I was lonely," she said. "It had rats. And I'd lived there just long enough. I know the landlord didn't really like me. But, you know, a lot of people don't really like me. I'm not everybody's cup of tea!"

One of the last phone calls Marianne received while at Shell Cottage was from her agent who told her of an offer relating to an incident in her past. "I was in Shell Cottage with Sandra Bernhardt, who is a great friend of mine, and her lover," said Marianne. "And my fucking agent called and said I'd been offered a lot of money – a really lot of money – to do a Mars Bar advertisement. I said 'OK, you're fired'. I've never had an agent since." Marianne moved initially to the seaside town of Dun Laoghaire, eight miles south of Dublin, before moving to the house in Waterford.

The success of *Faithfull* made it almost inevitable that Marianne would write another book. *Memories, Dreams & Reflections* was published by Fourth Estate in 2007. *Faithfull* had been a loyal rendition of her life, related in approximate chronological order but *Memories, Dreams & Reflections* was much more impressionistic. She lingered fondly on reminiscences of characters such as Henrietta Moraes and Lady Caroline Blackwood, and the chatty style worked well untied from a linear narrative. "It's a lot more positive than the first one," she said. "I think when I wrote *Faithfull*, I was still very angry. And really I'm not now, at all. I've gotten over it, and I wanted to correct that. I mean, I didn't feel that it was that urgent, but I wanted to show a more positive side, which I felt I kind of left out of *Faithfull,* which is a bit too tipped in the way of the negative." The book was again co-written with David Dalton and contained a dedication 'For François [Ravard]'.

By March 2007 Marianne felt well enough to return to the stage. A three-month European tour was organised called *Songs Of Innocence And Experience*, a title borrowed from the collection of poems published by William Blake. The music was stripped down, with Marianne backed by a trio of musicians. "It's more chamber music because I wanted to use my voice more, and I don't want to have to shout because that's not good for me. It's very emotional, but that's OK too," she said. The show featured songs she had not performed live before such as 'Something Better' and also included the Harry Nilsson song 'Don't Forget Me' and 'Spike Driver Blues', the blues standard made famous by Mississippi John Hurt in the late-1920s.

Touring was important to Marianne as a source of income. She explained this to Sylvie Simmons of *Mojo*: "It is the only way I've made money. I won't be able to go on touring like this forever. I don't want to retire, but it is hard work. And I never really made money from my records. I got a royalty cheque from Island in 1979, a big one, and I never had one since, and I left Island 10 years ago. They put everything on your bill – a tuna sandwich, a coffee, everything – and with me there were a lot of other expenses like rehab." Although Marianne benefited financially from the repackaging of her previous records (or it at least reduced the deficit, moving the figures closer to break-even), Marianne was disgruntled. "They have to stop bringing out these terrible Best Ofs because it really is bad for the back catalogue. The records are beautiful as they are. It's just wrong."

Marianne revealed a new-found pragmatic attitude to finance as she entered her sixties: "I'm not prepared to be 70 and be absolutely broke. I don't own *anything*. I haven't got a house or a mortgage or a car. I'm still renting! I realised last year that I have no safety net at all and I'm going to have to get one. So I need to change my approach to life, which means I have to put away 10 per cent every year. I want to be in a position where I don't have to work. I should have thought about this a long time ago but I didn't."

Hal Willner was again enlisted as producer and they spent the winter of 2007 sifting through material. "We always wanted to do another record in the studio, and I felt like part of my taking a break, really, was that I wanted not to write. So we started to look for songs," she said. "I started, and he started, and I found quite a few. Then he came over and I played him the ones I found, and he played me lots of songs, and we went through them all."

The recording sessions for the album that became *Easy Come, Easy Go* began in December 2007 at New York's Sear Sound Studio. The record was released as two versions, one a single CD containing 10 songs and the other across two CDs and boasting 18 songs. Once more, Marianne enlisted a host of collaborators, among them Keith Richards, Antony Hegarty, Nick Cave, Rufus Wainwright, Chan Marshall [Cat Power] and Sean Lennon. Evelyn McDonnell, writing for *Interview*, summed up the approach when she wrote that 'they had gone hipster hog-wild, scrolling through their address books to enlist musicians'. The choice of material was drawn from an equally eclectic pool and included songs written by Dolly Parton, Bessie Smith, Duke Ellington, Brian Eno, Randy Newman, Smokey Robinson, Merle Haggard, Morrissey, The Decemberists, Black Rebel Motorcycle Club and Leonard Bernstein/ Stephen Sondheim. "We didn't pick any one kind of music." said Marianne. "There's country, jazz, blues, rock 'n' roll, and folk on this record."

The track recorded with Keith Richards was 'Sing Me Back Home' which had been Merle Haggard's third consecutive American number one in 1967 and had been covered by The Byrds and the Grateful Dead. Marianne had sent a fax to Richards' manager, Jane Rose, asking him to contribute. "He agreed, and then he sent me this wonderful fax," said Marianne. "He said: 'I'll do it for you, baby, if you do it for me'. So I wrote back and said, 'Of course I will, darling'. The song we did together was a wonderful penitentiary song, and I actually learned it from Keith in the 1960s when he was singing it with Gram Parsons. So it was like a circle coming to its end."

A song on the album with particular resonance for Marianne was 'The Phoenix' written by Judee Sill and drawn from her second album,

Heart Food, released in 1973. Sill had signed to David Geffen's Asylum Records in 1970 but succumbed to heroin addiction. She died in November 1979, aged 35, of 'acute cocaine and codeine intoxication'. She had suffered great pain in her later years after a severe back injury and was thought to be self-medicating when she overdosed. Sean Lennon played the 12-string guitar on Marianne's version and provided backing vocals.

Such a varied collection of songs, moods and styles with no identifiable theme – beyond Marianne claiming an autobiographical thread – was almost guaranteed to confound critics. Neil Spencer of *The Observer* wrote: 'Its gravelly tones are certainly no thing of beauty, but when married to the right song Faithfull can still emote, still deliver. There's plenty of plain wrong material, though. The sultry 'Solitude' needs melodic precision, not croaking self-pity, and Smokey Robinson's 'Ooh Baby Baby' is a non-starter. So bring on 'Down From Dover', Dolly Parton's tragic tale of stillborn birth, or Randy Newman's bleak 'In Germany Before The War'. Best of all bring on Keef on Merle Haggard's 'Sing Me Back Home' for a ragged, defiant duet reminiscent of *Exile*-era Stones. A sprawling double album with a fine single album inside? You got it'. Andy Gill of the *Independent* wrote: 'The album is ultimately spoilt by the ghastly treatment meted out to Smokey Robinson's gorgeous 'Ooh Baby Baby', one of the most sublime endearments in pop history. Sadly, it's done as a duet with Antony Hegarty, whose vocal mannerisms are, if anything, more idiosyncratic and peculiar than Marianne's; together, they clash like an iceberg scraping away at the hull of the Titanic. A late attempt to salvage the track by funking things up only makes matters worse, compounding its lack of grace with charmless gaucheness. Elsewhere, the duets are more successful, with Nick Cave surprisingly restrained on the Decemberists' "The Crane Wife 3" and Keith Richards virtually inaudible on "Sing Me Back Home". Overall, then, another brave assault on musical diversity from Faithfull, in typically intriguing musical livery'.

Michael Quinn of *BBC Music* was impressed by the album's ambition, if not Marianne's voice: 'Let's be honest: she can't hold a tune. She misses notes by a musical mile and her voice is as cracked as an eggshell under foot, but that doesn't stop Marianne Faithfull making fabulous records. *Easy Come, Easy Go* isn't an instant Faithfull classic. *Broken English* it ain't. Nor does it get disconcertingly under the skin in the way *Strange Weather* did. But in the breadth of material on offer, in Faithfull's signature way with a song, and in Hal Willner's pointed and eclectically elegant production it gets pretty close, exerting its own peculiar fascination along the way.' Dorian Lynskey of *The Guardian* held a similar view: 'Weighing in at 18 tracks, culled from the Great American Songbook and the indie blogosphere alike, this Hal Willner-produced covers album (a kind of sequel to 1987's *Strange Weather*) is too baggy and diffuse to hold the attention, but Faithfull's formidable croak can really worm its way under a song's skin.'

Easy Come, Easy Go had a staggered release throughout the world and was licensed by Naïve to different record labels covering the various territories. It was released in Britain and the United States in March 2009. While Naïve lacked the recording or marketing budget of Marianne's previous labels, it granted her greater artistic freedom and autonomy. A metaphorical hand on the shoulder, however, may have been judicious. It is doubtful whether a major label would have sanctioned such a broad and diverse collection of songs as *Easy Come, Easy Go*, especially across two CDs, aside, perhaps, from the indulgence lent to a handful of global, millions-selling artists.

The value of a certain mystique and aura was known well to both Marianne and Ravard and it was noteworthy that over many years interviews were routinely conducted at 'neutral' venues such as hotels and restaurants, normally of a high standard. Also, as someone who had, for a brief but intense period at least, been pursued by the tabloid press and had her privacy regularly invaded, Marianne remained understandably protective of her personal life, and space. A clear policy of discretion was significantly relaxed in November 2007 when Judith Woods of the *Mail On Sunday* was invited to their home in Paris. The piece began with Woods as good as revealing the actual address before taking the reader on a tour of the apartment. It had 'glorious high ceilings, elegant white stucco and polished parquet floors' and was 'more shabby than chic'. The 'ancient sagging sofas' were strewn with mismatched cushions and a 'rather tatty, faux leopardskin throw'. Books, including *Memories, Dreams & Reflections*, were piled on the floor. DVDs were scattered by the marble fireplace with 'boho carelessness' and a handful of chocolate Florentines lay discarded on the bureau. Woods wrote: 'A run-of-the-mill celebrity might have fussed about in advance, emptying the ashtrays that overflow on every surface. A more petit bourgeois interviewee might have offered me a cup of coffee when I turn up after an eight-hour journey that began at 4am. Instead, when I arrive, offering my apologies and telling my tale of transport woe, Faithfull barely registers me, and I am informed sotto voce by her assistant [Ravard] that if I would like something to drink, there's a very serviceable café round the corner.'

She reported that Marianne was 'wrapped in a battleship-grey greatcoat'. She gazed out of the open floor-to-ceiling windows and 'alternately bosses and flirts with the photographer'. Woods visited one of the bedrooms and labelled it a 'testament to Faithfull's love of fashion', revealing: 'It is by far the most organised space in the apartment – every wall is lined with clothes rails. There are shelves of handbags, racks of heels. The labels ooze class: Chanel, Marc Jacobs, Stella McCartney, a gorgeous blue silk Galliano full-length frock tiered with beautifully tailored flounces'.

Marianne was among a curious group lending their name to a British horror film (despite its 'American' setting it was actually filmed in Redruth, Cornwall and Haywards Heath, West Sussex) that was produced over a number of years during the 2000s but not actually released until 2008. Marianne recorded a piece of narration for *Alone In The Dark* which evolved into *Evil Calls: The Raven* before a third name change to *The Legend Of Harrow Woods*.

Others contributing to the film formed a bizarre list: Rik Mayall, Jason Donovan, Eileen Daly, Norman Wisdom, Robin Askwith and Christopher Walken. It appeared that Richard Driscoll, the writer, producer and director, had purposely gathered together such disparate players – each with just a few minutes on screen – in the hope of engendering curiosity at the box office. In the film a group of students visit a haunted forest, Harrow Woods, in New England, to investigate the disappearance of horror novelist George Carney and his family who have been missing, presumed dead, for two years. They discover that in the 17th century the witch Lenore Selwyn was burnt at the stake within the woods and as she died in the flames she cursed the land her ashes fell upon.

There was doubt whether Marianne was actually involved with the film. Indeed, there was an exodus from it – Christopher Walken, the main narrator, asked his name to be removed from all publicity and others were reportedly unhappy with how it turned out. Marianne's name was not included on the cinema poster or the credits on the subsequent DVD. She did not include it in the filmography carried on her official website. Rik Mayall, however, said in a press interview that Marianne *had* provided a voice-over for the film which received unanimously bad reviews and was described as an amalgamation of *The Shining* and *The Blair Witch Project*.

Marianne definitely appeared in the documentary *FlicKeR*, made in 2008 by the Canadian film-maker Nik Sheehan. He had established himself in 1995 with *No Sad Songs*, the first major documentry about AIDs. *FlicKeR* was a biography of Marianne's old friend Brion Gysin, the British/Canadian painter, writer, sound poet, performance artist and inventor of the 'Dreamachine'. The device comprised a 100-watt light bulb, a motor and a rotating cylinder with cut-outs. Users would sit in front of it, close their eyes and experience visions caused by the flashes of light. Gysin, who died in 1986, believed that by offering the world a drugless 'high' the invention could revolutionise human consciousness. Marianne was among many prominent figures who had experimented with the invention. The other interviewees were Lee Ranaldo from the band Sonic Youth, Genesis P-Orridge (ex-Throbbing Gristle and Psychic TV), Iggy Pop and another name from Marianne's past, Kenneth Anger.

In July 2008 Marianne had 15 of her songs from 1965 and 1966 included on an album that formed part of the 'Live At The BBC' series. The songs were recorded for the BBC's flagship pop programme, *Saturday Club*. Across five sessions, Marianne performed with both the Mike Leander Orchestra and her regular guitarist, Jon Mark. Songs such as 'Come And Stay With Me', 'In My Time Of Sorrow', 'Go Away From My World' and, of course, 'As Tears Go By' showcased Marianne's perfectly pitched voice. If there were rumours at the time (and ever after) that her smooth passage was down purely to her face, name and famous acquaintances, this was the ultimate riposte. The girl could sing.

Also included on the album were snippets of interviews Marianne had done with the show's presenter, Brian Matthew. Sounding resolutely middle-aged [he was actually 37], he quizzed her about her aristocratic background, forthcoming wedding, motherhood and the inevitable 'plans for the future'. Marianne, just 18-years-old, sounded sweet and posh and confident in her answers, telling Matthew that she hoped to one day star in a film and make a jazz record. The album was recorded in mono and came with an excellent booklet, which helped form a sublime time capsule.

Marianne's speaking voice – often cited as being definitively English with its patrician vowels and precise diction – had been noted and utilised in several film and theatre productions, where she was invited to narrate. In 2003 she had provided the narration, along with Julie Christie, to the Bruce Weber documentary *A Letter To True*, a feature about the 'affection, loyalty and unconditional love' displayed by his four pet golden retrievers. In the autumn of 2008 Marianne's voice was put in greater focus than ever before when a tour was organised of small but prestigious European theatres where Marianne recited Shakespeare's sonnets. The undertaking was perfect on many fronts: speaking was much less damaging than singing on her increasingly weathered voice; it further cemented her image as an artist of gravitas and such a fleet-of-foot tour required little in the way of back-up which meant it was financially viable.

The sonnets were recited by Marianne while sitting at a desk with just her glasses and a tumbler of water to hand. Between readings, the cellist, Vincent Ségal, played short pieces especially written for the show which were designed to 'rest the ears'. A conservatory musician from the National Music Academy of Lyon, Ségal was known for taking on diverse projects. He had played with Elvis Costello, Blackalicious and the French reggae band Tryo. He later collaborated and toured with Sting to promote the album *If On A Winter's Night...*

Marianne had been imbued with a love of Shakespeare by her father and her English teacher at St Joseph's. In September 1960 she and her classmates were taken to the Old Vic to see Judi Dench and John Stride star in *Romeo And Juliet* directed by Franco Zeffirelli. After her long period of drugs re-habilitation in the mid-1980s, one of her first positive moves on becoming 'clean' was to enrol on a course studying the early plays of Shakespeare at the Harvard Extension School.

Before her reading at the Chateau de Chillon in Montreux in December 2008, Marianne visited the Martin Bodmer Foundation Museum in Geneva. During his lifetime Bodmer had amassed 150,000 works in 80 languages, focusing on what he considered were the 'five pillars of world literature' – the Bible, Homer, Dante Alighieri, William Shakespeare and Johann Wolfgang von Goethe. At the museum Marianne viewed a rare copy of Shakespeare's sonnets dating from 1609. "It gave me goose bumps," she said. Of the 154 sonnets written by Shakespeare, Marianne chose to perform those that dealt with love, beauty, fame, time and hate. "It's the big stuff," she said. The show, lasting just over an hour, visited Berlin, Basel, Milan, Geneva and Brussels. She recited 26 sonnets which were translated into different languages and projected on to a screen behind her. "I love doing it," she said. "Anywhere there's an audience for sonnets I'll go." Marianne would reprise the performance on an ad hoc basis over the coming years.

Unknown to her fans and the public in general, Marianne was suffering from writers' block through late-2008 into early-2009 which meant recording material written by others for *Easy Come, Easy Go* was a necessity. Her relationship with François Ravard was disintegrating and she was too distressed to stir herself to write. The first newspaper to report the break-up was the *Daily Mail* in April 2009 under the headline: 'After 15 Years, Marianne and her soul mate split'. "I felt very betrayed and lonely. I am much, much better now, but it is not good for your self-esteem," she told Richard Simpson of the paper. Details were sketchy at first but Marianne began to proffer additional information in subsequent interviews. She told Liza Ghorbani of the *Wall Street Journal*: "He fell in love with another woman, a younger woman – agony – and I didn't notice that this was going on, and when I found out it was just awful." She said her emotional life had been deeply affected by cancer: "It doesn't make you feel sexy," she told Chrissy Iley of *The Telegraph*. "It took me a long time to get over it. I went right off sex and that was a difficult moment because when I felt better again François had fallen in love with someone else."

Although acknowledging Ravard as her 'soul mate' (Marianne had used this term of endearment often in interviews), the British press had drawn a typically abridged portrait of him over the years. Fiona Sturges of *The Independent* referred to him as a 'a dishevelled character in Woody Allen specs'. Chrissy Iley had said he 'looks like a love child of Serge Gainsbourg and Woody Allen'. In the infamous article by Lynn Barber she had also made the Woody Allen connection, stating that he 'looks like Woody Allen but without his suavity and charm'. Judith Woods of the *Mail On Sunday* was more sympathetic, describing Ravard as 'a handsomely dishevelled straight-from-Central-Casting Frenchman, reminiscent of Serge Gainsbourg'. The condescending references to Ravard's appearance were obviously made as a counterpoint to Jagger's assumed cachet as a partner. Although he and Marianne had been together for nearly four times as long as she had been with Jagger, in the articles announcing their split Jagger was mentioned significantly more times than Ravard.

There had been spats and misunderstandings but these were unavoidable considering the amount of time Marianne and Ravard spent together and the additional stresses of the manager/artist dynamic. Ravard often attended interviews where they tried to pass off their relationship as strictly business. When Marianne was asked by Jenny Johnston of the *Daily Mail* in April 2007 whether Ravard was her boyfriend, she replied: "I'm not telling you. He is very private. He doesn't want his name in the papers. He is French. He has been my lover for 13 years. He is the man I love." The ruse habitually failed because the pair would throw each other a look or argue with the familiarity of lovers, providing the journalist with the additional line of 'outing' the couple.

Just two years before the split, Marianne was clearly very much in love with Ravard. She refused to refer to him as her 'partner' or 'boyfriend'. "He is my lover. He is exactly that," she said. "I don't like the word 'partner'. He is more than a friend. What else should I call him?" She was planning a life together. "When I look back on the people I've loved, they were nearly all great people, but there wasn't the sense that we would be together forever," she said. "You know how it is with these men. You're walking along the same path, you come together for a while, then you diverge. Mick and I weren't meant to be together forever. With my current lover, it's for life."

One of the first songs written by Marianne after she overcame writers' block was 'Why Did We Have To Part' which was included on her next album, *Horses And High Heels*. The song, with its refrain of 'Why did we have to part my love?/ Why couldn't life just stay the same?' was about the break-up. "That's so blunt [the lyric]. It's almost shocking for me that it should be so blunt. But what else can I do? I have to tell the story as it actually happened," said Marianne. Both Ravard and Marianne agreed that their professional arrangement should continue and he remained her manager. Incidentally, Ravard's new relationship was short-lived. In March 2011 Marianne told *The Independent*: "I don't know what to say. It didn't work out, the romance he had. Surprise, surprise."

19

Early in 2009 Marianne and Ravard became embroiled in two undignified episodes that probably reflected their moods as they struggled to deal with the breakdown of their romantic attachment. Ravard was arrested after a row with check-in staff at Gatwick Airport as he prepared to board a flight with Marianne to Bologna, Italy, where she was due to perform. A spokesman for British Airways said: "He appeared to be intoxicated on arrival at check-in. In such circumstances, an assessment is made as to whether the passenger is fit to travel. When he was refused travel, he became physically and verbally abusive. Police were called and he was arrested. Such behaviour will not be tolerated." A 'spokeswoman' for Marianne said her client [Marianne] was not involved 'in any way in the situation' and boarded the plane as planned. "Marianne hadn't been drinking at the time of the incident and she does not drink alcohol. She is enjoying life and loving it as she is sober and clean," she said.

A few days later Marianne's name was back in the British newspapers. 'Kate Moss is a vampire who stole my style' was the headline in the *Daily Mail*. In the article Marianne was quoted: "She's [Kate Moss] not really my friend. I thought she was, but she's very clever. She wanted to read me like a Braille book. And she did. It's a vampirical thing." She accused Moss of copying her choice of men in dating Jamie Hince, the singer with the band The Kills [he and Kate married in July 2011].

"Now I see pictures of her with a boy who looks like Mick Jagger, and her looking like me. So there was a reason. It's one of her gigs to do me," said Marianne. Before the spat, Kate and Marianne had reportedly been drawn to each other through a 'shared love of fashion and rock stars' and had once been 'regular night-time fixtures in Central London and even holidayed together in the Bahamas'.

Kate Moss had been close to Marianne for several years. She appeared extensively in the video for Marianne's single 'Sex With Strangers' released in 2002. Earlier in their friendship Marianne had said of Kate: "She's very complex – she's very like me. She's a Capricorn. I think she's great." This opinion was later revised: "We were very fond of each other," said Marianne. "And then it suddenly soured. She's very clever but she isn't at all educated. We don't have any common references, except music." Before the story could spread to the multitude of celebrity magazines and websites, Marianne issued an apology. "I'm just about to pick up the phone and call her. I done wrong. It doesn't matter who started it, I have to make amends," she told *The Sun*. She continued: "We are friends again, and we are going to keep it to ourselves." Marianne admitted she had criticised friends unfairly in the past. "It's a great shame when people don't speak for a few years. I am not banishing people any more. In the past I hurt people before they could ever hurt me; my whole life was founded on that. I was a very lost little girl but I'm better now, thank you."

A host of famous names including Marianne were involved in a fiasco played out in the grounds of the Sydney Opera House in January 2010. Hal Willner had invited concert-goers to 'leave terra firma behind and cast off on a pirate adventure'. Willner had previously staged the show *Rogues' Gallery* in July 2009 in Dublin, Gateshead and at the Barbican Centre, London. It was a collection of songs chronicling a life at sea from the perspectives of sailors, convicts, travellers and pirates. The idea was conceived by Johnny Depp and film director Gore Verbinski on the set of the film, *Pirates Of The Caribbean*.

The show in Australia took place on the forecourt of the opera house and included in the ensemble with Marianne were actor and musician

Tim Robbins, producer Todd Rundgren, Gavin Friday (ex-Virgin Prunes) and Peter Garrett, the former frontman with Midnight Oil and Australia's Federal Minister for the Environment, Heritage and the Arts. The music was provided by the Rogues' Gallery Band directed by Kate St. John, formerly of The Dream Academy, and with Roger Eno, the brother of Brian, on keyboards and harmonium.

As part of the Sydney Festival, the performance had been billed as the 'must-see' show of the event, with tickets priced accordingly at the equivalent of £80 each. Heavy rain fell throughout the performance which was allegedly so poor that it inspired an 'online mutiny'. The news was broken in Britain by *The Telegraph*: 'Australian audience lambasts "shambolic" Marianne Faithfull concert' followed by the sub-heading: 'An ensemble performance by singers including Marianne Faithfull and Tim Robbins titled *Rogues' Gallery* has more than lived up to its name after Australian concertgoers complained the show was "shambolic", "pathetic" and that the cast members appeared "disinterested". It was reported that one member of the audience posted afterwards: 'The weather didn't help and poor Marianne was pathetic. She needed the sheet music to keep up'. Another audience member posted: 'The performance frequently collapsed into amateur hour – tawdry panto and sub school rock musical'.

The festival organisers issued a formal response: 'While many visitors to the website are unhappy with the event, we have also had letters of support and positive feedback. We value and appreciate all feedback, both good and bad, taking our audience's opinions very seriously and finding it helpful for future programming.' Marianne moved on to play two concerts in her own right in Australia, at the Tivoli in Brisbane and the Forum Theatre in Melbourne. She appeared with a seven-piece band before sell-out audiences to excellent reviews.

Marianne decamped to the French Quarter of New Orleans in the autumn of 2010 to work on her next album, *Horses And High Heels*. Once more, she drew on an acclaimed and eclectic group of musicians on a record featuring eight cover versions and four new songs that she had co-written. Among the guests were Lou Reed who played guitar on

'Back In Baby's Arms' and 'The Old House'; the producer and old friend John Porter (guitar), with cameo appearances from Dr. John and Wayne Kramer of MC5. The songs had again been sourced by Marianne and Willner. "We just *do* find great songs," she said. "But there's no theme... well, the only theme is me. Conventional happiness isn't my way, you know, but this is a very happy record. I'm not depressed any more. And I think it's all been well worth it. I did have a bit of a bad time in the 1970s but I think things have been wonderful. So I suppose this album is a bit of a breakthrough. I'm incredibly lucky, don't think I don't know it. I'm so grateful to be able to still write songs and express my emotion in music. And the best thing of all is working with such great people. It's inspirational. It's all a very different style for me, much more rhythmic. And a very modern record, it's not looking back to the past at all. All the songs are about now."

By *Horses And High Heels* an identifiable pattern had been set across a series of albums by Marianne and Willner, with support from 'executive producer' Ravard. They were collecting up songs, often of different styles, moods, sounds and eras, and presenting them as a single body of work. *Horses And High Heels* had sublime moments – 'The Stations' written by Greg Dulli (Afghan Whigs) and Mark Lanegan (Screaming Trees) and the gentle 'Love Song' (the Lesley Duncan number covered by Elton John on *Tumbleweed Connection*) among them, but much of the rest made for uneasy bedfellows. Ragtime ('Gee Baby') collided with folk ('Eternity') before swerving to pedestrian boogie-woogie ('No Reasons' with its refrain: 'Ain't got no reason to be happy, ain't got no reason to be sad') and then a re-write of The Rolling Stones' 'She's A Rainbow' with 'That's How Every Empire Falls'. While the songs had an interesting back-story in their own right, it was difficult to gauge who among Marianne's existing and potential audience would have a sufficiently broad palette to appreciate such diversity.

Marianne's growing commitment to France had been duly noted in cultural quarters. She spent most of the year living in the city, had signed to a French record label, starred in a French film and, most importantly, was viewed as a definitive chanteuse by the people who had given this very noun and concept to the world. In March 2011 she was made Commandeur of L'Ordre des Arts et des Lettres. The honour was bestowed upon her by Frédéric Mitterrand, the French Minister of Culture and Communication, after she had performed at Le Théâtre du Châtelet in Paris. The award was presented in 'recognition of significant contributions to the enrichment of the French cultural inheritance' and 'Commandeur' was the highest of the orders. "I am very, very grateful to be so honoured," she said. "When a friend, Etienne Daho [famous French singer, songwriter and record producer], was presented with an honour a few years ago I went to the ceremony but never thought I would be a recipient. Since I started coming to Paris in 1964, the French have welcomed me and been very loving."

The professional relationship with Ravard had served Marianne particularly well in France. His contacts across the country were unrivalled and he had recognised her specific appeal in his home country. In Britain the notion of a 'torch singer' was alien while in France and most other mainland European countries, it was a long-standing institution. The importance of a singing voice's technical quality was a good distance behind the life story it imbued and the manner of performance. There was also a wider acceptance of the ageing process and, in fact, it was considered a badge of honour, especially for women.

During the time Ravard had overseen Marianne's career he had formed a master-class in management. He had networked superbly, ensuring she was associated repeatedly with esteemed figures, in all aspects of record production. The sleeves and packaging of the CDs were tasteful. The marketing campaigns were subtle. He was highly selective of her media engagements, with an instinctive feel for what was appropriate for his 'client'. While observers might say he was merely building on what Island Records had started and Marianne's previous 'cool' standing as an artist, he was, in effect, dealing with diminishing returns. Her voice, by her own admission, had been affected by the excesses of the past and the continued smoking but, between them, they dressed this up in many ways – setting it against folk, techno, orchestral, Weill-based material – turning a weakness into strength by claiming it was a signifier of authenticity and 'character'. The precise nature of their professional arrangement – who had the ideas, who supplied the contacts and where the credit (and occasional blame) truly lay – was known only to themselves but, as a pair, they had formed a branding like no other – a British female singer in her mid-60s still considered relevant and newsworthy on the cusp of her 50th year in the music industry.

The promotional duties for *Horses And High Heels* saw Marianne visit the BBC to be interviewed by presenter Susanna Reid on *Breakfast*. Afterwards Marianne was upset because she felt the interview had dwelled too long on her former drugs use. "That stupid woman," she fumed to Nick Duerden of *The Independent* later that day. "OK I shouldn't call her stupid, but she was banging on about drugs, which is completely irrelevant in my life now. It's not the point any more, is it? The awfulness of my previous life is no longer the point." Marianne was far happier discussing her new drugs-free state. "I'm having a great life and I want to go on having one," she told Chrissy Iley of *The Telegraph* in March 2011. "I'm not sure yet what my higher mission is but I have a feeling it might be great. Before, I thought my mission was death, but now my mission is life. I feel quite different now to that bad, stupid, silly girl. I feel that everything is before me like a wonderful banquet. I think it's really helpful if you don't drink and do drugs. It's frustrating sometimes. I can't say it's a bed of roses. But it's better for my wilder emotions and my self-sabotage if I don't. Drink breaks down your spiritual system, and then you go back on to the drugs and that would be awful."

Marianne had realised that staying clean was enabling her to be productive and extend her career. In *Memories, Dreams & Reflections* she wrote: 'Stuff like cocaine and alcohol and shit like that just aren't an option any more. For me. I'm not putting it down but in my band, nobody drinks, nobody smokes. They're bloody vegetarians. Touring is hard work at our age. You have to make a choice: are we going to work properly or just fuck around?' She also disavowed her earlier romanticised image of drug-taking. "Maybe it worked for De Quincey and Cocteau, and it sounds good when you're 15,' she wrote. 'But ultimately I think it's incredibly immature. It's practically *infantile*.' She said she agreed with Gustave Flaubert who proffered that the best art came from a bourgeois life of adequate sleep, food and exercise. "You only have to think about Marlon Brando in *Apocalypse Now* to see what a hellish place the Romantic illusion can take you to. It's a supreme form of narcissism," said Marianne.

Two supporting roles in films of reasonably high production values helped Marianne maintain her parallel acting career. She played the part of Dr Langenkamp in the thriller *Faces In The Crowd*, released in 2011. Filmed chiefly in Canada, on a budget of $11 million, by the French director Julien Magnat, the story centred on a school teacher, Anna (Milla Jovovich), who develops prosopagnosia (an inability to remember faces) after being attacked by a serial killer. As Dr Langenkamp, Marianne was one of several trying to help Anna through her ordeal. The character was thought to be named after Heather Langenkamp who starred in *A Nightmare On Elm Street* in 1984 and was stalked in real life.

During the same year Marianne spent time in Switzerland filming her role as Mariette in the film adaptation of *Belle du Seigneur*, the English-language adaptation of Albert Cohen's epic French novel of a fated love affair between a high-ranking Jewish official and the protestant wife of one of his employees. The film, starring the Irish actor Jonathan Rhys Meyers and the Russian model and actress Natalia Vodianova, opened in Russia in November 2012 and was set to reach the rest of Europe by the late summer of 2013. Marianne revealed that her role as Mariette lent itself to comedy. "I love making people laugh. I love performing," she said. "The best acting I do is in my life, not just on stage or film."

Invitations to perform with other artists, both live and on record, were still made to Marianne on a frequent basis. She reunited with Metallica in December 2011 for their 30th anniversary celebration at the Fillmore in San Francisco where she performed 'The Memory Remains' with them. Also in 2011 she recorded a version of 'Angel' from the album *Tusk* which was included on a tribute album to Fleetwood Mac, *Just Tell Me That You Want Me*. Marianne was in the company of many credible young artists on the 17-song album such as MGMT, The Kills, Best Coast and The New Pornographers.

She was among a host of established names contributing to *Monsieur Gainsbourg Revisited,* an English language tribute album to the late French singer Serge Gainsbourg. She covered his track 'Lola Rastaquouère' with her old friends from the Compass Point All Stars, Sly and Robbie. Also on the album, released by Virgin Records, were Franz Ferdinand, Portishead, Tricky and Michael Stipe.

Another French project saw Marianne co-write a new song for the gangster film *Truands* [also known as *Crime Insiders* and *Paris Lockdown*]. She wrote the lyrics to a piece of music by Bruno Coulais, singer with the band Ulysse, who were also signed to Naïve. The song 'A Lean And Hungry Look' was played over the end credits and featured Marianne speaking and singing. In 2007 Marianne had sung with British singer-songwriter Patrick Wolf on his album *The Magic Position.* They performed a duet on the piano/violin ballad 'Magpie'.

Marianne was one of scores of artists asked to contribute to one of the most extensive tribute albums ever produced. *Chimes Of Freedom: The Songs Of Bob Dylan* was a three-CD set comprising 73 songs with all proceeds donated to Amnesty International. Alongside Marianne on the record were, among others, Adele, Kesha, My Chemical Romance, Pete Townshend, Seal, Jeff Beck, Elvis Costello, Mark Knopfler, Sting, Patti Smith and Pete Seeger. Marianne recorded a new version of 'Baby, Let Me Follow You Down', the traditional folk song that Dylan covered on his debut album, *Bob Dylan,* in 1962. *Chimes Of Freedom: The Songs Of Bob Dylan* was released in January 2012 and entered the *Billboard* chart in the United States at number 11.

More than 40 years after they had separated, John Dunbar and Marianne were brought together again in April 2012 when they curated an exhibition at the Tate Gallery in Liverpool. "The person who first showed me how to look at pictures was John, when he was at Cambridge and doing his degree," she said. "We went to Rome and Florence together. We spent a lot of afternoons in the Tate and the National back then. And so we had a fabulous time going through the Tate archives for this show." Marianne dutifully conducted a round of interviews to promote a display which she said was 'something like the inside of my head'. She talked up her connections to the city with the *Liverpool Echo*: "I was here until I was six [Ormskirk], so it was very formative, at least if you believe the Jesuits. I remember a lot of it, particularly my mother taking me to the docks to show me the big American liners. She would say to me: 'That way is America' which set something up for me, for sure. I played Liverpool a lot as a performer on tour. And when I was there I would go to the Walker Art Gallery; I remember seeing Millais' wonderful *Ophelia* there."

The exhibition, 'Innocence And Experience', ran for more than four months and featured paintings by William Blake (*Pity*), Pauline Boty (*The Only Blonde In The World*), Balthus (*Sleeping Girl*), Marlene Dumas (*Stern*) and Francis Bacon (*Study For Portrait II*); photographs by Robert Mapplethorpe (separate studies of Marianne and William Burroughs) and Nan Goldin (*Greer And Robert On The Bed, NYC, 1982*); collages by Richard Hamilton (*Swingeing London '67*) and Edward Ruscha (*Roughly 92% Angel But About 8% Devil*). David Tremlett's installation, *The Springs Recordings* was set up in the gallery – a shelf of cassettes of nature recordings made chiefly in rural areas but also including London, each lasting approximately 15 minutes. "What makes it so interesting personally is my mixed blood," Marianne told the *Liverpool Echo*. "So I've got my dear English father and my great love of England and my country, and then I've got my strange Austro-Hungarian continental mother. So we have this real mix of George Grosz and continental stuff, and then John's stuff which is also very interesting, which is the Yoko Ono, Colin Sell, David Tremlett, all sorts of fascinating people that I really wouldn't have understood or known about. In fact, the project has turned into a true labour of love. The whole thing makes my heart sing actually. It's a lovely, lovely thing to do."

The *Daily Mail* and Marianne had shared a complex 'relationship' for many years. At times the paper had been very supportive – it carried some of the most sensitively written pieces about her cancer. These articles aside, it was perhaps unfortunate for Marianne that the paper considered her a perfect fit for an update of an age-old morality tale. In short, she would pay for a life of hedonism.

In June 2012 Marianne was photographed having a cigarette outside the BBC studios in London. She had called in to finalise arrangements to deputise for Jarvis Cocker on his BBC Radio 6 programme. She had been invited to fill in for four consecutive Sundays from July 8 while Cocker toured. She had promised to play 'my most favourite records across a variety of genres including jazz and blues'. The photographs were not posed and showed Marianne supposedly borrowing a lighter from a passer-by and then talking to a middle-aged man who was wearing a baseball cap and carrying a plastic carrier bag.

The pictures found their way to the *Daily Mail* and were run as a feature under the heading: 'Time has not treated her well... Former Sixties siren Marianne Faithfull is unrecognisable'. To emphasise her change in body shape, it ran photographs of Marianne from her stick-thin younger days alongside the contemporary ones and further made the point in the copy written by Tammy Hughes: 'These shocking photos taken in central London this week show the former Sixties icon as she has never been seen before. Standing outside the BBC studios, Faithfull looks significantly heavier than she once was, with her blonde hair wild and unkempt around her face. The 65-year-old singer is also seen attempting to hide her features behind a pair of oversized sunglasses'. Hughes spelled out definitively why this had happened to Marianne: 'Tales about her drug abuse and infidelity have spanned almost five decades. And now it seems as though Marianne Faithfull's rock and roll lifestyle may finally be catching up with her.'

On the *Daily Mail*'s website, readers were asked to post comments about the story and 305 did so – a huge number for a routine 'downpage' piece. Most condemned the paper's mean-spiritedness. One read: 'Quelle surprise, woman ages in 40 years, well I never!' A poster calling himself 'Benny the Dip' wrote: 'So it's OK to bring to the public attention – in a series of 'shocking' pictures – this woman's ageing/smoking habit/ weight gain because she was once a public figure, is it? Funny that, 'cos earlier this week, when a comedian made a rather childish joke about a footballer's appearance, you came over all righteous and condemned him for his lapse in manners. YOU ARE HYPOCRITES!' Inevitably Marianne's overweight state brought forth the customary quota of Mars bar jokes but others detected a misogynistic undercurrent. She was, they pointed out, a 65-year-old woman, unaware she was being photographed. She was not wearing any make-up and it was a windy day. 'Why are women always judged on their looks?' wrote 'Anna' from Perth, Scotland. 'Who doesn't look better when they are in their twenties? It's time to stop commenting on how women look and let us grow old gracefully and without fear of criticism!' The comments logged on the site had no effect – just a few months later the paper ran a story of much greater cruelty.

The 50th anniversary of The Rolling Stones was marked in November and December 2012 when they played two concerts at the O2 Arena in London; two at the Prudential Center in Newark, New Jersey; and one at the Barclays Center in Brooklyn, New York. These shows and the release of a compilation album, *GRRR!*, prompted a media frenzy which, with a certain inevitability, washed up against Marianne. "Oh God," she told *The Independent*. "It's another thing that makes me want to retire, the fact that everybody absolutely must discuss The Rolling Stones with me, again and again and again. It was all such a long time ago. It has nothing to do with me any more. I've gotten over it. I just wish everybody else would, too."

The *Daily Mail* dispatched Paul Scott to track down Marianne who was performing *The Seven Deadly Sins* at the Landestheater in Linz, Austria. His article was one of a four-part series undertaken by him on 'Jagger's women', looking at 'the very different fates of the Rolling Stone's past lovers. Of them all, Marianne, perhaps, has had the furthest fall from grace'. The resultant piece spared her little dignity and was headlined: 'Ruined by loving Jagger: Broke, alone and performing in seedy stage shows, at 66 Marianne Faithfull STILL pines for the Stone who sexually humiliated her 40 years ago'.

Scott had travelled to Linz, Austria's third-largest city and one noted for its cultural and architectural richness, and headed to the theatre where the 2013 programme included performances of Verdi's

Rigoletto, Mozart's *Cosi Fan Tutte*, Philip Glass' *Traces Of The Lost* and Shakespeare's *The Merchant Of Venice*. He wrote that the venue 'is not exactly Madison Square Garden' and described it as 'a curious, municipal-looking building in the centre of a one-way system that puts on obscure, low-budget, theatrical productions of the type frequented by bearded night-school lecturers and ageing bluestockings who pay as little as £3.20 for the cheapest standing tickets.'

The aim of the piece was to contrast Marianne's situation with Jagger's who was said to be earning £4 million from the five anniversary concerts. So, with little regard to veracity or context, Scott set about his work. Marianne was 'scratching a living in one of the more unglamorous corners of Europe' and 'bunking down in a tiny flat in a nearby tower block to save money'. Susanne Kuffner, the theatre's secretary, was quoted: 'You sometimes see Marianne walking around town like a grandma'. Her performances in the show were said to be affected by ill-health: 'Sometimes it has been a struggle,' he wrote. 'Recently, during her theatre run, she suffered a severe cold, but muddled through, coughing and looking unsteady. And during an ovation, one of her backing dancers, young men dressed only in skimpy leather shorts, had to support her to make sure she did not fall'.

Once again, scores of readers posted comments on the *Daily Mail's* website. 'Nikki' of San Diego best summed up a recurring theme: 'The story makes it seem as if she's a pauper, rummaging through garbage cans. What did I miss? She keeps two homes in different countries. That's lucky, I'd say. She's 66 and working. So are many Americans her age, but surely they're not getting her salary. Maybe she doesn't have the uber-comfy lifestyle of Mick, but she seems as if she's doing just fine.'

The picture of Marianne accompanying the article showed her to be clearly overweight. She was photographed next to a pair of young male dancers who were wearing only briefs, which obviously emphasised the difference in their physiques. On the short promotional video released by the theatre to publicise the show, Marianne looked thinner but was still noticeably heavier than she had been before in performance. "I did actually have liposuction a while back," she told Nick Duerden of

The Independent. "I'd developed this double-chin, you see, and I didn't like that, not at all. So I got rid of it. But I couldn't have plastic surgery. Someone with my drugs past would have trouble with the painkillers, for starters, but also I wouldn't want to look like everybody else. I just want to look like me."

Aside from the cancer and hepatitis C, Marianne had been dealing with other health issues. She developed an addiction to sleeping pills and spent time at the Crossroads Centre in Antigua, the drug and alcohol addiction rehabilitation centre set up in 1997 by Eric Clapton and Richard Conte, the CEO of the Priory Hospitals Group. While she was at this 'international centre for healing', she was diagnosed with depression. "I was told that I had very likely been clinically depressed for a long, long time, probably since I was 15, or even 14," she said. "It explained, to me at least, a lot of my behaviour over the years."

In January 2011 Marianne spent a weekend at the Pennsylvania Gestalt Centre to undertake an intensive course in Gestalt Therapy. The centre, founded in 1973, summarised its philosophy as 'a lively and holistic experiential approach to healing and personal growth that emphasises the development of awareness – emotional, physical, intellectual and spiritual, and the capacity to make healthy contact with one's self, others and the environment.' The centre's founder and clinical director, Mariah Fenton Gladis, had a more homespun definition: 'In terms of my work, people often ask me how I do it, listening to people's problems all day long. I tell them that I don't hear problems. I hear people wanting to change, wanting to be better human beings, wanting to create happier families. Over and over again I hear people wanting to love and be loved more effectively. I hear people wanting to remove the barriers in their life and provide more for their loved ones on every level. I hear people looking for ways to contribute and improve their contact skills in the world."

Marianne underwent the 'open chair' technique while at the centre. She had to sit opposite an empty chair and mentally place into it someone of significance and was then encouraged to express whatever it was she had felt unable to express before. "It's pretty amazing, actually," she told *The Independent.* "You focus on this decisive moment in your life

– and, no, I'm not going to tell you what mine was – and then you try, essentially, to change history by imagining a more positive outcome, which your unconscious accepts. I think it was very useful, but I don't see myself going again. I mean, I don't feel depressed any more. Really, I don't."

20

The media and public were given the chance to once more deconstruct the Marianne Faithfull story in January 2013 with the release of the 'deluxe' version of *Broken English*. The two-CD set included the original 'lost' band recordings, bonus tracks and the film made by Derek Jarman featuring the tracks 'Witches Song', 'The Ballad Of Lucy Jordan' and 'Broken English'. The release was a trigger for media discourses on a multitude of topics: excess, post-modernism, celebrity, ageing, drugs dependency, feminism, punk, fame, bohemianism, solipsism, idealism – all inspired by one woman. At such times, reading and hearing of herself this way, Marianne must feel breathless, overwhelmed. It is a lot to bear. She must know that she will forever remain a symbolic figure and a catalyst for sharp debate and opinion. No escape.

She long ago accepted that her relationship with Jagger would never end. The public, led by the media, won't allow it. She, and he to a lesser degree, are the nation's prodigal children. They were conduits through which millions lived another imagined life, one that was glamorous, nomadic and indulged. Jagger's name will feature evermore next to hers in print. The photographs of their younger selves will stand side-by-side, even when the obituaries are written. It is a mean paradox that while Marianne would prefer this particular element of her past to fade away, without the unyielding link, mainstream interest in her music and acting and 'story' would have receded long ago.

While for many years it was impossible to plan ahead, Marianne's creative life now has the broad brush of the routine. She finished a three-month run of *The Seven Deadly Sins* in Austria in January 2013. She has a concert planned in Paris and at the annual folk get-together, the Kate Wolf Music Festival, in California in June. Good health withstanding, the pattern of the last two decades should remain much the same: albums, tours, the occasional film and any projects along the way that ensnare her interest. This, after what went before, is a celebration. She talks constantly of the joys of working, of being creative, and has the evangelical zeal of someone who has let too much time slip away.

A short profile of Marianne was featured in the popular American television programme *CBS News Sunday Morning*. At the end of the film, the reporter, Anthony Mason, delivered a summing up in the stagy, faux-serious voice beloved of television folk, especially in the United States. He said: "She took the hard road to becoming a legend. But Marianne Faithfull, who once tried to end her life, now can't get enough of it." A piece of recent concert footage of Marianne singing – inevitably – 'As Tears Go By' flashed on the screen and then a voice-over from her: "Now I appreciate it. I think I have been very unconscious for a long time and only now have I begun to 'get it'. As long as I got it before I croaked I think that's the main thing."

Discography

Counting/I'd Like To Dial Your Number
Decca F12443, July 1966

Is This What I Get for Loving You?/Tomorrow's Calling
Decca F12524, February 1967

Something Better/Sister Morphine
Decca F12889, February 1969 (withdrawn)

Dreamin' My Dreams/Lady Madeleine
NEMS NES004, November 1975

All I Want To Do In Life/Wrong Road Again
NEMS NES013, September 1976

The Way You Want Me To Be/That Was The Day
NEMS NES 117, September 1978

The Ballad Of Lucy Jordan/Brain Drain
Island WIP 6491, October 1979

Broken English/What's The Hurry
Island WIP6542, February 1980

As Tears Go By/Come And Stay With Me
Decca F13890, August 1980

Intrigue/For Beauty's Sake
Island WIP6737, October 1981

Sweetheart/Over Here
Island WIP6752, November 1981

Broken English/Sister Morphine
Island 7" MF100, May 1982
(also on 12-inch with longer version of 'Broken English', MF100)

Broken English/Why D'Ya Do It
Island 12WIP6542, February 1980 (available as 12" only)

Running For Our Lives/She's Got A Problem
Island IS105, March 1983

As Tears Go By/Trouble In Mind
Island IS323, June 1987
(also on 12-inch, 12IS 323, with extra track 'The Hawk')

Don't Forget Me/20th Century Blues/Mack The Knife
EC Reverso/BMG Classics/RCA Victor 74321 420292,
September 1996

Hang It On Your Heart (single, TV and instrumental versions)
EMI 7243 8 84396 26, August 1997

Vagabond Ways/Electra/For Wanting You/Wilder Shores Of Love/
Incarceration Of A Flower Child
It Records/Virgin ITPROCD5, June 1999

Electra (one track)
It Records/Virgin ITRDJ005, November 1999

Sex With Strangers (original edit; Sly And Robbie Sex Ref Mix;
Sly And Robbie Dub Mix)
EMI Hut Recordings HUTTP147, January 2002

Easy Come, Easy Go
Naïve B001GAQPTI, October 2004 (CD single and 12-inch)

Horses And High Heels
Naïve B004DEKOWS, January 2011 (12-inch)

Extended Plays

Go Away From My World/The Most Of What Is Least/Et Maintenant/
The Sha La la Song
Decca FE8624, May 1965

As Tears Go By/Come And Stay With Me/This Little Bird/
Summer Nights
Decca F13890, August 1980

Albums

COME MY WAY

Come My Way/Jaberwock/Portland Town/House Of The Rising Sun/
Spanish Is A Loving Tongue/Fare Thee Well/Lonesome Traveller/
Down In The Salley Garden/Mary Ann/Full Fathom Five/Four Strong
Winds/Black Girl/Once I Had A Sweetheart/Bells Of Freedom.
(Extra tracks on CD – Blowin' In The Wind/Et Maintenant/
That's Right Baby/Sister Morphine)
Decca LK4688, April 1965
CD reissue – Decca 820629-2, August 1991

MARIANNE FAITHFULL

Come And Stay With Me/If I Never Get To Love You/Time Takes
Time/He'll Come Back To Me/Down Town/Plaisir D'Amour/
Can't You Hear My Heartbeat/As Tears Go By/Paris Bells/They Never
Will Leave You/What Have They Done To The Rain/In My Time Of
Sorrow/What Have I Done Wrong/I'm A Loser. (Extra tracks on CD
– Morning Sun; Greensleeves; House Of The Rising Sun
(Version 1); The Sha La La Song; Oh Look Around You; I'd Like To
Dial Your Number.)
Decca LK4689, April 1965
CD reissue – Decca 820630-2, April 1989

NORTH COUNTRY MAID

Green Are Your Eyes/Scarborough Fair/Cockleshells/The Last Thing
On My Mind/The First Time Ever I Saw Your Face/Sally Free And
Easy/Sunny Goodge Street/How Should I Your True Love Know/
She Moved Through The Fair/North Country Maid/Lullaby/Wild
Mountain Thyme. (Extra tracks on CD: The Most Of What Is Least/
Come My Way – alternate version/Mary Anne – alternate version)
Decca LK4778, April 1966
CD reissue – Decca 820631-2, August 1990

LOVE IN A MIST

Yesterday/You Can't Go Where The Roses Go/Our Love Has Gone/
Don't Make Promises/In The Night Time/This Little Bird/Ne Me
Quitte Pas/Counting/Reason To Believe/Coquillages/With You In
My Mind/Young Girl Blues/Good Guy/I Have A Love. (Extra tracks
on CD – Hang On To A Dream/Rosie, Rosie/Monday Monday)
Decca LK4854, February 1967
CD reissue –Decca 820632-2, October 1988

DREAMIN' MY DREAMS

Dreamin' My Dreams/Fairy Tale Hero/This Time/I'm Not Lisa/The
Way You Want Me To Be/Wrong Road Ahead/All I Wanna Do In Life/
I'm Looking For Blue Eyes/Somebody Loves You/Vanilla O'Lay/Lady
Madeleine/Sweet Little Sixteen
NEMS NEL 6007, January 1976
CD reissue (with the four extra tracks recorded for *Faithless*) –
Castle CMRCD 988, November 2004

FAITHLESS

Dreamin' My Dreams/Vanilla O'Lay/Wait For Me Down By The
River/I'll Be Your Baby Tonight/Lady Madeleine/All I Wanna Do In

Life/The Way You Want Me To Be/Wrong Road Again/That Was The
Day (Nashville)/This Time/I'm Not Lisa/Honky Tonk Angels
NEMS NEL 6012, March 1978
CD reissue – Castle CLACD 148, April 1988

BROKEN ENGLISH

Broken English/Witches Song/Brain Drain/Guilt/The Ballad Of Lucy
Jordan/What's The Hurry?/Working Class Hero/Why D'Ya Do It
Island ILPS9570, November 1979
CD reissue – CID9570 (90 039-2) IMCD111, March 1987

DANGEROUS ACQUAINTANCES

Sweetheart/Intrigue/Easy In The City/Strange One/Tenderness/
For Beauty's Sake/So Sad/Eye Communication/Truth, Bitter Truth
Island ILPS9648, October 1981
CD reissue – 842 483-2/IMCD, April 1995

A CHILD'S ADVENTURE

Times Square/The Blue Millionaire/Falling From Grace/Morning
Come/Ashes In My Hand/Running For Our Lives/Ireland/She's Got
A Problem
Island ILPS9734, February 1983
CD reissue – 90-066-2/IMCD206, March 1989

RICH KID BLUES

Rich Kid Blues/Long Black Veil/Sad Lisa/It's All Over Now Baby
Blue/Southern Butterfly/Chords Of Fame/Visions Of Johanna/It
Takes A Lot To Laugh, It Takes A Train To Cry/Beware Of Darkness/
Corrina, Corrina/Mud Slide Slim/Crazy Lady Blues/All I Want To Do
In Life/I'll Be Your Baby Tonight/Wait For Me Down By The River/
That Was The Day (Nashville)/This Time/The Way You Want Me To

Be/Dreamin' My Dreams/Wrong Road Again/Fairytale Hero/Vanilla
O'Lay/Lady Madeleine/Honky Tonk Angels
Castle Communications CCSLP 107, November 1985
CD reissue – Diablo DIAB 861, July 1988

STRANGE WEATHER

Stranger Intro/Boulevard Of Broken Dreams/I Ain't Goin' Down To
The Well No More/Yesterdays/Sign Of Judgement/Strange Weather/
Love, Life And Money/I'll Keep It With Mine/Hello Stranger/
Penthouse Serenade/As Tears Go By/A Stranger On Earth
Island ILPS9874, July 1987
CD reissue – CID9874/IMCD12, July 1987

BLAZING AWAY

Les Prisons Du Roy/Strange Weather/Guilt/Working Class Hero/
Sister Morphine/As Tears Go By/Why D'Ya Do It/When I Find My
Life/The Ballad Of Lucy Jordan/Times Square/Blazing Away/
She Moved Through The Fair/Broken English
Island ILPS9957, May 1990

A SECRET LIFE

Prologue/Sleep/Love In The Afternoon/Flaming September/She/
Bored By Dreams/Losing/Wedding/Stars Line Up/Epilogue
Island 524 096-2/IMCD225, March 1995

20TH CENTURY BLUES

Alabama Song/Want To Buy Some Illusions/Pirate Jenny/Salomon
Song/Boulevard Of Broken Dreams/Complainte De La Seine/The
Ballad Of the Soldier's Wife/Intro/Mon Ami, My Friend/Falling In
Love Again/Mack The Knife
EC Reverso/BMG Classics/RCA Victor 74321 386562, September
1996

THE SEVEN DEADLY SINS

Prologue/Sloth/Pride/Anger/Gluttony/Lust/Covetousness/Envy/
Epilogue/Alabama Song/The Ballad Of Sexual Dependency/Bilbao
Song/Pirate Jenny
EC Reverso/BMG Classics/RCA Victor 74321 601192, August 1998

VAGABOND WAYS

Vagabond Ways/Incarceration Of A Flower Child/File It Under Fun
From The Past/Electra/Wilder Shores Of Love/Marathon Kiss/For
Wanting You/Great Expectations/Tower Of Song/After The Ceasefire
Instinct/EMI ITR CD1, June 1999

KISSIN TIME

Sex With Strangers/The Pleasure Song/Like Being Born/I'm On Fire/
Wherever I Go/Song For Nico/Sliding Through Life On Charm/
Love & Money/Nobody's Fault/Kissin' Time/(bonus track –
Something Good – foreign editions only)
Hut/Virgin CDPHUT 71, March 2002

BEFORE THE POISON

The Mystery Of Love/My Friends Have/Crazy Love/Last Song/No
Child Of Mine/Before The Poison/There Is A Ghost/In The Factory/
Desperanto/City Of Quartz
Naïve NV800111, October 2004

LIVE AT THE BBC

Can't You Hear My Heartbeat/Come And Stay With Me/In My Time
Of Sorrow/Go Away From My World/The Sha La La Song/Go Away
From My World/Paris Bells/Summer Nights/Lullaby/The Last Thing
On My Mind/Yesterday/As Tears Go By/Cockleshells/Tomorrow's
Calling
Decca 5307959, July 2008

EASY COME, EASY GO

Down From Dover/Hold On Hold On/Solitude/The Crane Wife 3/
Easy Come, Easy Go/Children Of Stone/How Many Worlds/
In Germany Before The War/Ooh Baby Baby/Sing Me Back Home.
Disc 2: Salvation/Black Coffee/The Phoenix/Dear God Please Help
Me/Kimbie/Many A Mile To Freedom/Somewhere (A Place For Us)/
Flandyke Shore
Naïve NV814412, November 2008

HORSES AND HIGH HEELS

The Stations/Why Did We Have To Part/That's How Every Empire
Falls/No Reason/Prussian Blue/Love Song/Gee Baby/Goin' Back/
Past Present And Future/Horses And High Heels/Back In Baby's Arms/
Eternity/The Old House
Naïve B004DEKOXM, January 2011

BROKEN ENGLISH: DELUXE EDITION

Disc One: Broken English/Witches Song/Brain Drain/Guilt/
The Ballad Of Lucy Jordan/What's The Hurry/Working Class Hero/
Why D'Ya Do It/Witches Song/The Ballad Of Lucy Jordan/Broken
English – Short Film
Disc Two: Broken English (Original Mix)/Witches Song (Original
Mix)/Brain Drain (Original Mix)/Guilt (Original Mix)/The Ballad
Of Lucy Jordan (Original Mix)/What's The Hurry? (Original Mix)/
Working Class Hero (Original Mix)/Why D'Ya Do It (Original Mix)/
Sister Morphine/Broken English (7″ Single)/Broken English
(7″ Remix Version)/Broken English (12″ Remix)/Why D'Ya Do It
(12″ Remix)
UMC/Island 3711732, January 2013

Compilation Albums

THE WORLD OF MARIANNE FAITHFULL
Decca PA/SPA17, 1969

AS TEARS GO BY
Decca TAB 13, 1981

SUMMER NIGHTS
Decca TAB 78/810 234-1, 1984

MARIANNE FAITHFULL
Decca DOA 3, 1984

THE VERY BEST OF MARIANNE FAITHFULL (Decca recordings)
UK London 820 482-2, 1987

FAITHFULL – A COLLECTION OF HER BEST RECORDINGS
Island 524004-2, 1994

BEST OF MARIANNE FAITHFULL (Decca recordings)
UK Spectrum/Universal 544 180-2, 1998

A PERFECT STRANGER: THE ISLAND ANTHOLOGY (2-CD set)
Island 524 579-2, 1998

A STRANGER ON EARTH – AN INTRODUCTION TO MARIANNE FAITHFULL (includes both Decca and Island recordings)
UK Decca/Universal 585 152-2, 2001

THE COLLECTION (Decca recordings)
UK Spectrum/Universal 9824801, 2005

Other Appearances

Marianne has appeared on numerous albums as a guest singer or as a contributor to film soundtracks. Details are included on her official website.

Filmography/Theatrical Performances

Feature Films

Belle du Seigneur, Mariette, 2013

Faces In The Crowd, Dr Langenkamp, 2010

The Legend of Harrow Woods/Evil Calls: The Raven, Narrator, 2010

Irina Palm, Maggie, 2007

Marie Antoinette, Maria Theresa, 2006

Paris, je t'aime, visitor to print shop, 2006

Nord-Plage, 2004

Far From China, Helen, 2001

Intimacy, Betty, 2001

Crimetime, club singer, 1996

Moondance, mother, 1995

Shopping, Bev, 1994

When Pigs Fly, Lilly, 1993

The Turn Of The Screw, Narrator, 1992

Assault On Agathon, Helen Rochefort, 1977

Ghost Story, Sophy Kwykwer, 1974

Lucifer Rising, Lilith, 1972

Girl On A Motorcycle, Rebecca, 1968
I'll Never Forget What's'isname, Josie, 1967
Made In U.S.A, singer in café, 1966

Documentaries (as narrator)
A Letter To True, 2004
Trees, 2001

Theatrical Roles

The Seven Deadly Sins
Pirate Jenny
Landestheater, Linz, Austria
October 2012 – January 2013

The Black Rider
Pegleg
Barbican Theatre, London, May – June, 2004
American Conservatory Theatre, San Francisco, August – October 2004

The Threepenny Opera
Pirate Jenny
Gate Theatre, Dublin
July – September, 1991

The Kingdom Of Earth
Myrtle Ravenstock
The English Theatre, Vienna
February, 1975

The Rainmaker
Lizzie Curry
British tour, August – December 1975

The Collector
Miranda
Wyvern Theatre, Swindon, 11 February – 16 February, 1974
St Martin's Theatre, London, February – March 1974

Mad Dog
Jane Ludlow/Little Lord Fauntleroy (disguised)
Hampstead Theatre, London
August, 1973

A Patriot For Me
Countess Sophia Delyanoff
Palace Theatre, Watford
November, 1973

Hamlet
Ophelia
The Roundhouse, London
January – February, 1969

Early Morning
Florence Nightingale
Royal Court, London
March – April, 1968

Three Sisters
Irina Sergeyevna Prozorova
Royal Court, London
May – June, 1967

Acknowledgements

Thank you to my editor, Chris Charlesworth, for believing in me enough to commission the original book and for being there for me 22 years later. Enthusiastic, quick to make a decision and provide counsel, he's the sharpest kid ever to escape Skipton.

Richard Lysons supplied a study, a library of rock books, unrivalled knowledge and, for good measure, contributed the discography and index. Kindness and understanding were granted and encouragement offered by Paula Ridings; my parents, Jean and Roy; sons, George and Alec; and my sister, Karen and brother-in-law, Tony. Antony Harwood proffered great wisdom, steering me through a row over the book's cover that might otherwise have escalated. James Heward and James Wallace took care of other business for me, as reliable and trustworthy as ever. Geoff Read and John Abraham looked out for me, as did Guy Patrick, Richard Whitehead, Christian Brett, David Cooper, Dave Taylor, Jim Stringer, Jonathan Bregazzi, Michael Tomlinson, Trevor Hoyle and Gary Canning. David Hammond provided accommodation and good company, along with Ali.

The following kind souls agreed to interviews or assisted through other means, either with the original book, or this one: Peter Finn, Ben Brierley, Chris O'Dell, Glynn Faithfull, Mike Leander, Gerry Bron,

Peter Wells, Eddie Edwards, Rachelle Coward, Eamon Carr, Maureen Doughty, Monica Main, Paul Privetera, Maryan Hunter, Chris Salewicz, Terry Rawlins, Bett at Kennedy Street Enterprises, Alan Clayson, Jan Dielissen, Barry Miles, Oliver Musker, Mark Miller Mundy, François Ravard, Duncan Hall, Frida Keep, Michael Ackermann, Betty Bishop, Kathy Catterall, Tim Power, Neil Storey, Henrietta Moraes, Bill Gardner, Christopher Gibbs, Mike Grime, Alastair Lewthwaite, Terry Eves, Johnny Rogan, Allyson Morgan, Mike Cooper, Andrew Bennett, David Supper, Joan Van Emden, John Wallace, Annie Lowmass, Colin Larkin, Peter Betham, Peter Jones, Tony Michaelides, Cecil and Ida Rapley, S. Periwinkle, Keith Altham, Paddy Rossmore, Simon Wells, Barry Fantoni, Jonathan King, Donald Brooks, Mick Lynch, Gered Mankowitz, Sharon Blenkson, Regine Moylett, Chris Jerome and Eugene T. Robinson.

Special mention to the late Rob Partidge who, in 1990, was an interviewee but became a good and true friend. Also missed greatly are top blokes Stephen and Frank Hewitt, and my grandmother, Eveline Duffy.

Bibliography

Appleford, Steve. *The Rolling Stones, It's Only Rock 'n' Roll, The Stories Behind Every Song* (Carlton, 1997)

Atfel, Mandy. *Death Of A Rolling Stone, The Brian Jones Story* (Sidgwick & Jackson, 1982)

Brown, Peter, and Gaines, Steven. *The Love You Make: An Insider's Story Of The Beatles* (Pan, 1983)

Chapples, Steve. *Goin' Down Th' Imp* (Arncliffe Press, 2005)

Clayson, Alan. *Call Up The Groups* (Blanford Press, 1985)

Cohn, Nik. *Awopbopaloobop Alopbamboom* (Granada, 1969)

Dalton, David. *The Rolling Stones* (Amsco, 1972)

Elson, Howard, and Brunton, John. *Whatever Happened To...?* (Proteus, 1981)

Faithfull, Marianne. *Faithfull* (Michael Joseph, 1994)

Faithfull, Marianne. *Memories, Dreams & Reflections* (Fourth Estate, 2007)

Gambaccini, Paul, Rice, Tim and Rice, Jonathan. *British Hit Singles* (Guinness, 1990)

Glossop, Dr. Michael. *Living With Drugs* (Wildwood House, 1987)

Goldman, Albert. *The Lives Of John Lennon* (Bantam Press, 1988)

Halliwell, Leslie. *Halliwell's Film Guide* (Granada, 1989)

Hardy, Phil, and Laing, Dave. *The Faber Companion To 20th Century Popular Music*, (Faber & Faber, 1990)

Herman, Gary. *Rock'n'Roll Babylon* (Plexus, 1982)

Hoffmann, Dezo, with Jopling, Norman. *The Rolling Stones* (Hutchinson, 1984)

Hotchner, AE. *Blown Away: The Rolling Stones And The Death Of The Sixties* (Simon & Schuster, 1990)

Hunt, Marsha. *Real Life* (Chatto & Windus, 1984)

Jasper, Tony. *Great Rock And Pop Headlines* (Willow Books, 1986)

Jasper, Tony. *The Top Twenty Book* (Javelin, 1988)

Landis, Bill. *Anger, The Unauthorised Biography Of Kenneth Anger* (Harper Perrenial, 1995)

Lewisohn, Mark, and McCartney, Paul. *The Complete Beatles Recording Sessions* (EMI Records, 2006)

McCartney, Paul, and Miles, Barry. *Paul McCartney: Many Years From Now* (Vintage, 1998)

Meyer, David N. *Twenty Thousand Roads, The Ballad Of Gram Parsons And His Cosmic American Music* (Bloomsbury, 2007)

Miles, Barry. *In The Sixties* (Pimlico, 2003)

Norman, Philip. *Mick Jagger* (Harper Collins, 2012)

Norman, Philip. *The Life And Good Times Of The Rolling Stones.* (Century Hutchinson, 1989)

O'Brien, Lucy. *Dusty* (Sidgwick & Jackson, 1989)

Oldfield, Mike. *Changeling* (Virgin, 2007)

Oldham, Andrew Loog. *2Stoned* (Vintage, 2003)

Oldham, Andrew Loog. *Stoned* (Vintage, 2001)

Palacios, Julian. *Syd Barrett And The Pink Floyd: Dark Globe* (Plexus, 2010)

Richards, Keith. *Life* (Phoenix, 2011)

Rogan, Johnny. *Starmakers And Svengalis* (Macdonald, Queen Anne Press, 1988)

Salewicz, Chris, and Newman, Suzette. *The Story Of Island Records: Keep On Running*, (Universe, 2010)

Sanchez, Tony. *Up And Down With The Rolling* Stones (William Morrow & Co, 1979)

Schofield, Carey. *Jagger* (Methuen, 1983)

Seaton, Pete, with Down, Richard. *The Kaleidoscope British Television Music And Variety Guide II* (Kaleidoscope, 2007)

Shaar Murray, Charles. *Crosstown Traffic* (Faber & Faber, 1989)

Shelton, Robert. *No Direction Home, The Life And Music Of Bob Dylan* (Penguin, 1986)

Spence, Simon. *Immediate* (Black Dog, 2008)

Stallings, Penny. *Rock'n'Roll Confidential* (Vermillion, 1984)

Steward, Sue, and Garratt, Sheryl. *Signed Sealed And Delivered* (Pluto Press, 1985)

Tobler, John, and Grundy, Stuart. *The Record Producers* (BBC Publications, 1982)

Various. *The History Of Rock* (Orbis, 1984)

Various. *Turning On, Rock In The Late Sixties* (Orbis, 1981)

Ward, Ed. Stokes, Geoffrey, and Tucker, Ken. *Rock Of Ages* (Penguin, 1986)

Wyman, Bill, with Havers, Richard. *Rolling With The Stones* (Dorling Kindersley, 2002)

Wyman, Bill. *Stone Alone* (Viking, 1990)

Index

367

CPSIA information can be obtained
at www.ICGtesting.com
Printed in the USA
LVOW13s2259270817
546616LV00002B/9/P